The Rand McNally Series on the History of American Thought and Culture

The Red and The Black

Dwight W. Hoover
Ball State University

Rand McNally College Publishing Company/Chicago

The Rand McNally Series on the History of American Thought and Culture

David D. Van Tassel, series editor

THE NERVOUS GENERATION: AMERICAN THOUGHT, 1917–1930.
  Roderick Nash
THE PROGRESSIVE MIND, 1890–1917. David Noble
THE UNBRIDGEABLE GAP: BLACKS AND THEIR QUEST FOR THE
  AMERICAN DREAM, 1900–1930. June Sochen
THE RED AND THE BLACK. Dwight W. Hoover

76 77 78   0 9 8 7 6 5 4 3 2 1

Contents

Editor's Preface

The United States in its Bicentennial Year of Independence is awash in activities celebrating its anniversary jubilee. It is important to note, amidst the parades, polka parties, and panegyrics, that July 4, 1976, not only marks the 200th anniversary of independence, but also the beginning of the third century of our country's history. Therefore, it is appropriate that we use this occasion for reflection, analysis, and resolution. How far in these 200 years have we come towards the realization of the ideals of the Revolution as expressed in the Declaration of Independence and the Bill of Rights of the Constitution? How far have we come in realizing the self-evident truth "that all men are created equal"? As we celebrate the pluralism of this country and recognize the contributions of each individual ethnic group, we must also recognize the struggles of these groups to win social, economic and cultural equality. Running through this nation's history, like a dark thread interweaving events on a Belgian tapestry, is the problem of racial prejudice. This problem has affected all peoples, but was particularly pervasive and difficult in regard to Indians and Blacks as they bore the distinctive physical mark of skin color. They also played a role in the nation's history not shared by any other ethnic group; Indians and Blacks forced each generation of Americans to come to grips with the question of race in relation to American ideals. The Indians were the only native occupants of the land that Americans, of foreign origin, now claim as their own. Throughout history, seizure of this land has had to be justified and rationalized, and guilt has had to be absolved. Black Americans came to these shores in chains as chattel. This enslavement of fellow human beings has constantly piqued the American conscience. As each generation sought to deal with these two special groups of Americans, they created images of Blacks and Indians that included visions of the past and the future as well as explanations of the present.

An important key to understanding a culture is knowing how that culture perceives its problems and in what ways it goes about solving them. *The Red and the Black* supplies that key, clearly delineating the perceptions of each era and the evidence used to support the assumptions about race. Dwight Hoover has skillfully revealed these assumptions through an examination of novels and other literature and through association with the ideas of contemporary social and political theorists and the work of natural scientists.

This volume aims to fulfill a major goal of the Rand McNally Series on the History of American Thought and Culture, which goal is to help the general student to understand intellectual and cultural developments in American History. Many of the patterns of thought, assumptions, and evidence revealed in this volume are still present in America today. It is important that we assess, as Dwight Hoover has done, the questions of "where have we been?" and "how we have come to where we are?" in order that the generation now launching the third century of United States history may deal with the issues here raised with knowledge and understanding.

DAVID D. VAN TASSEL

Introduction

Various images of Blacks and Indians have been an integral part of American social thought from America's beginnings. This book is an attempt to describe these images and the ideological framework of which they are a part.

The questions about persons of different color that have been asked by Europeans and Americans have reflected their anxieties, concerns, and curiosity about themselves. The early preoccupation with the question of the origin of the Indians is one example of this phenomenon. Scholars agreed that Indians, as all other persons, had descended from Adam, but they also agreed that they had not yet uncovered all the circumstances of the journey from the Near East Eden to the New World. Similarly, the attention paid to the seemingly different levels of social development attained by the Indian and the Black indicated a general concern towards how people experience and maintain their own particular kinds of society. The questions about origins and cultural differences have persisted throughout the American experience and have not yet been settled. They will, I think, continue to be asked.

The failure to achieve full integration and equality for Blacks and Indians in America has led to questions about the nature of American society as well as to questions about group characteristics in general. Sometimes this failure has been blamed on society in general and at other times on individual groups themselves. The persistent assigning of responsibility for inequality to the supposed inferiority of differently colored races has led, in turn, to doubts about the ability of the larger society to absorb these races. Thus, theories on racial inequality have been concerned with theories on the shape of contemporary and future societies and on the place of diverse groups in these societies.

Images of Blacks and Indians, then, have been a part of the

visions of the past and the future as well as involved in explanations of the present. These images have revealed at least as much about the people holding them as about those represented by them and have been supported by the kinds of evidence considered most scientific at each particular moment in time.

I have called the prevailing assumptions of an era and the evidence used to support the assumptions paradigms after Thomas Kuhn's *The Structure of Scientific Revolutions.* I believe that Kuhn's analysis of the shape of scientific explanations applies to the shape of certain ideas of race and that these ideas (examples of which appear in shorthand form as the legend of Noah, naturalism, and cultural relativism) can be considered paradigms. While some paradigms may lead to morally offensive conclusions, they should be seriously scrutinized, nonetheless. The expression and evolution of these racial paradigms are the subject matter of this book.

The development of a full-scale paradigm of race, encompassing such ideas as biological and social evolution and nationalism, did not occur until the late nineteenth century. As George Stocking has said, earlier thinkers could not really distinguish among race, culture, and nationality because these thinkers lacked key concepts of genetics and sociology, involving biological and social transmission of traits. The earlier paradigms, which equated biological and characteristic qualities, differed from the later ones, which are better organized and argued.

Finally, I would like to make my own position clear. The question of human equality ought not, in my opinion, to be based upon physical and mental similarities or differences. Equality is an ethical conviction that lies deep in the Western tradition and that, violated often in practice, still remains a cornerstone of any social theory that attempts to create a "good" society. Such, I think, was the position of the Founding Fathers who, despite their own practices, labored to create a community that would take man's moral equality as given.

Throughout the book, I have used the terms Black and Indian to describe native Africans who came to the New World and native Americans who were there when the Europeans arrived. I realize that the terms Negro, Black, and Indian contain within them possible racist implications. These terms were bestowed on native peoples by outsiders and were not originally self-selected.

Acknowledgments

I am deeply grateful to Ball State University for providing me with a sabbatical leave to do research on and to think about this book, and to Dean Robert Carmin and Richard Wires who provided clerical help for retyping the manuscript. Susan M. Dygert and Darlene L. Droper typed it cheerfully. I also wish to extend thanks to the editor of this series, Professor David Van Tassel, who gave support and encouragement when needed, and to Larry Malley, who is committed to the publishing business but is also sympathetic to the problems of authors and who was always ready to listen and to understand.

My intellectual debts are immense. The students in my seminars on intellectual and black history provided insights on books and ideas that had eluded me. Mike Bidelman took time off from writing his dissertation in order to help me with recent sociological theory, a sacrifice he should not have made. My student secretary, Judy Nickel, typed and did bibliographical research with industry and cheerfulness. My colleague and friend, C. Warren Vander Hill, read the manuscript and gave me many useful stylistic suggestions. Robert F. Berkhofer, Jr. encouraged me at a crucial time and aided me with his considerable knowledge about Indians and about the problems of writing history. George Juergens encouraged me with his close reading and kind remarks. George Fredrickson caught a number of errors I had made in the original manuscript. As always, my interest in intellectual history and whatever competence I possess come from Stow Persons, an outstanding teacher and thinker, whose work I return to again and again only to discover that my new ideas were his old ones.

Writing a book is a lonely experience; some of the loneliness was relieved by my wife Peggy and my youngest daughter Elizabeth. Without Peggy, the work would not have been done; without Elizabeth, it would have been done sooner but would have been less fun.

I have deliberately chosen Stendahl's title for my book, not because this work compares in any way with that of the French master novelist, but because the title reflects better than any of my own choosing the theme of this book.

DWIGHT W. HOOVER

Chapter 1

Before the Mayflower

Europeans rediscovered Africa before they discovered America, encountering black men before red men. They then revived the institution of slavery, which was to become significant in black-white relations, in order to facilitate the production of sugar, a product originally acquired from both Asia and Africa.

By the twelfth century, Europeans could trust neither Muslim North Africa nor the Muslim Middle East for a stable supply of sugar; they needed, they felt, a Christian source. They found this source in Cyprus when the Venetians established sugar plantations there. The importance of Cyprus as a sugar producing area grew as the Muslims gained more and more control of the Levant in the thirteenth and fourteenth centuries. Entreprenurial groups from Venice, Catalonia, France, and Genoa began sugar plantations in Cyprus. Originally, these plantations relied upon a mixed labor force of free and slave labor, but the labor-intensive nature of sugar production demanded a more permanent labor force. Extensive slavery appeared to be the answer to this problem.

The Mediterranean slave trade first involved Islamic and Christian slaves taken from the north and east coasts of the Black Sea. By the early fourteenth century, black slaves from sub-Saharan Africa were added to the labor force. At first, the slaves were prisoners taken in raids by North Africans, but, later, professional slave-traders provided the bulk of black slaves. When Constantinople fell to the Turks in 1453, the Black Sea slave trade was effectively closed and Africa was left as the major source of slave labor. Meanwhile, sugar plantations had spread to the islands of Crete and Sicily and to the Spanish cities of Valencia and Málaga and had become international in scope, using capital from northern Italy and southern Germany and management from a variety of European states. The increase in amount of land and capital and the improvement of management techniques led to a greater demand for slaves at the same time that the Near Eastern sources had dried up.

The focus of the slave trade was shifting from the Mediterranean to the Atlantic by the middle of the fifteenth century. The reasons were in part technological; the new sailing ship was an effective means of transporting bulk cargoes over long distances as well as of exploration. The Atlantic slave trade began in 1441 when ten Africans from the Guinea Coast were sent to Portugal as a gift to Prince Henry the Navigator. In 1444, another group imported 235 black slaves to Portugal.

Originally, the slaves taken to Portugal from West Africa did not become plantation laborers but, rather, household servants. But when the production of sugar moved to Madeira and the Canaries in the 1450's, new plantation slaves were needed from Africa. As a result, the Portuguese founded the slave castle, Elmina, on the Gold Coast, and by 1500 they were growing sugar on the island of Sao Tomé in the Gulf of Guinea and relying entirely on African slaves.

The discovery of America in 1492 occurred simultaneously with the technological innovation, the sailing ship, and the expanding commercial enterprise, the growing of sugar, both of which combined to encourage the transportation of Europeans and Africans to the New World where they encountered the Indians. While black slaves first came to America in 1502, they were few in number as compared with those going to European homes and plantations. However, the production of sugar had begun by this time in the New World, and the need for slave labor gradually increased. Hispaniola first exported sugar in 1522 and by the mid-1550's so also did Puerto Rico, Jamaica, and coastal Mexico. The major production of sugar in the New World, however, began in Brazil in the latter half of the sixteenth century and utilized both Indian and black labor.

I

The English encountered American and African natives early in the sixteenth century. In the 1550's, the English first visited Africa when a group led by Captain Thomas Windham and a Portuguese guide went to Guinea and Benin. Windham's group entered, against his guide's advice, the Bight of Benin where one hundred of his ship's company died. The second group was led by John Lok who took an expedition of three vessels to Africa and brought ten black men back to England. While contemporary English accounts listed these black men as slaves, they also indicate that the men returned to Africa in a few years.

There was no major English involvement in the African slave trade until the reign of Elizabeth I, largely because Queen Mary disapproved of challenging Portuguese claims. However, in the 1560's, with the toleration and tacit consent of Queen Elizabeth, John Hawkins made three slaving raids in Africa. Having obtained the backing of English financiers, Hawkins made his first voyage in 1562. He fought for, traded for, and stole three hundred Negroes whom he then sold in the Canary Islands. His next voyage in 1564 (in which the Queen invested despite an earlier denunciation of Hawkins) returned a large profit, although African resistance and a difficult ocean voyage had made the expedition more hazardous than the first. The last voyage in 1567 ended disastrously. Hawkins lost four ships to a Spanish fleet along with many men and most of his treasure. Africans used poisoned arrows against him for the first time, which made slave catching more risky. English trade with West Africa continued, however; and, in 1588, Queen Elizabeth granted a ten-year monopoly to a group of London and Exeter merchants for trade to the Senegal and Gambian coasts.

The English were also acquainted with the inhabitants of the New World by this time. In 1568, John Hawkins put one hundred sailors ashore on the northern part of the coast of the Gulf of Mexico. One of these, David Ingram, returned to England and reported his impressions of the native population. Francis Drake encountered Negroes in Panama in 1572. These were "Cimarrons," runaway slaves who were sworn enemies of the Spanish. Joining together, Drake and the "Cimarrons" robbed a Spanish mule train carrying Peruvian treasure across the isthmus; Drake was after gold and the "Cimarrons" were seeking iron for tools. The success

of the endeavor encouraged Drake to arrange for further cooperative raids, but these never materialized. Richard Hakluyt, having
heard of Drake's experience, proposed the first English colonizing
scheme for the New World. Based at the Straits of Magellan and
populated by Englishmen and "Cimarrons," the first colony was to
control the sea route from the Atlantic to the Pacific. The proposal
also never materialized, but Sir Walter Raleigh utilized the principle of cooperation in his plan for a colony in Guiana. His colony
was to consist of Indians, who would be happy to receive English
law, and of Englishmen anxious to further English goals. Although
this project failed to even get started, Raleigh and Gilbert applied
the idea, a colony of diverse races unified by a mutual hatred of the
Spanish, in Roanoke, the first actual English colony in North America. The original plan called for Drake to populate the colony with
Blacks and Indians taken from Spanish sources. While he did
supply some Spanish Carribean slaves, he did not provide any Indians, and the failure of the colony ended the English dream of
a multiracial colony tied together by mutual antipathy to the
Spanish.

II

The Europeans did not approach new lands and new people devoid of preconceptions. Instead, they brought with them a whole
set of ideas concerning both the natural and historical worlds. They
also projected on America visions of what society and man could
be. The idea of America as a Garden of Eden was the culmination
of an ancient Western dream, just as the belief that the American
was a new Adam represented the ideal of the Renaissance man.
These two ideas combined to create one early sixteenth-century
European view of America as a place where all men lived together
in peace, harmony, and abundance. This aspect of the European
view of the New World was highly utopian.

Other views were less optimistic, particularly those that characterized the inhabitants of previously unknown areas as wild. To
Europeans, as Richard Bernheimer has shown, wild meant "everything that eluded Christian norms and the established framework
of Christian society, referring to what was uncanny, unruly, raw,
unpredictable, foreign, uncultured, and uncultivated." The wild

man, as seen in the art of the period, was hairy, covered with fur, naked, often armed with a club, and was at times crawling on all fours. This bizarre image appeared on the first packs of playing cards, where the wild man alternated with plants and animals and never with humans. Scholars depicted the wild man as mute, irrational, sometimes insane, and always pagan; they thought that he may originally have been human but, because of shock, loss of mind, poor upbringing, or extremely bad environmental conditions, had reverted to an animal-like state. Both wild men and wild women were described as displaying exaggerated erotic drives, searching after human lovers, and taking them by force if necessary. The wild man could supposedly be civilized and might then even resemble a gentleman; Orson, the mythical bear's son, demonstrated this process. The habitat of the wild man was said to have been in Africa; Herodotus had said that Libia was the home of wild men.

Below wild men on the biological chain were the apes. Christians had originally believed apes to be debased replicas of men; they had based this judgment on first-hand knowledge of three types of primates—the tailless Barbary ape of Gibraltar and North Africa, the baboon of Egypt, and the tailed simians of tropical Africa and India. They did not know of the anthropoid apes of Africa and Asia. Like the wild man, the ape was supposed to possess evil traits and often symbolized the devil, who in turn was called *simia Dei.* Since the baboon came from Egypt, Christian scholars felt he represented paganism. Thinkers concluded that the ape had lost his tail because of devilish experiences.

By the twelfth century, the Christian view had changed. The ape was then thought to have been the last animal created before Adam and to symbolize sin and the flesh. The twelfth-century artist depicted the ape as possessing human qualities, showing the mother ape protecting her child from predators and the male ape being attacked by demons or monsters. This view of the ape, as a human being under the burden of sin, evolved in part from Aristotle who had said, "some animals share the properties of man and the quadrupeds, as the ape, the monkey, and the baboon." In part this view sprang from the common misapprehension that miscegenation between men and the apes was possible and resulted in monstrous offspring. This view of apes and of monsters came first from Augustine who claimed that monsters were true men derived from Adam's seed and possessed of reason and mortality—the two valid tests of humanity. The monster, then, was thought to be the link between man and ape.

Saint Hildegard of Bengen, one of the first scholars of the twelfth century to study the ape's physical structure, noted certain features which were common to humans. The ape had a hot constitution (based on the humors of Galen), an unstable and weak nature, and a menstrual cycle governed by the moon—a characteristic not shared by any other animals except humans. Albertus Magnus, probably the leading thinker of the thirteenth century and the reconciler of Aristotelian logic with Catholic theology, placed man in the same category as apes and pygmies. His taxonomy included comparison of heads, hands, and posteriors. Like Augustine, Magnus believed the mental function to be the most striking difference between man and the apes and the pygmies (the latter were considered inferior to man despite their possession of memory, imagination, and judgment).

Jewish thinkers had also speculated on the origin of the apes. The *Rothschild Canticles* (1300) contains a passage wherein Adam warned his children against the use of certain herbs which would cause the conception of monsters. His advice went unheeded and seven monsters were born, the last of which was the ape. The *Talmud* has three explanations for the origin of apes, all based on the thesis that men degenerated into apes as a result of sin. In the *Talmud*, the first sinners to become apes were a few of the builders of the Tower of Babel; the next were Sabbath breakers punished by Moses; and the last were idolaters in the time of Enos. Both Jewish and Christian thought agreed on the close connection between apes and men and maintained that the supposed degraded appearance of the ape was evidence of the sin that had caused man to turn into ape.

By the fourteenth and fifteenth centuries, the ape had become for Christians the symbol of the fall of man. The new symbolization was sexual; along with the bear, the ape came to represent male sexual desire and female wantonness. There appeared, along with the belief that males apes raped women, a legend relating that the ape had helped Eve eat the apple in the Garden of Eden. The former belief may have come from the Near East since it also appears in the *Thousand and One Nights*. It was a curious legend for, of all the apes known to Europeans at that time, only the baboon was large enough to attack women. Anthropoid apes were first brought to Western Europe in 1640, but the belief in ape rape preceded them by many years. Indeed, a story that a male ape had kidnapped a black woman for sexual purposes circulated in Portugal as early as the fifteenth century. The net results of the newer ideas were to add a sexual dimension to the already unfavorable view of apes, to associate sex with animality, and to associate Africans and American Indians with apes and wild men.

The reports of early explorers of Africa and America contained descriptions of monsters, of wild men, of one-eyed giants, of Amazons, of cannibals, of tribes devoid of hair, of men with tails, along with more sober assessments. Because Columbus discovered America late, and since he assumed he had found Asia, he described the Indians in terms of the known Old World. They were naked, had no creed, and were not black—a fact that astonished some Europeans. Instead, they were the color of the Canary Islanders and had coarse black hair which resembled horses' tails. Not until Magellan's voyage around the world in 1519–21 did Europeans realize that the Indians were a new people in a New World and that a problem existed in explaining their origins.

III

A paradigm already existed to explain both the different men and the different customs encountered in the previously unknown world. It was a model that could be applied equally to Africa and America; and it was based on the best possible authority—the Bible and the biblical commentaries. The paradigm was the *legend of Noah* and had been widely accepted during the Middle Ages. Basically, the paradigm went as follows: God created Adam as the first man, the last and highest creature made. All men were descended from Adam; but, because of the flood, all men came from Noah as well. Man's cultural characteristics were affected three times: by Cain's sin, by the flood, and by the builders of the Tower of Babel. Each time God wiped out man's evil past along with most men. This explained why there were both physical and cultural varieties among human beings and human societies.

First, the physical varieties were explained thus: all people were descendants of Noah's three sons—Japheth, Ham, and Shem. The three sons and their wives embarked on the ark with Noah and his wife and with pairs of every living creature. The ark grounded somewhere in the Near East near the Garden of Eden, perhaps in Armenia but more probably in Mesopotamia. From that central location, the descendants of Noah and of the animals in the ark fanned out to repopulate the earth, which had been swept clean of all living things. Man was unified because of his descent from Noah; the idea of human unity through Noah was the first form of *monogenesis.*

Humans, however, differed in physical appearance, in color of skin, hair, and eyes, as well as in size and shape. This difference was thought to mirror the influence of varying environmental conditions—climate, altitude, and temperature—which humans encountered in their migrations to various parts of the world after the attempt to build the Tower of Babel. This attempt had angered God and caused Him to render men's languages incomprehensible to each other. Since humans could no longer understand each other, they drifted apart and went to the four corners of the earth. Both physical and cultural differences were thus products of human sin but could not deny man's fundamental unity from Noah.

Despite the equalitarian emphasis in this orthodox account, there were also built-in elements of ethnocentrism. If humans came from the Near East and if the present residents of the area were the original humans, the first (thus purest) humans were white. In addition and quite significantly, the Bible revealed that Noah cursed the children of his son Ham. This curse came to be connected with color; the sons of Ham were supposed to be black. The Biblical account of Ham's crime is cryptic and indicates a punish ment far out of proportion to the act, which was to see his drunken father's nakedness. Why should such an act even be considered wrong? Hebraic exegesis had early attempted to answer this question, and the answers derived centered on sexual themes. One version said that Noah had prohibited his sons from having sexual relations aboard the Ark, but that Ham had deliberately violated the prohibition so that his child would be first born and thus inherit the major part of the world. Another version said that Ham had castrated his father to prevent the generation of additional children who would share the patrimony. Whatever the explanation, the implications were the same. Blacks were cursed because of sexual guilt. By the sixteenth century, Christian scholars had accepted Jewish speculations on the basis for Noah's curse and had incorporated them into their understanding of the legend of Noah.

There were, of course, anomalies in the model. If there were four human colors—red, black, white, and yellow—how could these four come from only three sons? Another anomaly involved animals. Since animals, like men, were twice propagated, all animals must have originated in the Near East. But experience showed that not all animals in the Old World had their counterpart in the Near East, and the question of their origins plagued thinkers. The discovery of the New World added to the anomalies. How did men and animals get from the Old World to the New; when and why did they come; did they come together or separately? The distance across the oceans complicated these questions, particularly when the size of animal and human populations in the New World were realized. In addition, neither the Bible nor classical literature contained descriptions of some of these populations. With the beginning of colonization, these anomalies were recognized, necessitating new explanations. In 1520, for example, Parcelsus maintained that God had created a second Adam for the New World, that the biblical account of creation referred only to the Old World. While Parcelsus's idea of *polygenesis* avoided the problem of the transfer of animals and humans from one continent to another, it was not widely accepted. Most thinkers still clung to monogenesis, to the view that all life came from a single act of creation in the Near East.

An even more difficult problem, however, was related to the cultural, rather than physical, diversity among humans. The difficulty of categorizing human groups on the basis of anatomical, physiological, or color differences paled before that of arranging them by language and religion. In order to differentiate among these diverse groups, the word nation was used. Thus, animals were of different races, but humans were of different nations. Down through the eighteenth century the explanation was sustained: although humans were of different nations and behaved differently, they were fundamentally equal because of their descent from Noah. The idea of race for describing human differences was not yet accepted.

Cultural diversity, like physical diversity, was thought to be the end product of sin; as such, it could be used as a justification of present inequality. The Christian explanation of diversity included this possibility. Human behavior began to differentiate with Cain who, having slain Abel, built the first city, had plural marriage, and created bronze and iron tools. After the flood, Ham also provided innovations: he began to divine by the stars and to sacri-

fice children by fire. The major behavioral changes, however, came
with the failure to build the Tower of Babel. Nations were cursed
with separate languages and forsook old ways for new. Thus, Christian theology assumed that change was bad and that cultural differentiation, the agent of change, was also. Cultural differentiation
caused a decline from earlier cultural homogeneity; it broke up tradition, caused a loss of true religion, and promoted a general decline in language, morals, and manners. The greater the process of
differentiation the greater the decline. Those nations which were
geographically most removed from the original seat of creation, i.e.
in the New World, were likely to have degenerated most from the
original ideal way of life.

A major problem with theories of cultural, as well as physical,
diversity involved time. Sixteenth-century thinkers assumed that
the time span between creation and their own era was extremely
short; thus, physical and cultural changes must have occured rapidly. The histories of the time did not discuss the idea of development, and the process of change was little understood. Scholars
were not historically minded; they preferred to leave the direction
of history in the hands of God. Thus, while the origin of man was
known and the present was obvious, the path between the two
remained obscured.

The extent of cultural diversity was measured by means of cultural comparison. The standard of comparison was cultural similarities or correspondences, as the whole paradigm on diversity was
based on a belief in general cultural uniformity. Since the most
ancient nation known was the Jewish one, the nations of the Indians and Negroes were evaluated against the Jewish pattern to
determine how far they had declined from their origins. Discrep-
ancies in comparisons plagued thinkers. Compilation of lists of
words showing the relation of Hebrew to oral native languages
relied upon the transcription of these oral languages into acceptable written form. The lists varied with the ears of the transcriber.
Similar traits were hard to find and, if found, were often of little
significance. Significant differences were often ignored in the
search for similarities. Also, the belief that the devil might simu-
late resemblances between cultures in order to confuse the Christian scholar further complicated the study of societies.

Despite the problems, recognized and unrecognized, the writers of the sixteenth century did make the attempt. Travelers and

commentators, relying on Hebrew ethnology, wrote down Indian languages (all the while looking for Jewish words) and described Indian customs (all the while looking for Jewish counterparts). They found similar words and such similar customs as first-fruit ceremonies, sacrifice to God(s), lunar and ritual calendars, feasts, exorcisms, purification rites, fasting and food taboos, confession, pilgrimages, endogamy, and circumcision. Similarity of words and customs seemed to prove the common past of all nations; the only task remaining was to define fully the relation of each to the other.

IV

The original European observers in the New World were the Spanish. Although the reports of the first explorers were confusing—Columbus had supposedly reported seeing fair-skinned men near the equator and Balboa had reported Negroes in Panama—the general agreement of later explorers was that the Indians were dark, but not black, and were that color because of their environment. These witnesses agreed that Indians were human beings with inferior manners, descendants of Noah who were both rational and capable of being Christianized. Pope Paul III, in his *Sublimus Deus* in 1537, made this opinion Catholic dogma; he held the Indians to be truly men who could own property and be baptized. The first general historical treatment of the Indians, Oviedo's *Historia general* (1535), also affirmed the Indians' humanity. Oviedo, in addition, proposed two theses concerning Indian origins: either that the Indians came from Carthage or that they came from Spain. The first version, which was suggested by Aristotle, claimed that merchants from early Carthage discovered the New World, occupied parts of it, and were eventually forgotten by their contemporaries at home. The second maintained that the twelfth king of Spain seized and populated the Indies in 1658 B.C. The two versions were not necessarily contradictory; there could have been two waves of migration. Both versions attributed Indian origins to trans-Atlantic migration and Indian color to environmental conditions.

Other theories also appeared. In 1553, the first book to trace the origin of the Indians to Plato's lost continent of Atlantis was published. The evidence for this theory was linguistic; the Indian word "atl" meant water and so must have originated in Atlantis. A book by the Portuguese Galváo, *The Discoveries of the World, from their first Original Unto the Year of Our Lord 1555,* claimed that the Indians had originated from the Orient.

Two other theories of Indian origins emerged in the next two decades. The first came from a book published in Antwerp in 1567, Lumnius' *De Extremo Dei Judico,* which claimed the Indians were the Ten Lost Tribes of Israel. The theory was based upon the fourth book of Esdras, a book of the Apocrypha that had almost biblical authority. The second theory claimed the land of Ophir, described in the Book of Solomon, to be the original home of the Indians. This theory appeared in the Polyglot Bible of Antwerp in 1572 and was the work of Benito Arias Montana, Chaplain to Philip II. Both theories relied on the similarities between the language and customs of the Indians and the Jews for proof.

In 1589–90, Joseph de Acosta summarized all the theories of Indian origin and provided the first systematic critique of these theories. Acosta, a Spaniard, attempted a naturalistic explanation of Indian origins and migration—avoiding the linguistic comparisons of his predecessors, while still retaining elements of the legend of Noah. He rejected the possibility that the Indians came by sea, for they had neither compass nor lodestone; nor could animals have crossed the ocean, for there was no new ark. There was no physical evidence to prove that Atlantis existed or that the Indians were Jews—they lacked circumcision. The inhabitants of the New World must have come in a series of migrations via a land bridge from the Old World or across a narrow strait of water. Once in the New World, these people developed their own customs which were not comparable with older ones. Since the flora and fauna of the New World were unique, either they must have survived the flood or God must have created new ones in the region. Acosta's explanation, which—with modifications—remains today the most accepted theory of Indian origins, did not end the speculation or the use of the method of cultural correspondence.

The most orthodox explanation was best stated by another Spaniard, Geogorio García, in his *Origen de las indios de el neuvo* (1607). García had lived in Peru for nine years and was struck by many similarities between Indians and other nations. In his book he considered these similarities as well as the theories that accounted for the resemblances. García started with the idea that all men were descended from Noah; God gave Asia to Shem, Egypt and Africa to Ham, and Europe to Japheth. The Indians migrated to the New World from somewhere; they were not indigenous to the area. They could have come either by land or sea; he attacked Acosta's denial of the possibility of oceanic travel with biblical evidence. (Noah as well as Adam could navigate, and the Bible contained several accounts of long voyages.) García also disposed of the problem of unique American animals; they were monsters, accidental derivations from known European forms. The llama, for example, was the monster of the camel. This explanation, although it accounted for uniqueness, contained internal contradictions in that the biological theories of the day held that monsters were incapable of reproducing beyond three generations. García, however, invented another kind of monster, one produced from a pair of animals which, due to some stellar or natural influence at the time of conception, could survive and reproduce. This early definition of mutation was exceptional and useful.

García then considered each theory concerning the origin of the Indians and tried to prove all of them. That is, he found evidence to suggest that each was true but that each was related to a different migration occurring at a different time. García's compromise had the virtue of explaining why the Indians were such a composite population, why there were such differences in manners and languages among different tribes. In supporting all the theories of origins, Garcia used the comparative method to show how Indians might have come from Atlantis, Asia, Spain, Carthage, and Israel. Typical of his method of analysis was his testing of Carthaginian thesis. Both Indians and Carthaginians had picture writing, similar architecture, child sacrifice, idolatry, sun worship, and priests. Climatic influences had affected both in similar ways; neither had beards, for hot climates prevented the growth of facial hair. His longest proof was of the Ten Lost Tribes theory. The proof again centered on cultural similarities—there were graves in the Azores with Hebrew names on them; the Jews and Indians both had stories of floods; the Jews and Indians were timid; they used similar religious ceremonies, were idolaters, wore sleeveless robes, buried their dead in hills, called relatives of second and third degree of consanguinity brothers, sacrificed children, and kissed cheeks as a sign of love and peace. There was even a physical resemblance; both had large noses.

García also accounted for cultural dissimilarities. How could the Jews have lost their written language, religion, and law? His answer was that only the two best tribes of Israel had really achieved civilization; the others never had. While all men had learned writing from Adam, some lost the ability because of diet, climate, and social isolation. Parts of the past tradition were remembered, others forgotten, and the remnants of customs kept were incomprehensible to the possessors. The Incas had a ceremony like passover; there were Indians in Yucatan practicing circumcision; the Mexican Indians had eternal altar fires. But none of the Indians could explain the reasons for or the origin of their practices.

García's effort typified the sixteenth-century explanation of cultural and physical differences among people. Humans were supposedly homogeneous at the time of Noah, but the dispersion after the Tower of Babel led to people who looked and behaved differently. The paradigm served as a model for the reconstruction of historic events that occurred after the building of the Tower of Babel. Such was the utility of the model that competing paradigms could not seriously challenge it. The explanation could accommodate views of the Indian as either depraved or innocent, enemy or friend, all of which views circulated in sixteenth-century Europe.

By 1550, the Spanish had begun to debate whether the Indians should be enslaved and forcibly converted to Christianity. The major participants in this debate were Bartolome de las Casas and Juan Ginés de Sepúlveda. In 1548, Sepúlveda had written a treatise on the foundation of natural slavery, which was sponsored by the President of the Council of the Indies, the ruling body for Spanish colonies. The treatise was rejected by the Council and referred to the Council of Castile, where it was denounced by las Casas. In 1550, Charles V ordered all Spanish conquests stopped until theologians and counselors should decide upon the question. The decision was to be based on the results of a debate between Sepúlveda and las Casas. The central question concerned what Aristotle meant by natural slavery. Las Casas argued against enslaving the Indians, writing two books—*Apologetica historia* (1550) and *Historia de las Indias* (1559)—on the subject. Sepúlveda upheld the practice of enslaving the Indians.

Sepúlveda's basic defense was the proposition that Indian slavery was the result of a just war. This war was necessary because of the rudeness (primitiveness) of the Indians' natures, the need to spread the faith and to protect the weak among the natives, and the gravity of the Indians' sins—the chief of which was idolatry. He quoted Aristotle, who had defined natural slaves as those whose customs were barbarous. Sepúlveda concluded that inferior nations must serve their superiors.

Las Casas's position was a sophisticated one. Faced by one of the leading Aristotelian scholars of the day, las Casas did not attack the doctrine of natural slavery. He argued that this doctrine did not apply to the Indians but rather to mistakes of nature, individuals whose physical deformities—such as the possession of six toes—clearly destined them for their inferior role. Before a just war was waged against them, the Indians must be given a chance to accept the civilization of the conquering Spanish. If they rejected this civilizing influence, they risked losing their property, their liberty, and their lives. However, if they accepted civilization, while they still would not be equal to the Spanish, neither should they be made slaves.

The debate reached a deadlock, although the Crown announced a more liberal Indian policy that reflected las Casas's position. However, the argument continued. In 1552, Lopez de Gómara, a biographer of Cortez, published *Historia general de las Indies*. In this book Gómara vilified the Indians, describing them as filthy devil-worshippers, sodomites, liars, public fornicators, naked cannibals, and the givers of syphilis to the world. Because of these qualities, they were fit only to be slaves. While the King of Spain suppressed the book in 1553 because of its inflammatory statements, the ideas were not extinguished.

V

The English, who were part of the sixteenth-century intellectual community, knew the paradigm of the legend of Noah and accepted it. By the 1550's, they had translations of the Spanish and Portuguese books on the subject. They also read the accounts of English explorers which depicted the aboriginal American in various ways. Thus, they could believe Martin Frobisher who, after three unsuccessful attempts to locate a Northwest Passage, returned to England with stories of half-men who were crafty, brutal and loathsome, and who were cannibals who ate any dead flesh. They could also believe Nicholas Monarde's *Joyfull Newes out of the Newe Founde Worlde*...(1577) which pictured America as an earthly paradise where nature's bounty permitted the Indian and the European to live together in peace, leisure, and sensuality. The mixture of good and bad appeared in Richard Hakluyt's books, *Divers Voyages* (1584), and *The Principall Navigations,...* (1589), which contained much material taken from the Roanoke failure. The books claimed that the Indians were receptive to Christianity and the Europeans, were willing to submit to good government, were gentle and loving, and were faithful and without guile. Hakluyt also admitted that Indians had rude manners and lacked knowledge of God. He indicated that Spanish cruelty might prejudice Indian relations with the English, but, hopefully, peaceful trade with the Indians could be had. In the end, Hakluyt believed that the good qualities of the Indians would outweigh the bad ones so that commercial intercourse between the English and the Indians would be a success.

Leslie A. Fiedler maintains that the image of the Indian and the Negro merge in Elizabethan times. Using Shakespeare's *The Tempest* as proof, Fiedler shows how Caliban was conceived of as being black (his mother was from Algiers) and Indian (he was a descendant of Brazilians, Patagonians, and Bermudans) as well as being part fish. He was a savage (wild) man who rejected the conventions of courtly love; he was sexually a satyr who tried to rape Prospero's daughter. In Caliban, the fears and fantasies of the sixteenth century merge: the wild man, the ape, and the unregenerate primitive all become one.

Thus, on the eve of English colonization in America, the English had seen both Indians and Blacks and knew of the theories that explained both origin and cultural diversity. They accepted the biblical explanation of human differences which, although resting upon a foundation of human equality based upon a single origin of man, had an imperfectly worked out morphology of man and animal, associated blackness with sin, and connected savages with sexuality. Still, the hope persisted that Englishmen could create a new society which would include Indians and Blacks and which would frustrate the Spanish hegemony in the New World.

Chapter 2

Colonial Beginnings and Opportunities

The adventurers of the London Company of Virginia landed in an area already visited by Europeans. Verrazano and Gomez had landed somewhere in the Chesapeake Bay area as early as the first quarter of the sixteenth century; the French had touched land somewhere south of Virginia in 1562; and the Spanish were reported to have set up a mission on the York River in 1570, only to have it destroyed by the Indians. During the same time period, pirates of various nationalities used the Carolinas as bases for raiding Spanish ships unlucky enough to sail close by.

In all probability, then, the Indians of Virginia had either heard of Europeans or had had some contact with them prior to English colonization. The same was probably true of the Indians in New England. When Gosnold and Gilbert made their first voyage to the New England coast in 1602, they found some Indians with surprising facility in the English language; and when the Pilgrims came to Plymouth, they met an Indian named Squanto (Tisquantum) who spoke good English and who saved them in the first grim years of their settlement. Squanto's story is instructive. He was one of a group of twenty Indians seized by a Captain Hunt from the New England coast in 1614 and taken to Málaga to be sold as a slave. Squanto managed to return to Cape Cod via Newfoundland and to be present when the Pilgrims landed. The Indians, in fact, had probably had more contact with Europeans than the English had with the Indians.

While it is difficult to reconstruct the Indians' view of the English, events seem to indicate an initial tolerance of the English on the part of the Indians based upon a lack of fear. In Virginia, the first Indian war occurred in 1622, some fifteen years after the settlement of Jamestown; while in New England, the first war was not until the month-long Pequot War of 1637. Not until King Philip's War in 1675 was New England really tested. Had the Indians wished, they could have wiped out the few colonists soon after their arrival. That they chose not to reflects several possible Indian attitudes. In the first place, the English probably did not impress the Indians. These colonists were few in number, were often unable to compete against the hostile environment (indeed the Indians had to teach Englishmen how to survive), and were unlikely to remain very long in their settlements, judging from past experiences with other Europeans. In the second place, the cultural differences between the two groups were not great. The Indians worked copper and had fabrics, pots, and many artifacts—nets, weirs, and gardening tools—which were similar to those of the English. Description of English cities failed to amaze the Indians, who lived in villages and who were acquainted with the large Indian urban complexes in the lower Mississippi valley. Finally, there was sufficient land for everyone, and the English guns could help subdue rival Indians.

This is not to say there were no clashes between the two nations. Christopher Newport, leader of the 1607 Jamestown expedition, reported that the Indians attacked the expedition near Cape Henry upon arrival. Newport believed this would foretell Indian treachery, but later experiences proved him wrong as Powhatan, chief of the Pamunkey, desired an alliance with the English. In the first difficult year, the Indians saved Jamestown from starvation by supplying food, but even this gift and the overtures of Powhatan failed to overcome English suspicions. In 1608, Captain John Smith burned Indian canoes and corn in order to extort food from and frighten the Indians. He was convinced that Indians had stolen some English implements, and he believed the confessions of two Indians who claimed Powhatan wanted to destroy the colony. His experiences in Europe, Asia, and Africa had persuaded him that a firm policy was best, a persuasion unchanged by his rescue by Pocahontas. By 1609, partially because of Smith, English policy had changed from one of alliance with the Indians to one of military occupation with the purpose of exaction of tribute. This policy continued until 1613 when friction was again eased by Pocahontas.

Relations until 1622 were good; a few English settlers lived in Indian villages while Indian day laborers worked in white settlements. The death of Powhatan in 1618 and the succession of his brother Opechancanough did not alter the situation. However, hostilities erupted in 1622 when colonists killed a highly respected Indian and the Indians retaliated. The war proved disastrous for both sides. The Indians expected reprisal for their attacks, which bankrupted the Virginia Company of London and killed one-third of the white residents of Virginia, but they had not anticipated the extent of the colonial retaliation. Some tribes were scattered, others were destroyed. After their defeat, the surviving Indians managed to retribalize, but they never returned to the early easy contact with the colonists. The English fortified the areas between Chesiac and Jamestown and the direction of settlement was south, away from the Indians, rather than north or west. Through deliberate colonial policy, the Indians and settlers became more isolated. The English even considered eliminating all the Indians rather than using their labor. From 1622 to 1629, the settlers raided Indian settlements every summer to kill Indians and to destroy their crops. In 1629, a peace treaty was negotiated, only to be repudiated by the Virginia Council which argued that the enmity of Indians was preferable to peace.

In 1644, another major Indian attack occurred. This one was more successful than that of 1622 as the Indians, although reduced in number, killed as many men as they lost. The peace treaty of 1646, signed soon after the war, provided that the remaining Confederacy Indians, as they were called, were to act as scouts and allies against other Indians; that the Confederacy Indians were to pay annual tribute to the English in beaverskins; and that, while the movements of the Confederacy Indians were to be restricted, redress of wrongs done them was to be included in law.

The last Indian attack in Virginia came in 1676, the year of Bacon's Rebellion. This was to be the final resistance of the Confederacy Indians in Virginia and their last attempt at cultural independence. The inland Indians remained culturally intact longer because of their isolation and because they provided a profitable trade in beaverskins. The English experience with Indians in Virginia presaged that of other southern colonies; Indian attacks began late and lasted only into the third generation of settlers. After that, the Indians either moved beyond the reach of the colony or lived in the community in a subservient status.

In New England the pattern was similar, although the colonists there had longer periods of peace. The Pequot War of 1637 was short; the English troops with their Mohegan allies quickly and effectively eliminated the Pequot Indians. Although friendly to the settlers, the Mohegans reacted with astonishment to the English tactics, regarding the war as too furious and as killing too many. On the other hand, the English were contemptuous of their allies who fought as much for pleasure as for victory. One Puritan reported how an Indian, shooting from a distance at the Pequot fort, watched the flight of his arrow rather than preparing to shoot again. The conflict between the different cultural definitions of war was obvious. However, the Pequot War did not herald the breakdown of relations between the colonists and Indians as there had been Indians involved in both sides. The Narragansetts, Mohegans, Massachusetts and River tribes all fought against the Pequots.

King Philip's War in 1675 was as much of a shock to New Englanders as the attack on Jamestown was to the Virginians in 1622. The main cause of the war was Philip's concern about the growth of Puritan land claims (although Philip had sold some land to settlers himself), the failure to permit Indians to be jury men before 1673, and the restrictions on the sale of liquor and firearms to the Indians. Again, the war involved Indians on both sides. Friendly Indians accompanied the forces from Plymouth at the war's beginning, and a group of more than fifty Christian Indians from Massachusetts joined the Puritan army on July 16, 1675. These men served well, acting as scouts to detect ambushes. The Mohegans and Pequots of eastern Connecticut remained neutral, while the Narragansetts fought with the Confederacy Indians on the side of Philip.

Even though most Christian Indians in New England remained loyal, the colonists turned against them. At the onset of hostilities, a certain Captain Mosley took fifteen Indians from the town of Marlborough and marched them with ropes around their necks to Boston for trial. The evidence given at the trial proved inconclusive; the authorities tried to equivocate but failed and were forced to declare the Indians not guilty. The verdict enraged the colonial populace and produced a lynch mob that, however, failed to accomplish its purpose. Because of the resulting tension,

Indians were restricted to their home towns while the General Court of Massachusetts impounded 500 other praying Indians on Deer Island. These were kept there for a year, when they were released to fight against King Philip. Despite their war record, the Christian Indians were forced to live in one of four restricted Indian towns after the war. This was the first example of the reservation system in America.

King Philip's War was complete with atrocities on both sides. Indians displayed the heads and hands of victims from Swansea on poles, while at Brookfield they cut off the head of a captured man and used it as a football prior to displaying it. At the war's end, the Puritans punished the losers severely. King Philip, who was killed by an Indian, had his head cut off and his body quartered. His son was sold out of the colony as a slave, as were a number of others. Although there was resistance in Massachusetts to selling Indians, the sale was made through Plymouth in 1675. Other Indians were sold into local servitude for ten years for adults and up to age 25 for children.

The Puritan settlers had tied civilization and religion together; they had tried to convert the Indian to both simultaneously. To civilize the Indian, they taught the idea of private property. Among the Indian tribes in the New England area, land ownership rested in family units, although sachems (or chiefs) could claim individual ownership of tools, weapons, and clothing. The Puritans tried to substitute their views for Indian traditions of land ownership but were careful to require the signatures of all the Indians involved and their sachems in any land transactions. In addition, the General Court in Massachusetts tried to limit the sale of Indian land, beginning in 1643. The Court set these conditions: the Indians had to be willing to sell, cultivated fields could not be sold, prices had to be fair, the Indians retained the rights to hunt and fish on developed land and to plant crops on unused portions of sold property. The Indians agreed to these conditions and seemed to understand them. The great hope of civilizing the Indian lay in making him a property owner in the English sense; this hope was held throughout the rest of American history.

The second element of civilization, as taught by the Puritans, was law. Since English law was based both on experience and the word of God, it was held superior to the pagan and barbarous native customs. Puritans took on the responsibility of administering laws and of overseeing all peoples within their colony. To fulfill this responsibility, the Puritans divided the Indians into two groups. If a tribe were independent, an Indian law-breaker could be tried by the English only if his crime were made public and even then only if a sachem approved. Tribes dependent upon English authority had to obey English law, but could also follow native law if the two were in harmony. In most judicial proceedings, the Indian was equal to the white, except for the fact that Indians were prohibited from serving on juries. The prohibition against Indian jury service was removed in Rhode Island in 1673, in Massachusetts in 1674, and in Plymouth in 1675. Indian testimony could be used in any case, even if the Indian were not Christian and took no oath. There were no special penalties or crimes reserved for Indians; the nationality of the criminal made no difference. However, the Indian could not be banished from the colony as the White could. In time of war, he could be enslaved if he were an enemy captive; but then, so could Whites. Alden Vaughan, a student of the early New England-Indian relations, maintains that the Indians liked the English legal system, and that this system was administered fairly for the first fifty years of its existence.

The major goal the New Englanders had for the Indians was religious conversion. Once again, there was no double standard. The Indian convert had to meet the same criteria as the white, which consisted of a religious experience followed by a life led under the Covenant of Works. For the Indian, this way of life meant giving up polygamy, fornication, blasphemy, indolence, idolatry, and immodesty. The converted Indians had to form a congregation and, once formed, the congregation had to select a minister and decide upon its operating rules. All of this required time, effort, and money. The accomplishment of these tasks presumed outside help until such time as the Indian congregations were self-sustaining.

On July 27, 1649, the Long Parliament passed an act "for the promoting and propagating the Gospel of Jesus Christ in New England," which created the New England Company, the oldest English Protestant missionary society (after the Revolution, the society shifted its efforts to Canada where it exists today). The Company received corporate status, which empowered it to collect money in England for Indian missionary work in New England.

In 1651, the Indians of Natick received land from the General Court of Massachusetts Bay in response to their application to form a town. They built a meeting house but were unable to establish a congregation because they lacked the number of converted Indians necessary to form a church covenant. In 1652, neighboring elders, who came to Natick to hear about the regeneration experiences of the Indians, were unsatisfied with the Indians' spiritual progress. In 1654, the visit was repeated but, as three Indians showed up with ten quarts of liquor, the day was spoiled. Finally in 1660, enough Christians were found to begin a congregation. The Puritans also attempted to develop a viable economic system in Natick but had even less success. However, the Puritans were not easily discouraged, and thirteen more Christian Indian towns were founded by 1674.

Work progressed on other fronts as well, particularly in education as the Puritans aspired to create a group of educated Indian teachers and ministers. The first schools to admit Indians were common schools; John Winthrop mentioned that there were Indians in these schools as early as 1645. However, because the Indians were particularly susceptible to European diseases, the death rate of Indians in white schools was extremely high and these educational attempts were largely unsuccessful. Harvard provided a building for an Indian College in 1656 or 1657, but the first Indian candidate for the B.A. did not enter until 1660. No more than six or eight Indians ever entered the college, and only one, Caleb Chesschanmuk ever graduated. But he was of little use in Christianizing his fellow Indians as he died of tuberculosis in 1666, the year after his graduation. The Indian College building, largely unused, was torn down in 1693, and the Harvard Cooperation substituted the provision that Indians might live rent free in the other dormitories. Few took advantage of the provision. The failure to achieve mass Indian education meant that no Indian preachers or teachers were available for home missionary work.

Another attempt at Indian conversion came through the provision of religious writings in the Indians' own language. The New England Company spent a large part of the missionary funds it had raised during half a century on building "The Indian Library," a collection of books in the Indian language. Most of these were translations of Puritan books made by John Eliot, who had learned Algonquin. The first book issued was his primer or catechism in 1654; the next was Pierson's catechism, *Some Helps*, in 1659. The most famous book in the Indian Library was Eliot's *Indian Bible*, which was written in 1663. In 1666, Eliot wrote an *Indian Grammar* and, in 1672, *The Logic Primer*, which was an introduction to the rules of reason. Eliot's last translation was of Thomas Shepard's *Sincere Convert,* completed in 1689, a year before Eliot's death. After Eliot died, publication slowed. Translations of John Cotton's *Spiritual Milk for Babes* (1691) and Increase Mather's five sermons, *Greatest sinners called and encouraged to come to Christ* (1698), were the only two books issued in the decade of the 1690's. As the eighteenth century began, influential American Puritans like Cotton Mather claimed that the Indians should learn English and deemphasized the Indian Library. The last book published by the New England Company was *The Indian Primer* (1720). The cessation of new translations signaled the end of this pioneer effort at conversion.

Active religious effort had lasted an even shorter time; King Philip's War (1675) proved the effective end of it. Vaughan estimates that by this time twenty percent of the Indians in New England had been converted, a number which fell short of John Eliot's hope that all Indians be converted in the forty years from the beginning of Eliot's ministry in 1646. The reasons for failure were many. The Indian sachems resisted interference; the Indians lacked the time, money, and desire to change their ways of life; and they were dying of drink and disease. King Philip's War and increased English migration only hastened the demise of the Indian.

From 1675 on, Indian relations in New England were bad. In 1694, the General Court of Massachusetts reconfirmed the confinement of friendly Indians and offered bounties for hostile Indians' scalps. The General Court also provided a three-month prison sentence and a fine equal to double the bounty for one scalp for claiming the scalp of a friendly Indian as an enemy one. Although the bounty system might indicate otherwise, the Indian challenge was over; the Indian population declined and the Indian assumed subordinate roles. By 1750, only a few thousand Indians, out of 25,000 in 1600, were left in all of New England. Puritan hopes for a multinational community where Indians and white men would live in harmony had died.

I

While the Negroes in seventeenth-century America attracted less notice than the Indians, they, like the Indians, failed to be assimilated into colonial society on an equal basis. Although the trans-

Atlantic slave trade had grown in the seventeenth century, primarily through the efforts of the Dutch, Blacks had been brought to the English colonies largely by accident. Indeed, the first black slaves to come to Virginia, in 1619, were brought on a Dutch ship whose captain had seized them from a Spanish one. The unplanned arrival of these first Blacks typified the slave trade to the English colonies, which was only incidental to the trade to the West Indian sugar islands. In the 1650's, the Dutch, having learned the sugar business from the Portuguese in northeast Brazil went to the French and English controlled islands of the Caribbean—the lesser Antilles, Barbados, Martinique, Guadeloupe, St. Kitts, and Antigua—to offer a special package deal. The Dutch proposed to create sugar plantations, furnishing the technical know-how, the capital, the slaves, and the market. The planter need only supervise and grow rich. The offer attracted so many takers that the islands, which had originally contained small farms devoted to tobacco growing, changed to large-scale sugar production by 1660.

Three different societal models emerged in the New World: in highland Peru and Mexico the population was predominantly Indian but was controlled by a few Spanish; in North America, there was a largely white population with a few powerless Indians and Blacks; in the South Atlantic (the Caribbean area) the population was primarily black with a few Indians but was dominated by a white-planter elite.

By 1650, Blacks outnumbered Europeans in the New World. Although Europeans had not desired a predominantly black society, a system of black forced labor had become dominant in the South Atlantic. The local planters maintained that the reason for the Caribbean becoming predominantly black was the superior ability of the Negro to work and survive in a hot climate. The major reason, however, seems to have been the superior ability of the Negro to resist disease. Africans had been exposed to the greatest number of human illnesses; far fewer diseases existed in Europe; and America had been exposed to the fewest of all. This meant that the Indians were especially vulnerable to both African and European microbes, while the Africans were less vulnerable to most American and European diseases because of previous exposure to them. Europeans, on the other hand, were highly susceptible to the tropical diseases in both Africa and America. Disease, as a result, decimated the Indian population in the lowlands of the American tropics; a black population was substituted. The high European death rate in both Africa and tropical America discouraged white settlers. Europeans living in Africa suffered a mortality rate of 40 to 60 percent each year; if they settled in the West Indies, their death rate was 10 to 12 percent, compared with a 1 to 1.2 percent death rate if they stayed home.

This does not mean that life in the West Indies was either idyllic or long for black slaves. Because of the disparity between the numbers of male and female slaves—the slavers took two men for every woman—and because of black contraception and disease, there was a net natural decrease in the black population each year. This natural decrease amounted to 2 to 5 percent per year. The slave trade was maintained because of this decrease, the continuing need to augment the labor supply, and the relative cheapness of importing slaves. In 1695, a Jamaican slave cost about £20, the price of six hundred pounds of sugar or the amount of sugar one slave could be expected to raise annually. A slave, if he survived the first year, began to earn a profit for his master.

While there was an expanding slave trade in the South Atlantic to replace those Blacks who had died or those who had been prevented from being born, the opposite situation was true in North America. The black population there showed a natural increase almost from the beginning. In the seventeenth century the slave population in the English colonies was small, but it grew steadily through both natural increase and importation. The size of that growing population has been disputed. Wesley Craven, a scholar who has recently studied the question, believes that the estimates of earlier scholars, indicating that there were 16,000 Blacks in Virginia at the end of the seventeenth century, were too high. He arrives at a figure that is nearer half that number by using the following statistics. From 1630 to 1660, black slaves were imported at a rate of 20 per year; after 1660, the rate increased to almost 90 per year. The total number of slaves imported between 1630 and 1699, as shown by customs records, was 4,400. The total number of headrights (between 50 and 150 acres of land granted to a person who brought others into a colony at his own expense) of Blacks granted from 1635 to 1699 (when Governor Francis Nicholson ended the practice of granting headrights) also amounted to just over 4,000. The remaining 4,000, of Craven's estimated total of over 8,000, must have come from a natural increase. The reason for this natural increase would have been twofold: first, the sexual ratio of the slave population was nearly equal, unlike the West Indies; and second, the death rate for Blacks was lower than in the West Indies. Thus, while Virginia imported few slaves, the colony had a natural increase in population.

The status of Blacks in the English colonies has also been the subject of dispute. Alden T. Vaughan has recently analyzed the available materials on the Virginia colony from 1619 to 1629. One of the first references to Blacks occurred in 1624 when John Phillip, a Negro christened in England twelve years earlier, testified in court against a white man. Vaughan felt that Phillip was probably a member of a ship's crew in port. The muster lists of Virginia inhabitants in 1625 listed Negroes separately from Whites and gave abbreviated information about their origins. Few Blacks listed had two names; about half had no names at all. No age or date of arrival for most were given, although such information was required for all Whites, including indentured servants. As no Negroes were listed as free, all were probably slaves. There were three Negroes listed in the census of 1625, however, who had changed statuses in later records: one became a servant of Governor Sir Francis Wyatt; another asked to have headrights granted for Africans he had imported; and another owned servants of his own. Vaughan concludes from his study of the records that Blacks in Virginia were not of the same status as white indentured servants. The status of Blacks, however, was not necessarily permanently fixed; the possibility of freedom existed.

Even prior to 1660, a few Blacks in Virginia were free. They could sue and be sued in court; they could earn money; and they could buy and sell cattle. Edmund Morgan points out that the community of Northampton had ten free black households by 1668. He also describes the case of one Tony Lango, identified as a Negro, who was served with a subpoena but refused to appear in court because he was busy planting. Morgan believes this shows that Lango, at any rate, felt he was allowed enough freedom of action to reject a legal instrument.

There were statutes in early Virginia that indicated a differentiated status for Blacks, although they did not yet define Blacks as slaves. In 1640, for example, a master was held legally responsible for providing weapons for all servants except Negroes. Another indicator of the distinct status of Blacks in Virginia was the fact that Negro women were used as field hands while white indentured servants were spared from this. However, the kind of legal slavery that had developed in the English sugar islands, in Barbados for example, where all Negroes served for life unless they had contracts of indenture, did not exist in the North American colonies until later.

Laws against racial intermarriage are frequently cited as evidence of early prejudice and as evidence of an already fixed black social role. In 1662, Maryland passed a special law against interracial fornication, although a general law against fornication in the colony dated from 1630. In 1664, Maryland passed a law restricting marriages between black slaves and freeborn English women. This law did not specifically ban the marriage of black slaves and white women; rather it said that if such a marriage took place, the wife and resulting children would be slaves. In 1681, a supplementary law provided that if such marriages had been made at the instigation of the master of the slave in order to obtain more slaves, the wife could not be enslaved. Blacks were of a different status, but the exact status was unclear.

The dramatic change appeared in the southern colonies in the 1690's when a law prohibiting the private freeing of Negroes was passed in Virginia. Up to that time the proportion of free Negroes to slaves in that colony was greater than at any subsequent time. These free persons were indentured servants who had served out their time, were the descendants of such servants, or had been freed privately. The free Blacks could vote, possess property, have slaves, and have white servants. The first restriction was placed on free Negroes in 1670, when they were no longer allowed to have white servants. The prohibiting of private manumission in 1690 was followed by a law against black-white marriage in 1691. While the right to vote was not taken away from the free Black until 1723, slavery was already well established in Virginia by 1690, and the chance for the Negro to enter into full participation in the society was ended.

The reason for this was to be found in the white community and its past. The first years of settlement in Virginia were traumatic ones. Life was short and hard. Disease, a difficult climate, and Indian attacks kept the population low. Unlike the small black population, the white one was predominantly male. According to the census of 1625, the male-female ratio was four to one. Nor did the later migration to the colony improve the ratio; a typical ship coming to Virginia in 1635 had six men for every woman. In addition, the birth rate was lower than might have been expected, given the age of the settlers, because three-fourths of the white Virginians immigrated under indenture and were forced to delay marriage until their terms of servitude had expired. This caused the rate of population growth of Virginia to lag; it also meant that the population was composed of a large number of poor, white males.

Eighty-thousand Whites went to Virginia in the years 1630 to 1700, one-half of whom arrived between 1650 and 1675. Ten years of crop failure in England had encouraged their emigration. With the increased labor supply in the 1660's and 1670's, tobacco production increased and prices fell. As a result, planters drove harder bargains for new servants, terminating service for children at age twenty-four rather than age twenty-one. Because of poverty and debts, servants who had worked out their indentures and had purchased land were often forced to leave the land and to choose between working for others again or becoming idle. By 1676, the situation was potentially explosive. One-fourth of Virginia's white freedmen (former indentured servants) had neither houses nor land and were becoming troublesome. As a rule they were young, unmarried (because of the shortage of women), and armed (because of the need for colonial defense against Indians). They squatted on lands, they stole, and they enticed servants to their kind of life. They had become a major problem.

In 1670, both the crown and the colony took action. Universal male suffrage in Virginia was ended and property qualifications for voting were imposed. New legislation also increased the penalties for such servant crimes as running away and the killing of hogs, as well as limiting the free movement of servants. These laws, however, did not solve the problem, as Bacon's Rebellion showed in 1676. This rebellion began when a group of volunteer Indian fighters, composed in part of landless freedmen, turned their guns upon the colonial establishment with the avowed goal of plunder, land, and wealth. Bacon's Rebellion was the biggest uprising in Virginia prior to the Revolution and confirmed the colonial rulers' fear of the propertyless white poor. Caught between the threats of Indian raids and those of armed white men, the government chose the former. When William Byrd and Laurence Smith proposed to create semi-independent buffer settlements on the upper reaches of certain Virginia rivers, manned by landless freedmen, the assembly voted down the proposition through fear of white rebellion against the colonial government.

Slavery helped to ease the problem of the poor and rebellious white men. Savery had a number of advantages. The codes devised to control the Blacks seemed effective. Since slave mortality was decreasing, slaves were becoming less expensive. The slaves seemed more tractable than servants because they had no rising expectations. They were in sexual balance, under close supervision, unarmed, disorganized, and marked by their color for easy sur-veillance. Freedmen were free to serve as soldiers in the imperial army or to get land. After Bacon's Rebellion, migration from En-gland slackened, and the surplus of labor and the competition for land eased with this slackening. The European wars that followed the Glorious Revolution provided military employment for many able-bodied colonists.

Political developments also relieved social pressure. The rising class division in Virginia fostered representative government; the House of Burgesses became more tainted with democracy. The aspiring middle-class planter became a familiar member of this governing body which, from 1680 on, gained power at the expense of the Governor's Council. The poor white freedmen, in turn, projected their sense of inferiority onto the Blacks. Both planters and poor, white freedmen gained in status, and the familiar Amer-ican experience of the development of popular government at black expense had begun.

II

The Puritans in New England shared certain tenets of social philos-ophy with the Anglicans to the south. Both groups accepted the necessity and rightness of social gradation, but both believed that differences in social rank were not unalterable. A normal expecta-tion of colonial Americans was that their children would marry within their own social class. Until marriage, their children would serve an apprenticeship to a master in the role of a servant. If the family were poor, the children might, after finishing their appren-ticeship, take up an indenture. Indeed, the majority of indentured servants were children. Both Puritan and Anglican societies, then, recognized servitude as essential.

The Puritans did, however, have convictions that differed from those of the Anglicans and that had different social consequences; they disliked popery, avoided oaths, and were Sabbatarians. They emphasized work, implying that many Englishmen of the time were lazy. In attacking idleness, the Puritans encouraged the smaller employer, the self-employed, a certain section of the gentry-lawyers, and farmers particularly. Their Sabbatarianism also reflected a work ethic; when a man worked six days, he needed a day of rest. The Puritans posed an urban ethos, a set of principles to offset the southern rural ones, and a new discipline, which, articulated by William Cranshawe and other Puritan ministers, was to turn bad men into useful members of a commonwealth. The Puritans created a new class of evil men, the poor. The Puritans saw the poor as being wicked and outside the bonds of society; they believed that these poor must be brought back into the community and put under its discipline. The ideal Puritan social order consisted of a regular work force that was controlled by external and internal discipline but which was not equalitarian.

The principal institution of this social order was the household. The family was authoritarian; children of all ages stood or even knelt when talking to their fathers, and grown sons removed their hats. The family combined the functions of a corporation, a school, a vocational institute, a church, a house of correction, a welfare institution, and a poorhouse. In one or two medium-sized rooms, as many as twelve people might have lived, worked, and played together. The family functioned at the expense of the freedom of the child, who remained in a subordinate position until marriage or until obtaining land of his own. The home contained family and servants. The term servant "covered the whole spectrum of persons who might be resident in a given household but not a member of the immediate family," according to John Demos in his *The Little Commonwealth*. Unmarried children of other families might be considered servants, as well as children whose parents had failed to control them. There might be Indian children or servants who were being Christianized; sometimes there was a black servant. The servants were not permitted to marry and were treated like children; they were also assured of the necessary creature and spiritual comforts. Indian and black servants differed from white ones mainly in that their services continued without a time limit. The terms slave and servant were often used interchangeably. The meaning of the word slave encompassed prisoners of war, prisoners in jail, and rebels against the government. In the New England family, the servant, child, and slave possessed similar roles. However, some children and some servants could eventually escape the confines of the family.

Blacks could be found in Massachusetts Bay as early as 1633; Blacks were reported in Connecticut in 1639 and in New Haven in

1644. While their number was never very large (Massachusetts in 1715 had 2,000 Negroes out of a total colony population of 96,000) and while they experienced prejudice, the treatment of both slave and free Black appears to have been basically more liberal than in later times, according to a study by Robert C. Twombly and Robert H. Moore. In their study, Twombly and Moore reported that prejudice against Blacks was mostly displayed through derogatory language and imputation of inferiority. Cotton Mather, for example, complained because a naval lieutenant had named a slave after him, while Samuel Sewall adjudged that Mather's treatment of him was worse than if his father had been a "Neger." The record of administrative justice does not show that this kind of derogation was carried over into the courts. The free Negro had a right to police protection, to legal counsel, to trial by jury, to a fair and considered hearing, and to impartial justice. Whether or not the right was always honored, it (contrary to later practice) did exist. Black testimony, for example, was admissable in court against Whites. In 1679, Wonn, a Negro, testified against a white woman who was suspected of arson; in 1690, the Negro Mingo testified in a suit involving warehouse arson.

Skin color did not affect penalties for convicted felons. The matter of color did not prejudice appeals, testimony, or length of sentence. In 1692, Mary Black, a Negro servant owned by Nathaniel Putnam of Salem, was tried, convicted, and jailed for witchcraft. The next year, however, the governor pardoned her. At this same time, Whites were being hung for practicing witchcraft. The Salem witchcraft trials relied heavily on the testimony of Tituba, a Negro servant from Barbados. Although her testimony was very vivid—Kai Erikson calls it one of the most exuberant ever recorded —it was accepted at face value. An examination of the sentences of black and white criminals shows little differences in the main among penalties assessed for identical crimes.

Sexual crimes have often provided a good index to racial feeling (at least, this has been the southern experience). Although Massachusetts had a full complement of laws controlling sexual behavior, there were no racial provisions in these laws until 1705 when interracial marriages were prohibited. Fornication merited a penalty ranging from a fine of forty to fifty shillings or a whipping of ten to twenty lashes, regardless of the race of the individuals involved. The severity of the sentence depended upon the attitude of the judge, and mild or severe punishment was uniformly meted out to Black and White alike. Bastardy was punishable with the same penalty, and, in addition, the father had to contribute to child support. Again race made no difference. One white woman, Hannah Bonny, received the sentence of being "well whypt" for having a bastard, while her Negro lover got the same punishment with the addition of eighteen pence per week for child support. Rapists could suffer the death penalty, but neither of the two Negroes who were found guilty of rape in colonial Massachusetts were put to death. The first, Basto Negro, raped the three-year-old daughter of his master in 1676; because of his master's appeal for mercy, he received thirty-nine lashes and a rope to wear around his neck for the rest of his life instead of the death penalty. The second man, John Negro, pulled Sarah Phillips of Salem off her horse and attempted to rape her. He was fined £5 plus court costs and banished from the colony. On the other hand, an Indian named Sam in 1682 received a whipping and banishment for an accomplished rape, while two whites, convicted of the same crime, were hanged. The death penalty was meted out as well to a white boy, Thomas Granger, for "buggery" with "a mare, two goats, five sheep, two calves and a turkey." The element of race did not appear to enter into the penalties for sexual crimes in Massachusetts; the penalties reflected rather the circumstances of the offenses.

The same was true for cases of murder. In 1684, a Negro, Robert Troyes, shot and killed a white man. Troyes' defense in court consisted of his sworn testimony that he was aiming at the door of the house and had not intended to hit the victim. The jury believed him and only convicted him of manslaughter, for which the penalty was a £5 fine or a whipping. The only case on record of a white man killing a Black was in Maine in 1694. In this case the white man, who killed his own servant, received a £10 and 10 shilling fine on conviction of manslaughter. Interracial violence was seen as being no different than other violence.

Discriminations against Indians and Negroes did exist. No Black or Indian could serve in the militia after 1656, and legislation for the regulation of Negroes, mulattoes, Indians, servants, and apprentices first appeared in 1680. Three laws applied to persons in these five categories: the first prohibited buying or selling liquor, the second forbade dealing in stolen goods, and the third disallowed going aboard a ship weighing over twelve tons without a permit. The major restrictions on Negroes, however, did not emerge until the first decade of the eighteenth century. In 1702, the

General Court tried to eliminate the use of black slaves and to encourage white servants to come to Massachusetts. The stated motives for this move were both social and economic. Masters wanted to import black servants because taxes on black servants were lower, because black service was for life, and because these servants did not have to be equipped for militia duty. Black slaves were cheaper than white servants, although they supposedly needed more clothes in winter and were less productive. When black labor replaced white labor, owners expanded their land holdings, making it more difficult for white servants to take up land after their term of service ended. These frustrated white servants often became runaways and thieves; thus, there were fewer persons to share the burden of military defense. Because of these facts, the General Court believed that black slaves must be more strictly controlled and that fewer black slaves should be admitted into the colony.

In 1703, two more laws were enacted: the first set a curfew of nine o'clock for Negroes, Indians, mulattoes, slaves, and servants (no individual in these categories was allowed on the streets after nine without a permit); the second provided that manumission of slaves had to be accompanied by a £50 security bond from the master. In 1705, the importation of a Negro servant cost £4 duty, and conviction of interracial fornication resulted in the banishment of the black partner from the colony. In 1707, free Negroes were prohibited from entertaining nonwhite servants and were given alternate service—working on highways and streets—in lieu of militia duty.

The black man lived either as a slave or a second-class citizen in English North America in the seventeenth century. Although he was degraded, a roughly equal position in the lower stratum of the social system was potentially open to him. But this possibility was fading by the end of the century; the Negro, like the Indian, was not destined to live in peace and harmony in a society of equals.

III

Scholarly speculation continued in the seventeenth century on the origin, character, and future of both Indians and Blacks. Affected by, and yet remote from, the social experiences of the time, thinkers developed the paradigm based on the legend of Noah and tried to reconcile it with religious expectations of the time that the Last Judgment might be near. Scholars tried to build an anthropology, a history, a taxonomy, and a cosmology all on a single framework.

The Indian was incorporated relatively easily in European thinking into the legend of Noah. Travelers had reported back to the Europeans at home stories of such things as circumcision, legends of floods, and devil-worship among the Indians, all of which were taken as evidence that the Indians were heirs to Jewish tradition and thus descendants of Noah.

Another, more secular, legend about the Indian also appeared in Europe during the seventeenth century. It was the legend of Pocahontas, the Indian princess, and concerned the uniting of the races through sexual means. The legend started with Captain John Smith's *General Historie* ... in which he reported an incident where he was surrounded by thirty naked young girls, whose bodies were painted different colors and decorated with a few feathers. Led by Pocahontas, these nubile maidens, after dancing around a fire for an hour, supposedly escorted Smith to his house and tormented him with the question, "Love you not me?" Pocahontas, having developed an affection for Smith, then saved him from a head bashing. Smith had used this same story line before; while in Turkey, he claimed to have been saved from death in somewhat the same manner by the wife of a high Muslim official. Despite its lack of originality, the myth of love in the woods, as Leslie Fiedler called it, persisted, and the Indian princess became the European symbol for America. As portrayed in pictures, she was handsome, vigorous, naked to the waist, and armed with a bow and arrow. She was believed to be a descendant of the Indian Queen, who was a symbol for the Western hemisphere and who was depicted as an Amazon carrying a club with the arrow-pierced head of a man lying near her feet. The legends of the Indian Queen and Pocahontas demonstrate the fascination of the European with the physically attractive but savage woman who could bridge the gap between red and white.

In 1613, two masques were performed at the Inns of Court in England to celebrate the marriage of Princess Elizabeth. One of these, written by Chapman, had an Indian theme and incorporated the conventional anthropological wisdom of the day. The masque proclaimed the Indians to be descendants of Noah because their legends contained a flood, because they worshipped one God, and because they had worshipped devils. In the same year, a famous travel account, *Purchas his Pilgrimage*, appeared. This book contained a critique of earlier accounts of the origins of the Indians and was the first such definitive work by an Englishman. (The book became a favorite of James I who claimed to have read it seven times.) Purchas, an educated scholar who had served as chaplain to the Archbishop of Canterbury, decided that no one could be certain as to which nation came from which son of Noah and that although many nations had come and gone since the time of Moses, all had originated after the flood. In the first edition of his book, he rejected the idea that the Indians were descendants of the Carthaginians; in the third edition, he said they came from Asia.

The opinion that Indians came from Asia was shared by most Englishmen as well as by Edward Brerewood in his *Enquiries touching the diversity of languages, and religions through the chiefe parts of the world,* published in 1614. Brerewood, a professor of astronomy at Gresham College in England who studied languages as a hobby, used a process of elimination to decide upon Indian origin. The vast expanse of the Atlantic and the color and primitiveness of the Indians were factors which convinced Brerewood to eliminate Europe and Africa as places of Indian origin. Indians had no ships and would have been more sophisticated, in his opinion, had they come from Europe or Africa. Brerewood considered the evidence for Indians being the Ten Last Tribes of Israel as weak. The physical evidence of circumcision among Indians was limited and relatively recent. Brerewood, like Purchas, believed that the reported smallness of the Indian population proved that the Indians were latecomers to America and that their Asian origin accounted for their barbarism.

Sir Walter Raleigh spent his last years in the Tower of London writing a *History of the World.* Published in 1614, his history began with Adam and was concerned with the legend of Noah. Like Purchas, Raleigh believed that the Indians could not be traced to any one son of Noah because the derivation of ancestry was impossible beyond the first few generations following the flood. Raleigh, like Purchas and Brerewood, denied those theories which indicated that the Indians had come from Atlantis, Ophir, Spain, or the Near East. He also claimed that the Indians came from Asia, probably when the Old and New Worlds were connected by a land bridge or separated by only a narrow body of water. The similarities among the views of Purchas, Raleigh, and

Brerewood reflect the general qualities of the commonly accepted English view of human origin and history, which was derived from a biblical account of man's creation and dispersal and contained implicit assumptions about human unity.

The first settlers in New England also shared the belief in man's unity based on a common origin. According to Alden T. Vaughan, they had no clear-cut Indian policy "because they seldom thought of the Indian as a race apart." The Puritan settlers believed that the Indian was originally white but had been darkened by weather and skin dyes and that he was a descendant of the Ten Lost Tribes of Israel. (It is curious that more credence was given this last theory by Englishmen in the New World who knew the Indian than by Englishmen in the Old World who did not). The Indian was not considered a natural enemy of the colonist but rather an unfortunate heathen, one who had been subverted either by his physical environment or by the devil and who deserved to hear the message of Christ. The moral challenge for the colonist was to convert, civilize, and educate the Indian as rapidly as possible. The early Puritan settlers believed that Satan had a hold on the Indians and that the Indians were sinful but regarded them as less loathsome than certain Christians, such as the Catholics and Quakers who failed to recognize Puritan truth.

The Indians were seen to have weaknesses: they lacked ambition and loved liquor; they wore few clothes and greased their bodies. The early New England settlers tried dutifully to keep white temptations from the Indian and the Indian temptations from the wayward settler. The Puritans sent Thomas Morton back to England because he had sold firearms and liquor to the Indians and because he had harbored lawless and irresponsible persons and runaway slaves. Morton later returned to New England where he once more got into trouble with the Puritans by shooting some Indians with hailshot to get their canoe. The Puritans punished him by seizing his goods and burning down his house in public view of the Indians.

The risk of unconventional sexual relations was ever present (in most cases, the Indian seems to have been the passive party and the white the aggressor). In 1631, John Dave endured a whipping for enticing an Indian woman to lie with him. The woman and her husband had protested to the Massachusetts General Court, which convicted Dave. According to testimony in 1639, Mary Mendome seduced an Indian man, despite the fact she was married. She was whipped through the town at a cart's tail and given a scarlet letter to wear. Her lover was whipped at a stake with a halter around his neck. The most serious problem, however, was neither the presence of the Indian in New England settlements, nor interracial sexual relations, but the alternate way of life represented by the pagan Indian. John Winthrop in 1642 lamented the fact that some Englishmen, who traded powder with the Indians, lived alone without government on the frontier. Both actions presented a serious threat to social order. In 1652, the General Court of Plymouth ordered Joseph Ramsden to move into a town rather than to continue to live without community discipline among the Indians. This period was not the last time that the Indian way of life unsettled the settled Whites.

The Puritans believed that they were destined to bring Christ and civilization to the Indian and to give order to the land; but they also believed the Indian experience to be a providential lesson from God. The Puritans had little faith in contemporary accounts of Indians in New England as these accounts explained Indian behavior in natural rather than religious ways. Thomas Morton's *New English Canaan* (1632) showed the Indian to be a slightly tarnished noble savage; Philip Vincent's *True Relation* (1638) made the Indian a vigorous warrior; and Thomas Lechford's *Plain Dealing* (1643) pictured the Indian as a natural person. None of these books revealed God's plan for the world and were rejected by the Puritans. Also rejected was John Cotton's *The Way of Congregational Churches Cleared* (1648) because its message was overly pessimistic. Cotton warned that the prophecy in Revelations 15 meant that the Indians could not be converted until after both the conversion of the Jews and the appearance of the anti-Christ. The Puritans preferred to believe that the Indians could be converted and that God's plan called for the Puritans to do it.

In order to communicate with the Indians the colonists had to learn their languages; the first aid to that learning was Roger Williams's *A Key into the Language of America*, published in London in 1643. Williams's book not only provides an insight into the Algonquin language but also into the colonial view of the Indian. Williams divided his book into the following parts: origin and descent of the Indians; Indian religions; their manners and customs; and the possibility of conversion. He began with the assertion that while everyone grants that Indians were descendants of Adam and Noah, no one can agree on how they came to the New World. The

Indians did not know; they believed they were indigenous and that their Creator had placed them where they lived. Although the Indians lacked knowledge of their own origin, Williams concluded that they were descendants of the Ten Lost Tribes of Israel. He based his conclusion upon the evidence provided by comparative linguistics and cultural correspondences. The Indians used words similar to those of the Jews, and the Indian customs of annointing heads, giving dowries, and isolating menstruating women were the same as Jewish ones. Williams did not know how the Indians got to the New World; but he speculated that the Southwest was their first American home.

He recounted many Indian customs, using them to draw universally applicable morals and to attack the follies of his own nation. He claimed that Indian society was superior to the drunken, gluttonous societies of Europe, and even decided that Indian sexual practices were not pernicious. According to him, Indians regarded fornication but not adultery as acceptable; they had several wives because of economic necessity (the wives were needed to work in the fields) and sexual convenience (the Indian women did not have sexual relations while nursing a baby, a period of several years). The Indians smoked more tobacco than Europeans only because God had not given them beer and wine. They regarded dreams as messages from God and prayed at any time or place, as David had. While male Indians' hair was long, it was not as long as that of degenerate Englishmen. Williams traced the Indian kinship system much as a modern social anthropologist might have done, noting the relationships of uncles and nephews to the family and noting the duties of brothers to pay each other debts of money and honor. These relations and duties, plus the inordinate love of children shown by the Indian parent, caused Williams to conclude, "In the *ruines* of deprave *mankinde* are yet to be founde *Natures destinctions,* and *Natures affection*" (1643). In his view, the Indians were already prepared for conversion in their hearts. Although they were full of sin and did such barbarous things as to eat the brains of their enemies, Williams felt that Indians might expect God's call. Thus he wrote, "Nature knows no difference between *Europe* and *Americans* in blood, birth, bodies, etc. God having of one blood made all mankind [Acts 17] and all by nature being children of wrath" (1643). True, the Indian woman was naked except for a small apron, but she was less wanton in Williams's view than the European woman, and "the best clad English-

man, not cloth'd with Christ, more naked is; than naked Indian."
Williams began with the conviction that all men were equal in
their sins and ended with the belief that Christ's grace could transform anyone.

Williams's interest in the Indian was paralleled in Massachusetts Bay by the concern of John Eliot, pastor of the First Church
of Roxbury. Like some other Puritan missionaries to the Indians,
Eliot took time from his regular parish duties to preach to the Indians and to the whites about the Indians. His efforts proved quite
successful; the General Court of Massachusetts, at his behest, approved the idea of creating Indian towns in 1647. This kind of
effort was not confined to the New World. In 1643, a pamphlet
appeared in London called *New Englands First Fruits* whose purpose was to raise money in England for missionary work to the
Indians. In 1647, an anonymous tract, *The Day-Breaking if not the
Sun-rising of the Gospel with the Indians in New-England*, became
available on the streets of London. This tract described Eliot's
work, without mentioning him by name, and asked for financial
help from England. In 1648, another tract, *The Clear Sun-Shine of
the Gospel breaking forth upon the Indians in New England*, appeared; in 1649, still another, *The Glorious Progress of the Gospel,
amongst the Indians in New England. Manifested by three letters,
Under the Hand of that famous Instrument of the Lord Mr. John,
Eliot. And another from Thomas Mayhew jun.* All requested money
to buy medicine, clothes, and tools for the Indians and reminded
Englishmen of their Christian duty.

This interest in Indians continued in 1650 with the publication
of a book in London that combined the ideas of Roger Williams
with the millenial fervor aroused by the English Civil War. The
book was Thomas Thorowgood's *Jewes in America*. Thorowgood
revived the idea that the Indians were the Ten Lost Tribes. He
based his ideas on material from a book published in Amsterdam
called *Spes Israelis*. This book, by Manasseh ben Israel, told
the story of a Portuguese Jew who reported in 1644 that he had
found Indians who were Jews in New Granada and Cartagena.
According to this report, these Jews had originally come from Asia,
had been the first settlers in the New World, but had been driven
into isolated areas by later settlers who were Gentiles. Supposedly,
not all of the ten tribes had come to the New World, nor was
America to be their final home. The discovery of these Indian-Jews

in America signaled to Manasseh ben Israel the start of God's redemption. These Jews were to rise up, cast out the Spanish, and return to Israel to be united with the other tribes.

Thomas Thorowgood's book had a different purpose from that of Manasseh ben Israel. While the major part of his book consisted of evidence of the Jewish origin of the Indians, its aim was to further the Christianizing of the Indian.

Using the work of Roger Williams, Thorowgood pointed to linguistic parallels between the Indians and the Jews, to similar kinship relations and marriage restrictions (e.g., the Indians were endogamous, marrying only into their own tribes and kindred), and to the Indian legends about a fair God and about wandering great distances before finding their home. But, above all, he relied upon common customs of Indians and Jews (he found twenty-six in all) and common religious rites (twenty-five in all). To disarm the critics of his thesis, Thorowgood advanced three propositions: the Jews had come to America over a land bridge from Asia in the same way that "bears, lions, tigers, and wolves" had come (this eliminated the problem of the second ark); the Jews had been in America 2,000 years (this was sufficient time for the Indians to have populated the immense areas of North, Central, and South America); and the Jew in America had backslid and God had punished them (thus answering the question of why the Indians were primitive). After proving his thesis to his satisfaction, Thorowgood turned to prophecy. He claimed that the end of the world was near, and to fulfill the biblical injunction that all will be reached by the Gospel before that day, he urged that greater missionary effort be spent in the New World. The agency of conversion must be Puritanism, whose superiority was shown in Eliot's work. Thorowgood's thesis of the Jewish origin of the Indians assumed the validity of both the legend of Noah and the use of cultural correspondences.

Even those who denied that the Indians were Jews based their arguments on the legend of Noah model. Haman L'Estrange's *Americans no Jewes* (1651), published to rebut Thorowgood, utilized biblical proof to support another theory that Indians were Asians. L'Estrange used geographic explanations as well as cultural ones to back his argument. He argued that America became more populated by the Indians as one moved westward because that was the side closest to Asia. L'Estrange held that the customs and rites of the Indians that Thorowgood had thought were Jewish were common to many other peoples and merely reflected common environmental factors—the practice of the Jews and Indians of wearing few clothes, for example, was a function of their hot climates.

As the seventeenth century progressed, the Indian missionary effort slowed and the Puritan attitude changed. King Philip's War was seen as a kind of Divine retribution for the sins of the present, degenerate younger generation. The older generation had planted the colony and prospered, a sign of piety. But the new generation had backslid, according to the ministers, and was experiencing God's wrath, manifested by King Philip's War and by the lack of success in Indian conversion. This was clear to Increase Mather who said in a sermon in 1679 that the errand into the wilderness had been forgotten.

King Philip's War was not only an example of God's retribution but also showed the Indian as agent of the Devil. There were two commonly held images of the Indian during the war—one, the skulking, treacherous enemy and, the other, the friendly protector from enemy Indians—but the image of the hostile Indian prevailed and can be found in the writings of Increase and Cotton Mather. Increase Mather's *Brief History of the Warr with the Indians* (1676) said that the Indians were little better than beasts, while Cotton Mather preached in 1689 that hostile Indians were wolves worthy only of extermination. In another sermon, he denounced the Indians as being lazy drones, liars, and overindulgent parents to their children; this latter example was considered subversive to Puritan family government, the base of the Christian commonwealth. The Indian was seen as a more and more diabolical figure.

While the Indians had suffered heavy losses in King Philip's War, they recovered enough to participate in the imperial wars that followed—King William's War (1689–97) and Queen Anne's War (1702–13). These war years were the years of greatest Indian depredation in New England, years when Indians captured approximately 600 white women and children. Only 29 percent of those captured ever returned. Of the remainder, 25 percent were converted by the French or by converted Indians to Catholicism, 15 percent became Indians, and the other 31 percent, whose ultimate status is unknown, refused repatriation. Serious questions were raised about the success of Indian conversion and the relative attraction of Indian and Puritan life. Puritans began to ask the question which was to become common in the eighteenth century, to be asked by Benjamin Franklin in 1753 and by Crévecoeur in

1782. It was, "Why, given the choice, did the converted Indian always revert to savage ways, while the converted white, given the taste of savagery, so seldom wanted to return to civilized society?"

The captives themselves articulated some of their reasons. A few indicated spiritual motives, saying that the Indians were morally superior. Others found Catholicism, taught to Indians by the French, more emotionally satisfying. Personal problems also influenced some persons; Eunice Williams, daughter of Reverend John Williams of Deerfield, did not return to her home because her father had remarried and she did not wish to be subordinate to a stepmother.

The Indian's way of life appealed to many and for a number of reasons. In the first place, the Indians often adopted captives, with impressive ceremony, to replace lost children. As one converted Indian asked, did the Whites adopt their enemies? The answer was, of course, no. In the second place, the Indian way of life seemed a more natural one, free of artificial wants and absent of care. Puritans lived a more hectic life. The Indians required no obligations from converts, while captives ransomed from the Indians had to work out their ransoms as indentured servants on their return to the colony. For all these reasons, captivity aroused concern and fear in the New England community.

These emotions led to a new kind of literature, the captivity stories, the most harrowing of which were written by women. The first to appear was Mary Rowlandson's account, published in 1682, of her capture during King Philip's War. In her book, Mrs. Rowlandson recounted how she was first afraid for her life and the lives of her loved ones and then afraid of the potential Indianization and Catholicization of her children. Rowlandson's story, however, was not nearly as harrowing as that of Hannah Duston, the most famous captivity story and one, according to Leslie Fiedler, that helped begin another American myth. Hannah Duston's experience, as told by Cotton Mather and retold by Hawthorne and Thoreau, became the archetype of the legend of the avenging white woman, the anti-Pocahontas. A band of Catholic Indians raided Haverhill, Massachusetts, on March 15, 1697. The family of Thomas Duston was attacked; one of Duston's eight children, his wife Hannah, and a nurse were captured. The Indians almost immediately killed the baby child, but they did not harm the others. Hannah Duston pretended to be docile and, catching the Indians off guard, killed them all with an axe. As she was returning home, she recalled that the ten Indians' scalps would fetch a £50 bounty, so she backtracked and scalped them. She returned to Haverhill, petitioned the reluctant government into giving her £25, and became a celebrity. Cotton Mather, in *Duodecennium Luctuosum* (1714), called her an Old Testament heroine and justified her bloody deed on the grounds that her own child was killed.

In addition to citing actual evidence of Indians torturing captives and killing children, Mather hinted at the danger of Indian rape, although there was no record of this ever occurring. Like his father, Increase, and his fellow minister, Solomon Stoddard, Cotton Mather used Indian captivity as a metaphor for man's bondage in sin. Redemption from Indian captivity he equated with man's redemption from sin through Christ. Mather provided a symbolism for the Puritan counterattack on the Indian way of life. Mather's Indian was no longer the representative of natural man; he was an agent of the Devil.

By the end of the seventeenth century, the Puritan in America had changed his view of the Indians. No longer was he hopeful for the redemption of the native American; rather he feared the reversion of the colonist to savagery. But he still clung to the belief in man's basic equality because of his descent from Noah, and he still respected the theory that the Indians were remnants of the lost tribes of Israel.

In Europe, the situation was changing. The model based on the legend of Noah had been questioned by the French Huguenot La Peyrere, who advanced a polygenetic explanation of human origin based on the idea of the creation of men before Adam. La Peyrere's book *Prae-Adamitae*, written in the 1640's but not published until 1655, focused on two anomalies in the legend of Noah model. The first concerned the length of time humans had lived in America; there seemed to be evidence that this was longer than the time that had supposedly elapsed since the flood. The second anomaly involved the ages of civilizations in Egypt and Mesopotamia, both of which seemed older than Jewish civilization. La Peyrere declared that humans had existed in the New World before the flood and that Egypt was older than Israel. In his view, Adam was not the first man; he was only the first Jew, for God had created the Gentile first. Noah's flood was a local one and destroyed only the Jews; the Gentiles in other parts of the world—Egypt, Mesopotamia, and America—survived. La Peyrere used both biblical and historical sources to support his theory and to attack the traditional explanation. His book, translated into English in 1656, incited twelve attempts at refutation in that same year. While the polygenetic theory at first attracted few supporters, it did question the sufficiency of the explanation commonly held.

English scholars also added their weight on the side of doubt for the completeness and accuracy of the popular paradigm. Sir William Petty, in a speech before the Royal College of Physicians (1676) and in his book *The Scale of Creatures* (1677), divided men into several races, groups that were not made by God and were not related to the flood or creation. (Margaret T. Hodgen, a historian of anthropological theory, claims that Petty was the first to replace the word nation with race.) Another scholar, Thomas Burnett, in his *Theory of the Earth* (1681), also denied the existence of a world-wide flood and supported his denial with evidence indicating that the world could not have been repopulated in the short period of time after the flood. He did not attack the authority of the Bible, but he said it was ambiguous. Nor were the accounts attributed to Adam and Noah necessarily wrong; according to Burnett, these individuals lacked full knowledge of what was happening to them and had erroneously assumed that no one else existed elsewhere.

Still another tack, which questioned the paradigm, was taken by Sir Edward Tyson who brought anthropoid apes to the attention of the English and European intellectual community in his "*Orang-Outang, sive Homo Sylvestris*" or, "*The Anatomy of a Pygmie* compared with that of a Monkey, an ape, and a Man." To which is added a "*Philological Essay* concerning the Pygmies, the Cynocephali, the Satyrs, and the Sphinges of the *Ancients,* wherein it will appear that they are all either *Apes* or *Monkeys,* and not *men* as formerly pretended" (1699). Tyson accounted for the monsters of legend in a naturalistic, biological way and compared man to the newly discovered apes through anatomical resemblances. Tyson said that the ape was close to man and the pygmy was a link holding the two together. He helped begin the construction of a naturalistic explanation of the origin of man that was finally to replace the Providential explanation altogether. His construct, however, placed the black man in a subordinate position to the white man. The modern study of man, the animal, began with the Black believed to be nearer the ape.

The seventeenth century was one of disappointed hopes. The vision of a society where different men of different nations could live together in peace and harmony, whether Negro or Indian or English, failed to materialize in practice. As the century ended, the Indian on the Atlantic coast was dying from diseases and drink and living in a limbo between white and Indian societies. The Black's chances for living outside of slavery were diminishing. Thinkers of the time explained these events in terms of God's will, but this explanation, like that of the origin of man, was in the process of being challenged.

Chapter 3

Freedom for Some, Slavery for Others

The eighteenth century was one of high population growth for colonial America. From 1700 to 1860, the rate of population growth, which was twice that in England, is estimated to have been 34 percent per decade. (This figure, however, is unreliable since records are uncertain, particularly those prior to the census of 1790 when the main enumerations were done by colonial governors at the request of British authorities). In particular, the records are questionable regarding Indians or Negroes since neither the colonial nor the Imperial governments were initially much interested in the fate of either. However, the general trend is clear; the Indian population declined and the black population expanded greatly.

By 1770, Negroes made up 21.8 percent of the total colonial population, which was the highest proportion of Blacks to Whites at any time in American history. This figure reflects the rapid growth of slavery in the eighteenth century. The contribution to population made by the importation of slaves has been estimated in Table 3.1.

However, Philip Curtin, the leading scholar on the demography of the slave trade, disagrees with these figures. He indicates that the slave who was imported from Africa to the West Indies often was counted a second time as he went from the West Indies to the colonial South. Despite the possibility of double counting, the list of figures indicates a trend. There was an increase during this

TABLE 3.1

Year	Number of Slaves	Percent of Total to British America
1701–10	9,000	9.2
1711–20	10,800	9.4
1721–30	9,900	8.5
1731–40	40,500	23.9
1741–50	58,500	28.0
1751–60	41,900	21.4
1761–70	69,500	29.8
1771–80	15,000	13.5

Source: J. Potter in "The Growth of Population in America, 1700–1860," in D.U. Glass and D.E.C. Eversley, eds., *Population in History* (Chicago, 1965).

period in both the total number of slaves sent to the Americas and the percentages of slaves destined for the North American colonies. The reasons for the increase lay in the political situation in Europe. The British had gained the *asiento,* a monopoly on the shipment of slaves to Spanish America, from the Treaty of Utrecht at the end of the War of the Spanish Succession in 1713. This meant that there was an expansion of British interest in the slave trade. At the same time that the importation of slaves was highest in the North American colonies, the British Empire was engaged in wars with Spain—The War of Jenkins's Ear and the French and Indian War. To avoid Spanish naval forces in the Carribean, British slave ships sailed instead to the Carolinas, Maryland, Virginia, and Georgia. The result was a blacker America.

White Americans were ambivalent toward the increase in the number of Negro slaves. On the one hand, they wanted and needed cheap labor; on the other hand, they were concerned about the impact that Negroes would have upon the new society. This ambivalence can be seen in Benjamin Franklin's pioneering demographic study, *Observations Concerning the Increase of Mankind, Peopling of Countries, etc.* (1751). Franklin made what appeared to be shrewd and accurate population estimates. He showed that the American population was increasing rapidly, doubling every twenty years. The major reason for this, he claimed, was natural increase; Americans had an average of eight children from each marriage while Europeans had only four. Franklin attributed the differences in numbers of offspring to the earliness of American marriages— which appears to have been a misconception on his part—and to the greater availability of land in America. He correctly saw that America was becoming less urban and more rural as time passed.

Of all the colonies, the two tobacco colonies, Maryland and Virginia, had the largest populations. This concerned Franklin because of the number of black slaves in these colonies. Using short term figures, he estimated that the black population of the North American colonies, which had tripled between 1730 and 1750, would double again by 1770. His extrapolation, which was incorrect, projected an even larger black population than there was to be. He suggested ending the slave trade, not because he was opposed to slavery but because he did not want more Blacks. It should also be pointed out that he objected to the entering European immigrants, particularly the Germans. The crown, however, did not heed Franklin's warnings, and most of the colonial laws that rejected transported convicts or regulated the slave trade by the imposition of duties were disallowed by the Board of Trade and the Privy Council in England.

While the increase in black slaves occurred at the expense of the number of white servants, one-half of the white immigrants still came as servants in 1750. There was still no large gap in actual practice between white servant and black slave; both could be bought and sold, rented out, and inherited. The white servant could sue and be sued but could not vote even if he owned property. He, like the slave, could not marry without his master's consent. Neither slave nor servant were much respected; both were considered idle, irresponsible, unhealthy and immoral.

The earlier problem with freed white servants had continued up to and even into the eighteenth century; Jackson Turner Main has estimated that one-third of the work force in the South was landless at the time of the Revolution. Some of the free laborers were industrious, but most were considered the "vicious" poor. Both British and American authorities perceived the threat of armed revolt.

In the eighteenth century, however, the threat to the social order from landless Whites diminished while the threat from black servants and slaves increased. More land was available for Whites and provided more work opportunities. The first instance of active revolt by nonwhite groups occurred in 1712 in New York City. This revolt aroused concern because it involved both Blacks and Indian servants and raised the specter of the two groups combining into one threatening force. The plotting servants bound themselves to

secrecy through a blood oath and rubbed their bodies with a powder, supplied by a black "sorcerer," supposedly giving them in-
vulnerability. They fired an outhouse and attacked the volunteers
who came to put it out, killing nine and wounding several others.
The white reaction was severe. Although some servants escaped,
many were captured and 24 were condemned to death (the governor
pardoned six); 18 died either by being hanged or burned.

There were repeated alarms of this type in Virginia, although
no white persons were killed by Negro rebels until the Nat Turner
Revolt of 1831. From 1700 to about 1720, there was general unrest
in the colony. Suspected rebels were killed or deported: a supposed
plot in 1709 resulted in the hanging of three slaves; a plan for an
uprising in 1722 led to a demand for stronger laws; in 1730, the
gathering of 200 slaves from Norfolk and Princess Anne counties
for the supposed purpose of electing officers and plotting rebellion
resulted in the hanging of four slaves.

While the 1730's was a relatively quiet period in the North
American colonies, there were over a dozen bloody revolts in Jamaica during the period. News of these traveled to the mainland,
adding to the uncertainty caused by the rapid increase in slave
population. The Stono revolt in South Carolina in 1739 also aroused
fear. Enticed by the freedom offered in Spanish colonies, a number
of South Carolina slaves ran away from their owners and headed
for St. Augustine, Florida. In the ensuing fight, 80 slaves and 30
Whites were killed. The Stono Rebellion confirmed the reality of
the threat of slave revolt and convinced Whites of the need for
stricter social control of the Blacks.

The effort to control Negro slaves was complicated by the small
size of plantations and by informal living arrangements. While
there were large plantations in South Carolina after the 1740's
(with the rise of indigo as a cash crop), the majority of plantations
in the other colonies were small. In 1745, in Lancaster County, Virginia, seven out of ten white farmers owned slaves, but only three
out of ten owned more than 21 taxable slaves. By 1780, 40 percent
of all slaveowners in Virginia had fewer than five slaves and only 23
percent had more than 200. The small scale of slavery meant that
there were nonsegregated living facilities in many areas. Thad W.
Tate's study of Williamsburg in the eighteenth century showed that
slaves slept in outbuildings, in second floor rooms, or on pallets in
hallways, landings, and staircases in the main house. The physical

separation of black and white sleeping facilities in the South arrived only with the growth of large plantations.

Because of the danger of slave revolts, landowners consented to some limitation of the slave trade. The first of such measures limited the importation of slaves by imposing duties. In 1699, Virginians placed a 20 shilling tax on each slave imported. The English government disallowed an attempt in 1724 to impose a 40 shilling duty, but another tax, based upon the value of the slave and enacted in 1732, went unchallenged. In 1772, the colony tried (unsuccessfully) to end the slave trade by petitioning the crown. None of the Virginian efforts at limitation, however, succeeded in reducing the influx of Negroes very much; by 1790, Virginia had 40 percent of the slaves in the United States.

Along with attempts to limit the importation of Blacks was a tightening of the slave system in Virginia. Slaves were denied the right of trial by jury in 1692; those accused of crimes were tried by a judge commissioned by the governor. In 1705, a Virginia statute provided compensation for the owner of an executed slave, which implied that slaves were considered more as property than as human. In 1723 and 1748, comprehensive legal codes involving both free and unfree Negroes were passed. Among the provisions of these codes were: the denial of the right of the free Black to vote, the refusal to allow the benefit of clergy to Blacks plotting rebellion, the restriction of the right to possess arms to black householders and militiamen; and the increase in the severity of penalties for felonies particularly associated with Blacks—hog stealing and murder by poisoning. Black testimony was restricted, by the provision of the 1723 act, to capital crimes involving Blacks. Punishments for all black crimes were severe. Runaway slaves could have a foot amputated. Giving false testimony earned the punishment of nineteen lashes and the cutting off of both ears.

In the newer lower South, additional tactics for controlling Blacks emerged. The growth of the market for pitch and tar in the 1720's and for indigo in the 1740's in this area meant a concomitant need for black laborers. As a result, Blacks came to outnumber Whites in the Lower South by a factor of two to one. In 1750, the population of the South Carolina consisted of 30,000–40,000 Whites, 60,000 Indians, and 70,000–90,000 Blacks. The fear of an armed coalition between Negroes and Indians was complicated and intensified by the possibility of a coalition among Negroes, Indians, and neighboring Spaniards. To prevent such a combination, the colony of South Carolina tried to keep half of its soldiers on call in Charleston at all times to discourage revolts; it tried to limit the contact between Indians and Negroes; and it attempted to set the Indians against the Blacks. Indian visits to colonial towns were regulated; detribalized Indians could not marry Blacks; settlement Indians became trackers for slave catchers; and provisions for the return of slaves became standard clauses in Indian treaties. The colony used Negro slaves to fight the Indians in the Yamassee War of 1715–17; and the Whites blamed the smallpox epidemic of 1739, which decimated the Indians, on the Blacks. South Carolina solved the problem of a minority white population controlling two larger racial groups by turning the two groups against each other.

Paradoxically, the attack on the institution of slavery in the North American colonies came at the same time as the greatest growth of the institution. There had always been conflicting opinions on slavery, even among slaveowners, who believed that slavery was the base of both the colonial and imperial economy and yet that slaves endangered public safety. One of the first controversies over slavery occurred in colonial Georgia. The Germans of Ebenezer, a pioneer settlement, did not want slavery because they feared that marauding slaves would rob their houses and gardens. Oglethorpe, the major proprietor of the settlement, believed the Spanish would subvert slaves and weaken the colony's pivotal role in the imperial defense system. Other settlers objected to slavery on moral grounds. Although the original charter for Georgia in 1732 did not forbid slavery, a special law in 1735 did. But the colony was unable to grow without slavery, and pressure for the repeal of the law proved overwhelming. Arguments by proponents of slavery, including George Whitfield, a noted evangelist, resulted in the legalization of slavery in Georgia in 1750.

John Woolman and Anthony Benezet, both American Quakers, had begun to attack slavery by the mid-eighteenth century. Benezet reprinted, for American readers, George Wallace's *A System of the Principles of the Law of Scotland* (1760) which attacked the idea that slavery brings prosperity to a nation through the production of exportable crops; indeed, he said a nation might be richer with less foreign trade. Wallace also noted the social consequences of slavery and argued that equality was an ideal toward which all societies should strive. Benezet, in two of his own books, *A Short Account of*

That Part of Africa Inhabited by the Negroes... and The Manner by Which the Slave Trade is Carried On (1762) and *A Caution to Great Britain and her Colonies in a Short Representation of the Calamitous State of the Enslaved Negroes in the British Dominions* (1766), attacked slavery as man-stealing and advocated that the slaves resist by either running away or revolting against their masters. Unlike Wallace, Benezet concentrated on moral arguments and ignored the economic ones. His fellow Quaker, John Woolman, traveled in the American South to persuade Quakers of the wrongness of slavery. His testimony and his refusal to wear cotton clothing or use sugar succeeded in moving the Quakers toward an antislavery position by the time of the Revolution.

The Revolution gave Americans an opportunity to end the institution of slavery. The Founding Fathers believed slavery to be an evil and impermanent institution, but their primary concern was the creation of a viable white republic. Abolition of slavery conflicted in theory with their belief in property rights and provoked their fear of a propertyless mob. Even their personal efforts were equivocal. Washington freed his slaves, but only in his will; Jefferson did not free his slaves because of debts and because he felt that the newly freed slaves could not support themselves. The Revolutionary generation, according to William W. Freehling, assumed that the dangers to the Union, property, or the social order were so acute as to demand their full attention, and they did little to end slavery. However, they tried to set conditions so that slavery would be eliminated in the long-run.

What did they do? They tried to terminate the interoceanic slave trade, but only succeeded in postponing the end until 20 years later. The new constitution provided that the slave trade could not be outlawed until 20 years after ratification. They also attempted to limit the extension of slavery. In 1784, Jefferson proposed prohibiting slavery in all Western territories, including the future Southern states of Alabama, Mississippi, Kentucky, and Tennessee, but his proposal was defeated by a one vote margin. The Northwest Ordinance of 1787 did forbid slavery in the states of Ohio, Michigan, Illinois, Indiana, and Wisconsin. Slavery was not a major issue at the constitutional convention as the argument over whether the people or the states possessed ultimate sovereignty dominated the convention; the counting of slaves for purposes of representation was used to support the people's side of the argument. In 1789, the new constitution was not considered illiberal on the slavery issue;

no antislavery activists condemned it. But, once again, the new
government had put white interests over black ones. As Howard A.
Ohline says in "Republicanism and Slavery: Origins of the Three-
Fifths Clause in the United States Constitution," *William and Mary
Quarterly* (1971):

Slavery and the fears of slaveholders acted to assure a more democratic
political system for white men. The regretable paradox of American
Revolutionary Republicanism was that the new nation had to acknowl-
edge the existence of slavery in its legislature in order to be republican
and that the major dispute in the convention was not whether this
should or should not be, but *how* it would be done.

Slavery in the North died during and after the Revolution.
Vermont ended slavery in 1777, Pennsylvania in 1780, Massachusetts in 1783, Rhode Island in 1784, and Connecticut in 1787. New
York and New Jersey delayed the abolition of slavery until the
nineteenth century. Even with abolition, legal disabilities remained
in the North to limit the freedom of free Blacks.

It would be useful here to reflect upon the difference between
Latin America and the United States at this time. In the Spanish
colonies in the seventeenth and eighteenth centuries, the free Blacks
could penetrate white society by becoming members of the artisan
class, by serving in the militia or the police, by entering the pro-
fessions, or by buying patents of legal whiteness. The Spanish government used the free black population to balance that of the
Creoles and Penninsulares; by the end of the colonial period, the
number of free Blacks equaled or exceeded that of slaves and their
lot was steadily improving in relation to that of the slaves. The
English crown did not use the Blacks to balance the population of
native-born Englishmen. In the United States the number of free
Blacks declined from the time of the Revolution, and their lot
became worse. Without question, the Blacks' position in the United
States deteriorated as their numbers grew.

I

The Indians' condition in the colonies continued to be miserable as
their numbers shrank. Benjamin Franklin went so far as to say in
1751 that Providence seemed to have designed their extirpation.

Franklin had concluded that Indians living near colonists not only died of disease and drink at a higher rate but failed to match the natural increase of white Americans. The Indian male supposedly had a cold nature and was not driven by sexual urges. Also, the Indian woman would not have sexual relations with her husband from the time she was pregnant until she weaned her two-and-a-half- or three-year-old child, creating at least a four-year gap between children. Thus, the Indians could not equal colonial reproduction rates.

Missionary interest had flagged since the time of King Philip's War. The New England Company had received money through bequests which it had proposed to use by employing Harvard graduates to teach Indians and by endowing scholarships for Indians at William and Mary. The Company failed, however, to find individuals willing to teach the Indians or Indians willing to go to school. Two other groups from Great Britain had entered the missionary field, with equal lack of success. The first was The Society for the Propagation of the Gospel in Foreign Parts, an Anglican organization that was competitive with the Puritan New England Company and that received a royal charter in 1701. The second was the Scottish Society for Propagating Christian Knowledge, a Presbyterian missionary effort, which was chartered in 1709, but only able to send representatives to the New World in 1730. Despite the new organizations, missionary efforts for the Indians from Britain remained small and unsuccessful.

In the colonies, the earlier Puritan effort to Christianize Indians had diminished. Separate meeting houses for Indians were closed and Indian rooms in white churches opened. Students who had received financial aid at Harvard on the condition that they preach to the Indians were admonished with the threat of having to repay this money if they failed to do so (however, few students did either). In the 1730's, the impetus for converting the Indians had passed to revivalists who were involved in a new movement called the Great Awakening. These revivalists had a vigor not matched by their more rationalistic contemporaries. In 1734, an Indian town was established at Stockbridge, Massachusetts, with John Sergeant as the missionary. A colleague of Sergeant, David Brainerd, served as a minister to the Indians on the upper Delaware in Pennsylvania and New Jersey. The most famous American Indian school, Dartmouth, began as Moor's Indian Charity School in the 1750's; its founder was Eleazar Wheelock, a "New Light" (Great Awakening) revivalist, who originally was supported by the New England Company.

The Great Awakening included a millenial atmosphere best shown by Jonathan Edwards, the most sophisticated American theologian of the period. Edwards said that the discovery of the New World might prove to be the final act prior to the coming of the millenium, the one thousand years of Christ's rule that is to precede the Last Judgment, for the Americas were the last territories on earth where the Gospel had never been heard. In Edwards's version, the Devil knew this and had established a formidable American redoubt against the spread of Christianity; he had obtained control of the unhappy Indians and had instigated their resistance to conversion. For a time, it appeared as if the Devil had won; however, Edwards stated that God's will would finally prevail. The newly invigorated missionary work among the Indians was seen as furnishing additional proof that the last days were near. Even more than his forefathers of a hundred years earlier, Edwards contemplated the coming end of the known world and saw the conversion of the Indians as the sign of that end.

A millenial atmosphere also existed among the Indians. Pontiac's War of 1763 was started because of a religious vision of a period of peace at the end of the known world. The Delaware prophet, Neolin, had pleaded to the Indians to return to the old way of life, to give up liquor and plural marriage; another prophet, an Onondaga, had predicted that the Great Spirit would punish Whites if they kept taking Indian lands. Pontiac combined the plea and the prophecy to which he and added his own injunction, that the Indians had an obligation to drive out the Whites. Pontiac's war marked the first appearance of a phenomenon which was to reappear again and again in the Indian experience. This phenomenon encompassed a call to arms preceded by an appeal to return to the simplicity of a lost culture, both of which had Divine approval and would bring an age of peace and plenty upon successful accomplishment. This theme recurred several times in the eighteenth century. In 1777, the Continental Congress published a book entitled *Apocalypse de Chiokoyhekoy, Chief des Iroquois*, which purported to be a translation of an Iroquois prophecy made in 1305. The book, which combined the sixteenth-century ideas of a Huron prophet with eighteenth-century Christian apocalyptic ones, was probably a clever hoax designed to counter the influence of British agents among the Indians. In any case, it revealed much about both white and Indian millenialism.

The story of the sixteenth century prophecy has two versions. The one held by modern Indians is this: Deganwida, father of the Iroquois Confederation, had a vision. In this vision, a great white serpent came to the Indians, who first accepted it as a friend but who were later attacked by it. Next a red serpent arrived which fought the white one and which was later joined in his attack by a black one. The Indians remained neutral, although in great fear, and prayed for a prophet, who arrived as a great light. The prophet, in conjunction with the Indians, the red and the black serpents, and half of the white serpent, succeeding in driving away the remaining half of the white serpent. The Indians became a great people again, living in their old ways. In the eighteenth-century version, Deganwida saw a fiery cloud in the West which divided into five monsters—each supposedly representing one of the Great Beasts of Revelation as well as one of the Indian-conquering nations. The beasts fought and the worst beast, which symbolized England, lost to one representing the United States, according to the interpretation of the dream by a Prophet-bird, a parrot. The millenium then arrived, and there was an era of peace overseen by a supreme deity in which Americans became true friends of the Indians. In both versions of the prophecy, the hope of a return to the old Indian culture was tied to the success of the American Revolution.

In 1799, a new religion, which also combined the call to return to an old culture with the expected coming of the millenium, emerged among the Iroquois. This was the Longhouse religion—named for the dwellings of the Iroquois—which was begun by the Indian, Handsome Lake. Handsome Lake's religion reflected both the Indian's struggle with alcohol and his contact with Quaker reformers. In 1799, Quakers were alarmed by an incident where some Indians, returning home after selling their furs in Pittsburgh, became drunk and commenced fighting among themselves. Some of the Indians were killed in the fighting; others, lying in a drunken stupor, died from exposure to the cold. Because of this tragedy and the fact that the Indian sacred dances were becoming orgies, Quakers prevailed on Cornplanter, an Indian leader, to call an Indian council and to ban liquor. Because of the ban, Handsome Lake, a Seneca Indian who had been a heavy drinker for years, stopped drinking and soon after became ill. During his illness, he had a series of visions which foretold the future and set rules for attaining the good life. Following his visionary instructions, he became a minister to the Indians, wandering around villages in upstate New York. His sermons implored Indians to give up drinking, to stop gossiping, to be hospitable, to discipline children, and to have family unity. He told of an Indian Heaven; it was a place of good berry-picking where Indians lived according to the old ways and where no Whites could come (except for the Destroyers of Villages, the American presidents, who lived just outside of the Indian part of paradise). The new converts met in longhouses and celebrated four Thanksgiving festivals: Mid-winter, Thanks-to-the-Maple, Strawberry, and String Bean. The religion of Handsome Lake grew slowly because of Catholic opposition, but it represented an original Indian answer to the challenge of white society.

English and American Indian policy presaged a dismal future for the Indian. By the mid-1750's, the English had realized that a new direction in Indian affairs was needed. They implemented the Edmond Atkin Plan in 1755, which set up a governmental superintendency system for supervising the Indians, a line of protective frontier forts, and a rigidly controlled trading system monopolized by government agencies. In addition, the plan called for a variety of officials—including missionaries from the Society for the Propagation of the Gospel in Foreign Parts, frontier rangers, gunsmiths, interpreters, and commissioners—to provide necessary services to the Indian. The English later enacted the Proclamation of 1763, which prohibited further settlements in the areas heavily populated by Indians until relations could be regularized. Whether the new policy could have been successful is questionable; however, the Revolutionary War ended the experiment too soon to tell.

From the start, Indian problems plagued the new government of the United States. The first difficulty concerned the settlement of lands between the Appalachian Mountains and the Mississippi River. Should the English policy of limiting settlers be followed? The answer was no; the American government decided against following English policy. The Indians, for the most part, had supported the British during the war and were to be punished. The Americans believed the Indians to be so impressed by the strength of the United States that they would not resist settlement. Their lands were needed both to reward worthy veterans and to pay the national debt. A proposal was advocated by General Philip Schuyler of New York in 1783 to take over only part of the Indians' land. The Treaty of Fort Stanwix of 1784, signed with the Iroquois Nations, allowed only the Oneida and Tuscarora tribes to keep their lands because of their friendship during the war; the other Iroquois tribes were forced to relinquish their title to the lands west of Pennsylvania. In the Treaty of Fort McIntosh in the following year, the Americans appropriated the Delaware, Ottawa, Chippewa, and Wyandot lands north of the Ohio river. In 1786, the Shawnee, in a treaty signed at the mouth of the Great Miami, gave up their claims as well.

This coercion of the Indians, however, inspired their resistance; they did not believe that they had been defeated, and they were jealous of their lands. The U.S. government, realizing that the policy of naked power had become too difficult to implement, returned to the British model of purchasing land for expansion and of closely regulating Indian trade. On August 7, 1787, the United States government created the Indian Department under the jurisdiction of the Secretary of War. Trade with Indians was limited to citizens of the United States who possessed federal trading licenses. Congress provided funds for buying Indian lands, and in 1789 the first Indian treaties were made under the new policy.

Henry Knox, Secretary of War and spokesman for the United States government, said in 1789 that there were two alternative possibilities for the United States; it could either kill the Indians or make treaties in which Indian rights and obligations were clearly defined. Knox preferred the latter course both in the interest of fairness and of cheapness (since he estimated that treaties cost less than armies). He projected a cost of $1500 per year for Indian land claims. This cost was only supposed to last fifty years, because Knox believed that by 1830 most of the Indians would have vanished. Knox based his prediction of Indian extinction on a version of history which claimed that when Whites built cities, Indians disappeared, either through death or absorption. The best hope for the Indian, according to Knox, was assimilation into American civilization (and subsequent loss of Indian identity). He believed confidently that this was to be the fate of the American Indian.

During the presidency of George Washington, the peaceful assimilation of the Indians did not occur. Although the Trade and Intercourse Act of 1790 provided funds for buying Indian land, the Indians in the Old Northwest refused to sell; they were reinforced in their decision when they defeated the military expeditions of Harmar and St. Clair, who had tried to force them into selling. However, the Indians were defeated by Mad Anthony Wayne at the Battle of Fallen Timbers in 1795 and were coerced into selling. In 1796, Congress set official boundaries to the Indian lands and empowered the president to maintain these limits. Congress also initiated a governmentally controlled system which monopolized trade with the Indians. The government hoped these measures would result in the early assimilation of the Indian into American society.

Succeeding presidents held to that hope. Jefferson's position was typical of presidential positions. Jefferson argued that while in a primitive state, the Indians were originally equal to Whites, the merits of civilized life were such that the Indians had become unequal. Ignorant of the fact that the Indians had been agricultural at the time of the first European contact, Jefferson believed that the acquisition of farming skills, private property, and American law would civilize the Indian, enable him to live in peace and to multiply, and make possible the ultimate intermixture of the Indian blood with white. He stated this belief in his annual message to Congress in 1803 when he said that the federal government should encourage the Indian to farm and to trade. At the same time, he declared his Indian policy to be a success as demonstrated by the rapid progress of Indians toward civilization. His optimism, however, was belied by two developments. With the Louisiana Purchase of 1803, Jefferson himself began to talk about Indian removal across the Mississippi. The second development was the encroachment of white settlers on Indian lands in the North and Southwest. Both developments signaled the impending failure of federal Indian policy.

Thus, by the end of the eighteenth century, the futures of Blacks and Indians in America were perceived differently by white Americans: the Indian was expected to disappear, either through amalgamation or through death; the Black, however, would survive but would remain a second-class citizen.

II

While the paradigm of human origin and development based on the legend of Noah continued to hold a dominant position in the eighteenth century, certain modifications had evolved. The most important of these was the idea of degeneracy. Stow Persons, a noted intellectual historian, calls this modification the most significant feature of eighteenth-century thought because it provided an explanation of origin lying somewhere between "traditional religious loyalties and new scientific imperatives" ("The Cyclical Theory of History in Eighteenth-Century America" *American Quarterly* [1954]). The idea of degeneracy developed from the thesis that all living things and all social institutions were created perfect but had subsequently deviated from that perfection. This thesis accounted for present physical and cultural differences between nations and provided a means of comparing these nations.

Incorporated into the idea of degeneracy was a theory of organic cycles. This theory held that human societies replicated the life stages of living organisms, such as youth, middle age, and old age, and originated in England in the eighteenth century in such works as Viscount Bolingbroke's *The Patriot King* (1738). Incorporated into a view of social degeneracy, the theory of organic cycles held that societies were born (near perfect), grew old, and died (degenerate). The theory came to be held by America's Founding Fathers who believed American society to be superior to European ones because of its youth, but who anticipated the future senility and corruption of their society.

The concept of the Noble Savage, which appeared in eighteenth-century religious and popular thought, was also connected with degeneracy. Because of his closer contact with nature, man's original state, the less sophisticated man was thought by some to be physically superior to a more civilized person. The Noble Savage was also believed to retain more of original, natural morality and thus to be morally superior. This idea of the Noble Savage was supported by the findings of a new onset of geographic exploration by the English in the eighteenth century. Expeditions were sent to remote areas of the world, reawakening the interest in geography and ethnography of both the popular and educated publics. Commodore Byran went to Patagonia, where he saw giants; Captain Wallis rediscovered the South Seas, naming Tahiti "King George III's Island"; Captain Cartwright reintroduced Eskimos to England; Captain Furneau brought Omai, a South Sea Islander, to England. The visits and reports of these exotic persons, most of whom were physically impressive and who invited invidious comparison with Englishmen, seemed to support the idea of the Noble Savage.

The idea of the Noble Savage could have applied both to the African and the Indian. In England the Black was portrayed as such in Aphra Behn's *Oroonoko; or the History of a Royal Slave* (1688). The plot of this work was simple (and unlikely). The African hero, a Cormantee, fell in love with Imoinda, a woman destined for the king's harem. As a result of their forbidden love, Imoinda was sold as a slave and Oroonoko was accused of treason. After being pardoned, Oroonoko was captured by English slave traders and sent to Surinam, where he found Imoinda. Oroonoko, despite the enlightened treatment of his owner, led an unsuccessful slave revolt. In imminent danger of capture, he killed Imoinda and tried to commit suicide. Failing this, he was horribly tortured at the stake, burned, and dismembered. His nobility under torture and his handsome physique stamped him a hero, and the tradition of the captured African prince became a staple of eighteenth-century English theater.

In America, however, after the early military threat had passed, the Indian became the Noble Savage. The first book to reflect this romantic view was Robert Beverley's *The History and Present State of Virginia* (1705). In his book, Beverley praised the Indians for their physical attractiveness, and he contrasted Indian behavior with that of members of civilized society. While Indians were strange and remarkable people, he considered them neither savage nor primitive. Rather, he believed them to be like early Europeans, resembling the Spartans in their customs. These virtuous customs had been replaced by the vices of civilization, which had reduced the Indians of Virginia from a population of 18,000 to that of 2,000 in one hundred years. Doubting the real possibility of returning to the original virtuous Indian society, Beverley advocated intermarriage between Indians and Whites to bring to the Indian the virtues of civilization. (Beverley later rejected this solution in his 1722 edition.) In his comments on Indian-White relations, Beverley noted that there had been little intermarriage although the Indian women were attractive and the Indian males were not adverse to marrying Whites. He also observed that even though the Indian males treated their wives badly, white women captives who had married Indians had not chosen to return to white society (thus voting with their feet). Beverley concluded that the history of the Chesapeake area would have been improved had the settlers chosen to amalgamate with the Indians, and to share civilized virtues as well as vices.

The next book to incorporate the Noble Savage idea, *A New Voyage to Carolina* (1709), written by John Lawson, also advocated intermarriage as a desirable end. Like Beverley, Lawson saw Whites perverting the Indians, debauching them with rum and educating them in thievery, avarice, and immorality. The uncorrupted Indians were naked and frankly sexual but were not immoral. While fornication was acceptable to the Indians prior to marriage, they held marriage vows to be sacred. White men, however, persuaded Indian women to prostitute themselves despite their married state. The white men then generalized from their experiences, creating the tradition of Indian promiscuity. The European was seen as bringing about the loss of what was best in Indian society—cleanliness, equable temperament, bravery, loyalty, hospitality, and concern for the welfare of the group. His society destroyed by the white man, the only way left for the Indian to survive was through intermarriage with Whites.

A third book in the Noble Savage tradition was William Byrd's *History of the Dividing Line* (1728). Byrd, writing about Virginia, echoed Lawson and Beverley. Like them, he took a new position on the character traits of the Indian, a position that used the pre-settlement descriptions of Indian bravery and hospitality, cleanliness, and physical attractiveness. Unlike the captivity narratives in the northern colonies, the histories of the colonies to the south emphasized the primitive virtues of the Indians and suggested intermarriage to civilize the Indians whose societies had been destroyed. The verbal promotion of intermarriage appeared, interestingly enough, in those areas which prohibited it legally; North Carolina and, for a time, Virginia both had laws against Indian-white unions.

Meanwhile, in the New York colony, Cadwallader Colden, the leading American moral philosopher of the time, had written a history of the Indians called *The History of the Five Indian Nations Depending on the Province of New York in America,* the first part of which was published in 1727 and the second in 1747. This pioneering effort, dedicated to the Royal Governor William Burnell, was frankly didactic. Its purpose was to show how the French had successfully undermined the alliance between the Iroquois and the English, thus reaping the benefits of the fur trade. Colden wanted the English to regain the fur trade and the Iroquois alliance. While Colden did not advocate miscegenation like observers in the South, he also found virtue in the Indians. Colden was particularly impressed by their willingness to be tortured and their stoicism under torture. Here they outdid the Romans. The one major vice of the

Indian as seen by Colden, revenge, was also a classic one. If the Indians could rid themselves of the desire for revenge, in Colden's view, they would no longer be barbarians but could easily become civilized. Colden was optimistic about this possibility, using the history of Greece and Rome for confirmation. Colden wrote of the Iroquois as Beverley and Byrd had written of the Virginia Indians, as representatives of an earlier, virtuous society that would be amenable to civilization.

The idea of the Noble Savage still competed with the idea in lesser works of the bad Indians. Samuel Penhallow's *The History of the Wars of New England* (1726) portrayed the Indians as treacherous, ferocious, and cruel and said (like the works of the Mathers) that the Indian Wars were a scourge from God to punish the settlers for neglecting Indian souls. Samuel Hopkins' *Historical Memoirs* (1753), a study of the missionary work of John Sergeant, depicted the Indians as ignorant and without virtue. Charles Thomson, in *An Enquiry into the Courses of the Alienation of the Delaware and Shawnee Indians from the British Interest, And into the Measures taken for recovering their Friendship* (1759), blamed proprietory officials, Indian traders, land-hungry settlers, as well as some overbearing members of the Indian tribes for the failure of amiable relations in Pennsylvania. William Smith's *A Discourse Concerning the Conversion of the Heathen Americans, and the Final Propagation of Christianity and the Sciences to the End of the Earth* (1760) repeated the connection between the failure of Indian conversion and the coming millenium. All of these writers denied the natural virtue of the Indian and concentrated upon the problem of conversion.

The most famous history of the Indians in the eighteenth century was James Adair's *The History of the American Indians* (1775). Adair had been an Indian trader in the regions of east and west Florida, Georgia, North and South Carolina, and Virginia. He was an astute observer of the Indians and knew the intellectual trends of his day. In his book, Adair painted Indian life as one of classical simplicity in contrast to the decadence of white luxury. Adair praised the even tempers and physical attractiveness of Indians; he emphasized that Indians were red and not Whites who made themselves red (although Adair conceded the Indians tried to improve their redness with paints). Furthermore, they liked being red. Adair commented on the Indian ethnocentrism, using a common anti-Negro stereotype:

If a deformed son of burning Africa was to paint the devil, he would not do it in black colours, nor delineate him with a shagged coarse wolly head, nor with thick lips, a short flat nose, or clumsy feet, like those of a bear: his devil would represent one of a different nation or people.

Adair attributed the Indian's color to the climate, to winds and sun, to bear grease and red root, and to a desire to be red, all of which had operated over a long period of time to turn the Indian from his original white color.

Adair believed that the Indians originated in the Orient. His study of Indian languages and customs convinced him that the Indians were originally Jews, and he offered proof through cultural similarities. The Indians worshipped one God and had marriage regulations, punishments, ornaments, clothes, funeral rights, and menstrual prohibitions that were similar to those of the Jews. Adair even claimed that the Indian name for God was Yo He Wah and was an obvious corruption of Jehovah. He attacked the idea that the Indians resembled the Chinese, citing the lack of Chinese customs among the Indians and the inability of the Chinese, who were not a maritime people, to sail to the New World. He also argued against the belief that the Indians were pre-Adamites. He felt that the power of Indians' oratory and their use of language must prove their common brotherhood with other humanity, that only persons descended from Adam and Eve could possess such a facility.

Adair approved of the social arrangements of the Indians. Their society was simple, encouraging patriotism and emphasizing equality. It rewarded merit while other aspects of Indian life enhanced physical beauty. The Indian women were pretty and there were no fat, helpless young Indian men who could not fight (unlike the white men in Charleston). Adair admitted that the Indians were barbaric, but he believed that the Indian, with proper instruction, could shed his barbarism and become civilized.

Adair's Indian history included the ideas of two centuries. The Indian was supposedly of the tribe of Noah that had degenerated into barbarism, but he was also a Noble Savage with natural virtues worthy of imitation.

These ideas can also be found in the literature of the early American republic. Philip Freneau, sometimes called the father of Indian poetry, wrote poems entitled "The Indian Student," "The Indian Convert," and his most famous, "The Indian Burying

Ground," which depicted the Indian as nature's nobleman. However, the first American novel, *Edgar Huntley, or Memoirs of a Sleepwalker* (1791) by Charles Brocken Brown, cast the Indian in the role of the villain and emphasized the savage rather than the noble elements. Thus did conflicting images of the Indian enter into American literature.

Both the concepts of degeneracy and of the Noble Savage could be fitted into the legend of Noah; indeed, certain elements of these ideas were already present in the Christian explanation of man's origin. Both concepts depended upon the assumption of the perfection of man as originally created, an assumption necessarily supported by the legend of Noah. Both the concepts could also undermine the biblical legend. The Christian model would not use a naturalistic mechanism such as degeneracy to explain men's differences; sin was the proper explanation. Also the legend of Noah assumed that the significant loss that man suffered after his dispersion was a religious loss, while the degeneracy theory assumed the change to be social, behavioral, and even physical. In the Christian view, natural men, or Noble Savages, might be superior to evil Europeans, but they could not be superior to regenerate Christians. Yet the whole idea of the Noble Savage argued the absolute superiority of the natural man over the civilized one. Thus, both the concept of degeneracy and that of the Noble Savage, carried to their logical conclusions, eroded the defense of a biblical paradigm.

Two other eighteenth-century developments further complicated the paradigm. The first was the realization that fossils were the remains of long dead organisms. Both discoveries extended the boundaries of time. Mastodon bones were found at Big Bone Lick in Kentucky by George Croghan in 1765. Croghan sent the bones to the naturalist John Bartram who sent half to Benjamin Franklin and half to Lord Shelburne. Thought to be the remains of an elephant, the bones posed a real problem to naturalists for no elephant had been seen outside of tropical regions of Africa or Asia. The puzzlement was increased in 1796 when a workman dug up the remains of a giant sloth in what is present-day West Virginia and sold them to Thomas Jefferson, who named the specimen the Great Claw. These bones presented an even more difficult problem than did those of the mastodon, for they represented an animal not known to exist anywhere in the world. Neither the legend of Noah nor the thesis of degeneracy included the possibility of species extinction. Jefferson was forced to rationalize, saying that the Great Claw must exist somewhere, probably in an isolated or still unexplored area of the New World. The New World fossils posed a threat to the prevailing scientific orthodoxy.

The second development was the discovery of ruins and a beginning realization of the age of civilizations. Settlers were rediscovering Indian mounds in upstate New York and southern Ohio. The question of who built the mounds became pressing, particularly since the artifacts in them appeared to be more advanced than those of contemporary Indians. An argument for degeneracy could have been made, but Benjamin Franklin and Noah Webster held that the mounds were built by the Spanish explorer, Hernando de Soto, while Benjamin Barton said that the builders were probably descendants of Danes who had supposedly discovered the Americas long before Columbus. The interest in the possibility of lost civilizations increased with the translation of Volney's *Ruins: or a Survey of the Revolutions of Empires* (1791) by Thomas Jefferson and Joel Barlow. The book, a best seller in America by 1795 and popular many years after, presented a romantic account of the rise and fall of civilizations. Thus, more and more evidence pointed to the possibility that New World life forms and societies were much older than

III

anyone had thought. New developments in biology in Europe emphasized a connection between humans and other primates. One of the most significant figures in the development of this idea was a Swede, Carl Linnaeus, who in 1735 published the first edition of his *System of Nature*. In his book, Linnaeus presented the proposition that there was economy, infinite variety, and a rationally ordered system in nature. He devised a taxonomic system that influenced science strongly. On one level of the Linnaean system were species; Linnaeus defined these as biological types which were created by Divine wisdom and which were fixed from creation. Varieties were temporary forms within a species that were produced by different environments. Linnaeus vacillated somewhat between the definitions of fixed and changing types and, at times, seemed to admit the possibility of change within or extinction of species. He emphasized the closeness of man to the primates, classifying man in the same order—*anthropomorpha*—as the ape and the sloth and finding no in-

Table 3.2

Kingdom	Class	Order	Family	Genus	Species	Variation
Animal	Mammalia (1st ed.) Quadruped (10th ed.)	Anthropomorpha	Primates	Homo	Sapiens	Wildman American European Asian African
					Monstrous	Mountaineers Patagonians Hottentot Chinese Canadian
				Symia (Apes, Monkeys, etc.)	27 Species Including: Satyrous Sylvanus Sphinx (Baboon) Silenus Faunus Diana Oedipus	
				Lemur	Tardigradus Catta Volans	
				Vespertilio	Vampyrus Spectrum Perspicillatus Spasma Leporinus Auritus Murinus	

Note: Linnaeus did not use the classification "Phylum". At times he did not use "Family" and listed "primates" under "Order" instead.

herent characteristics by which to separate men from the apes. Table 3.2 shows Linnaeus's system of classification.

Linnaeus divided the genus (a category composed of species) Homo into two species, *Homo sapiens* and *Homo monstrous,* and these two species into several varieties. Each of these varieties could be differentiated by physical and/or cultural characteristics. His scheme follows in Table 3.3.

TABLE 3.3

	HOMO	
Sapiens		*Monstrous*
1. Wildman—four footed, mute, hairy		1. Mountaineers—small, inactive, timid
2. American—copper colored, choleric, erect		2. Patagonians—large, indolent
3. Europeans—fair, sanguine, brawny		3. Hottentot—less fertile
4. Asian—sooty, melancholy		4. Chinese—head conic
5. African—black, phlegmatic, relaxed		5. Canadian—head flattened

Note that Linnaeus included the wild man as a variety of *Homo sapiens,* but put two groups of Indians, the Patagonians and the Canadians, as well as Chinese and Hottentots in *Homo monstrous.* He was handicapped in his classification of men by his lack of specimens and, because of this lack, relied upon travelers' accounts for information. Although it might seem that Linnaeus's taxonomic effort was little better than the sixteenth-century collection of rumors, his system survived his errors and became basic to biological classification.

Linnaeus' system did not go unchallenged. Another scientific giant of the age, the Frenchman Comte de Buffon, presented a system of his own in his *Natural History* (1749) and *Epochs of Nature* (1778). In his books, Buffon claimed that the most significant characteristic of nature was the endless proliferation of different forms. The purpose of natural history was to describe and compare these forms as they existed in a natural system that was always in balance between fecundity and death. Buffon believed that no species could become extinct. Unlike Linnaeus, he believed that only species existed in nature; all of the other biological divisions— those of genus, family, class—were human inventions. Species could be identified only by studies over time testing whether two individuals could mate and produce fertile offspring. According to Buffon, each species had a particular climatic and environmental condition for which it was suited.

While Buffon classified apes into three groups (the *orang-utan*, the *pithecus*, and the *gibbon*) and said that the apes lack of a language proved their brute nature, he felt that man was a member of a single species who could adapt to any climate and condition. According to Buffon, only man required civilized society and possessed the faculties of thought and speech. Therefore man was separate from the apes.

Whatever resemblance, therefore, takes place between the Hottentot and the ape, the interval which separates them is immense; because the former is endowed with the faculties of thought and speech (quoted by Marvin Harris in *The Rise of Anthropological Theory: A History of Theories of Culture* [New York, 1968]).

All men, however, were not considered equal in their abilities or their societies. The invidious reference to the Hottentot was not the only reference Buffon made to the inferiority of Blacks. He believed that white was man's original color, that Africans had degenerated, that the Blacks were physically inferior, and that the orangutan mated with black women.

Buffon attempted a naturalistic explanation of the origin of life, claiming that there had been spontaneous generation of life rather than Divine Creation. If all life were extinguished, according to Buffon, new forms would emerge. Buffon thus tied life to energy and presented an early version of the idea of entropy. Unlike Linnaeus, he personally attacked the prevailing view of God's creation of man upon which much of the idea of human brotherhood rested.

Abbé Raynal applied Buffon's ideas and general theories of degeneracy to the New World in *Histoire philosophique des établissements et du commerce des Européens dans des deux Indies* (1770) and implied the inferiority of the American environment. European scholars had claimed that the animals common to both the Old and New Worlds were smaller in the New World, that those taken to the New World degenerated, and that the total number of species was smaller in the New World. The Indians in America supposedly indicated human degeneracy by their smaller and weaker sexual organs (as reported by explorers) and by their lack of sexual drive and facial hair (for Buffon, hairiness equaled sexuality).

The German J. F. Blumenbach, who elaborated on the Buffonian environmental explanation of human differences, was credited with being the first scientist to teach natural history through comparative anatomy. Blumenbach asserted that the people in the region of the Caspian Sea were the most perfect anatomically and that all other peoples had degenerated from this physical ideal. Other scientists, using his techniques, explored the anatomy of the orangutan. The Dutch were pioneers in this effort; adventurers to Borneo had sent a number of specimens back to Europe. Two of these appeared in Holland in the 1770's; using these specimens, Peter Camper, a Dutch scholar, published a detailed study of the orangutan in 1778, a study which gained him a reputation as the leading authority on the subject. Camper denied that sexual relations between humans and orangutans were possible. In his *Dissertation on the Natural Varieties which Characterize the Human Physiognamy*, published posthumously in 1791, he described physical measurements by which he believed human groups could be differentiated from each other and from the apes. These measured the facial line—a line drawn from forehead to lip—and the facial angle—the angle made by the facial line and a line drawn parallel to the chin. The degree of the facial angle was thought to be correlated with intelligence; the greater the angle the higher the intelligence. Apes, Negroes, Chinese, and idiots had low facial angles and were placed in inferior categories.

Concurrent with the scientific categorization of physical characteristics was the growth of secular explanations for historical change. The historians of the eighteenth century reconstructed the human past into three stages—civilization, barbarism, and savagery. These stages were described in terms of economic and social development in Adam Ferguson's *An Essay on the History of Civil Society* (1767). In William Robertson's *History of America* (1777), archeology was utilized to show a connection between the level of technology and the stages of society. In both these histories, the authors assumed that man had begun civilized, degenerated into savagery; but both authors failed to settle two pressing questions. Who were the most primitive peoples? Could the retrogression to savagery be reversed? There was no agreement on the answers to these questions. Some said the most primitive peoples were the Fuegians, others the South Sea Islanders. While a few believed the regression to savagery could be reversed, most European theologians, missionaries, travelers, and historians denied the possibility. The evangelist John Wesley, for example, said that the Indians had regressed so far that he doubted whether they could be civilized. His doubt extended to black men as well. Savages were thought to have lost moral sense, the necessary quality for civilization.

Other European thinkers displayed more optimism and argued that history also showed evidence of ascent from savagery, although at the cost of physical degeneration. One such thinker was Lord Monboddo, James Burnett. Burnett argued in his *The Origin and Progress of Language* (1774) the proposition that the age of savagery was a golden age and that it still lingered on in the South Seas. His most famous theory, however, was that the great apes had turned into men through the acquisition of language. In defense of this, he cited sailors' reports and rumors about men who had tails; these rumors referred to a Scotsman in Inverness and a group of men in the Dutch West Indies. Just as man resembled the ape (in more ways than one) in physical appearance, so the society of apes was seen to resemble that of man. Orangutans lived in groups, built huts, and supposedly enslaved men, played the flute, and showed such human emotions as remorse and sensitiveness. Their lack of language did not disqualify them from membership in the human race in Burnett's opinion. Burnett used his belief that human and primate differences were small in a severe attack on English society. In his opinion, Englishmen had physically decayed below the level of the orangutan and the savage. The savage, at least, possessed keener senses and more physical strength, patience, and forbearance.

While belief in monogenesis was shaken by the new scientific ideas in Europe, polygenetic ideas persisted and became stronger. Certain English writers especially used the findings of scientists and historians to promote the polygenetic explanation. Among these men was Lord Kames who in his *Sketches of the History of Man* (1774) argued that different species of men had been created by God for different climates. Kames carried the Buffonian idea of environmental suitability to its logical extension; he denied any human ability to adapt to an environment and argued that each human group belonged only in the climate for which it was created.

In the same year, Edward Long's *The History of Jamaica* appeared. Long, an Englishman, had lived in Jamaica for twelve years. He was no naturalist, but he utilized the ideas of Buffon to argue that the Negro was a member of a separate and inferior species to that of Whites. He justified his argument by claiming that the offspring of a cross between a Negro and a White was infertile. (Although his claim was manifestly contrary to fact, it persisted.) In addition, he argued that Negroes lacked a moral sense and had a mental level that apes could approximate. Long accepted Buffon's belief in the possibility of ape-Negro intercourse and argued that the Negro was a member of a species located somewhere between the white man and the ape. Thus, by extension, Long implied that there had to have been at least two original creations to account for the two different species of man.

In 1799, Charles White, a Manchester physician, wrote *An Account of the Regular Gradation of Man,* which postulated four human species—European, Asian, American, and African. Although opposed to slavery, White believed in African inferiority, saying that Blacks had smaller brains, larger sexual organs, an ape-like odor, and animal immunity to pain. All of these supposed characteristics put them lower on the Great Chain of Being than other humans. Again, the postulation of the separate species implied polygenesis, whether biblical or natural.

In England, these arguments for polygenesis were countered with the orthodoxy of the day. Scientific evidence was not conclusive, and scholars reiterated the beliefs that man was of one species and that African history showed African progression (not regression). The strongest refutation of polygenesis, of course, was religious; a belief in man's natural inequality and nonunity denied the literal truth of the Bible. Christians attacked the notion of natural inequality as subversive of that truth.

One of the more interesting refutations of the claim of African inferiority came from a black man who had lived both in America and England, Olaudah Equiano whose *The Interesting Narrative of Olaudah Equiano, or Gustavus Vasa* came out in two volumes in London in 1789. Equiano was born in Benin, but was kidnapped at age 11 and sent to Barbados. He became the servant of a British naval officer who named him Gustavus Vasa. In 1763, he was sold in the West Indies, but his purchaser, a Quaker, helped him gain his freedom. He went to London in 1767, became a barber, and worked to end slavery and to colonize Sierra Leone. He wrote his book both to tell his story and to attack slavery. In it, Equiano portrayed Africa as others had been portraying it for two centuries. The Africans were described as simple people who did not drink, believed in one creator, practiced circumcision like the Jews, and had similar religious festivals. Equiano concluded that Africans were in the same stage of development as the Jews had been in the time of Moses and were literal descendants of the Jews. Africans were darker than the Jews because their hot climate and harsh environment had turned them black. Equiano finished his book by declaring that though slavery had depressed the African and though refined nations had advantages, all men came from the same origin and were therefore equal.

IV

The ideas of European intellectuals created a dilemma for Americans. The intellectual elite in America was nominally Deistic at this time but preferred, like Franklin, to avoid religious discussion. These intellectuals did not, therefore, attack Creationism, the literal belief in Adam and Noah as the unifying ancestors of all men. On the other hand, they were environmentalists, believing that individual populations were changed by their environments, and they wished to deny that the American environment was an inferior one. This put American intellectuals in the position of refuting claims of Indian inferiority (as it was attributed to the American environment), while they wobbled on the question of black equality (as was implied in the belief in man's one origin).

The Jeffersonian circle, the American Philosophical Society, reflected on the origins of man and his natural equality. They speculated on both the black man and the Indian, and their ideas were, in the main, not original. They believed in monogenesis; the majority of the Jeffersonian circle believed in the legend of Noah. Thomas Jefferson provided a good example of the ideas of this group. Without a good grasp of history, geology, or archeology, he tried to understand the Indian and his history. In his *Notes on the State of Virginia* (1781), Jefferson refuted Buffon's assertion of Indian inferiority. In Jefferson's opinion, the Indian was neither sexually weak nor hairless. (Jefferson had seen too many Indians painfully removing facial hair to believe that.) The Indians had few children because child bearing was inconvenient to their social relations. Jefferson believed that the Indians had come from the Orient via the Bering Straits and that they had been dispersed from a common source, an idea based on his analysis of Indian languages. Because of the proliferation of Indian tongues, Jefferson considered the possibility that the Indians were older than Asiatics and that the original home of man was America. However, he did not push this idea. He did, however, publicize his belief that the Indian was equal in mind and body to the White.

About the Negro, Jefferson was less sure. He suspected that Negroes were innately inferior but withheld judgment, thinking that slavery had caused inferiority and that, given enough time, Negroes could reach civilization. Yet Jefferson was troubled by the historic fact that Greek slaves of Romans had accomplished much while black slaves of Americans had not. Jefferson accepted the Linnaean system—in which Africans, Americans, and Europeans were of one species—and yet at times he hinted a belief that the Negro had been created black, which would mean created as a separate species. At other times, Jefferson described Blacks as falling between a species and variety (a category possibility Linnaeus had not contemplated). While he believed that the Negro had a greater sexual appetite and a lower intellectual capacity than Whites, Jefferson never openly argued that Negroes were members of a different species. Although he was accused, and was possibly guilty, of having a black mistress and mulatto children, Jefferson opposed miscegenation. (In his proposed revision of Virginian laws, Jefferson suggested that a white woman who gave birth to a mulatto child should be given the option of leaving the state within a year or being outlawed.) He could not make up his mind; he hoped his views on black inferiority were wrong; but on balance, he believed that while all men were created equal, the Negro had degenerated into inferiority.

Other Americans believed in the natural equality of the Negro and in an environmental explanation of color. Such was the position of Dr. Benjamin Rush who claimed the dark skins, thick lips, flat noses, and insensitive nerves (supposedly characteristic of Negroes) were the result of leprosy. If the Negro could be cured of the disease of blackness, he would return to his natural white color. Rush neatly combined the ideas of man's original equality with the idea of change through the environment.

Others had similar ideas about the Indians. Although Benjamin Smith Barton had claimed that the Indian mounds in Ohio were Danish in his *Observations on Some Parts of Natural History* (1787), he returned to a belief in an Indian origin in his *New Views of the Origin of the Tribes and Nations of America* (1798).

In these books, Barton reiterated the Buffonian belief in geographic or ecological zones that set environmental boundaries for the organisms found within them. According to Barton, only humans could live in any zone or climate, for God, in His infinite wisdom, allowed them the freedom to find their own homes. Indians had descended from Noah; men of wisdom—Acosta, Brerewood, and Adair—all recognized this. For both Rush and Barton, the old beliefs that human equality came from a single origin and human differences from varying environments remained firm.

The penultimate defense of monogenesis as the basis of equality and of environmentalism as the reason for human physical differences came from an American, Samuel Stanhope Smith. Smith, a Presbyterian minister, taught moral philosophy at the College of New Jersey (present day Princeton) in 1779, becoming president in 1795. The 1810 edition of his *An Essay on the Causes of the Variety of Complexion and Figure in the Human Species* ... contained material specifically designed to refute the ideas of Lord Kames and Charles White, who had argued that there were different species of men designed for different climates. Smith believed in only one human species. According to Smith, species of animals had geographic limits but man did not; God had different laws for different species. Only humans had a moral faculty and their moral choices could not be geographically determined. Species were again defined as those individuals who possessed the ability to interbreed. The differences in physical appearance among members of the same species was explained as a product of a degenerative factor among some of these members.

Smith attacked the idea that man originated as primitive and savage. The monuments of nations in the mid-regions of Asia (such as the Egyptian pyramids), showed that humans were already civilized at the start of history. Humans could not survive without civilization, in Smith's view, as they lacked the animal instincts with which to preserve themselves. Smith's most telling defense of the idea that humans did not begin as savages made use of the American Indians. The Indians were classified far above primitive peoples—the bow and hook that they used were considered high and noble inventions. Yet despite these accomplishments, Indians could master only two or three simple arts, and only master them with much effort. From this, Smith concluded that Indians could not have created their inventions but could only have retained them.

While God had created civilization, man lost most of it. Thus, Smith stated the classic case for degeneracy and rejected savagism as a necessary prior state for civilization.

Smith gave the idea of polygenesis short shrift. To believe in polygenesis, Smith insisted, meant to believe in *equivocal generation* as opposed to Divine Creation. To a true believer, God's singular Creation was dogma. Smith accepted one creation and claimed that different human colors came from the effects of climate. Men were originally created white, but some became brown and others black. (The sun supposedly made people black by giving them a universal freckle and by causing an excess of bile which turned the skin yellow and then dark.) Smith tried to anticipate objections to his hypothesis, such as the question: if skin color was due to climate, why were the Indians in tropical America not the same color as Negroes? Smith answered that the process took time and the Indian was a relative newcomer to America. Besides, the clothes worn by the Indians prevented the full action of the climate and delayed change. Smith argued that the different hair colors in different nations also came from the climate. According to his argument, Negro hair was kinky because the sun pulled the hair into tight whorls and stimulated the production of bile which made hair curly; this bile also accounted for the supposed bad smell of Negroes. (Smith also said that different nations smell differently because of their physical and social environments. Indians in the southern part of America smelled badly because of their filthy habits, poverty, poor food, and the use of rancid seal oil on their bodies.) Other physical characteristics were also products of living habits and states of society; the black man supposedly had big feet and a gibbous leg shape because the black child was allowed to wander at will. Color was seen as a function of social discrimination; the poor everywhere were darker than the rich, as in Scotland, France, and India. In the South, field slaves were darker than house slaves (Smith never mentioned miscegenation as a possible cause). Smith argued that Negroes in America were losing their dark color, kinky hair, and bad smell because of a new environment. Smith referred to Henry Moss, a Negro in Maryland who supposedly turned white, as proof of this ongoing process. According to Smith, given sufficient time, a different environment would produce a physically different individual.

In his final section, Smith refuted the ideas of Charles White on the inferiority of Negroes. Smith denied that Blacks were ugly; he submitted data on two black women whose proportions were the same as the Venus de Medici. The supposed characteristics of the Negro which White used as proof of inferiority were disposed of by Smith as either wrong or explainable in environmental terms. When White used some of Jefferson's statements to bolster his case, Smith simply said that Jefferson was correct when he defended Indians and Americans against the implication of environmentally induced debility and that he should stick to that.

On the ideas of Lord Kames, Smith was equally rejective. Kames had criticized the biblical account of man's dispersion and differentiation, arguing that men's languages were not of one common source, that men were unable to live in all climates—using as examples, Charleston, South Carolina, and the Caribbean where Whites died so fast that depopulation was prevented only by continued immigration—and that different men's behaviors were so different that the only possible explanation was multiple origin. Kames combined this criticism with Long's thesis of mulatto infertility and with his own belief that Indians were naturally cowardly and had a nervous system more tolerant of pain, all indicative of separate species. Smith answered with a passionate defense of man's equality. Men had begun with a common language, but lost it after the Tower of Babel. Men could and did live everywhere. The mulatto was disappearing in America, but the reason was not infertility but rather that racial mixture and civilized life made offspring white. The Indian was the most noble savage; he was not as degenerate as other nations living in more severe climates. Indian customs and environment accounted for his behavior. He fought from ambush because he lacked forts and large armies; he withstood torture not because his nerves were different but because his moral condition was that of a Spartan.

Smith's defense of Indian and Negro equality revealed an eighteenth-century position that, while still in ascendancy, was under attack. Despite lack of success with civilizing the Indian and abolishing slavery, white Americans clung intellectually to the biblical account which said that men were of one species and were equal at creation. Americans had incorporated into this account such ideas as those of the Noble Savage and degeneracy (although the latter eventually proved more persuasive than the former). The Indian fared better than the Negro; he was seen as nature's nobleman in America while the Negro never was.

The American social thinkers of the eighteenth century were responsive to intellectual opinion from abroad. While well-informed, Americans were not yet the leaders in the formation of social theory. Although Smith's ideas became obsolete in the nineteenth century, with the addition of a new concept of culture and the deletion of the concept of degeneracy they were akin to those of twentieth-century anthropology, although not, one must hasten to add, to twentieth-century biology.

Chapter 4

Broken Promises; Fallen Hopes

The American view of the fate of the Indian, on the surface at any rate, was optimistic at the beginning of the nineteenth century. Although the Indian population continued to decrease, the Jeffersonian hope of assimilation persisted. However, by the end of the War of 1812, the belief that the Indians could become civilized if they lived together with white men was under attack even though there was evidence that assimilation was working. The optimistic belief collapsed completely in the 1830's with the forced removal of the Civilized Tribes—Cherokee, Creeks, Choctaws, and Chickasaws—from Georgia. In the end, greed triumphed over theory and Indian Removal replaced Indian assimilation.

The Civilized Tribes had become farmers at least as early as the middle of the eighteenth century and had willingly received missionaries after the War of 1812. They thus fulfilled the dual requirements for assimilation of becoming capitalists and Christians. Sixty thousand strong, they owned twenty-five million acres of land in northeast Georgia, in addition to lands in western North Carolina, southern Tennessee, eastern Alabama, and northern Mississippi. White settlers in the region were desirous of this land and, in their haste to obtain it, pressured the state and federal governments to remove the Indians. The Indians, in turn, were faced with the choice of removal or complete submission to the state and federal law.

Beginning in 1816, Secretary of War Crawford proposed allowing the Indians to reserve in treaties all the land that they had improved by cultivation. Crawford's proposal was applied in the Cherokee Treaties of 1817 and 1819 and in the Choctaw Treaty of 1820. Although few Indians (311 Cherokees and 8 Choctaws) obtained private allotments under these treaty provisions, a precedent had been established. By this arrangement, restrictions on the sale of Indian land were lessened, and although the treaties supposedly discouraged white speculators from purchasing land, these speculators acquired land even before the Indians received final title.

A legal precedent for dispossessing the Indian was established by Supreme Court Justice John Marshall in *Johnson and Graham's Lessee* vs. *McIntosh* (1823). The case involved the question of whether the Indians had a natural right to land or whether the settler's grant from the Crown took precedence. Marshall ruled that the Indians lacked unqualified sovereignty because they failed to utilize the land, that discovery of unused land gave the English title to it, and that this title was strengthened through use of the land. The Indians, through Marshall's decision, became vulnerable to further land alienation.

Further attempts in the South to make Indians like Whites increased. State laws made Indians liable to civil suits—mainly in cases of debt and trespass—although few states permitted an Indian to testify on his own behalf. In Mississippi, Indians had duties of citizenship—to muster with the militia, to work on the roads, and to pay taxes—although they could not vote. State laws nullified the authority of tribal government and superceded all Indian laws except those on marriage. In addition, states prohibited persons from advising Indians against signing treaties or migrating.

The complete assimilation of the Indian failed, however, because the Indians refused to relinquish totally all tribal ways and to become totally white. This refusal was felt as a real threat by white settlers. If the Indians remained in cohesive groups, the possibilities for obtaining their lands diminished. As a result, a new policy began to emerge, one which made Indian lands more available while still retaining the rhetoric of civilizing the Indian. This new policy called for voluntary Indian Removal to newly acquired lands across the Mississippi. Supposedly, Indian progress to civilization would be unimpeded in the West, by the two corrupting forces which delayed it in the East—whiskey and evil Whites. The Indian, in isolation, could develop at his own rate. Indian Removal originated with white fears and greed but took on an aura of humanitarianism.

The policy of voluntary removal of the Civilized Tribes failed; white Americans blamed the failure on the half-breed. According to these critics, the half-breeds in the Civilized Tribes controlled opinion, took pride in the idea of Indian nationalism, and discouraged other Indians from either selling their lands or leaving. In order to strike at these Indian leaders, states began attacking tribal government and tribal leadership. Although the Cherokees had established a tribal government by constitutional convention in 1829, in the following year the state of Georgia declared all statutes and ordinances of the Cherokees void and started alienating Indian land. The Cherokees asked President Jackson for federal protection against state action but failed to obtain it. They turned next to the Supreme Court where they were more successful. In two decisions, *Cherokee Nation vs. Georgia* (1831) and *Worcester vs. Georgia* (1832), Chief Justice Marshall held that the Indians were "domestic dependent nations" under the United States and that the laws of Georgia did not apply to the political community of the Cherokees. However, President Jackson refused to enforce the mandate of the court and Georgia continued to force the Cherokees out.

The officials responsible for Indian affairs during President Jackson's administration believed that the Indians would not leave their lands voluntarily because of the manipulations of the half-breeds and because of the white traders with Indian wives. Hence, these officials applied pressure (through whiskey, bribery, and verbal persuasion) to force the Indians to sign treaties and to leave the Southwest Atlantic states. The Choctaws ceded their lands to the U.S. in the treaty of Dancing Rabbit Creek in September, 1830. The treaty provided land allotments for those who wanted to stay (those who did not want land were considered savage and were expected to leave). Provisions were made for individual allotments of from 80 to 480 acres of land to Indians, the amount dependent on the size of the family and the number of slaves owned. Land owners received title in fee simple (without restriction on heirs or transfers of ownership) and had to become citizens of the United States after 5 years. The white negotiators of the treaty had estimated that only 200 Indians would wish to take up private ownership; however, thousands indicated a desire to stay and the ensuing land claims took 12 to 15 years to settle. The Creeks presented even more of a problem. They refused to emigrate. Although they signed a treaty in March, 1832, the Creeks maintained they had not sold their land. The treaty with the Chickasaws, which was signed in May, 1832, was more liberal because of the Creek and Choctaw experience. Chickasaw Indians were allowed to receive from 640 to 3200 acres per family in privately owned land. Although the treaties with the Indians maintained the pretense of voluntarism, in 1838 the federal government forcibly moved Cherokees without land to Oklahoma where they suffered dislocation, cultural shock, and death. Those who stayed behind quite often lost their lands through others' fraud or their own drunkenness, despite attempts by the federal agencies to police land sales.

The humanitarian idea of assimilation still echoed in public and private circles as people insisted that the transfer of Indians to the West had certain advantages. There, the Indian territory could be well defined, the evil White could be prohibited, the Indian could govern himself. Further, teachers and missionaries might, in the cultural isolation of the Indian territory, teach the Indians the civilized way of life along with the Christian religion, thus preparing the way for ultimate reintegration of Indians into American society.

In his farewell address in 1837, President Jackson maintained that he had saved the Indians from degradation and destruction by moving them beyond the reach of white injury and oppression. But the solution of removal had the opposite effect on the Indians. From 1830 to 1860, four epidemics of disease swept through the Indian Territory in Oklahoma as Indians came into contact with new germs and a more hostile environment. Removal also exacerbated old tribal rivalries and helped begin new ones. As the technological gap between American and Indian widened, tribes became increasingly dependent upon white technology, money, and amenities, and many Indians became indigent camp followers of white military posts and Indian agencies.

American religious groups continued to profess confidence in the possibility of civilizing the Indians. At the beginning of the Republic, there were only about a dozen missionaries to the Indians in the field; but interest after the Revolution in the conversion of all pagans resulted in new missionary groups. These included the Society for Propagating the Gospel among the Indians and Others in North America (1787), the Society of the United Brethren for Propagating the Gospel among the Heathen (1787), the American Board of Commissioners for Foreign Missions (1810), and the

United Foreign Missionary Society (1817). All the groups agreed that the Indians needed to practice economic individualism, freedom, political democracy, and Protestant Christianity. But the priority of conversion was a matter of dispute. Should the Indian be civilized first by the establishment of schools, and political and economic systems, or should he be converted first and then civilized?

The American Board of Foreign Missions said that conversion and civilization were mutually re-enforcing and should occur simultaneously. A certain level of economic self-sufficiency was requisite to becoming Christian and the consequence of conversion was further self-improvement. Both conversion and civilization, however, were dependent on education. The ability of the Indian to read and write seemed crucial to the Indians' further progress, but educational attainment proved difficult to achieve. Indian children failed to attend schools in tribal areas because of cultural conflicts—family disapproval or lack of relevance of the curriculum—and had to be bribed with food and clothing when they did come. Better attendance was one of the reasons why Indian boarding schools became the key to Indian education. The first such institution was the Foreign Missionary School, opened by the American Board of Missionaries in Connecticut in 1817. The next was the Choctaw Academy in Kentucky in 1825. The boarding schools accomplished a certain amount of assimilation because of their ability to isolate Indians from their families. Students received haircuts, baths, clothes, new names, new manners, and new trades. (The regime resembled that used successfully at Hampton and Tuskegee after the Civil War to make black students middle class.) Not all Indians could be persuaded to enroll their children in the schools as they objected to enforced work requirements and to the corporal punishment, both of which they thought cruel.

Religious conversion encountered other cultural barriers as well. Adult Indians attended church infrequently; they, like students, had to be bribed with clothes or food. Once at church, the Indians found the sermons difficult to understand as most ministers lacked proficiency in Indian languages. Those few ministers who spoke Indian languages complained that these languages failed to present religious concepts properly. Missionaries believed that the lack of an Indian sense of sin was a handicap, so they went about encouraging such a sense of sin. The difficulties encountered by missionaries rendered mass conversion unlikely; for example, the

Moravians worked twenty years and converted only eight Indians. In teaching their views of civilization, the missionaries emphasized the essential art of farming. Here, the barrier of culture intruded once more. The collective agricultural efforts of the Indians might best have been served by setting up farming villages; but believing in private property, the missionaries tried to persuade the Indians to take up individual plots. They also tried to convince the Indian man to take up the hoe despite the tradition in many tribes that cultivation was women's work. At the same time the male Indian was being taught to become a farmer, he was encouraged to create legal and governmental systems patterned after the white American ones. Those Indians who became Christian farmers living in a self-governing society of laws could become American citizens.

Missionaries were divided on both the question of whether the Indian would learn better in complete isolation from white society and the question of Indian Removal. Isaac McCoy's *Remarks on the Practicability of Indian Reform, Embracing Their Colonization* (1827) urged that Indians be sent west of the state of Missouri, be given farms, and be taught civilization. Jeremiah Evarts, corresponding secretary of the American Board of Commissioners for Foreign Missions, wrote in *Essays on the Present Crisis in the Conditions of the American Indians* (1829) that the Indian would be civilized faster in his familiar, native area. However, the latter opinion was held by a minority; most missionaries supported the principle of Indian Removal.

The Indian reaction to attempts to civilize and Christianize him involved both acceptance and rejection. Often, the Indians argued that the Great Spirit had ordained two ways of life, one for the Whites and another for the Indians. If He had desired the Indians to be Christian, He would have given them the Bible Himself. In addition, Indians claimed that their ways were more appropriate for them and even superior to white ways. Conversion was hampered because, as a Christian, an Indian had to wear a shirt, tend a garden, marry one wife, clear fields, build a house, attend church, and send his children to school. Once converted, the Indian had to become anti-Indian, denouncing the "wild Indians," nakedness, and the ways of the savage; he had to reject his former friends. This required change often resulted in physical violence between Christian and pagan Indians. Sometimes villages were split; the Moravians encouraged this division as they felt contact with pagan Indians encouraged backsliding. However, the social isolation of Christian Indians deterred new conversions.

Despite the problems, missionaries had nominally converted about 40 percent of the Indians among whom they had worked by 1860. However, the superficiality of the conversions was recognized, and there was doubt as to whether the Indians would remain Christian if white missionaries left. Although some groups claimed success—the American Board closed its missions to the Tuscarora and Cherokees in 1860, saying that its work was accomplished—the majority opinion was that the Indian had become neither Christian nor civilized.

I

The historic image of the nineteenth-century Indian had a popular counterpart based on first-hand traveler's accounts. The nineteenth century was also the heyday of romantic racialism for by this time the terms *nation* and *tribe* had been replaced by *race*. Romantic racialism insisted that the significant differences between groups were innate and natural rather than products of the environment, and that each race had its own peculiar gifts. Thus the qualities of the Indians were unique and could never be shared with the Whites (and vice-versa). This popularly held romantic view often conflicted with first-hand experience of the Indians.

One of the most significant first-hand accounts of Indian life was *Alexander Henry's Travels and Adventures in the Years, 1760–1776* (1809). Born in New Jersey in 1739, Henry accompanied Lord Amherst to Canada in 1760, experienced Pontiac's Rebellion, prospected for copper in the Lake Superior area, traveled to Montreal, and left for France when the American Revolution started. After the war, Henry returned to the New World to become once again an Indian trader. Henry's accounts proved a storehouse of information for later writers; Francis Parkman used material from Henry in his *The Conspiracy of Pontiac*, and Henry Thoreau drew on Henry for his writings on Indians.

Alexander Henry's Travels and Adventures in the Years, 1760–1776 told of Henry's adoption by a Chippewa and his subsequent capture by an Ottawa. He was later recaptured by the Chippewa tribe, who insisted that he dine on the body of the Ottawa. After further adventures, including the discovery of a cave full of bones that he believed to be the remains of sacrificial victims, Henry became to all intents and purposes an Indian ethnologist (a specialist in the study of races), and he began to record Indian customs. Henry's book made Indian practices seem natural and vivid.

Between 1765 and 1767, Henry had encountered the Assiniboine tribe near Lake-of-the-Woods. An informant named Great Road explained to him a number of rituals, such as the Indian way of selecting sacred objects. Henry also learned about the marriage and burial customs of the Assiniboines, which he felt were common to all Indians. To marry, a man selected a girl and visited her in the family lodge at night. If she talked to him, he brought his own blanket back to stay the night. (Henry compared this practice to New England bundling, noting that the Indian practice was more openly sexual.) Following this, the two fathers of the couple met in the sweating house (an Indian sauna) to determine the details of the match (which usually included service of the groom to the father-in-law for three years). Having other wives was no deterrent to marrying again as long as the groom could support the new wife. Funeral customs were as simple as marriage ones. The dead were buried, seated along with their necessary property; a relative pronounced a eulogy and food was placed on the grave, concluding the ceremony.

Henry's book contained no overt didactic thesis. He portrayed the Indian as virtuous but also as primitive. He drew no moral from his adventures nor did he speculate on Indian origins. His factual account did not particularly promote a view of romantic racism. It was left to others, who had little contact themselves with the Indians, to promote such a view, basing their arguments on Henry's works and ideas.

In 1818, John Heckewelder, a Moravian minister, wrote a first-hand *Account of the History, Manners, and Customs, of the Indian Nations, Who Once Inhabited Pennsylvania and the Neighboring States.* Heckewelder analyzed Indian life and showed that the cultural center of that life was hunting. He distinguished both good and bad Indians, a dualism later utilized in the fiction of James Fenimore Cooper. While Heckewelder amply demonstrated the savagery of the Indian, he also said that the best Indian was better than the corrupted civilized man. Heckewelder, however, maintained essentially eighteenth-century ideas; his book was not a good example of the nineteenth-century romantic view of race.

More congenial to the romantic view of the Indian was Thomas L. McKenney's and James Hall's *History of the Indian Tribes of North America*, 3 vols. (1836). The books contained 120 portraits from the Indian Gallery of the Department of War. McKenney had begun to collect Indian portraits in 1821 when he was Superintendent of Indian Trade, prior to becoming Chief of the Bureau of Indian Affairs. Hall joined the Bureau of Indian Affairs in the 1830's and decided to collaborate with McKenney. The two men wished to document the physical appearance of those Indians who were becoming extinct.

The first two volumes of the history contained pictures while the third had narrative descriptions. The general impression maintained in all the volumes was that of the wild, unsettled Indian, the savage. The first picture, that of Red Jacket (called the last of the Senecas), carried the appellation the perfect Indian. Red Jacket refused to wear white men's clothes, hated missionaries, and venerated ancient customs. He claimed that even if the Indian could become civilized—which he said was impossible—he still would be treated no better than the Negro. The third picture was of Mohongo, an Osage woman. She was one of seven Indians taken for display to Europe by a Frenchman who later abandoned them. The seven made their way home with money donated by Lafayette, three dying before reaching the West. McKenney and Hall claimed that the portrait of the Osage woman showed both the limited mental power of the Indian and the submissiveness of the Indian woman. The sixth portrait was of an Indian called the Prophet; his face supposedly showed that Indians lied and exaggerated, were cowards—he had run from his first battle—but possessed some genius. The twelfth picture, that of Nawkaw, a Winnebago chief who remained neutral in a war between the United States and the Sauks and Foxes, was accompanied by the comment that "the Indian has some heroic traits of character; he is brave, patient under fatigue, generous, tenacious, etc. In social intercourse with Whites lack of versatility and deficiency of intellectual resources degrade him into meaness and puerility" (1836). The twenty-sixth picture was of an Ojibwa mother and child. In this portrait the woman was shown nursing a suckling child from elongated breasts. The description concluded that the Indian woman nursed her child while the child was on her back.

Although a result of first-hand experience, the tenor of McKenney's and Hall's book resembled that of Samuel Stanhope Smith's theoretical moralizing. All three had concluded that the Indian was capable of civilization, but that he must be deprived of his natural liberty until he earned it. They all felt that the federal government should help in the civilizing process, as should the churches. Unlike Smith, however, McKenney and Hall included hints of a belief in the existence of innate racial characteristics.

Others who were in contact with the Indian were less optimistic about the possibilities of civilization. The fur traders of the period, according to Lewis O. Saum, wavered between the image of the Indian as a Noble Savage and that of an evil spirit. Despite these prejudicing stereotypes, the fur traders were, in general, quite objective. They did not believe that the only good Indian was a dead one, partly because their livelihood depended upon a symbiotic relationship with Indians. They lacked much interest in the question of Indian origins, although some traders said that the Indians were Jews, a few believed they were from Asia, and one—James Mackay—said they were from Wales. The fur traders tended to be environmentalists, to attribute Indian characteristics to the Indians' surroundings. Philip Turner of Hudson's Bay Company said that the Indians became more peaceful the further north they lived. The traders preferred Indians who hunted over those who fished. The worst Indians were supposedly the "Diggers" of the Great Basin, who survived by eating plant roots. The best Indians were the Flatheads and the Nez Percé, the former being closest to the ideal of the Noble Savage. Contrary to the position held by some twentieth-century anthropologists (such as Kroeber and Benedict), little variance appears to have existed among the attitudes of traders of different nationalities.

The trader found the Indian to be insensitive to suffering, indolent, reluctant to fight, and sexually immoral. The Indian practice of plural marriage bothered the traders, as did their exchanging of wives. Despite the bad reputation of Indian women, or maybe because of it, the traders often lived with them. The traders confirmed the fears built up over more than a century that contact with the Indians converted Whites into Indians. Traders also found virtue in Indian life; Jebediah Smith commented in 1822 that the pastoral setting of a Sioux camp almost persuaded him to go native, and John McLean used the image of natural nobility to protest the practices of Hudson's Bay Company. Concomitant with a belief in Indian virtue was the acceptance of an adaptation of the concept of degeneration, as traders said that the red man learned only the vices of civilization.

The Indians' appearance hardly promoted a romantic viewpoint. While some Indians were tall, especially the Cheyennes and Arapahoes, many others, particularly the Pacific coast tribes, were short and unimpressive. Those few Indians who were affluent and had horses were physically most prepossessing, but all seemed dirty. Indians had, the traders admitted, characteristics that were superior. They possessed great endurance; stood up to torture, weather, and wounds; and survived gluttony, rotten food, and polluted water. However, these qualities were believed to be learned traits; white men were considered as capable if trained (traders claimed that Whites were already better hunters and street brawlers). Other Indian traits were less desirable. Indians were thought to be selfish; they rarely displayed any hospitality. They also were great bargainers, resisting even drink and other temptations when determined to get a better deal; but they supposedly lacked principle, were dishonest, refused to answer questions directly, and were too polite.

In general, the fur traders believed that Indian characteristics came from their environment but, once acquired, were permanent. The traders believed that when white and red men met, both degenerated; liquor ruined the Indian, and primitiveness ruined the trader. The offspring of a red and white liaison was thought to share the vices of both races. The Indian's destiny was not civilization as only a few might ever be civilized. To be successfully civilized they had to be separated from Whites on reservations (in Kit Carson's view) and to learn to farm; they then could be Christianized. While the trader's priorities differed from those of the missionaries and while they were less optimistic, the views of both groups were similar.

II

Professional anthropology began in America in the nineteenth century with the study of the Indians, inspired by the belief that Americans had the unique opportunity to record a vanishing race. The new anthropology was concerned with the question of Indian origins and the evidence of Indian mounds especially. In 1818,

De Witt Clinton, in an address before the Literary and Philosophical Society of New York, outlined the dilemma for those persons seeking the truth of the Indian past. Indians did not know their own history, he said; they were too engrossed in war or hunting to reflect on their own beginnings. On the other hand, Indian mounds revealed an "inhabitation by nations much further advanced than present tribes of Indians" and were considered not much inferior to the pyramids in Mexico and Peru. How could the discrepancy between the sophistication of the past and the ignorance of the present be resolved?

In 1820, Caleb Atwater's *Description of the Antiquities Discovered in the State of Ohio and other Western States* attempted to answer this question. Atwater, a postmaster at Circleville, Ohio, and one of the first American archeologists, said that the serpent mounds in Southern Ohio had been built by Hindus and Southern Tartars who had then moved south to construct the pyramids in Mexico and Peru. Speculation of this sort also appeared in the work of an Englishman, John Ranking. His *Historical Researches on the Conquest of Peru, Mexico, Bogata, Natchez, and Talomeco, In the Thirteenth Century, by the Mongols, Accompanied with Elephants* (1827) combined several phenomena into a general theory of Indian origin. Ranking claimed that the few Indian cities in America—Natchez, Talomeco (an Indian city near the serpent mounds in Ohio), and those in Mexico and Peru and Bogota—had in common their location near the remains of elephant's (Mastodon) teeth. This fact, plus the sophistication of these cities and the primitiveness of the rural Indian populace, led Ranking to divide the original inhabitants of America into savage and civilized groups. The civilized mound and city builders had supposedly descended from the survivors of a 100,000 man army that Kublai Khan had directed against Japan in 1283 A.D. but which had disappeared along with its war elephants. Ranking believed that this army's ships had been blown off course and had come to the New World (the usual historical explanation for this disappearance was that a typhoon had sunk the ships). There the elephants died, depositing their bones to be discovered by Croghan, and there the Mongols built cities. Atwater and Ranking illustrate how the renewed interest in Indian ruins led to the kind of fanciful theorizing that had been current in the sixteenth century.

More significant than this intellectual whimsy was the attempt to resuscitate the idea that the Indians were the Ten Lost Tribes of

Israel. In England, Edward King (Viscount Kingsborough) wrote a nine-volume work, entitled *Antiquities of Mexico* (1830–48), dedicated to this theory. In the United States, the thesis gained great notoriety as part of a Mormon religious proposition. Joseph Smith's *The Book of Mormon* (1830), purported to be a pre-Columbian history of the New World, claimed the Indians to be descendants of the Jews. According to Smith, the founder of the Church of the Latter Day Saints, the Jews migrated to the New World in several waves from the Old World. The Jaredite tribe supposedly left the Near East at the time of the building of the Tower of Babel and was destroyed in the second century B.C. The Israelites came to the New World in 600 B.C. and split into two groups, the Nephites and Lamanites. The Nephites remained faithful to Old Testament ways and built the pre-Columbian cities of Middle America as well as the Indian mounds of North America. The Lamanites degenerated and became the ancestors of the present-day Indians. Although Christ had ultimately appeared to save the Nephites, Smith claimed, they too backslid and because of their degeneracy, were overpowered in a final cataclysmic battle with the Lamanites. Smith neatly packaged certain ideas of his day—such as lost tribes and degeneracy—and added an idea of his own, that of the second appearance of Christ in the New World. Smith's religion provided a rationale for the Indians' position in America; he argued that their primitiveness was a result of their sin. Smith's religion also justified the elimination of the Indians and warned against the association of civilized peoples with savage peoples.

Samuel G. Morton, in his *Crania Americana* (1839), approached the question of Indian origin and future through the science of phrenology, through comparing the cranial measurements of skulls of different races. On this basis, he divided the Indians into two families, the American and the Toltecan. The American family included the more primitive Indians of both North and South America; the Toltecs included the less primitive tribes of Central America as well as the Natchez. Morton's basis for division derived from accounts of Indian life written by such authors as Heckewelder. Morton compared skulls of contemporary Indians with those of Indians found in mounds in Ohio and Virginia and in burial sites in Mexico and Peru. Morton concluded that contemporary and historic Indians were of one race, created in the New World. Morton believed that American Indians were of a race which was supposedly cautious, taciturn, warlike, indolent, and lacking private property and religious complexity. Morton noted the accounts of Mayan ruins just published by Stephens but said these ruins failed to disprove the thesis of Indian inferiority. The Toltecans were of a superior Indian family and could have developed the urban complexes themselves or, perhaps, could have been aided by the Japanese. Morton also attacked Ranking's theory of American city development by the Khan's army, saying that Ranking knew neither history nor geography. If there had been successive waves of Mongol migration to the New World, written records would confirm it since the Mongols had been literate. He applied the same test to the Ten Lost Tribes theory; the Jews would not have forgotten their literature, language, or religion. There was, Morton concluded, no connection between the people of the Old and New Worlds. Each race had originated in a distinct climate and locality; each race had not changed but was fixed with peculiar physical and mental qualities.

Morton's book contained an appendix written by George Combe which, based on a comparative study of Indian skulls, classified the abilities of various tribes. The extinct Hurons had the smallest skulls, and the Cherokees and Chippewas, who were the most civilized of tribes, had the largest. From this comparison, Combe provided a natural explanation for American historical development. He justified Indian extermination by saying that the Indians lacked the mental resources to be civilized.

In 1841, John Lloyd Stephens, in his *Incidents of Travel in Central America, Chiapas, and Yucatan*, agreed with the obvious theory, claiming that the mounds in Central and North America had been built by the ancestors of those Indians who still lived in the mound areas. The book enjoyed immediate popularity, selling 20,000 copies in three months. Its thesis was expanded by E. G. Squier's *Aboriginal Monuments of the State of New York* (1849), which linked the mounds in that state with the known history of the Iroquois. Stephens's and Squier's position soon was taken as scientific orthodoxy; the belief that races other than the Indians had built the mounds or pyramids began to dwindle.

Archeology, however, seemed to provide only ambiguous answers to the question of Indian origins. It was believed that linguistics might reveal Indian origin by analyzing the deviations of Indian languages from one general language. Because of this hope, John Pickering reprinted the extant works on the American Indian languages and, in 1820, published his own *Essay on a*

Uniform Orthography for the Indian Languages of North America. In this essay, he proposed a phonetic alphabet for transcription of Indian languages. Using his technique, Albert Gallatin then made the first systematic attempt to compare and classify Indian languages in his *A Synopsis of the Indians within the United States East of the Rocky Mountains and in the British and Russian Possessions in North America* (1836). These efforts revealed the vast number of Indian dialects and did much to make possible the more objective approach to the Indian past and present; but they failed to answer the question of origins.

Others proposed to study the Indians for reasons unrelated to discovering Indian origin. Lewis Cass, Governor of the Michigan Territory from 1813 to 1831, encouraged the collection of data on the Indians because he was convinced that they were vanishing. He circulated a 64 page questionnaire designed to collect information about the Indian's way of life in 1820 and published the results in *Inquiries Respecting the History, Traditions, Languages, Manners, Customs, Religion, Etc. of the Indians, Living within the United States* (1823). Cass believed that his book depicted the reality of Indian life in contrast to the idealized picture in Heckewelder's works and in the popular and literary images of the day. Cass's major contribution to Indian studies, however, was not his own book but rather his promotion of the work of Henry Rowe Schoolcraft.

Schoolcraft, whom H. R. Hays, a well-known historian of anthropology, calls the first social anthropologist and the first genuine field anthropologist in the world, was born in Oneida, New York. Schoolcraft met Cass on a trip to the headwaters of the Mississippi and, with Cass' support, became the Indian agent at Sault Ste. Marie, Michigan, in 1822. More than fifty years before the founding of the American Folklore Society, Schoolcraft began a study of Indian legends and folktales as well as of Indian languages. He founded the Algic Society in 1832 to collect and disseminate information about the Indians and helped found the American Ethnological Society in 1842 for the same reason.

Schoolcraft wrote a number of books, among them *Algic Researches* (1839)—on which Longfellow based his "Hiawatha"—*The Indian in His Wigwam* (1844), *Notes on the Iroquois* (1847), and a six volume work, *Historical and Statistical Information Respecting the History, Condition and Prospects of the Indian Tribes of the United States, Collected and Prepared under the Direction of the*

Bureau of Indian Affairs (1851). (The Secretary of War, who still controlled the Bureau of Indian Affairs, sponsored the last study and helped distribute the 348 item questionnaire Schoolcraft devised.) Schoolcraft based his conclusions about the intellectual life of the Indians upon his knowledge of the Algonquin and Iroquois who, he felt, were only savage because of their wild experiences. These experiences had been translated into myths, which enabled the Indians to symbolize experiences; the myths provided clues to the mental characteristics of the Indian.

In Schoolcraft's study of myth, he found what he believed to be Oriental influences; he also discovered sexual taboos similar to those of the Jews in the Old Testament. Despite these similarities with eastern and western societies, Schoolcraft believed that evidence was insufficient to prove any of the theories of origins. The resemblance of an Indian platform pipe to Etruscan ware did not mean the Indians had come from Italy; nor did the inscriptions on the West Virginia Indian mounds, which seemed to be in Pelasgi (an early Mediterranean language), prove that the Indians had migrated from the Mediterranean Sea.

Schoolcraft had little use for earlier writers on the Indian as he believed them to have been both uneducated and prejudiced. They had failed to comprehend both the scope and the genius of Indian languages and civilizations; they had ignored Indian myths because they had lacked the ability and the desire to understand them. They had regarded the Indians as wild animals without a past.

Schoolcraft coined the term *Algic family* by combining Alleghany and Atlantic, which represented the Algonquin Indians. The Algonquin tribes that had welcomed Europeans had achieved considerable cultural growth in his view; they had built canoes, woven bark nets, made pots, and conducted public affairs with dignity. He did feel, however, that they had failed to develop long-range political goals, that they were men of impulse but not endurance, that their actions originated from nervous tension and not intellectual excitement. In Schoolcraft's view the Indians were not savages; rather they had a developed culture.

The Algic language, according to Schoolcraft, was a simple tongue whose hieroglyphic nature resembled Egyptian but whose major character seemed Semitic. Algic myths were homogeneous and of vernacular origin; they were transmitted orally, with great care. He believed that they were old because guns, knives, and blankets were not included. The myths showed that the Indian was polytheistic. In addition, they contained a great variety of geographical, astronomical, and cosmological materials. The myths, Schoolcraft thought, resembled Oriental ones, although they were not exact duplicates.

Schoolcraft's favorite Indians in the Algic family were the Iroquois. In 1845, after taking a census of the Iroquois in New York State, he conceived the idea of updating Cadwallader Colden's 1727 and 1747 histories; the result was *Notes on the Iroquois* (1847). The book showed an appreciation of the Iroquois, whom Schoolcraft praised as the outstanding Indian tribe, surpassing even the Incas, because of their heroic love of liberty, true art of government, and great personal energy and stamina.

The Iroquois spoke of a mythic origin which consisted of creation, a flood, and subsequent political confederation, but they could not account for any of their history after that point (Schoolcraft dated the Confederation at about 1539 and estimated that the Iroquois had constructed the mounds in New York State at a later date). The Iroquois said that the mounds had been built earlier to protect themselves from the attacks of monsters, giant men, and animals who had early inhabited the area. A study of Indian language was of little help in understanding Indian history, according to Schoolcraft, for there was nothing in the Algonquin language which resembled the ancient languages, Hebrew, Greek, or Egyptian. Nor did Indian political or kinship organizations shed much light. The Iroquois kinship organization was unique. The Iroquois were exogamous; they had to marry into a clan whose totem differed from theirs. The line of descent lay in the female, but their government was patriarchal. Marriage was personal and did not involve property transfer.

Schoolcraft showed more confidence in predicting the future than in unraveling the past. He realized that the Indians were dying. Schoolcraft estimated from his census data that there were 2,108 less Iroquois in 1845 than in 1775. Except for the Iroquois, in his view, Indians were in a state of barbarism, misled by false religion and false views of government. The Indian lacked the conscience and gentle affections of civilized man. Schoolcraft thought that those who had given up hunting for the cultivation of maize were superior mentally and physically, proving that the Indian could be civilized if he gave up his bark lodge, his blanket, his paint, his orgies, and his liquor and became a farmer. His only other choice was extinction.

In an article in the *Democratic Review,* reprinted in *The Indian in His Wigwam,* Schoolcraft argued that barbarism and civilization could not coexist. Civilization was fatal to barbarism; the farmer replaced the hunter. The Anglo-Saxon race, which was vigorous and bent on improving the world, could not tolerate those who were not vigorous and so bent. As proof, Schoolcraft quoted President Monroe who said in his special message to Congress on January 27, 1825, both that it was impossible to incorporate Indians into American society and that, if not incorporated, "their degradation and extermination will be inevitable." Schoolcraft compared the 97,000 Indians who had lived on 77,000,000 acres of their own land in 1825, with the 40,000 on government reservations and the 21,774 on their own land in 1843; he concluded Monroe was right on both counts.

Schoolcraft anticipated much of what later anthropologists were to say; he independently constructed an evolutionary mechanism that tied social development to technological progress. He maintained that the invention and use of physical artifacts paralleled the development of sophisticated social arrangements. In addition, he connected racial characteristics with social development. The implicit progressivism in Schoolcraft's ideas (that barbarism must progress toward civilization or cease to exist) did not negate his acceptance of man's unity in Adam; but Schoolcraft's interest lay in the mechanisms of social change.

Schoolcraft was soon eclipsed by another self-taught anthropologist, Lewis Henry Morgan. Morgan was also born in New York State and began his professional life as a lawyer in Rochester. While there, Morgan became interested in Indians through a combination of professional and personal reasons. The Tonawanda Senecas hired Morgan to represent them in an ongoing land dispute. Out of gratitude for his legal efforts, the Indians made Morgan an honorary Seneca in the Hawk Clan of Tonawanda and gave him the name "One Lying Across." At approximately the same time, Morgan joined a secret society of young white men. Morgan then met the Indian Ely Parker, a Grand Sachem of the Iroquois, who persuaded Morgan to change his secret society's name to The New Confederation of the Iroquois and to substitute Indian ceremonies for those already in use. From these chance events, Morgan was on the path to becoming an Indian scholar, a path that was to lead eventually to his selection as the first anthropologist president of the American Association for the Advancement of Science.

Morgan presented a series of lectures to his secret society during the years when he was involved in Indian litigation; the lectures appeared in the *American Review* in 1847 in the form of fourteen letters to Albert Gallatin, the President of the New York Historical Society. Morgan published these letters and an added report on Indian artifacts in *The League of the Iroquois* in 1851. The work was hastily done, as Morgan erroneously believed it was to be his first and last Indian book. *The League of the Iroquois* is an inaccurate if exalted view of the Indians. Morgan knew little of Indian history or even of contemporary Indian customs. He claimed that the Iroquois League had originated 150 years before the Dutch arrived in the New World, that the Confederation and the clan system of the League had been deliberately formed by Indian legislative action, and that the Iroquois were and had been hunters rather than farmers (despite Schoolcraft's evidence to the contrary). Morgan romanticized the Iroquois, praising their democracy and claiming that they exceeded the Greeks in the nobility of their religion.

Morgan's purpose was to answer the question he posed in *The League of the Iroquois,* "can the Residue of the Iroquois be reclaimed, and finally raised to the position of citizens of the state?" Morgan believed the Indians could and should be reclaimed from degeneracy; to support his position, he proceeded to describe the Iroquois and their institutions. Relying upon Schoolcraft, Morgan depicted the gradual depopulation of the Iroquois after the Revolution. In his opinion, this depopulation accounted, in part, for the lack of progress toward civilization. Economic, political, and social factors also contributed to Indian backwardness. Morgan described the customs of the Iroquois, including the tribal system, which he compared to that of the Jews and Greeks. Using Montesquieu's political categories, Morgan characterized Iroquois government as an oligarchy (see Table 4.1 below) superior to that of the Greeks because of its greater freedom. The basic and fatal deficiency of the Iroquois, however, in Morgan's view, was the lack of progressive spirit; the hunting state was considered the lowest level of human society.

Of all the Indians' customs, religious ones interested Morgan the most, and *The League of the Iroquois* contains more material on religion than on any other topic. According to Morgan, the Iroquois had "a firm hold upon the great truths of natural religion." They believed in the Great Spirit; they confessed their sins and

TABLE 4.1

Political Category	Perversion of Original
Monarchy	Despotism or Tyranny
Aristocracy	Oligarchy (corrupt or selfish people rule by a small group)
Democracy	Ochlocracy (mob rule)

believed in an after-life. They had little crime and had always honored their treaties, considering lying a heinous offense.

Morgan concluded his book with a look at the destined future of the Indian. Since civilization was both aggressive and progressive, the Indian, to survive, must be reclaimed and civilized. This could be done by education and Christianity; Morgan pointed accusingly to the failure of New York State to provide for Indian education out of the common school fund prior to 1846 and the denial of admission of Indians to the State Normal School prior to 1850. Morgan believed that, once educated, the Indians would desire property. Once Indians possessed property, they would become citizens and would "cease to be Indians, except in name." Failing this, the Iroquois would suffer the fate of the Indians of New England; they would vanish.

Morgan had little concern for ultimate Indian origins, nor did he talk of degeneration at this time. Rather, the idea of progress was implicit in *The League of the Iroquois* as was the idea of progressive stages of civilization, which Morgan was to apply to all societies. The belief that certain qualities were inherent in certain races also permeated *The League of the Iroquois*.

In 1855, Morgan visited the Chippewas and discovered a kinship system similar to that possessed by the Iroquois. As a result of this discovery, Morgan embarked upon a detailed study of human kinship systems, resulting in a study published by the Smithsonian Institution in 1866 entitled *Systems of Consanguinity of the Human Family*. Morgan argued that kinship relations were natural rather than cultural products, were transmitted through heredity, and provided the best evidence for historical connections among people.

Morgan had, by this time, devised a progressive series of stages through which societies passed on the way to civilization. The stages were classified as to marriage arrangements, family structure, and property holding. They were:

1. promiscuous intercourse
2. brother and sister cohabit
3. communal family
4. clan organization
5. marriage between single pairs
6. patriarchal family
7. polyandry
8. private property
9. civilized marriage

Morgan argued that the Indians had come from Asia, because their kinship systems and clan organizations were similar to those in Asia. The Indians needed to accept private property, civilized marriage, and a new kinship system in order to be civilized. Morgan failed to explain how this could be accomplished if, as he insisted, the kinship system was natural and hereditary.

Morgan might have argued that kinship systems, assuming they were hereditary, could be gradually changed through intermarriage. However, Morgan rejected this solution in his *Systems of Consanguinity and Affinity of the Human Family*. He also rejected the idea of polygenesis, which could have explained the origins of the different kinship arrangements of Indians and Whites. Morgan devoted considerable time to the question of intermarriage. He believed that because of incompatible levels of passion—the Indian having too little and the European too much—the offspring of mixed marriages lacked the physical ability of the Indian while retaining all the passion of the white. While Morgan believed all Indian-white mixtures to be superior in intelligence to pure Indian, these individuals supposedly lacked the moral qualities of either race. Thus Morgan discouraged intermarriage.

By 1866, Morgan believed in a racial explanation of Indian society and development. He became later a full-blown evolutionist, arguing that societies progressed according to uniform laws. He had entered the intellectual arena with a grand scheme, one which explained human progress in naturalistic terms. Morgan believed in one origin for all people, but he disposed of Providence as a necessary element in the model.

The historians, philosophers, novelists, and dramatists of the day also incorporated a romantic racism, a belief in inherent racial characteristics, into their explanations of Indian behavior. Typical of the historians were George Bancroft, whose ten volume *The History of the United States* took him forty years to complete, and Francis Parkman, whose *The Conspiracy of Pontiac* was one of eight volumes describing the conflict between the English and French in America. Both historians predicted the inevitable demise of the Indians because of the antiprogressive nature of their race. Both held that the triumph of the Teutonic race and civilization spelled the end of the Indian.

Bancroft had to reconcile a belief in the virtue of natural simplicity with a recognition of Indian barbarism. Like Ralph Waldo Emerson, Bancroft believed that men, at their best, were products of nature who lived in harmony with it. By this definition, the Indian was the most natural of men. Why then did he not qualify as nature's nobleman? Bancroft's answer was familiar; the Indian had not improved upon nature, he had not cultivated it. Natural simplicity was inherent in the farmer, not the hunter. Despite the Indian's lack in the arts of cultivation, Bancroft believed he had virtues which placed him above degenerate Europeans. The Indian tolerated different religions, was honest, had democratic government, respected marriage vows, and was courageous. In resisting the French or the English, the Indian was seen as facilitating progress; but when he resisted American expansion, he was seen as a barrier to progress and a tragic figure. In the end, Bancroft said, the Indian would either be destroyed or exiled. Bancroft fit the Indians into a Divine scheme; they were pawns in the hands of a God who cared only for white Americans.

Parkman was more ferocious. In *The Conspiracy of Pontiac,* Parkman called Pontiac the perfected savage who did not want his people civilized and who would use any means to frustrate civilization. Parkman portrayed other Indians as being without honor or religion; he pictured them almost as the Mathers had, as agents of the Devil. Physically, they were described as dirty and grotesque, without sexual restraints. Before the Republic began, the Indians supposedly possessed courage and endurance; they helped defeat the French. But afterwards they were seen as degenerate and doomed to die as the Anglo-Saxon relentlessly advanced.

The wild Indian is turned into an ugly caricature of his conqueror; and that which made him romantic, terrible, and hateful, is in large measure scourged out of him. The slow cavalcade of horsemen armed to the teeth have disappeared before parlor cars and the effeminate comforts of modern travel.

Henry David Thoreau also believed in the eventual demise of the Indian, though for different reasons. He, like most writers of the time, based his ideas on first-hand accounts on the Indians but ended with a symbolic image of the Indian that was almost unrecognizable. Thoreau used Alexander Henry's account to draw conclusions about the future of Indian-White relations in the United States. Thoreau indicated that the dream of red and white men living in peace in the primeval woods was doomed to failure because the Indian was a serpent in a Christian paradise. Echoing an older belief in America as a new Eden, Thoreau believed that Eden was not a permanent state and that the Indian would tempt the White to sin and to progress. The concern with the theme of Indian and White friendship in the wilderness was to become standard in American literature as was use of the metaphor of the Indian serpent in an American Eden.

The theme of Indian-White relationships in the wilderness could be seen in the dramatic literature of the day, existing even before the birth of the Republic. Robert Rogers's play *Ponteach, or the Savages of America,* was published in London in 1766 but was never performed in America. The first notable Indian play to be performed in the New World was *The Indian Princess: or La Belle Sauvage,* written by James Nelson Barker. It opened in Philadelphia in 1808 and in London in 1820 and had the distinction of being the first American play to be performed overseas. Based upon Smith's *General History of Virginia,* the play portrayed the Indian as a noble red man and Pocahontas as a kind and merciful woman.

George Washington Parke Custis, son of John Parke Custis (George Washington's stepson), wrote three Indian plays during the 1820's which became quite popular—*The Indian Prophecy, The Pawnee Chief,* and *Pocahontas: or the Settlers of Virginia.* The first eulogized George Washington; in it an Indian spokesman claimed that Washington had had Divine protection. Custis adapted parts of Smith's *General History of Virginia* but transformed Pocahontas into a civilized person who saved Smith because she was a Christian. Custis's other Indians also were vehicles for displaying white values.

The play that became the most popular Indian drama, until those of the Civil War, was John Augustus Stone's *Metamora, or the Last of the Wampanoags* (1829). Stone wrote the play as an entry for a contest for the best tragedy. *Metamora* won the $500 first prize. The play's hero was King Philip, who was portrayed as possessing considerable nobility. Ironically, King Philip became the epitome of the Noble Savage at the very time the United States government was moving the Civilized Nations out of Georgia.

Stone's success encouraged others to write similar plays. *The Battle of the Thames* appeared in 1836; and, although the character of the Indian Prophet showed elements of superstition and vice, he also contained many manly virtues. Robert Dale Owen, the son of the founder of a Utopian community in New Harmony, Indiana, contributed *Pocahontas: A Historical Drama* to the repertory the following year. Owen's Pocahontas was kind and good, but his Powhatan was crafty and revengeful. With these entries, the Indian had become a stock figure on the American stage.

Nondramatic fiction of the era on Indian subjects relied upon the themes of the Indian princess who saved white men in the woods and on the vanishing Indian who possessed noble qualities. On occasions, the anti-Pocahontas also emerged, in the guise of Hannah Dustin.

The fictional depiction of the Indian had begun with history but ended in allegory. Daniel G. Hoffman, a noted literary critic, says that Hawthorne and Melville were right in saying that the early masters of American fiction wrote romances and not novels. The result had been "an historical depiction of the individual's discovery of his own identity in a world where his essential self is inviolate and independent of such involvements in history." The novelist was ambivalent about the role of the Indian in his creation; was the Indian a comrade in the woods, was he a Noble Savage illuminating the corruption of civilization, or was he a sexual symbol?

Regardless of their answers, authors uniformly denounced Indian-White miscegenation. James W. Eastburn's and Robert Sands's *Yamoyden, A Tale of the Wars of King Philip* was a case in point. A long narrative poem, *Yamoyden's* thesis was that Indians and Whites ought not to marry. Yamoyden, the Indian hero, had a white wife and child and was harassed on the one side by King Philip, who coveted Yamoyden's wife and child, and on the other side by his white father-in-law, who hated Yamoyden for marrying his daughter. This long poem attracted the attention of Lydia Maria Francis (Child), who was later to become an antislavery advocate, and prompted her to write her first novel, *Hobomok, a Tale of Early Times* (1824). The setting was Salem and Plymouth in 1629 and the heroine was a white woman who married an Indian, Hobomok, after mistakenly assuming that her first husband was dead. When the first husband returned, the noble Hobomok voluntarily left his wife and child and entered Cambridge University. Thus, Francis managed to warn against interracial marriage, to portray a Noble Savage, and to have a happy ending.

Another novel involving Indians was James Kirke Paulding's *Koningsmarke, The Long Finne* (1823), which was a kind of American *Tom Jones*. The hero, Long Finne, wandered through Delaware and Pennsylvania in the 1660's. Long Finne's adventures included capture by the Indians and enslavement to an Indian widow. While among the Indians, he witnessed all kinds of horrors but came to no harm because of his Indian mistress. In the end, his mistress graciously freed him in order to permit him to marry a white girl. The moral of this work was that it was better to live with the Indians than to marry them.

The ultimate and most influential portrayal of the Indian in the literature of the period, or indeed in all of American literature, was drawn by James Fenimore Cooper, whose works on Indians have been the object of literary criticism since their creation. Cooper, who lived from an early age in Cooperstown, New York, personally encountered only the marginal Indian, the Indian caught between two societies. He became a novelist of the Indian by accident. Cooper tried several occupations but only found his vocation when he was 30 years old after successfully writing a novel in response to a challenge from his wife. The book, *Persuasion* (1820), failed to bring him fame but his need of money pressured him to continue. His third book, *Pioneers* (1823) was the first to involve Indians and was the first in the *Leatherstocking Tales* series. His fifth book was the second and most famous of the series, *The Last of the Mohicans* (1826). After writing it, Cooper went to Europe, where he remained for over seven years and where he wrote *The Prairie* (1827), the third book in the *Leatherstocking* series. After his return to the United States, he completed the *Leatherstocking Tales* series with *The Pathfinder* (1840) and *The Deerslayer* (1841). The *Leatherstocking Tales* traced the story of Natty Bumppo and his Indian companion Chingachgook, "Big Serpent." Cooper wrote other Indian novels, including *The Wept of Wishton-Wish* (1829), *Wyandotte* (1843), and *The Oak Openings* (1848), a trilogy: *Satanstoe* (1845), *Chainbearer* (1845), and *The Redskins* (1846). None of the latter works were as successful as the

Leatherstocking Tales, although *The Wept of Wish-ton-Wish* was made into a play.

The plots of Cooper's secondary works were instructive. *The Wept of Wish-ton-Wish* involved King Philip's War. The hero was an Indian who was married to a white woman, an Indian captive who had become Indianized. The Indian hero was truly noble; he pledged and kept his word to return to his enemies, the Mohicans, even though it meant his death. *Wyandotte* was set in New York State and concerned an outcast Tuscarora chief who killed a man in revenge for having flogged him thirty years before. The trilogy, *Satanstoe, Chainbearer,* and *The Redskins,* was a history of the Littlepages, a white family in New York State, from the French and Indian War to the 1840's. The theme of the trilogy was the battle between the landowning Littlepage family and the white squatters who attempted to seize parts of the land. Most of the Indians in the trilogy played a supporting role. The Hurons sided with the squatters, but an honest Onondaga, who came to the aid of Mordaunt Littlepage in his struggle against land pirates, almost dominated the last volume of the trilogy.

In the *Leatherstocking Tales,* the Indians were idealized. Cooper admitted this when Lewis Cass accused him of relying too heavily upon the works of Heckewelder. Cass charged that the idle traditions of the Indians were too frivolous for sober historical discussion and that Indian superstitions were too often accepted as serious religion by white reporters. Cooper retorted that both he and Heckewelder were correct to pick out the most elevating characteristics of the Indians to describe. Cooper never maintained that his Indians came from nature; his purpose was not to realistically depict Indian life but rather to write an allegory of American life.

The Indians in Cooper's works were either very good or very bad (as they had been in Heckewelder's). The Huron tribe represented evil; the Chingachgooks and Uncas represented virtue. Cooper did not, however, permit even the good Indians to survive. Their lives of war and hunting were shown as limiting their development and character. Indians could not enter into white society through miscegenation. In all his books, Cooper asked himself the rhetorical question, "has the flight from Europe and the expropriation of the Indians' lands bound white man and red in such an inextricable knot of mutual interest and guilt that they must eventually blend into one accursed race?" (Daniel G. Hoffman, *Form and Fable in*

American Fiction [New York, 1961]). His answer was no. In *The Last of the Mohicans*, the Indian Uncas loved the mulatto Cora, but he was not to marry her; an Indian could not marry an even partly white woman. Nor could the white male live with or marry an Indian woman in Cooper's works. Leslie Fiedler, a recent critic, concluded that the only companion Cooper permitted the white man to have in the woods was male, and that the Indian Chingachgook, who had a death's head for a totem, stood symbolically as an enemy to women. The *Leatherstocking Tales* represented an escape from society and an avoidance of women and sexuality, all of which were to become traditional in the Western literary genre. Cooper's Indian heroes were anticivilization and anti-Christian, but were destined in the end to die. Cooper, like writers before him, saw both the Indian's nobility and his savagery, foresaw the degeneration but not the civilizing of the Indian, and believed that the answer to the Indian problem was extinction and not assimilation into American society.

In the Indian novels written after Cooper's, the character of the white hero in the woods changed into that of the Indian Hater. The Indian Hater, unlike Cooper's Deerslayer (Natty Bumppo) who was native to the woods, was a civilized man gone savage to defend civilization. James Hall used this stock figure in his *Legends of the West* (1832) and *Tales of the Border* (1835), but the outstanding work in this tradition was Dr. Robert Montgomery Bird's *Nick of the Woods or the Jibbenainosay* (1837) a book which almost approached the popularity of Cooper's best novels. The work was a powerful one; the critic R. W. B. Lewis said that Bird "came closer than he knew to breaking through the conventions of fiction and producing a novel of honesty and stature." Bird portrayed the Indian as neither noble nor heroic. Bird conceded in his introduction that his image of the Indian was not a favorable one; in fact, his intent was to attack the favorable image of the Indian found in Cooper's works.

The story was set in frontier Kentucky and the hero was a Quaker pacifist who was neutral toward the Indians until his wife and five children were killed by a Shawnee. This experience turned the pacifist into a secret killer, Nick of the Woods, who carved crosses on his scalped Indian victims. The hero was a kind of inverted Christ figure, possessed of both saintly and devilish qualities. The Indians in Bird's work had no good qualities; they were ignorant, violent, debased and brutal.

Herman Melville had another image of the Indian; in *Moby Dick* (1851), the Indian was the oldest man aboard the Pequod and symbolized the antiquity of the American continent. In this role, the Indian was not without heroic qualities. In *The Confidence Man* (1857), the Indian Hater appears as Melville speculated on the phenomenon. Melville asked, why did Indian hating persist after Indian rapine had ceased? His answer lay in the character of the frontiersman and the Indians. The former was seen as strong, unsophisticated, impressive, self-willed, and self-reliant, and possessing instincts which prevailed over his weak precepts. The frontiersman, Melville said, was to America what Alexander was to Asia, a captain in the vanguard of a conquering civilization. Having fulfilled that role, the frontiersman retained his hostile, aggressive attitudes toward the Indian and inculcated these in his children. Melville believed that the Indian was depraved, that there was an essentially Indian nature, and that this was not that of the Noble Savage. Melville's suspicious frontiersman believed that the concept of the Noble Savage was used to lull him into a sense of security, when he could be attacked. He vehemently rejected any claim of virtue in the Indian and held an implacable hate for him, a hate which foretold Indian demise. Melville described the problem of the Indian situation fairly accurately but offered no solution.

While Melville discussed the metaphysics of Indian hating, Longfellow bolstered the Noble Savage image in an epic poem, "Hiawatha" (1855). The poem was instantly popular, selling 50,000 copies in the first one-and-a-half years. Longfellow based his tale on the history of Heckewelder and Schoolcraft; he shared their confusion over whether Hiawatha was Algonquin or Mohawk. He borrowed his meter, style, and some ideas from the Finnish national epic, "Kalevala." Thus combining American and European elements, Longfellow wrote what was to become one of the most well known and often quoted nineteenth-century poems; his idea of the Indian became a part of the consciousness of American society. The Indian, as Longfellow described him, was a noble child of nature who possessed the virtues of strength and manliness; but he was also of a society left behind in the past. He had never encountered civilization; his virtues were uncorrupted by European vices. Longfellow gave no clue as to the ultimate fate of the Indian in America. His Indian was removed from reality and had entered the realm of legend.

By the time of the Civil War, the American view of the Indian had changed from the more favorable eighteenth-century one. The Noble Savage idea persisted but with considerable modification, divorced from reality and immersed in allegory. It was challenged by the conflicting idea that the Indian represented natural wildness and evil. The earlier advocacy for intermarriage disappeared; writers now uniformly denigrated such unions. While missionaries clung to the possibility of Christianizing and civilizing the Indian, even they confessed their lack of success in achieving the goal. The official policy of the federal government at this time was to try to civilize the Indian by isolating him from the corrupting influence of bad Whites. Public opinion, however, held to the belief that the Indian was doomed to extinction. This belief prompted the beginnings of social anthropology in the United States through Schoolcraft and Morgan, who looked for new answers to the old questions: what were the origins of the Indians? what was their destiny? In all aspects of thought, the Indians served as a foil for American society, showing its progress through their primitiveness.

Chapter 5

Slavery Ends but Race Begins

Benjamin Franklin's prediction of estimated population trends was quite accurate until the time of the Civil War. As he predicted, the rate of American population increase was approximately 34 percent each decade. With this rate of increase, the white population gradually outstripped the black. The major reason for this was immigration. The slave trade ended in 1807; some 70,000 slaves had been legally imported prior to that date, and 54,000 were illegally imported afterward. White immigration during this period, on the other hand, increased significantly. The census of 1820 (the first to include questions about places of birth) estimated that two percent of the 1810 to 1820 increase in American population was the result of immigration; in 1840, the census showed that 25 percent of the increase came from immigration. This caused the percentage of Blacks in the total American population to drop, as the figures in Table 5.1 show.

The most significant question arising from the data is not why the percentage of Blacks declined but why, given the rigors of slavery and the lack of black immigration, did the black population remain such a significantly large part of the total population?

One answer seems to have been a decline in the birth rate of native white Americans to a figure more nearly approximate that of Europeans; the decline was probably a result of the spreading knowledge about contraception and the imbalance in male-female

TABLE 5.1

Date	Total Number of Blacks	Percent of Population
1790	760,000	19.3
1800	1,000,000	18.9
1810	1,380,000	19.0
1820	1,770,000	18.4
1830	2,330,000	18.1
1840	2,870,000	16.1
1850	3,640,000	15.7
1860	4,440,000	14.1

ratios. Francis Place's *Illustrations and Proofs of the Principle of Population* (1822) and his *Contraceptive Handbills* (1823) arrived in America in 1828, and American contraceptionists, such as John Humphrey Noyes, also published birth control information. Census data revealed that, at the time of the Civil War, the white population still contained a preponderance of males while the black population contained a majority of females, thus indicating the potential for a greater natural increase among Blacks. The potential for black population increase in the United States meant that social theorists of the time had to come to grips with the problems implied by the existence of a permanent multiracial population and had to construct a social system which could accommodate this situation.

Contemporary analysts viewed black increase with alarm and made fantastic predictions of future growth. William Darby, in his *View of the United States: Historical, Geographical, and Statistical* (1828), projected the growth figures (Table 5.2) for the decades before the Civil War.

TABLE 5.2

Year	Negro Population
1810	1,528,270
1820	8,096,518
1830	11,149,333
1840	14,114,709
1850	15,756,079
1860	17,860,118

Darby's projections of black population erred mostly because he overestimated the natural increase of Blacks from 1790 to 1820. Besides errors committed by those who anticipated the censuses, the actual censuses lent themselves to misinterpretation because of their imperfections and inaccuracies. The census of 1840 enumerated, for the first time, the mentally defective and ill (under the rubrics of idiot and insane) and indicated that free Negroes suffered insanity at a rate eleven times that of slaves. Proslavery apologists hailed these findings as proof both that slavery protected the Negro from the emotional stresses that caused insanity and that the northern climate adversely affected Blacks. Dr. Edward Jarvis, a physician specializing in mental disorders, attacked the census, showing how the definition of insanity had differed with each respondent, demonstrating also that the census-takers had reported insane Blacks in towns where no Blacks had existed, and declaring that both the methods and conclusions of the census were wrong. Jarvis failed, however, to convince Secretary of State Calhoun, who was responsible for the census of 1840, of its errors. The erroneous census of 1840 survived to embarrass abolitionists and other friends of the Blacks.

Slavery within the United States in the nineteenth century had developed a particular demographic pattern; it had moved South. In 1790, 20 percent of all slaves were in border areas; in 1860, only 10 percent lived there. In 1790, 20 percent of all slaves were in the lower South; in 1860, 54 percent were.

The opposite pattern was true for free Blacks. After 1830, there was an increase in the number of free Blacks in the border states but not in the number in the lower South. Maryland, for example, had 103,000 slaves and 8,000 free Blacks in 1790; in 1860, she had 87,000 slaves and 84,000 free Blacks.

While slavery was becoming confined to the South, racial incidents were increasing in the North. In 1819, a Negro woman was stoned to death in Philadelphia; in 1829, 1,000 free Negroes fled Cincinnati, Ohio, after a white mob had roamed, killing and looting through the Negro area. In 1834, New York City had a major racial disturbance precipitated by a charge, printed in the *Courier and Enquirer*, that abolitionists favored intermarriage. Racial friction in the North became a fact of life in nineteenth-century America.

The major American social and political issue in the first half of the nineteenth century was slavery. The issue concerned both conservative and liberal northerners as well as southerners.

While the northern liberals attacked the institution of slavery, the conservatives attacked the expansion of it, since expansion might bring more blacks to the North. Southern apologists for slavery were expansionistic as they perceived that expansion meant increased political and economic power for the South. Perennial pressure to annex Cuba, the Caribbean Islands, and Latin America as slave territories came from the South as planters talked of an American empire in the Gulf of Mexico. Some writers justified acquisition of these additional slave territories in humanitarian terms; J. C. Reynolds, writing in *De Bow's Review in* 1850, argued for the annexation of Cuba in order to improve the lot of the Cuban slaves; Mathew F. Maury, of the Navy Hydrographic Office, promoted naval exploration of the Amazon in the 1850's with the goal of taking Brazil as a haven for slaves who might be expelled from the United States. The expansionist schemes floundered, however, because they would have effected a marked increase in the population of blacks in the United States; only the most rabid defenders of slavery wished for such a result.

There were persistent efforts to reintroduce slavery in the new North. While some northerners in the older established states were concerned with the abolition or restriction of slavery, prior to 1809, Indiana settlers, led by William Henry Harrison, petitioned again and again for the federal government to permit slavery. In 1809, the Illinois Territory (the most proslave part of the Indiana territory until division into a separate territory) tried to legalize slavery. In 1818, the Illinois Constitutional Convention included a provision in the new constitution permitting indentured servitude (although slavery would have been preferred). The fear of not gaining statehood if slavery were instituted limited them to this provision. Although hopes that Illinois would become a slave state persisted until 1824, they were unfulfilled.

At the same time, no established state voluntarily gave up slavery and no new state, after the admission of Maine in 1820, granted political rights to the free Black. By 1860, only five states—all of them in New England—had equal suffrage for black men as well as white. In the rest of the North, the extension of the white franchise was accompanied by restrictions on black suffrage. In 1821, the New York Constitutional Convention enfranchised any free white male who possessed a freehold, paid taxes, and served in the state militia or worked on the highways. At the same time, the property qualification, which formerly applied to all voters, was raised from $100 to $250 and applied only to black voters. Other states took similar steps. Pennsylvania ratified a new constitution in 1838 which prohibited black voting altogether. The new states to the west uniformly placed disabilities on black suffrage. In addition to limiting the voting of Blacks, some states restricted their freedom of movement, their access to schools, and even their protection by the laws. In 1842, the Indiana Senate proposed establishing separate Negro schools to prevent racial mixture. Few states went as far as Missouri, whose constitution prohibited the entry of any mulattoes or free Blacks to the state; but the newer northern states often required the posting of bonds in cases of black immigration.

A few states had more liberal records; while these states proved to be the exception to the rule, even they showed only limited gains. A good example of a liberal state was Massachusetts. In 1832, an attempt to prohibit the entrance of black paupers into the state was frustrated; in 1839, the prohibition on racial intermarriage ended; in the 1840's, the segregation of railroad passenger cars ceased; and in 1855, school authorities abolished all-black schools and integrated the public schools. While the strong pattern of segregation, which developed in most northern states, diminished in the New England states, only in Maine did Blacks have full civil rights.

Prior to the Civil War, the federal government had relegated the black man to an inferior status. In 1790, Congress enacted legislation which prohibited black naturalization, thus restricting the immigration of free Blacks. In 1792, Congress restricted the national militia to Whites (although Blacks served in it in both the later, undeclared war with France and the War of 1812). In 1810, legislation excluded Blacks from carrying the U.S. mails; in 1820, legislation was passed in Washington, D.C. (which was under federal control) implementing slave codes as well as restrictions on free Blacks.

Ambiguity existed in the granting of black citizenship. Only a limited number of states afforded state citizenship to Blacks. The State Department of the federal government granted or denied passports depending upon the citizenship status of Blacks in their home states. This resulted in inconsistency. In 1839, a Philadelphia Black failed to get a passport because Pennsylvania limited its suffrage to white males; but, in 1854, a black man from Massachusetts received a passport. The final resolution of all questions on federal citizenship came with the Dred Scott decision in 1857, which held that Blacks were not citizens and, hence, could claim none of the privileges of citizens.

The Republican Party attacked the Supreme Court's decision in the Dred Scott case but refused to support equal rights for Blacks. The Democrats approved the Dred Scott decision and attacked the Republicans as being pro-amalgamation (or intermarriage)—an anti-Republican political cartoon of the day showed a black man hugging a white girl—Republicans defended their party by declaring it a white man's party. This was the position of Lyman Trumbull, Republican leader from Illinois and close friend of Lincoln, who said that the Republican party favored free labor and opposed the extension of slavery. He denied that the party wished equal political or social rights for the Negro. Even the so-called radicals within the party, who were for equal black political rights, denied wanting black social equality.

One proposed solution to the problems of both the free Black and slavery was the old one of African colonization. The pro-colonizers visualized both the free Black and the slave as dangerous to the social order (thus maintaining the fears of the eighteenth century) and believed that the only way to reduce the danger was to remove the Black. The proponents of colonization believed slavery to be a passing phenomenon and prejudice to be an enduring one. Like Jefferson, they felt the slave experiences to have been too compelling to be easily forgotten by the Black; they felt that white ideas of black inferiority were too deeply rooted to be eradicated. The colonizers also shared the belief that men's social and behavioral differences were environmentally determined. They believed the Negro to be biologically equal to Whites but culturally inferior. As George M. Fredrickson says in *The Black Image in the White Mind* (1971):

Colonizationist thought illustrates the sometimes forgotten fact that social environmentalism—the belief that human character and values are shaped or predetermined by social and cultural conditions—can be put to extremely conservative uses.

Many Whites, in the North and South, were attracted to the colonization movement and proposed different schemes of colonization.

English colonization schemes had predated the American attempts. The African colony of Sierra Leone was begun as a refuge for English Blacks, many of whom had been ex–Revolutionary-War loyalist soldiers and had been taken from the slums of London in 1787. Sierra Leone inspired American attempts. Dr. William Thornton and Reverend Samuel D. Hopkins of Newport, who were both Whites, influenced the foundation of two black colonization societies, which appeared in Newport and Boston. In 1795, these societies sent delegates to Africa to find suitable locations for settlement. President Jefferson attempted, without success, to induce the Sierra Leone colony to permit the entry of free American Negroes in 1800. While Jefferson's attempt failed, other private efforts did not. Paul Cuffe, a black Quaker, made two colonizing trips to Sierra Leone, one in 1811 and another in 1815, with a total of 38 black emigrés. Despite these efforts, black opinion was largely anticolonization; in 1817, black leaders meeting in Philadelphia unanimously rejected colonization as a solution to American race problems.

The first national white antislavery organization was the American Colonization Society, founded in the chamber of the United States House of Representatives in December, 1816, by a Presbyterian minister, Robert Finley of Bashing Ridge, New Jersey. Its first president was Justice Bushrod Washington, a nephew of George Washington. The Society planted a colony in Liberia after the purchase of land in 1821.

Colonization schemes in the 1820's, while White-inspired and financed, were supported by a few cooperating Blacks. Among these Blacks was Daniel Coker, one of the founders and first bishop of the African Methodist Episcopal Church; he was sent to Africa as an agent of the American Colonization Society. John B. Russwurm—a Jamaican-born Black, one of the first black graduates of an American college, and the coeditor of the first American Negro newspaper, *Freedom's Journal* (1827)—migrated to Africa in 1829. He founded a newspaper there and became the first black governor in Africa to have come from the United States. Both of these black men believed that prejudice made the United States an unfit place for Blacks to live (a belief shared by their white sponsors) and that the duty of the American Black was to Christianize Africa. Believing that God had permitted the Black to be enslaved only as part of His plan to spread the gospel through the world, these deeply religious men considered themselves to be the spearhead of African conversion.

In the 1830's, however, the rise of two new movements, immediatism and Garrisonianism, eclipsed colonization sentiment. Immediatism was the demand for immediate and uncompensated emancipation. William Lloyd Garrison carried immediatism furthest and converted many, Black and White, to the belief that a genuine, equalitarian, multiracial society could be formed in the United States. He said that white Americans could overcome prejudice and that, although Negroes were now inferior, they would become equal if freed. His most telling argument, however, was his demonstration of the impracticality of colonization, showing that the proportion of Blacks taken to Africa represented only a fraction of their yearly natural increase.

Black interest in colonization revived in the 1850's. Edward Wilmot Blyden—a Virgin Islander who, after being refused entrance to Rutgers University, went to Liberia—wrote a pamphlet, *A Voice from Bleeding Africa* (1856), designed to encourage black migration to redeem Africa from paganism. The leading protagonist of colonization at this time was Martin R. Delany, a black doctor who had attended Harvard Medical School. Delany originally argued for colonization of either the Caribbean or Central America but shifted to a support of Africa after a visit there in 1859.

The majority of black and white abolitionists never supported colonization. Convinced that the home of the Negro was America, they agitated to end slavery and to change the image of the free Black in American society. They claimed that the supposed cultural inferiority of the Negro was not inherent but resulted from the disadvantages accrued from the slave system and poverty. White and black abolitionists strove to portray the Negro as hardworking and sober and formed societies to inculcate these virtues. In 1831, for example, the Coloured American Conventional Temperance Society, an offshoot of the Negro Convention movement, tried to induce Blacks to become teetotalers. Mutual aid societies, schools, and libraries for Blacks attempted to reduce the environmental gap between the free Black and the free White. All these efforts, however, failed to convince most white Americans.

The debate for and against slavery, based on racial grounds in the United States, could have been argued quite differently. According to Carl Degler, a noted historian, the discussion over abolition in Brazil was not based upon the racial character of the slave but centered on the economic consequences of abolition and on the importance of political rights. Brazilians debated whether the prosperity of their country depended upon slavery and whether the right of property should overshadow the right to freedom. In Brazil, the slave was feared, but the Black was not. Even defenders of slavery approved of social arrangements that permitted Negroes and mulattoes to achieve high social position.

The institution of slavery varied little between the two countries. Both had similar laws, indifferently enforced; both permitted slave families to be separated; and both had a certain amount of slave resistance—although Brazil had more numerous and more severe slave rebellions. "Maroon states," autonomous enclaves of runaway slaves, existed in Brazil but not in the American South. In some cases, Brazilian law and practice permitted more severe treatment of slaves. Slaves in Brazil were rented as prostitutes; they had to wear masks to prevent them from eating dirt and drinking liquor; and older, infirm slaves were often cruelly abandoned. These latter practices rarely occurred in the American South.

The reasons for the differences in the ideologies of the two countries lay in the social systems of the two slave economies. In Brazil, the mulatto had independent status; society was hierarchical by tradition and antidemocratic in practice; and lower-class Whites lacked the right to vote. Miscegenation in Brazil occurred primarily as an outcome of slavery, as in the United States; but the status of white women in the United States prevented open philandering by their husbands. In the American South, mulatto children were not acknowledged by their white fathers. In Brazil, white men kept their wives under close physical and psychological restraint while openly acknowledging their black mistresses and their mulatto offspring and giving illegitimate offspring economic and political advantages. In Brazil, racial miscegenation was more common and more significant than in the U.S. As a consequence, Brazilians practiced integration despite discriminatory laws, while in the United States the social practice of segregation was accompanied by legal restrictions. Class in Brazil became nearly as significant as race. Marvin Harris, an expert on the sociology of Latin America, illustrates this in his collection of Negro and White class definitions in Brazil (Table 5.3).

TABLE 5.3

Considered Negro	*Considered White*
Poverty-stricken white man	Wealthy white man
Poverty-stricken mulatto	White man of moderate means
Poverty-stricken Negro	Poor white man
Poor mulatto	Wealthy mulatto
Poor Negro	Mulatto of moderate means
Negro of moderate means	Wealthy Negro

Color in Brazil, as reflected in the terms Negro and white, depended upon the wallet.

In the United States, the black man rather than the slave was feared. Slavery was supported by many poor, non-slaveholding whites as a necessary means of controlling dangerous Blacks. This was the usual theme of proslavery pamphlets, such as *Abolitionism Unveiled!, Is the North Right?, The Laws of Race,* and *Free Negroism,* which were written and circulated in the North. As Carl Degler says in his *Neither Black nor White:*

In a mobile, individualistic, loosely structured society the poor white man on the make had much to gain in status as well as material goods if he and his fellows could single out Negroes as inferiors. As they gained political power, they used it to enhance their own position by legally and otherwise reducing the status of Negroes. To that extent segregation statutes were popular as well as racist measures. In a fluid, competitive social structure, all devices are called upon to assist in the gaining and maintenance of status and economic advancement.

While the Civil War ended slavery in the United States, it did not solve the problem of the Black in white America. During the decades prior to the war, the romantic racism in American society had developed into ideological racism, the belief that Blacks were permanently inferior because of racial characteristics. Until the nineteenth century, Americans had had racial prejudice but had not firmly believed the Black to be permanently and innately inferior. Nor had earlier Americans denied that the black man could become a full member of society; but in the mid-nineteenth century, according to the historian George M. Frederickson, Americans believed Blacks to be disqualified from full membership in American society because of their permanent inferiority.

I

The questions raised by the problems of slavery and by the new ideas of race cast doubt upon the prevailing paradigm of monogenesis, which explained human differences through environmental influences. Once again polygenetic ideas challenged the accepted view of human origins, this time with the addition of the concept of race. Defenders and attackers of slavery used monogenesis and polygenesis respectively to prove their different points. Both proslavery and antislavery proponents relied heavily upon environmental arguments to demonstrate the importance of servitude or freedom; a minority on each side went so far as to say that innate racial differences made either slavery or freedom necessary.

Pierre L. van den Berghe defines the racial attitude in nineteenth-century America as a *"Herrenvolk* democracy," a belief in white equality and black slavery. In the South, most whites desired some form of white domination over the Black. Because of this presumed social necessity, racial theory became a necessary ideological tool.

The beginning of the racial defense of slavery occurred in the 1830's. The Nat Turner Revolt in Virginia and the subsequent slavery debates in the Virginia legislature stimulated the publication of many pamphlets and books on the topic. One of the racial defenders of slavery was Thomas R. Dew; George Frederickson calls Dew a transitional figure, standing between eighteenth-century environmentalism and nineteenth-century racism, because of his conservative environmentalist position. Dew accepted the biblical account of creation but claimed that Blacks were an inferior race because they came from primitive backgrounds or environments. While slavery civilized the savage and Christianized the Black, the hold of savagery was strong. If freed, the black man, according to Dew, would revert to type and become a savage again. For Dew, savagery was not noble; the black savage was a fearsome creature. With his distinction between the black savage and the Christian slave, Dew provided what was to be a significant and long-lasting contribution to racist imagery, the idea of the duality of the black character. It was claimed that the Black was an asset to white society when controlled by slavery but that freedom made him a threat to society. Dew never explained why the pull to savagery proved so irresistible. Presumably, two explanations were possible. Perhaps the African experience had lasted too long to be counteracted by only two hundred years of slavery (the environmental argument) or perhaps the African experience had been a product of hereditary factors (the racial argument).

Two developments added to the racialism in American thought. In England, two men anticipated Darwin with early versions of the natural selection process. The first was James Prichard who was the most influential British anthropologist in the first half of the nineteenth century. The second was William Charles Wells, who was born in Charleston, South Carolina, but who, alienated by the Revolution, settled in London in 1784.

James Prichard's ideas are summarized in his *The Natural History of Man* (1843). Prichard believed in monogenesis, saying that "mankind" and the inferior tribes (he still used the eighteenth-century word *tribe*) had similar physical structures while varying immeasurably in mental endowment and intellectual capabilities. He believed that all humans had souls and feelings. According to Prichard, the fact that Europeans felt guilty about enslaving Negroes proved that the Black was of the lineage of Adam, for humans supposedly would not have felt this same guilt from enslaving the pongo (ape).

In developing his theory of man's origin, Prichard defined species as original categories formed at creation and varieties as temporal variations. Again, the test for common species was the ability of two individuals to produce fertile offspring. Prichard believed it to be impossible to have new and intermediate races. Using evidence from the United States census of 1820, Prichard showed that 1,769 persons of black-white mixture had had children. Hence, he concluded that man was of one species and that what were called tribes or races were merely varieties, temporal variations.

Prichard next considered the sources of temporal variations and concluded that the major cause was climatic intervention. Thus, when organisms moved or were moved to different areas, they had to adjust to new temperatures and other new circumstances. This adjustment produced changes, temporary deviations from the original, which lasted as long as the organism remained in its new environment. Returned to its first environment, the organism would revert to its former state. According to Prichard, climatic intervention changed plants most and domestication wrought the greatest alteration in animals. Domestication produced changes that were physical, physiological, and psychological. However, Prichard believed that civilization had an even greater influence than domestication on humans. Still another agent of human change, Prichard said, was a kind of social selection, the fixing of certain human physical traits because of selective mating. Prichard believed that the original man was black, but because lighter color was more aesthetically pleasing, Whites gradually evolved from Blacks.

Prichard was not a racist. His arguments were conservative, attempting to defend the ideas of monogenesis and original human equality. He denied the fixity of race. He admitted that there were physical differences among different races, but he thought that the differences in primitive peoples probably corresponded to a hunting stage of civilization and would change when civilization overtook them. Using evidence from many sources, Prichard indicated that variations of skin color, skull shape, and behavior were functions of climate, domestication, and civilization rather than of race.

Prichard concluded that, physiologically and psychologically, all humans were equal. Physiologically, humans lived about the same length of time; their body temperatures and their pulse rates were the same. Differences which others called racial were really cultural; the Eskimo was fat because he ate blubber, not because he was an Eskimo. Psychologically, all people had similar rites and customs that demonstrated universal needs.

William Charles Wells's fame rested on less substantial foundations than Prichard's. Wells was born in the United States but went to England to live during the Revolution. He was a doctor. In 1818, he published an "Account of Female of the White Race of Mankind, Part of Whose Skin Resembles That of a Negro." The woman referred to had been a patient of Wells; from her case, Wells derived a theory of color differentiation. He discounted the effects of the climate on color, arguing that great heat did not turn skin black. Instead, Wells suggested a theory of natural selection that relied on chance. According to this theory, men were white but could become black because of disease. Black skins had proved to be adaptive, thus Blacks had multiplied.

As the theory of natural selection was being developed in England, the American Richard H. Colfax initiated what was to become an integral part of racial theory in the American South; he argued that the Negro had a differently shaped head and a different facial angle from the White. These different physical characteristics were supposedly accompanied by different mental and personality characteristics. Colfax lacked a scientific explanation of the connection between the physical and behavioral characteristics. But such an explanation was coming.

The French, who had contributed much to the romantic idea of the Noble Savage, began in the nineteenth century to evolve a theory of racial differences based on skull shapes. In 1800, Francois Peron headed an expedition to Australia, Timor, and New Holland to test the theory of degeneracy that stated that primitive men possessed superior health, strength, and physical development because of their closeness to nature, man's original state. Peron, like the fur traders in the United States, found evidence that the hypothesis was wrong. His conclusions undermined that theory of degeneracy and bolstered the notion that human physical structure was the key to group differences.

The development of physical anthropology accelerated in the nineteenth century as anthropologists concentrated upon cranial differences among men. The man who contributed to the development of cranial comparison was the Frenchman, Georges Cuvier. Cuvier, who was the leading European anatomist of his time, had begun to collect skulls in the late eighteenth century. In eighteenth-century Europe, there had been a paucity of human anatomical material: Count de Buffon, for example, had never seen an Oriental, alive or dead; Peter Camper had seen one live Chinese and had examined one Chinese skull. No detailed comparison had yet been made of skeletons of Negroes and Whites. Cuvier's attempt to remedy the lack effected his own personal collection, which served as a beginning for European physical anthropologists. In 1817, Cuvier, commenting upon the French description of Egyptian antiquities (Napoleon's invasion of Egypt had rekindled French interest in Egyptology), said that the ancient Egyptians had had skulls resembling Europeans. Judging by cranial capacity, Cuvier also said that the Mongol race had reached a plateau of development sometime in the past and that the Negro race had never progressed beyond barbarism.

While Cuvier was studying skulls in France, Franz Joseph Gall originated the study of phrenology in Vienna. He developed a psychological system that was both authoritarian and deterministic. Gall argued that an individual's personality was determined by the shape of his skull and that an individual's skull shape was a fixed characteristic, not affected by environment. Gall, however, incurred the censure of the Australian government in 1802 and was forced to leave. Along with his colleague, Johann Gaspar Spurzheim, Gall roamed Europe for five years before settling in Paris, where he died in 1828.

The new phrenologists considered the concept of mind as too vague an explanation for human behavior and attempted to develop a precise science based on skull shape and size. Originally, as John D. Davies has said in his *Phrenology: Fad and Science* (1955), it was a respectable science:

In its own time phrenology, like Freudianism, was a serious, inductive discipline, accepted as such by many eminent scientists, doctors, and educators; its aberrations were the results not so much of charlatanism or credulity as of the limitations of early nineteenth century scientific method and medical techniques.

Phrenology divided the brain into 37 faculties, each located in a different region of the skull. These faculties were considered potentials; only the individual possessing them could convert potentials into realities. Phrenology incorporated Peter Camper's cranial angle as a method of categorizing all creation; the lowest animal had the smallest facial angle and the highest the greatest. The angle increased from snake to ape to human idiot to bushman to Caucasian.

Phrenology contributed to racist thought; phrenologists believed that different races had distinctive skull shapes. The practice of phrenology encouraged the collection of human skulls which were invariably compared. George Combe, who wrote the most famous book on phrenology, claimed that Negro inferiority was a product of a narrow anterior portion of the skull, although he also argued that this natural inferiority neither justified slavery nor rendered the Negro unfit for freedom.

Another scientist who contributed to the development of phrenology was Charles Caldwell, an American doctor. Caldwell was a pioneer in medical education who helped found medical schools in Lexington and in Louisville, Kentucky. Caldwell deservedly is given credit for the introduction of the formal study of medicine in the Midwest. In 1821, Caldwell traveled to Europe to collect medical specimens and books for Transylvania University in Lexington, Kentucky. While in Europe, he encountered the science of phrenology and was converted to its precepts, which he brought back to America and popularized. Caldwell prepared the ground for the ideas of Johann Spurzheim (who had been a colleague of Gall) and, in fact, became known as the "American Spurzheim."

Spurzheim, himself, came to the United States in 1832 to study American skulls; he showed particular interest in Indians and Negroes. Spurzheim's phrenology attracted a wide audience, including the two pioneer educators Horace Mann and Henry Barnard. Spurzheim had converted Gall's deterministic, psychological base for phrenology into an idealistic, perfectionist one. He believed that an individual's faculties could be improved. Through education, he felt, an individual could be led away from insanity, crime, and drinking. Thus phrenology became connected with the treatment of the insane, prison reform, and temperance.

In 1830, Caldwell published *Thoughts on the Original Unity of the Human Race,* which attacked the prevailing monogenetic paradigm of human origin. Caldwell denied that his attack of the belief in the original unity of man was an attack on revealed Christianity. Nor did he feel his disbelief in man's natural equality to be equated with thoughts of injustice, acts of unkindness toward Negroes, or feelings of superiority on the part of the white race. "Inferior beings became objects of kindness, *because* they are inferior," Caldwell said. Caldwell claimed that no evil could come from his book.

Caldwell attacked Samuel Stanhope Smith, Buffon, and especially James Prichard for their reliance upon natural history and scriptural analysis rather than on physical science. The question of defining species and hybrids (the result of the crossing of species) occupied Caldwell greatly. Caldwell believed, in the first place, that all races were separate species. Animals had many species, why not man? The differences among various animal species appeared less striking to Caldwell than those among races of men. Caldwell agreed with the naturalists' definition of a hybrid that said different species could interbreed but that their offspring would be infertile. Caldwell claimed that mulattoes were less prolific than either Blacks or Whites and that this proved that races were separate species. While Prichard said that hybridity could occur only in a state of domestication and that natural repugnance prevented species from intermixing in nature, Caldwell responded by saying that man had always been a domesticated animal; he had never been in a natural state. Caldwell also claimed that animal species lusted after other species. He used the old story of the ape desiring a human female for proof.

Caldwell's biggest target was the legend of Noah as used by Prichard. While Prichard averred that the continents had been populated after the flood by offspring from single pairs of plants and animals (he failed to explain how this had happened), Caldwell offered an alternate hypothesis for origins, that of spontaneous generation. Thus, given certain conditions of soil, climate, and exposure to the sun, vegetables, animals, and humans could supposedly be generated. As proof, Caldwell referred to the pine lands of New

Jersey and the Carolinas. These lands had originally contained oak and hickory, which the settlers cut down. When the land was abandoned, however, only pines grew. Yet when the pines were felled, the oak and hickory returned. So Caldwell argued, had all species re-emerged from their natural areas after the flood.

Caldwell claimed that Prichard's beliefs in the insignificance of human color and in the product of chance were wrong. In order for one human pair to have produced different races, Caldwell said, several improbable events would have had to occur. The descendants of Adam would have had to commit incest and would have had to give birth to pairs of Mongolians, Indians, or Africans. Caldwell refused to accept Prichard's description of the original human pair as black because the Garden of Eden was supposedly located in Asia, a climate he believed unsuitable to the black race. Finally Caldwell asked how Prichard explained the existence of only a few races rather than an unlimited number, since Prichard's mode of racial differentiation seemed a relatively simple process and one easily duplicated.

The greatest difficulty with the old paradigm, however, was time. This difficulty was to prove insurmountable and to become the foundation of the new paradigm of evolution. Caldwell posed this question: if the flood had occurred 4,179 years before, as conventional chronology would have it, how could the races have become differentiated so rapidly? Descriptions of black Ethiopians appeared in the earliest histories and Blacks were portrayed in monumental remains dating back 3,445 years. In the 3,445 years since the earliest known descriptions of men, there appeared to have been no racial changes of any great moment. The climate had not changed the Jews who had populated Malabar for 1,700 years, nor the Negro who had existed in the United States for 200 years. Caldwell had found a significant weakness in the legend of Noah, which could only be remedied by either changing conventional estimates of biblical time or by arguing that special conditions had operated in the first 634 years of human history. Neither remedy was completely satisfactory either to scientists or biblical literalists.

Caldwell ended his *Thoughts on the Original Unity of the Human Race* with a paean to the natural superiority of the Caucasian. He said that the Caucasian bent was toward civilization, the African and Indian toward savagery. The African was cannibalistic and sexually promiscuous. The Indian, like the buffalo, could not be civilized and was doomed to extinction. Perhaps, said Caldwell, the Indians could have been saved by returning them to the forest or through intermarriage, but neither of these had happened. Therefore, he believed that neither Indian nor Negro had a future in white America.

Caldwell's advocacy of polygenesis, based on a belief that humans and animals developed in and were best suited for particular climatic zones, had some impact on the scientific community. More telling, however, was his critique of religious orthodoxy. Caldwell's efforts influenced a fellow phrenologist, Samuel G. Morton, who was a physician from Philadelphia. Morton pioneered the American school of ethnology, the most significant anthropological movement of the time. Morton was a Quaker who had encountered the ideas of George Combe as a medical student in Edinburgh. Impressed by the significance of cranial measurements, Morton began to gather skulls; he eventually owned the largest collection (with skulls of 918 humans, 278 other mammals, 271 birds, and 88 reptiles and fish) in the world. Morton collaborated in his research with Josiah Nott, a doctor from Mobile, Alabama, and with an Englishman named George R. Gliddon, an Egyptologist who had come to the United States in 1837.

Morton began the argument for separately created races in 1839 in his *Crania Americana*, a book based upon his skull collection. Morton subtitled his book "A comparative view of the skulls of various aboriginal tribes and also an essay on the variety of human species." Believing in the phrenological principle of a harmonious relationship between mental character and cranial development, Morton showed that skulls of different races varied.

Morton identified three skull types, Caucasian, American, and Ethiopian. The first was large and oval, the second was smaller and wider, and the third was long and narrow. The skull shape supposedly correlated with social character. The Caucasian was intellectual; the American was restless, revengeful, fond of war, and resistant to cultivation; the African was indolent, joyous, and lacking in intellectual achievement.

In 1842, Morton read a paper at the annual meeting of the Boston Society of Natural History; the paper was published as *An Inquiry into the Distinctive Characteristics of the Aboriginal Races of America*. It was a theoretical statement which defined ethnography as the analysis and classification of the races of man and claimed American primacy in the field of ethnography because of available resources and able scholars. Asian ethnography relied on fables; African ethnography still included monsters; but American ethnography was scientific.

By the 1840's, Morton had become interested in Egypt through the agency of George R. Gliddon, a businessman who was a scholar in his own right and who collected skulls for Morton in Egypt. Gliddon's skulls were used as the base of Morton's *Crania Aegyptiaca* (1844), which speculated on the origins of Egyptian civilization and which denied that this civilization was a black one. Basing his argument on cranial measurements, Morton concluded that the Egyptians were a race somewhere between the modern European and Semitic ones; the Copts were mixtures of Caucasian and Negro; the Nubians were mixtures of Arabians and Negroes; and the Negroes, descendants of Ham, were members of the Libyan family of nations. His descriptions of the racial background of Egyptians, however, were less significant for anthropological thought than his attack on monogenesis and his claim that races existed at the beginning of time. Morton said, "the physical or organic characters which distinguish the several races of men are as old as the oldest records of our species."

Morton died in 1851, but his collaborators, Nott and Gliddon, continued his work. Morton had also made other converts to phrenology, the most notable of whom was Louis Agassiz, who became the leading popularizer of science in America in the mid-nineteenth century. Agassiz was Swiss; he originally studied to become a doctor but turned to embryology while attending the University of Munich. His interest in fossil fish led him to the Museum of Natural History in Paris, where he heard Cuvier lecture. While disagreeing with Cuvier's premises, Agassiz admired his empiricism, as indicated by the fact that Cuvier actually tried to find specimens to study. Agassiz became a student of Cuvier and, after Cuvier's death, of the German scholar Von Humbolt before returning to Switzerland to teach and write. His own book, *Recherches sur les poissons fossiles* (1843), earned Agassiz an international reputation and an invitation to lecture in the United States. He responded to the invitation in 1846 and proved an instant success, so much so that, in 1847, Agassiz was asked to become one of the two original professors of the newly created Lawrence Scientific School of Harvard. In 1859, he became curator and director of the Museum of Comparative Zoology at Harvard.

Agassiz became an American citizen and married an American wife; as he changed his citizenship so he changed his ideas. In

1845, Agassiz had believed that man belonged to a single species but that there were special "zoological provinces" suited to different human types. But later Agassiz argued that men were products of successive, separate, and independent creations. His change in attitude came, according to Edward Lurie in his biography, *Louis Agassiz: A Life of Science* (1960), from contacts with Blacks, on the one hand, and with Morton's skull collection, on the other. In an article in the *Christian Examiner* in 1850, Agassiz advocated a theory of polygenesis but tried to retain a biblical framework. He maintained that Adam and Eve had been white (and only the ancestors of Whites) and that biblical silence concerning the New World did not mean that the contention that groups had existed there before the creation of Adam and Eve contradicted revealed truth. He also traced differences in races back to the time of the Egyptians and claimed that these differences were not produced by climatic modification.

In 1854, Nott and Gliddon edited a book called *Types of Mankind* which included essays by a number of writers, among them Agassiz. *Types of Mankind* was dedicated to Morton; its purpose was to memorialize his views. Agassiz contributed an essay on the natural provinces of the animal world showing how animals and men fit into their special environments. Agassiz said that the major divisions of the animal kingdom were primordial and independent of climate but that local species varied according to conditions of temperature, soil, and vegetation.

Nott's introduction covered many bases; he attacked Prichard's defenses of Genesis, and he presented a scale of civilized traits by which races could be judged. The scale indicated that the Negro had no civilization; that the Mongol had semicivilizations in China and Japan; that the Indian had feeble ones in Peru and Mexico; and that the White had all the great civilizations. In addition, Nott claimed that racial war was the agent of human progress.

Types of Mankind contained descriptions of the geographical distribution of animals and man, based in large part on Agassiz, as well as descriptions of human interbreeding that indicated that each contemporary race was a combination of an infinite number of primitive stocks. The infusion of the blood of one race into another had supposedly created physical and mental modifications. Thus, white blood supposedly improved black intelligence and morality while black blood protected against yellow fever (a conclusion based on Nott's study of the disease). It was believed that without racial mixing, the Negro could not live in temperate areas and the Indian could not be civilized. The terms race and type were used interchangeably; they were defined as primordial organic forms. Contemporary human groups were believed to be proximate races or species that resembled each other. The Jews were supposedly a mixture of races but were still predominantly Caucasian. Africans were also a mixture of races but the most superior African had the most white blood. Africans from below the equator were described as human beings "with intellects as dark as their skins, and with a cephalic conformation that renders all expectance of their future melioration a utopian dream, philanthropical but somewhat senile." The best Africans under this system were the northern tribes of Senegambia, the Mandingos, Fulahs, and Iolofs.

Types of Mankind included an abundance of illustrations of Egyptian art to show that Negroes had existed in historic Egypt, that they had been enslaved even then, and that they had not created Egyptian civilization. The book defended the proposition that the Indians were native to America and that the mound builders had been Indians. It discussed the hybridity of man, arguing that mulattoes were the shortest-lived of the human groups and were intermediate in intelligence between White and Black, and that the males were incapable of withstanding hardship and the women were delicate and of low fertility. After asserting all of these canards about racial inferiority, the book ended with an attack on the Bible. Gliddon called much of the Old Testament merely allegorical and insisted that the history of man did not fit into the accepted religious chronology.

In 1857, followers of the American school of ethnography published another book, *Indigenous Races of the Earth,* with selections by Alfred Maury, Francis Pulszky, J. Aitken Meigs, J. C. Nott, and George R. Gliddon as well as a letter from Agassiz. In his letter, Agassiz supported his idea of natural provinces with new data drawn from animal studies. Using the study of orangutans made by Richard Owen, an English anatomist, which divided the ape into three species, Agassiz maintained that men who occupy the same zoological regions as these apes must vary in species in the same way. Agassiz said that the orangutans in Malaya resembled the Malays in color, while the other species in different areas did not. Further, there were social resemblances as well as physical. The monkeys in South America were split into many minor groups just as the Indians were split into many tribes.

Additional findings on apes and humans appeared in *Indigenous Races of the Earth*. Two American doctors, Thomas S. Savage and Jeffrey Wyman, had made the first anatomical study of the gorilla in 1847, capitalizing on the recent discovery of the gorilla in Africa. In their study, they concluded that the gorilla and the chimpanzee were of different species, that the gorilla was on the highest level of brute creation and nearest to man, and that the Negro was the closest human to the gorilla. Savage and Wyman based their racial classification on a study of pelvic shapes, which had been developed by the German scholar Weber. Weber insisted that Europeans had oval pelvises, Americans had round, Mongolians had square, and Africans had wedge-shaped ones. Savage and Wyman said that the Negro pelvis, as described in Weber's thesis, resembled that of the gorilla. This comparison, along with other measurements, led them to conclude that "it cannot be denied, however wide the separation, that the Negro and Orang (gorilla) do afford the points where man and the brute, when the totality of their organization is considered, most nearly approach each other."

An historical development of considerable moment to the American school of ethnology was the successful decipherment of cuneiform, ancient bone writing, by a number of Europeans, including the Englishman Henry Rawlinson. Rawlinson, in his books, *A Commentary on the Cuneiform Inscriptions of Babylon and Assyria* (1850) and *Outline of the History of Assyria* (1852), like the others, argued that the age of Babylonian and Assyrian civilization had rivaled that of Egyptian. He forced reconsideration of both the accepted historical chronology and the theory of historical origins that named Egypt the cradle of world civilization.

Indigenous Races of the Earth attempted to incorporate these newer ideas. Agassiz, as we have seen, used the speciation of anthropoid apes to prove that humans were of several species. Francis Pulszky added illustrations from the monumental remains of Sumer and Assyria to show that the Negro in those areas had closely resembled the contemporary African Negro and claimed that Blacks had never created any art. Pulszky took the surprisingly equalitarian position that all men were entitled to "life, liberty, and the pursuit of happiness, all possess reason and conscience and are responsible to the Creator, mankind, and themselves."

J. Aitken Meigs, who was a Fellow of the College of Physicians and who had helped arrange and classify Morton's skulls, was less equalitarian. Meigs compared the skulls of men and apes and announced that the greatest resemblances were between the lowest type of each, not between the highest ape and the lowest man. Meigs then attacked both Monboddo and Rousseau for their ignorance of anatomy and physiology and their belief in environmentalism. After tracing a history of the study of craniology—beginning with Blumenbach and ending with J. S. Philip's essay in Henry Rowe Schoolcraft's *Aboriginal Races of America*—Meigs defined the premises that had become the basis of physical anthropology in America. The premises of racial differences and physical confirmation of intellectual capacity were fundamental and interconnected; cranial shape was believed to be permanently fixed. A racial type was an ideal invention, which embodied the mean or average of a series of statistics. Anatomical differences were valuable to the scientist, not because of their magnitude, but because of their constancy. Quoting Knox, Meigs concluded that fossil men, when discovered, would show that humans belonged to different species even though they might possess similar characteristics. Quoting Blumenbach, Meigs maintained that racial traits were apparent early in a child's life. Further, he insisted that there was a correlation between climate and cranial forms. The shape of the head of the so-called lower races was best suited to arctic or tropical climates and the shape of the so-called higher races to temperate climates.

Josiah C. Nott's chapter discussed the impact of climate and disease on races of men. Unlike Knox, Nott believed that races could survive in any climate, but like Agassiz, he said that races had particular zones in which they survived best. He claimed that a temperate climate would not change Black into White, but would handicap the Black just as Whites were handicapped in the tropics. Unlike Prichard, Nott maintained that tropical climates did not shorten life; the Black lived to an old age in Africa because it was his home. Utilizing the census of 1850 and its analyses, Nott showed that the black population of the United States had increased to a figure ten times the number imported, while the black population of the British West Indies was only 40 percent of the number imported. Since the climates of the American South, where the majority of the American black population lived, and of the British West Indies were similar, climate was not considered a significant factor in the failure of Blacks to maintain themselves in the Caribbean. The cause was believed to be race mixing. The first generation of mulattoes were supposedly prolific while the fertility of succeeding generations of mixed-bloods declined. Nott concluded that Blacks should be content in Africa and the American South, that they should live naturally, abjuring civilization, and that, barring miscegenation, their life expectancy should be as long as that of Whites.

Gliddon's observations on polygenesis completed the book. Gliddon was the only contributor to attack the biblical account of man's origins, claiming that the story of Ham had been created by Europeans during the Age of Exploration and had become popular as a justification of slavery. Despite Gliddon's belief in polygenesis, he agreed with Thomas Jefferson on man's original moral unity. Gliddon denied that man was of different species; he believed that there was one human species but that there were several human types (a word Gliddon preferred to race). The types that appeared in the present had existed in the past, as demonstrated by fossil evidence and despite the denial of so-called reputable scholars. Fossil evidence showed that the same types of men and monkeys lived in the same areas in the past as they live now. Fossils of the gorilla and chimpanzee were found together with those of the Negro, those of the orangutan with those of the Malay. This proved the natural connection between humans and apes.

The work of the American school of ethnology is best understood as a largely successful attempt to attack the anomalies of the prevailing paradigm of the legend of Noah using the most precise scientific and historical data available. The existence of Blacks at the beginning of history was not easily explained by the legend of Noah, and the problem of the lack of time for the transformation of races proved difficult to surmount. As no great differences in racial characteristics had developed throughout historic time, doubt was cast on the possibility that climate was a causative factor of race.

By 1854, the new paradigm of man's origin, polygenesis, had won acceptance among the English intellectual community as it had among the American. It was supported in *The Races of Men* (1850) by Robert Knox, a physician and honorary member of the ethnological society of London. Knox was a racist, claiming that human character was solely a product of physical inheritance and believing that races had originated in particular geographic locations and could not survive in any other. Knox defined races as permanent and unchanging but as capable of extinction. They were believed to be neither accidental variations nor the product of the gradual evolution of one into another (as Prichard had said). In Knox's view, race was not nationality; Blacks could become English but not Saxon. Races could not permanently amalgamate; no new varieties could arise. If races interbred, the mixture supposedly either died out because of infertility or reverted back to one of the original strains. As he held that races could not be transplanted, Knox refuted the idea that Europeans could survive in America; he even claimed that when European immigration stopped, the white American population would become extinct. Thus, climate did not change men permanently; it just killed them. America had a bad environment, Knox agreed with Buffon. According to Knox, the eventual future of the New World was uncertain; the Indians had been on the decline when the Europeans arrived and would probably become extinct as would the Blacks. Knox concluded that the ancient Greeks had been the best of all races; all humans since then have been degenerate and have shown that "variety is deformity."

Knox's position was a curious blend of the ideas of degeneracy —albeit from a classical rather than biblical standpoint—with the doctrine of separate creations and a belief in environmentalism. Knox's pessimism about primitive people's ability to achieve civilization negated eighteenth-century optimism. His polygenetic point of view swept British anthropology; by 1863, the leaders in anthropological theory had become converted to it. This conversion delayed for a decade the acceptance of a new theory provided by Charles Darwin, that of evolution through natural selection.

While most of the American ethnologists reflected implicit American white prejudice, they were not dedicated to proving black inferiority. Rather, they were intent upon constructing a new paradigm to explain human origin and racial differences. In the long run, their attempt was unsuccessful; the biological theories of separate racial creation were superseded by those of evolutionism and monogenesis. The polygenetic paradigm advocated by the American school suffered from a major deficiency: no one could suggest a really plausible scientific explanation as to how separate creation occurred. While Charles Darwin offered both an opposing theory— evolution—and a mechanism—natural selection—by which the theory operated, the belief in polygenesis and zoological provinces persisted in the scientific community long after the publication of his *On the Origin of Species* (1859). Agassiz never gave up his ideas, even though his inflexibility lost him students at Harvard; his last book, *A Journey to Brazil* (1868), still claimed that the physical differences between Indians, Blacks, and Whites proved separate creation.

The defenders of monogenesis in the scientific community of the United States seemed to have been in the minority. They did exist, however. Perhaps the most significant critic of the American school of ethnology was John Bachman, a fundamentalist Lutheran minister, who served as professor of natural history at the College of Charleston. In *An Examination of the Characteristics of Genera and Species as Applicable to the Doctrine of the Unity of the Human Race* (1850), Bachman, relying on Cuvier, argued that man was of one species. As proof of the single species nature of man, Bachman showed that there was an identical number of bones and teeth in all humans and that there was interracial fertility. He believed that man was divided into varieties, but these were products of natural circumstances and domestication. He denigrated the arguments based on the evidence of the monumental records of Egypt and Assyria, saying that these portrayals of Blacks were the product of artistic imagination and not of historical reality. Bachman's defense of monogenesis relied heavily on Prichard and Cuvier, referred seldom to the Bible, and utilized naturalistic evidence.

There is some dispute as to whether the polygenetic ideas of the American school of ethnology received popular support in the larger American community. W. R. Stanton, in *The Leopard's Spot*, denied that they did and indicated that even southern slavery apologists refused to abandon the biblical accounts of creation and human differences. The historian George Fredrickson, however, in *The Black Image in the White Mind*, sees the matter differently. He says that all those who argued that polygenesis was rejected relied on the fact that Moncure Daniel Conway was unable (as he says in his *Autobiography, Memories, and Experiences* [1904]), to get support for his thesis that the Black was not a man. According to Fredrickson, however, a belief in polygenesis did not necessarily mean a belief that Blacks were inhuman.

In order to achieve greater popular support for polygenesis, southern popularizers like Samuel A. Cartwright, a doctor in New Orleans, tried hard to make it compatible with the Bible. Cartwright did this by reverting to a version of the pre-Adamite thesis, the same compromise that Agassiz had made. Cartwright maintained that Blacks and Indians were not human, that they were created prior to Adam, and that they were included in the "living creatures" over whom Adam was given authority. Cartwright also claimed that the name of the serpent in the Garden of Eden was "Nachash," a word meaning black, and that the serpent was not a serpent but was rather a black gardener. Blacks inhabited the Land of Nod, where Cain moved after killing Abel; Cain's wife was black. Cain's miscegenation supposedly caused God to send the flood. Cartwright's interpretation of the Bible left many questions unanswered. Did the flood destroy all of life or only that in the Near East? Did the pre-Adamites survive? Was the contemporary Black a descendant of Ham? Cartwright did not seem to be bothered with these questions or with the fact that the American school attempted to refute the biblical account totally. His racism was virulent, and he used the idea of separate creation to deny that Blacks were human. Like a mule, a Negro could not be overworked; he had diseases peculiar only to his race, according to Cartwright. One of these ascribed diseases was drapetomia (running away) and another was rascality. Cartwright's attempt to fit polygenesis into a biblical framework drew support from prominent southern officials such as Jefferson Davis, who was later to become President of the Confederacy.

The belief in polygenesis was not confined to the South. Horace Bushnell, a leading American theologian and northern conservative, believed that Blacks "were separately created as inferior beings." Bushnell was not a defender of slavery; in 1830, he blamed slavery for the neglect of black religious instruction and the disintegration of black family life and advocated the reform of slavery and the improvement of these deficiencies. By 1850, Bushnell had ceased to believe that slavery could be reformed, but because of a belief in black inferiority, he still opposed abolition on the grounds that freedom would hasten the extinction of Blacks because of their inability to compete with free white laborers.

Other northern conservatives, while disagreeing about polygenesis, arrived at a similar anti-Black position. For example, Charles Eliot Norton, who was editor of the *North American Review*, feared that the natural increase of Blacks in the South could be replicated in the North. The South had become a "trans-Atlantic Africa," where the Blacks outstripped Whites in population growth and where barbarism recurred. Norton believed that because of the Black, the South was doomed; the North must be saved. But curiously enough, Norton supported both the abolitionist John Brown, whom Norton thought showed superior character, and the Civil War, which Norton felt would purge the North of some of its acquired vices.

By 1861, most conservative northerners were anti-Black and

pro-Civil War. Even abolitionists—such as Samuel Gridley Howe, husband of Julia Ward Howe—had doubts about black talents and future. When Howe solicited an opinion from Agassiz about the consequences of abolition, Agassiz predicted that mulattoes would gradually vanish and northern Blacks would go to the South because of a natural inability to withstand the harsher climate. This opinion confirmed a study Howe had made of black refugees in Canada whose high mortality rate had caused Howe to conclude that eventually no more Blacks would be left in that nation.

Abolitionists also often believed in the existence of racial differences and natural climatic zones for human groups. These persons emphasized the environmental conditioning of slaves as the reason for the different behavior of Blacks and suggested that the poor environment in cities was responsible for the free Blacks' debasement. Abolitionists argued that a new environment would produce Blacks who would possess greater knowledge and thrift, who would be desirous of improvement, and who would demand admission to schools, museums and lyceums. Then, Black and White would be truly equal. Few abolitionists advocated full social equality under the existing conditions. One exception was Frances Wright, a Scotswoman who established an utopian community, Nashoba, in Tennessee in 1827. Here, black slaves could work out the price of their purchase and men and women could live and love equally, Black and White. The resulting free mulatto, Wright thought was the answer to the racial question. However, it was not a popular answer and the colony failed. Few abolitionists believed in the equality of Black and White; many believed that the Black was best suited to a tropical climate. Few advocated racial mixing.

A more typical abolitionist position was what George Fredrickson has called romantic racialism. This view held that Blacks had special personal qualities because of their race, that they had a Divine mission to fulfill in America or Africa, and that racial intermixture was a mistake. Theodore Parker, a leading abolitionist theologian, said the Blacks had a greater natural aptitude for true religion than did Anglo-Saxons, whose nationalism, prejudice, materialism, and individualism subverted Christianity. Alexander Kinmont, another well-known abolitionist, in *Twelve Lectures on the Natural History of Man* (1839) described Blacks as light-hearted people with a talent for music and a willingness to serve humanity. The abolitionists, in addition, quite often described Blacks in feminine terms, as composing a softer, simpler, less aggressive race, as a necessary balance to white masculinity. The question of the destiny of the Black occupied these abolitionists; some said that Africa was to be his final home while others said that America needed him more. Theodore Parker said that Anglo-Saxons would not stand for the Africanization of America, while Alexander Kinmont and Anglina Grimké, one of two sisters prominent in the antislavery movement, said that God had given Blacks the Christ-like task of spreading a pure and undefiled Christianity in the heathen world of Africa, which would then fulfill its destiny as a great nation.

Romantic racialism can also be found in Harriet Beecher Stowe's *Uncle Tom's Cabin* (1851), one of the most popular American novels of that, or any other, time. Harriet Beecher Stowe disclaimed authorship of the book and credited God with writing it. In it, the black race, as exemplified by Uncle Tom, was an "affectionate, magnanimous, and forgiving one." Despite the moral superiority of the black race, intermarriage was shown to be a mistake. Black destiny, as represented by the mulatto George Harris, was to return to Africa to spread Christianity, to be forgiving of those who had wronged the Blacks, and to prepare for the coming millenium. In the years after the publication of *Uncle Tom's Cabin*, when colonization schemes failed and abolitionists attempted to justify the continued black presence in the United States, several people asked Mrs. Stowe to change her ending and leave Harris in the United States. She never did.

II

Most black authors refuted charges of racial inferiority. One such author was Robert Benjamin Lewis, who was born in Boston of mixed Negro-Indian parentage. Lewis's book, *Light and Truth* (which bears a copyright date of 1836 but was not published until 1844), is usually considered the first history written by an American Black. Lewis believed in the old religious paradigm and began his history of the world with the Old Testament. He accepted the biblical account of human dispersion and said the Indians were descendants of the Ten Lost Tribes of Israel. He asserted that all civilizations were offshoots of an original Ethiopian one and that many famous persons of antiquity, including Hannibal, Pompey, Homer, and Euclid, had been Blacks.

James W. C. Pennington, in *A Text Book of the Origin and*

History, etc., etc., of the Colored People (1841), also utilized a biblical account of the history of man, traced Blacks back to Ham, and explained human color environmentally. His emphasis, like Lewis's, was upon the natural unity and equality of man. The books of Lewis and Pennington began a tradition of black history that was to persist through most of the nineteenth century, one based upon the older biblical paradigm and which asserted black equality.

Another black writer, William Wells Brown, used a similar point of view in his *The Black Man* (1863). Brown, an escaped slave, claimed to have been descended from a daughter of Daniel Boone and became active in the Western New York Anti-Slavery Society. He wrote several other books: *The Anti-Slavery Harp* (1848), a collection of antislavery songs; *Three Years in Europe* (1852), an account of his travels overseas; and *Clotel, or the President's Daughter* (1853), the first black novel in America. Brown believed that prejudice resulted from slavery and that the world black did not have an intrinsically bad connotation; he gave examples of black being beautiful. Black clothes were best; black eyes and hair were admirable in women; older persons preferred to dye their hair black rather than retain the natural white. Brown believed that if slavery ended, the prejudice against the Black would vanish and American society would become truly equalitarian.

Brown discussed miscegenation in *Clotel,* which was based on an alleged mulatto daughter of Jefferson. The story did not originate with Brown; it had appeared both in a book by Captain Frederick Marryat and in Mrs. Lydia Maria Child's "The Quadroons" (1839). Brown's story detailed the misadventures of a beautiful mulatto woman and centered on the problems of being sold and victimized by white slaveowners. In Brown's novel, mulatto women were the heroines and the villains were white. Brown favored interracial mixing, saying that prejudice against the Black in the South was less than that in the North because of interracial sex. He did not believe that the Black should return to Africa, although he did support a scheme for colonization in Haiti. Wells combined a belief in human unity and equality with a belief in the possibilities of making America a truly equalitarian society.

The image of the black man as morally better than the white man was not a popular image among Whites. Nor was the image of the black man as the creator of civilization much accepted. The most popular white image of the Negro was that of the Sambo, childish, comical, nonviolent, humble and a "natural" servant or slave. Sambo shared some of the qualities of the Christ-like figure seen in the romantic racialism of the abolitionists, but these qualities in Sambo were demeaning rather than elevating.

The Sambo figure first appeared on stage in England in such plays as Isaac Bickerstaff's *The Padlock* (1769), George Colman's *Inkle and Yarico* (1791), and *The Africans; or, War, Love and Duty* (1780). In the United States, the black comic figure was first used after the War of 1812 and was the creation of Mical Hawkins, an American composer who wrote such songs as "The Siege of Plattsburg" and "Back Side Albany," which were meant to be sung by persons with faces blackened with burnt cork and wearing sailor suits. By 1820, the character of Sambo was commonplace in American plays; by 1830, two new songs identified two black stage charters—"Coal Black Rose" and "My Long-Tail Blue." The stage image had split into two characters, the stupid plantation hand and the citified dude. Thomas D. Rice used the latter image, one he had helped to develop and one that was patterned after the stereotype of a white dandy, to create the minstrel. The solitary minstrel was soon replaced by the minstrel show, which spread from the United States across the Atlantic. The minstrel shows' most popular years were those from 1830 to 1880, but neighborhood productions could be seen in the United States as late as the 1940's and the Black and White Minstrels still perform in London. The minstrel show, more than any other medium, spread the image of the Negro as a comic figure.

The Sambo image appeared elsewhere, in novels, plays, and travelers' accounts. It became a matter of controversy with the publication of Stanley Elkin's *Slavery* in 1959. Elkins held that the Sambo stereotype was a realistic representation of the result of a successful program of slave depersonalization. Many scholars disagreed, saying that the slave only played the role of Sambo and that the need for a Sambo image told more about Whites than about Blacks. These scholars held that the slave acted like a Sambo but did not become one. They were justified by the fact that slaves were not docile; rebelliousness became part of black culture as slaves participated in slowdowns, sabotage, escapes, and revolts. The rebelliousness was portrayed in the slave songs, which expressed a desire for freedom and for the end of slavery, which attacked white indolence, and which parodied slave behavior. Such songs as

"Massa Had a Yaller Gal" poked fun at the white master and his mulatto girl; "Run, Nigger, Run" did the same for a slave stealing corn. Both reflected a realistic assessment of plantation life and a keen appreciation of inappropriate behavior.

By the beginning of the Civil War, the white majority had a pernicious view of the black man. The older, biblical view, which held that humans were naturally equal and that their physical and behavioral differences were a product of varying environments, was being severely questioned in intellectual circles; scientifically, at any rate, it was considered inadequate. A new explanation based upon the natural origins of several races reinforced the belief in black inequality. The popular image of the Black also furthered this idea, portraying him as childlike, docile, and stupid. Even those who believed that the black man should be free and argued the belief in black moral superiority portrayed the black race as feminine, passive, and forgiving, possessed of qualities vividly contrasting to the vigorous, masculine ones of civilized mid-nineteenth-century white America.

Chapter 6

Indian Wars
and "The Survival of the Fittest"

Pushed beyond the Mississippi and threatened with extinction, the Indian in the late nineteenth century assumed the role of savage attacker, a role already ascribed to him in earlier white literature. There were a series of military engagements beginning during the Civil War and lasting until 1890, when the Plains Indians were defeated. The Indians achieved some military victories, such as closing the Bozeman Trail in Montana in 1868 and depriving Custer of his army and his hair at Little Big Horn in 1876, but the massacre of Wounded Knee in 1890 ended hostilities.

The Indian Wars had a profound effect upon the white imagination. Because of the struggle that became the great American epic, the image of the Plains Indians, who were only two-thirds of the approximately 300,000 surviving Indians in the United States, displaced all others. In a sense, this was unfortunate because the culture of the Plains Indians was not typical of Indian cultures.

Prior to the introduction of the horse into New Mexico by the Spaniards, even the Plains Indians had not been primarily hunters nor had the different tribes had many similar social practices. The horse changed the way of life of thirty different Indian tribes in Western America and provided them with common customs and values. The result was that the new institutions resembled those of no other Indians. The new basic social organization of the Plains Indians divided them into composite tribes where descent could be reckoned either through the father or the mother, where marital residence could be with either parent, and where tribes functioned primarily as political entities in summer camps. Indian identity derived less from tribal affiliation than from membership in nonkinship sodalities—fellowships—which united dancing, feasting, or fighting men. The Cheyennes had six sodalities, including one for contraries, men who did everything backwards. The Plains Indian culture came to require war and enemies. The horse, the gun, and the buffalo—the bases of their culture—all fostered aggressive, violent traits. Indian tribes raided each other to get guns and horses. An inflationary spiral resulted as wealth in horses increased and prices for other commodities went up. Advancement in sodalities required ever more horses. The culture fed on itself; as a result, the Indian came to live a life centered on hunting and war, a life that was to be portrayed in hundreds of movie houses long after the Plains Indians had been confined to reservations.

The defeats suffered in the Indian Wars provoked a certain amount of religious fervor among the Plains Indians. Like the earlier expression of the Indians in the Eastern woodlands, this response was either apocalyptic—predicting a great disaster to be followed by a return to a better past—or accommodationistic—displaying a surface acceptance of white institutions in order to escape from hostility. The apocalyptic response came from the dreamers, who incorporated white religious ideas into, and whose visions culminated in, the Ghost Dance. An example was an Indian Shaman named Smoholla, who was born in the Rockies in 1820 and who had a Roman Catholic education. The crucial turning point in his life was when he was left for dead by fellow Indians; Smoholla believed he had died and had talked to the Great Spirit. In response to God's instruction, Smoholla wandered through the American Southwest and into Mexico, preaching about the origins and history of the world. The burden of his message was that Indians should not cultivate the land but should use it for hunting, resisting the attempts of Whites to make them farmers. Smoholla's influence was considerable, reaching as far north as the Nez Percés and Chief Joseph in Idaho, and his ideas and dream were institutionalized by various Indian tribes into dreamer societies. In 1870, a variation on the dream appeared among the Northern Paiutes who lived on the California-Nevada border and whose leader was an Indian named Wodziwol. The variation (which was not unlike the Cargo cults of the post–World War II Pacific islands) predicted that a big train would appear in the West, carrying all the formerly dead Indians. Its coming would coincide with a cataclysm that would destroy the Whites but would leave their goods untouched and would bring back the Great Spirit. Wodziwol persuaded the Paiutes that the coming of the millenium could be hurried by song and dance, and the movement became known for these expressions. The dream reflected contact with the Mormons who believed that the Messiah would appear in 1890. In addition, an assistant to Wodziwol, an Indian called Wovoka, had a vision which confirmed the earlier promise that all the dead Indians could be brought back by a sacred ghost dance. The Ghost Dance spread through the West, but was extinguished at Wounded Knee; there, Peter Farb, a student of Indian history, says, "The Ghost Dance had proven as make-believe as the rest of their [Indians'] improbable culture."

Accommodationism took several forms, one of which was peyotism. The first use of peyote by Indians in the United States occurred in 1770 when wandering Apaches brought the drug back from Mexico. The use of peyote did not become popular among American Indians until about 1850; the principal users were not the Indians of the Southwest where the drug originated but, rather, the Plains Indians. The Indian using peyote could escape from white reality while appearing to conform to it. And, as peyotism was emphasized as particularly Indian, it became an affirmation of Indian ways and permitted Indians to conform outwardly to American society while still experiencing Indian visions. Because its use was concealed from the Whites, peyotism persisted after the Ghost Dancers had vanished.

Meanwhile, unthinking white assumptions about Indian assimilation continued. The Indian Bureau was transferred from the Department of War to the Department of Interior in 1849, but little progress was made on the problem of Indian-White relations. There was little agitation for Indian rights during the 1850's when the nation's attention was focused on the problem of slavery.

This stalemate was changed in the 1860's. The men responsible were two pioneer reformers, Henry Benjamin Whipple, an Episcopalian Bishop who worked among the Chippewa and the Sioux in Minnesota, and John Beeson, an Englishman and transplanted Illinois farmer who knew the Rogue River Indians in Oregon. Beeson pleaded the Indian cause in *The Calumet,* a journal he created to speak for the Indian in 1856, and in his book, *A Plea for the Indians* (1858). Bishop Whipple, at about the same time, wrote a letter to President Buchanan detailing the inequities of the Indian system and making suggestions for improvement. He proposed establishing four reservations—the Indian Territory, the White Earth Reservation in Minnesota, the Yakima Reservation in the Washington Territory, and another in either Colorado or Arizona. Both Beeson and Whipple blamed Indian trouble on the white intrusion into Indian land. They urged reform of the Indian Bureau and proposed that the Indian be taught agriculture and Christianity. In these ways, their pleas were similar to those of the missionaries of an earlier era.

In 1862, the Sioux Uprising in Minnesota focused national attention on the still unsolved question of the fate of the Indians. Whipple and Beeson went to Washington; Whipple saw Lincoln and reiterated his belief in the possibility and desirability of Christian conversion and education of the Indian, and of reform of the Indian Bureau. Lincoln asked Congress for action, but none was forthcoming. The Indian War of 1864 in Minnesota and the Sand Creek Massacre of 1864 in Colorado emphasized the urgency of the Indian question. In 1865, a special joint committee of the House and Senate began an investigation of Indian affairs. Two years later, the federal government asked missionary societies to establish Indian vocational schools and promised federal aid for that purpose. The Indiana Yearly Meeting of Friends received the first contract for the establishment of an Indian school among the Kansas Shawnee to teach English, the use of agricultural implements, and the domestic arts of knitting, sewing, and housewifery. Other contracts followed.

The joint congressional committee investigating Indian affairs reported in January, 1867, that the Indian ways were being destroyed—the railroads had severed their tribal bonds, the bison were disappearing, and the Indians were dying from smallpox, measles, cholera, scrofula, and syphilis. The Indians had not been assimilated; they had been depraved. The report concluded that time was short; for 40 years Congress had failed to take action to save the Indian, and the frontier was rapidly becoming settled. If the Indians were to be assimilated, action had to be taken immediately.

The report suggested two possible alternatives for accomplishing assimilation. The first resembled the policy of military reconstruction in the South in that it relied on the army and treated the Indians like the defeated southerners. This alternative recommended transferring the Bureau of Indian Affairs back to the Department of War and confining the Indians to reservations by force through the administrative agency of military districts. The second alternative was to leave the Bureau of Indian Affairs in the Interior Department, to coax the Indians back on their reservations, and to place them under the tutelage of Christian teachers. The second alternative appealed to the congressional committee, which created a Peace Commission composed of three Senators, four generals, and the commissioner of Indian Affairs. The commission was instructed to investigate further the practicality of the peaceful plan. The Peace Commission Report, which was made public a year later, placed the blame for frontier war on neglect of the Indian by the government and claimed that protection of Indian land rights and the development of civilization among the Indians would bring lasting peace.

The Peace Commission Report provoked popular support. Indian reform became an issue among the people who had formerly pushed for black rights. These reformers were eastern, middle class, and idealistic; while they were religious, they wished to save the Indian from extermination and not necessarily to convert him. Although they believed in racial equality in principle, they also believed that the Indian possessed singular, innate racial qualities—integrity, loyalty, and bravery. Although the reformers' view was romantic, they neither conceived of the Indian as a Noble Savage nor rejected civilization as a goal for the Indian. The Indian was considered to be on a lower stage of cultural development than the White, but he had the potential to advance to a higher level. His primitivism was attributed to his natural and social environment, his vices to the Whites who surrounded him—the army, Indian agents, and post traders. His warlike nature was supposedly a response to injustice and white threats of extinction.

In 1868, Lydia Maria Child's "An Appeal for the Indians" appeared as an article in *The National Anti-Slavery Standard* and as a separate pamphlet. In the essay, Child pleaded for Indian reform and suggested that the Indian be coaxed down the road to civilization by gradually transforming Indian cultural practices. Rather than eliminating Indian dialects, as the Peace Commission had proposed, Child urged that Indian languages be used in lower-level schoolbooks and that English be gradually introduced. Child was joined by other reformers, among them Peter Cooper who helped found the United States Indian Commission, a private agency dedicated to ending frontier warfare. Cooper attacked fraudulent treaties, whiskey peddlers, and other corrupters and exploiters of the Indian.

President Grant, reacting to public pressure, inaugurated his Peace or Quaker Policy in 1869, which was to end in failure seven years later. The Congressional Act of July 20, 1869, provided a commission made up of military and civilian personnel to make peace with the Indians, to settle all Indians on reservations, to educate Indians for citizenship, and to do all of this outside tribal organizations. Grant had originally intended to use only military officers on the commission, but a committee of concerned Friends persuaded Grant to include civilians. He agreed to permit the various Friends groups to submit a list of names from which he would nominate Indian agents and superintendents. The Hicksites, a splinter group of Friends, were to oversee the northern region in Nebraska, while the Orthodox Quakers controlled the central region, which included all the tribes in Kansas and the Indian Territory except for the Five Civilized Tribes. In 1870, Congress reinforced Grant's Quaker Policy by forbidding the use of army officers as Indian agents; at the same time, various other religious denominations asked for the privilege of nomination.

Meanwhile, Congress proceeded to attempt Indian detribalization. In March of 1871, the treaty system of dealing with the Indians was ended by congressional enactment. The intent of the legislation was clear; Grant and Congress wanted the Indian civilized and Christianized. Since the tribal system was in the way, it would be circumvented. The Indian was supposed to finally become a full participant in American society, but he was to do it as individual, not as a member of a tribe.

In 1870, the American Anti-Slavery Society was changed to the Reform League, a general organization designed to eradicate caste spirit and to advance the causes of Indian civilization, temperance, labor and prison reform, and the enfranchisement of women. But the reformers of the new organization were old and times had changed. Despite the claim of the abolitionist Frederick Douglass that the new group was created in the spirit of the old, the Reform League failed to kindle the imagination of the American people.

In addition to the lack of public support, certain problems with the policy of peacefully civilizing the Indians became apparent. In the first place, the Catholic Church displayed little interest, although some of the Indians were Catholic. In the second place, the settlers in the West felt that the destruction of the Indian was both necessary and desirable. In the third place, the army, which was the major instrument of the policy, lacked the necessary resources to meet the task. The army had to herd the Indians on to reservations and then to supply them with food—an expensive and lengthy process. The Peace Commissioners had estimated that the process of civilization would take twenty-five years (the length of time the buffalo was estimated to survive, but the buffalo lasted only ten years). The soldiers tended to sympathize with the anti-Indian feeling of the white settlers, and Indian wars provided the only path of advancement in a peacetime army.

Continued skirmishes agitated public opinion against both the Indian and the army. The Piegan Massacre of 1870 and the Camp Grant Massacre of 1871 roused antimilitary opinion in the East, and the Modoc killing of two unarmed Indian commissioners in 1873 led many persons in both East and West to question the Peace Policy. To add to this, the investigations of scandals in the Department of the Interior and the Indian Bureau culminated in the exposure of the "Indian Ring," a group guilty of having looted the treasury. This corruption turned many reformers against all the policies of President Grant. Even Bishop Whipple attacked the administration of reservations in 1874 and advocated granting each Indian an inalienable patent for 160 acres of land. Whipple's agitation, along with that of other reformers, prepared the way for the Indian Homestead Act of 1875, which signaled the end of the Peace Policy. The crowning blow to the Peace Policy, however, was Custer's last stand at Little Big Horn. Critics blamed the Peace Policy or, alternately, the ineptness of the army for the conflict and demanded a new effort to solve the Indian question.

Various generals, in defending the army against its critics, suggested their visions of the future of the Indians. General James H. Carleton, commander of the Military Department of New Mexico, said, "the Races of the mammoths and mastodons, and the great sloths, came and passed away: the red man of America is passing away." General William T. Sherman, the most influential general in the army, was more optimistic. He believed that if the Indians would remain on reservations, and if the army could successfully keep out whiskey peddlers, the Indians could be civilized to the point of becoming citizens. Many civilian reformers still shared this belief. In 1877, Stanley Pumphrey, a Quaker reformer from England, gave a series of lectures on the Indians in which he claimed both that Indians were becoming civilized and that their numbers were increasing. In the same year, John Greenleaf Whittier defended the notion that the Indian could be civilized in an essay entitled "Indian Civilization."

President Hayes appointed Carl Schurz as Secretary of the Interior just as another controversy over Indian affairs was arising in the spring of 1877. The United States Indian Commission had charged the chief clerk of the Indian Bureau with irregularities and Schurz ordered a general investigation of Indian conditions. The investigation found much wrong; the Indian-army contact stimulated miscegenation, while other assimiliation had not worked. The informal liaisons between soldiers and Indians caused much moral concern, and reformers charged that the Indian needed to be isolated even more in order to be protected from white sexual pressures. However, the pressure to separate Indians from contact with the army was resisted because the army believed its survival depended upon its role as keeper of frontier peace.

As a result of the Schurz investigation, religious administration of Indian reservations ceased, partly because of its assumed failure and partly because of Schurz's hostility. In 1879, the Orthodox Quakers terminated their Indian administration, and, in 1880, the Methodists ended theirs. Schurz, with the removal of religious influences, emphasized educational reform through boarding schools, believing that separation from parents would make the civilization of Indian children easier. An effort to place Indians in boarding schools began in 1878 with the dispatch of 17 students to Hampton's Institute, an industrial school originally designed to train black freedmen. In 1879, a new Indian school opened at Carlisle Barracks in Pennsylvania, and in 1880, another one began at Forest Grove, Oregon.

At the same time, the movement to commit all the Indians to reservations continued unabated. President Grant had wanted to confine the Indians in a few large reservations; but he had not succeeded. By the end of his administration, there were 76 reservations outside the Indian Territory. Despite the failure to achieve consolidation, the little that had been accomplished exacerbated tribal hostilities. One of the examples of this friction was the Ponca Removal in 1877. The Ponca tribe lived in the Dakota Territory on the Sioux Reservation, but the Sioux wanted them out. The army, on the orders of the Indian Bureau, moved the Poncas to the Indian Territory. In December, 1878, 30 Poncas began a trek back to the Dakota Territory under the leadership of Standing Bear. The group got as far as Nebraska where an army unit intercepted it and took it to Omaha. There the Poncas attracted the attention of Thomas H. Tibbles, an ex-abolitionist minister and reporter for the *Omaha Daily Herald.* Tibbles obtained a writ of *habeas corpus* to free the Indians and then sued the army. The ensuing case, *Standing Bear vs. Crook,* established the legal right of the Indians to litigate. More importantly, Tibbles organized a lecture tour to publicize Indian grievances and took with him three Indians. The speakers all demanded a new legal status for the Indians including the privileges of citizenship, equal protection by the laws, and individual land patents. In Boston, the lecturers spoke before a number of people, including Wendell Phillips and Helen Hunt Jackson.

A new phase of Indian reform began in 1880 with high hopes as President Hayes promised eventual Indian citizenship through Indian education, equal protection by the laws, and a land policy of individual allotment with transferable title. In the same year, an influential book appeared; it was George W. Manypenny's *Our Indian Wards.* Manypenny, who had been commissioner of Indian affairs in 1850 and chairman of the Sioux commission in 1870, urged justice for the Indian.

An even more influential book, *A Century of Dishonor,* was published in 1881. *A Century of Dishonor* was written by Helen Hunt Jackson, who was born in Amherst, Massachusetts and was a contemporary and friend of Emily Dickinson. After the deaths of her husband (in an experimental submarine during the Civil War) and her two children, Mrs. Hunt turned to writing as a kind of personal therapy and became one of the most prolific women writers in the United States. She was remarried in 1875 to a Pennsylvania-born Quaker, William Sharpless Jackson, and turned to the cause of the Indian after hearing Tibble's Indian lecture in Boston in 1879. After spending a year doing research in the Astor library in New York City, she wrote *A Century of Dishonor,* which enjoyed immediate success following its publication in 1881.

In her book, Mrs. Jackson traced American Indian policy from the American Revolution to 1880. She devoted one entire chapter to white massacres of the Indians, another to the differences between Indian and American legal concepts, and seven chapters to the description of various Indian tribes, including the Poncas. She concluded that the Indians had been victims of white greed, of broken treaties, and a bad press. The Indians could learn to be industrious and, with time, become both Christians and good citizens, claimed Mrs. Jackson. However, until such time, they should be protected from white depredations. A *Century of Dishonor* was intended to influence congressional policy and succeeded in arousing the American public as well.

As a result of the book, Helen Hunt Jackson received an appointment as special commissioner of Indian affairs from President Chester A. Arthur to investigate the condition of the Spanish Mission Indians in California. She wrote a novel, *Ramona* (1884), based on this experience. The novel traced the Indian path to vagrancy, despair, and degeneracy and became a best seller, going through 300 printings, several movie versions, and inspiring a popular song in the twentieth century. Mrs. Jackson's announced aim was to arouse as much sympathy for the Indian in *Ramona* as Harriet Beecher Stowe had for the Black in *Uncle Tom's Cabin;* she very nearly succeeded.

Ramona, the heroine of the novel, was a half-breed Indian girl whose father was a Scot and whose mother was an Indian. Pure of heart, she married an Indian, Alessandro Assis, who was equally pure of heart. The two fine people, however, encountered other Indians who were incapable of caring for themselves, who had lost their lands and possessions to white exploiters, and who demonstrated the failure of a paternalistic governmental policy. The love story of Ramona was a vehicle for a plea for the reversal of a policy which had failed.

Impressed by *A Century of Dishonor,* Herbert Walsh formed a major organization for the Indian cause, the Indian Rights Association, in 1882. Mary L. Bonney, who had responded sympathetically to Helen Hunt Jackson's description of the Poncas, organized the Women's National Indian Association the following year. Alfred Meacham and Theodore Bland founded the National Indian Defense Association in 1885. These agencies all advocated the granting of citizenship to the Indian.

Others took up the refrain. Beginning in 1883, a series of conferences at Lake Mohonk concerned themselves with the Indians. Among the participants were Senator Dawes, a leading congressional spokesman, and Dr. Lyman Abbott, one of the most articulate religious leaders of the day. Abbott, who took an extreme position, advocated terminating the reservation system, distributing land to individual Indians, providing industrial tools and education, and then leaving the Indians alone. The other members of the conference accepted the goals of eliminating tribalism and extending citizenship; Senator Dawes incorporated these goals into a bill bearing his name, which became law in 1887.

The Dawes Act began as an act to give citizenship to the Indians but ended as a bill for private land ownership. Although the Supreme Court had ruled in *Elk vs. Wilkins* (1884) that the Indians were not citizens, the Dawes Act gave the president the prerogative to decide on individual cases. The president could extend citizenship to any Indians, with or without their consent, depending upon their achievement as farmers, with the exception of the Five Civilized Tribes and a few others. The Dawes Act further provided that the heads of Indian families would receive 160 acres of land from the reservation and that the land would be held in trust by the federal government for 25 years. Single persons over 18 years and orphans of any age received 80 acres, while children under 18 received 40 acres. If land was only suitable for grazing, the allotment was doubled. The Indian Allotment Act, as the Dawes Bill was also called, provided that if an Indian did not file a land claim in four years after passage of the act, the Indian agent could file for him. Those living on individual farms became subject to state or territorial law, rather than tribal law, and could become citizens. Any reservation land remaining after the allotments had been made and not needed by the Indians could be sold to white settlers. By these measures, the Dawes Act culminated 250 years of faith that the Indian could be converted into a European-style farmer.

The Act failed to do what reformers envisaged. The amount of land in each allotment proved insufficient to support a family in the arid West and land sale to Whites depleted much needed reservation land. For example, the Blackfeet, Blood, Gros Ventre, Piegan, and River Crow of Montana lost 17,500,000 of their 21,651,000 acres because the land was declared surplus and sold. Many individual Indians also sold their land after they received title; the Burke Act of 1906 made the sale easier as it abolished the 25 year trust provision. The public sentiment towards the Dawes Act varied; the Indian-rights advocates, in general, were for it; the Indian reactions were more mixed. But most white Americans either forgot the Indians after the Battle of Wounded Knee, or thought that the Indians were becoming civilized farmers.

I

Meanwhile, a scientific theory to account for inferior races was evolving in England. This theory came from Charles Darwin's *On the Origin of Species* (1859) and his *The Descent of Man, and*

Selection in Relation to Sex (1871), and from Herbert Spencer's *Social Statics* (1850) and *The Principles of Sociology* (1877). Alfred Russel Wallace also articulated the theory in *Contributions to the Theory of Natural Selection* (1870). The theory was that of evolution of living organisms through the agency of natural selection; it replaced both the monogenetic paradigm of the legend of Noah and the half-developed paradigm of polygenesis. It argued that Nature produced races through the same process by which other natural organisms were produced.

Chevalier de Lamarck, an early nineteenth-century zoologist, was a forerunner of Darwin. Lamarck thought that the inheritance of acquired characteristics caused evolutionary change. Lamarck offered a moral answer to the question of survival: those individuals who, through their own efforts, adapted to their environment would be rewarded; they and their offspring would survive. Lamarck's ideas gained wide acceptance; Darwin, himself, originally favored them. Lamarckian principles explained why men had varying intelligence, as certain men and races supposedly tried harder than others, and how races were formed. Races were formed as a result of prior biological selection as well as through a continuing process of social selection.

The basic assumptions of Charles Darwin's theory, or Darwinism, were these: living organisms produced more offspring than could survive; the survival of these offspring was limited by finite food resources and other environmental conditions; there were chance variations in these offspring; and some of these variations proved more adaptive than others to environmental circumstances. Darwinism was based on the premise that organisms changed through time, thus attacking the concept of the fixity of the species, a concept that was vital to Creationists, and explaining how many species of animals had become extinct. While the agent of change, natural selection, or the process by which certain chance variations operated to the advantage of those possessing them, was not in itself necessarily progressive, it came to be so regarded. Darwinism became identified with change, development, and progress.

Darwin's *The Descent of Man* explicitly outlined the development of humans in relation to other animals. Darwin believed that the difference between humans and other animals existed mainly in gradation of feelings and emotions. In *The Expression of Emotions in Man and Animals* (1873), Darwin described animal emotions as more rudimentary than human ones, but he always insisted that humans shared many primitive animal instincts. Darwin believed that man had evolved from the apes but was undecided as to whether man originated from a single species of ape—monogenesis—or from several species—polygenesis. He was also uncertain as to whether man was of a single species or whether races represented separate species.

Alfred Russel Wallace, another pioneer evolutionist, proposed a compromise solution on human origin in an 1864 article in the *Anthropological Review*. He said that theories of monogenesis and polygenesis could be combined in the following way. All men came from the same primate root, but before the acquisition of the intellect that made man human, natural selection created separate races. Natural selection of humans ended with the achievement of humanity, and was replaced by sexual selection, human choice based on aesthetic preference. Thus man began as one species but ended as several. In addition to this theory of origins, Wallace raised two questions concerning the adequacy of an evolutionary paradigm. How long did it take to turn an ape into a human, and by what means could it be accomplished? Granted intelligence was adaptive, why did the human mind develop one hundred times more than appeared to be necessary for survival?

Darwin opposed Wallace's racial ideas. He denied that natural selection had been completely supplanted by sexual selection in humans. Darwin used intellect as a criterion for humanity and held that some races had not yet become human. He believed that humans evolved from savagery to civilization and that the savage races declined in fertility when exposed to civilizing influences. This, combined with the "poor constitution" (1871) of children of savage races, led to their extinction. Darwin failed to answer Wallace's questions as to how man had evolved or why his brain had developed more than was necessary for adaption to his environment, but provided a natural explanation of racial differences.

The major monogenetic competitor of Darwinism was not the biblical paradigm but was rather the paradigm of degeneracy. The most significant proponent of this latter paradigm was Richard Whately, Archbishop of Dublin, whose *On the Origin of Civilization* (1855) had enormous impact on the scientific community. Whately held that primitive man had degenerated from a semi-civilized condition at the beginning of history while civilized men had continued to advance. Primitive men were condemned, he said, unless they received outside help; without assistance they were doomed to remain forever primitive.

Darwin and Darwinists disagreed with the degenerationists, denying that some men had degenerated from civilization and insisting that all had been primitive at the start of human history and had developed from there. While the theory of developmentalism, an integral part of Darwinism, finally won out over the theory of degeneracy, the struggle was difficult. Darwin had to argue his thesis without adequate fossil evidence; he was forced to rely on logic and other nonbiological sources for support. One source of support was the work of E. B. Tylor, an English anthropologist who also attacked Whately. Tylor wrote two major books, *Researches into the Early History of Mankind* (1865), and his most famous, *Primitive Culture* (1871). In the latter book, Tylor used the concept that was to become the keystone of twentieth century anthropology, the concept of culture. Tylor did not use the word culture (which incidentally did not enter dictionaries for another fifty years) as modern anthropologists do, referring to the complex of ideas and artifacts possessed in common by a group. Rather, he used it in a nineteenth-century sense as the quality of human development in civilized societies. According to George Stocking, a historian of anthropological ideas, Tylor's definition of culture was influenced by Matthew Arnold's "Culture and Anarchy" essays in *Cornhill Magazine* (1867 and 1868), which essays distinguished between civilization, which was outward and mechanical development, and culture, which was inward and spiritual progress. Tylor combined the two kinds of development under the single rubric of culture.

Tylor used his concept of culture to attack the idea of degeneration. *Primitive Culture* was written to show that man's cultural development had followed the same evolutionary laws as his biological development. Tylor's basic premises were that all humans had a common human nature, that history indicated progress not decay, that societies went through three stages of development—savagery, barbarism, and civilization. Cultural change was effected through inheriting various cultural elements from ancestors living in distant regions, cultural diffusion from other races, and invention of new cultural elements. Tylor also derived the "doctrine of survivals." This doctrine held that all humans had originated with the same mental organization and that remnants of primitive mental states might still be found in civilized society in such cultural survivals as games, riddles, proverbs, and certain religious practices. Tylor found enough evidence of primitive survivals to convince many anthropologists of the correctness of his theory. Tylor's explicit developmentalism also became popular although his "doctrine of survivals" seemed to negate natural selection since survivals were old and, by definition, nonadaptive.

Tylor's ideas, as several scholars have noted, rely more on the eighteenth century than the nineteenth for both methods and goals. Tylor encouraged a comparative method in his doctrine of survivals, in his view that all groups necessarily have similar histories, and in his belief that primitive peoples were not intrinsically inferior to civilized ones. However, social evolutionists after Tylor failed to share his eighteenth-century optimism that all people could reach the level of European civilization. Their theory of evolution, according to George Stocking, put together "Darwinian evolution, evolutionary ethnology, and polygenesist races" to conclude that only large-brained Whites were fully civilized.

One man who popularized evolutionary ideas in America was Herbert Spencer. In his *Principles of Sociology* (1876), Spencer argued that natural selection operated on both human individuals and human societies, which he called social organisms and which were considered the superorganic parts of culture. Evolution supposedly modified social organisms until an equilibrium between environment and culture was reached. The selective factors that operated to change the superorganic societies were intrinsic—physical, emotional, and intellectual—and extrinsic—environmental. The intrinsic factors were believed to be more significant than the extrinsic and were associated with race. According to Spencer, "the more-evolved societies drive less-evolved societies into unfavourable habitats and so entail on them decrease of size, or decay of structure."

Spencer postulated a parallel relationship between intelligence and fertility. An increase in human fertility meant that more mental activity was required in order for the existing individuals to survive. The least intelligent individuals and races supposedly died out, through lack of ability and fertility, thus raising the general level of intelligence and population. There would result, it was believed, a competition between mind and body cells. But it was predicted that intelligence would win over fertility and population pressures would end.

Spencerian evolution began with Lamarck rather than Darwin.

Spencer argued that heredity, the quality of the characteristics inherited by a population, determined the quality of a social organism and that this heredity could be modified by the conscious effort of a race; those men and races who tried hardest could become superior.

While Tylor and Spencer emphasized developmentalism and evolution in England, European physical anthropologists were still relying upon polygenetic explanations for racial differences. French physical anthropology, following the tradition of Cuvier, was the most impressive European school of thought. The leading figure of the time was Paul Broca, who founded the Paris Anthropological Society in 1870, discovered the speech center in the human brain, and edited the *Revue Anthropologique*. Broca, in such books as *The Physical Character of Prehistoric Man* (1868), *The Comparative Anatomy of Man and the Primates* (1869), and *On the Phenomena of Hybridity in Genus Homo* (1869), insisted that culture was tied to race, that racial differences were at least as old as historic time, and that the most significant determinant of race was skull shape. He also claimed that physically similar races were interracially fertile but that dissimilar races had a high degree of infertility. Strangely enough, Broca said that the offspring of a black female and white man were as fertile as any race but those of a black male and white female were not, while the offspring in both cases were infertile among themselves.

Broca's successor as editor of the *Revue Anthropologique* and as leader of French anthropology was Paul Topinard. Topinard elaborated the ideas of Broca in *Study of the Indigenous Races of Australia* (1872), *Anthropology* (1876), and *Elements of General Anthropology* (1885). Topinard asserted that human mental faculties were located in particular areas of the brain, although he denied the validity of the results of phrenologists' efforts to pinpoint these faculties on the skull's exterior. Since Topinard assumed that the development of skulls varied from race to race and that the mental capabilities of each race could be determined through sociological study, he felt that skull shape and mental capabilities could be correlated. This correlation indicated that humans were of three original races that were separate species and that came from different anthropoid ancestors. Topinard admitted that the primary races had divided into many secondary ones and were hard to distinguish in modern times, but he felt that persistent effort could disentangle them. This effort involved the use of several criteria. Color could be used to distinguish between the black and Caucasian races but not among various European ones where the significant difference was skull shape. French physical anthropology continued the tradition of the American school of ethnology in that it was polygenetic, convinced of the existence of permanent racial differences, and supportive of the importance of skull comparisons.

II

Americans were offered the choice between British cultural anthropology and French physical anthropology, which meant a choice between monogenesis and polygenesis. For the most part, they followed Britain's lead. The Peabody Museum of American Archeology and Ethnology was established at Harvard in 1866. Its director was Dr. Jeffries Wyman, the first man to describe the gorilla scientifically and a convert to Darwinism. Wyman became a significant American anthropologist, and the Peabody Museum became a leading institution for the study of the physical anthropology of the American Indian. John Wesley Powell, who was an explorer of the West, helped create a similar organization, the Bureau of American Ethnology, under federal auspices in Washington in 1879.

Lewis Henry Morgan was still the leading American anthropologist after the Civil War, and he became president of the American Association for the Advancement of Science in 1880 and inaugurated the first section on anthropology in that society's annual meeting in 1882. Morgan had participated vigorously in the discussion of Indian affairs in the 1870's; he defended the Sioux after Custer's defeat in an article in the *Nation* entitled "The Hue and Cry Against the Indians," saying that the Sioux were only defending themselves. In a subsequent issue of the *Nation,* Morgan's article "The Factory System for Indian Reservations" outlined a plan for Indian preservation and civilizing through a revival of the factory system. Morgan was optimistic; although the Indians were still barbarians, he believed that they had advanced toward civilization as evidenced by their improved treatment of women (the Indian woman could now sit at the same table with her husband). Morgan also recommended that an independent Department of Indian Affairs be created in the cabinet.

Morgan, while reviewing a book by a popular historian of the time, H. H. Bancroft's *Native Races of the Pacific States of North America* (1874–75), took umbrage at Bancroft's elevated views of the Aztecs, Mayas, and other Indians of Central America. Bancroft had claimed, justifiably, that these Indians had possessed civilizations that were hardly inferior to contemporary civilizations in Europe and Asia and that they had had sophisticated political systems with monarchical forms of government. As these claims did not fit into Morgan's evolutionary scheme, he denied the validity of Bancroft's work.

Morgan became an evolutionist reluctantly; he had not originally been interested in the problem of social change. His reluctance was due, in part, to his opposition to Spencer's secularism and emphasis on absolute individualism. However, his *League of the Iroquois* was implicitly progressive, and he had never accepted the theory of degeneracy, an idea that he dismissed as contrary to the known facts of human existence.

Morgan's *Ancient Society* (1877) contained a comprehensive scheme of human progress, which was applied to the history of Greece and Rome. Morgan took man's psychic unity and his common origin as given but rejected the biblical account of Creation because he believed that man was at least 100,000 years old and that man had evolved from an animal-like beginning. He thought that the human population, however, had originated in a single center in Asia; that much of the "Mosaic Cosmogony" he retained. Man's subsequent social development he compared to geological strata, "like the successive geological formations, the tribes of mankind may be arranged according to their relative conditions, into successive strata." Social development could be charted; shown in Table 6.1, in truncated form, is how Morgan did it.

TABLE 6.1

Savagery	Barbarism	Civilization
1. Lower—No fire; fruits and nuts	4. Lower—Pottery (Indian tribes east of the Mississippi)	7. Practice of writing
2. Middle—Fire and fish (Australians and Polynesians)	5. Middle—Irrigation, adobe, and stone building (Village Indians of New Mexico)	
3. Upper—Bow and arrow (Indians of Columbian River Valley)	6. Upper—Iron and phonetic alphabet (Grecian tribes in Homeric Age)	

Morgan maintained that each of the seven stages was successive and that human groups had gone through each state prior to achieving their present levels.

Social evolution supposedly operated in human institutions as well and was focused upon marriage and property relations. Morgan charted this kind of progress in *Systems of Consanguinity of the Human Family* (1866), as shown in Table 6.2.

TABLE 6.2

1. promiscuous intercourse
2. brother and sister cohabit
3. communal family
4. clan organization
5. marriage between single pairs but not exclusive cohabitation
6. patriarchal family
7. polyandry
8. private property
9. civilized marriage

Morgan thus tied civilization to monogamy and to private property. He assigned most of the Indians and the ancient Greeks to the stage of clan organization and argued that further development depended upon an evolution of mind and morality. The Greeks had accomplished this; Morgan believed the Indians could also do it.

Evolution occurred, according to Morgan, through the agency of three kinds of forces—biological (race), psychological (mind), and culturological (culture). He considered the second force the most significant as the evolution of human society supposedly paralleled the evolution of mind. The evolution of the mind could be demonstrated through physical evidence of the gradual enlargement of the brain. Savage men had smaller skulls and, therefore, smaller brains, thus indicating a feebler intellect and a less developed moral sense. Morgan did not assume that the skull sizes of different races remained constant; he said that nutrition, not heredity, was the key to the larger heads of the civilized races. The Aryan and Semitic races, for example, supposedly owed their preeminence to the domestication of the cow and the goat and to a diet based on milk and meat. If the village Indians of New Mexico had smaller brains, they were the result of a vegetable diet operating over long periods of time.

Morgan described the different Indian tribes as having arrived at different evolutionary stages. The North American Indians, in general, were in the upper stages of savagery because they had the bow and arrow but lacked horticulture. The Iroquois, however, had supposedly advanced to the lower stage of barbarism while the Village Indians of New Mexico were even higher, in the middle stage of barbarism. Despite their technological primitiveness, the Indians were thought to possess political organizations worthy of emulation; Morgan expressed the hope that that Indian example would revive "the liberty, equality, and fraternity of the ancient gentes." He said that all American Indians were of the same racial origin; Morgan claimed credit for settling that question once and for all. Finally, Morgan believed the Indians could advance to civilization if they changed their attitudes toward private property, marriage, and land tillage. Once this happened, the Indian was expected to disappear into the American mainstream as the historic Greek had disappeared into the mainstream of Western Civilization.

Morgan had problems in fitting black societies into his developmental scheme. Some African societies smelted iron, which qualified them for the upper stage of barbarism, but lacked an alphabet, which was also requisite for that stage. Morgan was unable to find virtues in African society which would reflect credit on the American Black as the virtues in Indian society reflected credit on the American Indian. Morgan assumed Africans had failed to achieve civilization and were inferior in cultural terms to American and European peoples.

Two other American anthropologists shared Morgan's evolutionism. One was John Wesley Powell, who helped create the Bureau of American Ethnology in 1879 and who was primarily interested in the languages of the Indian—as witnessed by his *Introduction to the Study of Indian Languages* (1877) and *Indian Linguistic Families of America North of Mexico* (1891). Powell rejected Spencerism and claimed that cultural evolution was separate from biological evolution. He argued that similarities between cultural groups reflected independent invention or similar environments rather than diffusion from one cultural origin. For example, individual groups probably each invented bows and arrows themselves.

The other anthropologist was Daniel G. Brinton who, like Morgan, found the Indian more absorbing than the Black. In *The Myths of the New World* (1868), Brinton provided conclusions about the Indian which paralleled those of Tylor and Morgan, utilizing Schoolcraft's method of studying myths. Brinton took as given the facts that Indian languages were all of one family and that all the Indians were related. He used as proof of the relationship, the cranial resemblance shown in Daniel Wilson's "The American

Cranial Type," in the *Annual Report of the Smithsonian Institution* (1862), and in J. A. Meigs' *Cranial Forms of the American Aborigines* (1866). Brinton found no cultural connection between the civilizations of North and South America nor, for that matter, between those of America and either Asia or Europe (Brinton believed, contrary to the informed opinion of his day, that the Indians had originally come from Europe). He believed that the Indians had been in America for a considerable period of time and that this accounted, in part, for their lack of progress—geographical isolation, coupled with the absence of domestic animals resulted in a lack of civilization. The Indians' failure to develop a written language also prevented progress, although the Indians had stood on the threshold of such a development when they were first discovered.

The lack of Indian records, caused by the absence of a written language, was partially rectified by the tenacious quality of Indian myths which persisted from generation to generation and from tribe to tribe. In the myths of the Indians, Brinton found a religious quality shared by all men. Attacking the assumption of degenerationists that Indian religion was a corruption of an earlier, purer faith, Brinton said that the Indian had not developed his religious ideas as much as Europeans had but that Indian religions had evolved, at least somewhat, from a more primitive stage. To Brinton, the symbolism of the Indians, their use of birds and serpents, showed the influence of a natural environment, not, as the early Christians had thought, the influence of the Devil. The Indians had not chosen totemic symbols to portray their allegiance to the Prince of Darkness but rather to show their connection with nature. Brinton believed that their myths concerning the animistic qualities of water, fire, and air originated from observation of physical events and showed "that primitive man was brute in everything but the susceptibility to culture" (1868). (Brinton's use of the word culture pre-dated Tylor's use by several years but conveyed approximately the same meaning.) Some Indian myths centered on human creation and the flood; and these myths paralleled those of other religions, as did Indian concepts of the soul and an afterlife. Finally, Brinton denied that Indian religion hindered the Indian in his struggle to survive, a position argued by the German historian George Waitz in his *Anthropologie der Naturvoeker*. According to Brinton, the Indians' religious sense had no necessary effect on morality or behavior; it showed only their common humanity.

Brinton had criticized Indian languages as uncongenial to abstract thought; but, in a paper read before the Congress International des Americanistes in Copenhagen in 1883 and later published as *Aboriginal American Authors and Their Productions,* Brinton changed his mind. He decided that Indian language had an ample vocabulary and could express abstractions and that Indian literature showed a love of story telling and the use of vivid images. Brinton listed Indian literary works, beginning with David Cusick's *Ancient History of the Six Nations* (1821) and mentioning Peter Dooyentate Clarke's *Origin and Traditional History of the Wyandotts* (1870) and Chief Elias Johnson's *History of the Six Nations* (1881). Brinton lauded the accomplishments of Cusick, Clarke, and Johnson and concluded that the languages and literature of the American Indians ought to have as high a claim on European anthropology as "Chinese documents, cylinders of Assyria, and papyri of Nilotic tombs."

Brinton, like Morgan, had a high opinion of the Indians despite their alleged primitiveness. He believed that the Indian societies could evolve and that their religion and literature showed the quality of the primitive mind to be no less than that of the civilized mind. Brinton, like Morgan, typified nineteenth-century American anthropological interest, which still centered upon the Indians partly because of an urgency to record the Indians' way of life before their extinction.

Despite the work of these scholars, America had lost its ascendancy in anthropology. Jeffries Wyman, John Wesley Powell, and Daniel Garrison Brinton lacked the training and the students to develop a national school of anthropology. And as Lewis A. Morgan did not attempt to train new anthropologists or to teach his view, American anthropology remained disorganized and diffuse until the twentieth century.

The image of the Indian in popular American literature remained unaffected by anthropological speculation. Joaquin Miller, who first encountered Indians in Indiana and Ohio before moving to Oregon, included Indians in a fictionalized account of his adventures in the West, *Life Among the Modocs* (1873). Miller portrayed two kinds of Indians, the mountain Indians who were Nature's Noblemen and the lowland Indians who were Nature's rejects. The story line traced the adventures of a 14 year-old white boy who lived with the Modocs, married an Indian woman, and tried unsuccessfully to organize the Indians into one single tribe so as to resist white pressures. Miller's book contained a typically American theme of an individual who flees civilization to find happiness in a life of primitive virtue. His hero was a younger Leatherstocking type who possessed political skills but (unlike the original type), was willing to marry an Indian.

Another writer, Edward Eggleston, continued the literary tradition of the Noble Savage. Eggleston is best known for his *The Hoosier Schoolmaster* (1871), a novel of frontier life in Indiana; but in order to support himself, he also wrote juvenile books in collaboration with Lillie Eggleston Seelye, his daughter. Among these juveniles were *The Shawnee Prophet; or the Story of Tecumseh* (1880) and *The Indian Princess; or the Story of Pocahontas* (1881). The first book portrayed Tecumseh as the highest type of Indian genius, an individual who combined courage with political wisdom. Tecumseh's tribe, the Shawnee, however, was shown as lacking identity because of past intermarriage with Whites and other Indian tribes; this resulted in the loss of their proud and warlike character as well as their lives. In the story of Tecumseh, Eggleston combined the eighteen-century idea of degeneracy with the contemporary one of the impending extinction of the Indians. He could have written this book a hundred years earlier and it would have contained few surprises.

The Indian Princess was a simplified version of John Smith's *General History of Virginia*. Eggleston included the gory details of Smith's story but left out the sexual ones. Pocahontas, though an uncivilized savage, was portrayed as a friend to the Europeans; after Smith's capture, she saved him because of this friendship. Eggleston's Pocahontas was a preadolescent girl, between 10 and 12 years of age, when she rescued Smith; she became a Christian only after her capture and a woman only after her marriage. Eggleston's account followed Smith quite faithfully and could have been written in the seventeenth century.

The Indian problem, for anthropologist, novelist, and reformer, seemed after the Civil War to be solvable through the assimilation of the Indian into American society. Although the Indians were supposed to be in a lower stage of cultural development, they were believed to be rising through the acquisition of private property and monogamous marriage. Indian reformers rested comfortably with the notion that legislation had finally assured Indian conversion to civilization. It was only in the literature of the time that the stock image of the Indian as the Noble Savage remained, along with the older view that primitive Indian traits were the degenerate remnants of an older more civilized state.

Chapter 7

Could Blacks Survive?

Emancipation, though helpful to Blacks, also had a grimmer side. John Duffy, a medical historian, estimates that approximately one million black persons died in 1865 after the conclusion of the Civil War. Freed from the plantation, Blacks ventured to new areas and encountered new diseases for which they lacked natural immunity and which were rendered more deadly by poverty, limited diet, and inadequate medical facilities.

The census of 1870, reflecting this black mortality, showed little absolute increase in black population and a relative decrease in the proportion of black to white population. However, errors in the census made the amount of black increase in proportion to white increase seem less than it was; thus the increase indicated by the subsequent census of 1880 seemed to reverse the trend of the census of 1870. Suddenly, it again appeared that Blacks were proliferating. Census figures from the Civil War to 1900 are listed in Table 7.1.

The censuses of 1870 and 1880 became objects of intense scrutiny and analysis; many statisticians attempted to explain the data. For some, the census of 1870 proved that Blacks could not compete in a free society; for others, the census of 1880 aroused fears that the black population growth would eventually produce a black South. The censuses also seemed to prove Agassiz's theory of zoological provinces to be correct for, despite the increasing

TABLE 7.1

Year	Black Population	% of Blacks in total U.S. Population	% of black increase in decade	% of white increase in decade
1860	4,400,000	14.1	22.1	37.7
1870	4,880,000	12.7	9.9	24.8
1880	6,580,000	13.1	34.9	29.2
1890	7,490,000	11.9	13.8	27.0
1900	8,830,000	11.6	18.0	21.2

urbanization of American society as a whole, Blacks remained overwhelmingly rural residents of the South.

Dr. Edward W. Gilliam predicted in 1883 that the black population of the United States would reach 192,000,000 by 1980, based upon the rate of increase shown in the 1880 census, and that this population increase would result in a race war. Albion W. Tourgee said in *An Appeal to Caesar* (1884) that all the Southern states from Maryland to Texas would have Negro majorities by 1900 and unless Southern whites moderated their attacks on Negroes, racial conflict might occur.

After the census of 1890, which showed a relative decline in the black population, thinkers began to change their views and proclaimed a belief that Blacks could not survive in the United States, although the climate of the South was favorable to them. Henry Gannett of the United States Geological Survey, geographic consultant to the United States Census Bureau for the censuses of 1880, 1890, and 1900, confirmed an observation that Blacks were concentrated in the Gulf states and in areas of high temperatures, which indicated that tropical United States was the natural home of the Blacks. Gannett predicted the reduction of black population in other, more temperate areas and that all but tropical America would become a white country.

The most significant demographic speculation in America was made by Frederick L. Hoffman, a German-born insurance statistician. Hoffman's book, *Race Traits and Tendencies of the American Negro* (1896), was published and backed by a new organization, the American Economic Association. Hoffman claimed that he was unprejudiced because he was German-born and that his work was both scientific and definitive. He concluded that:

The Negro is subject to a higher mortality rate [than that of the White], but especially so at the early age periods .... The natural increase in the colored population will be less from decade to decade and in the end a decrease must take place. It is sufficient to know that in the struggle for race supremacy the black race is not holding its own; and this fact once recognized, all danger from a possible numerical superiority of the race vanishes.

For proof, Hoffman extracted data from the census of 1890 which showed that in 1890 there were 13.24 percent more Blacks in the South than in 1880 but that there were 23.91 percent more Whites in 1890 than in 1880. In the United States as a whole, the black population increased 13.51 percent and the white increased 26.68 percent. He tried to show why earlier predictions had erred so badly, using the figures in Table 7.2.

TABLE 7.2 Negroes in the United States

Year	U.S. Census	Darby's View of the United States 1828	De Bow's Review	Kennedy
1830	2,328,642	2,893,731		
1840	2,873,648	4,114,709		
1850	3,638,808	5,756,079		
1860	4,441,830	7,860,118	4,319,452	
1870	4,880,009	10,669,236	5,296,235	5,407,130
1880	6,580,793	14,329,701	6,494,334	6,591,292
1890	7,470,040	19,209,740	7,962,004	7,909,550
1900	(est) 8,458,952	25,825,878	9,766,884	9,491,454

He attributed the errors to the failure to consult mortality tables for Blacks and to the use of only birth data for estimates. Hoffman seized upon a higher black death rate as a significant variable, a variable recognized by many White-run insurance companies, including his own. His company, the Prudential, refused to write policies on Blacks (this refusal stimulated the growth of black insurance companies, one of the few avenues for black economic success after the Civil War). The White-owned insurance companies had known what population experts had not; a Black's life expectancy was lower than a White's.

Hoffman analyzed other demographic data and found that the black population was increasing in certain cities—Philadelphia, New

Orleans, Baltimore, and Washington—and in rural areas in the South but not in the North as a whole. Hoffman concluded that Blacks would remain in the South as they could not survive in the North, where the death rate exceeded the birth rate. Nor could Blacks compete permanently with Whites in the South in Hoffman's opinion; because of a high birth rate, the black population was temporarily increasing, but a high death rate meant that the black population would decrease as the birth rate fell.

Why was there such a high black mortality? The first reason Hoffman discussed was high infant mortality; in Richmond, Virginia, Hoffman found that only one out of two black babies survived the first year of life. Also, black adults had a shorter life span than white adults. The third factor of black mortality, according to Hoffman, was that black men died younger than black women. Hoffman claimed that the data indicated racial weakness; he denied that the higher mortality rate of blacks resulted from poverty and poor housing. Citing reports of the Surgeon-General of the United States Army in 1889 and the physician of the Alabama penitentiary, both of which reported higher death rates for Blacks than Whites in the army and in jail, Hoffman insisted that given equal environments, Blacks still lacked Whites' longevity. Not only was the black mortality rate higher than the white; the disparity between rates was increasing, according to Hoffman. To prove his point, Hoffman used statistics from Charleston, South Carolina (Table 7.3).

TABLE 7.3

Year	White Mortality*	Negro Mortality*
1822–30	32.73	28.16
1831–40	25.24	25.02
1841–50	16.17	19.77
1851–60	29.79	34.12
1866–75	25.56	41.98
1876–85	24.32	43.82
1886–94	22.26	44.06

* Individuals per thousand

Hoffman indicated that the Negro mortality rate had increased after emancipation and that it was especially high in age groups up to 30 years—the years of highest reproductive potential.

Hoffman conceded that some of the reasons for higher Negro mortality were social; people died because they lacked access to medical care; they died of diarrhea because of poor sanitary conditions. However, he believed that the major reasons were constitutional, that Blacks had an inferior physical structure that was particularly susceptible to pulmonary diseases, scrofula, and venereal diseases. Black resistance to all of these diseases had weakened since the Civil War; even such diseases as yellow and typhoid fevers, to which formerly the Black had greater natural immunity, now took as great a toll of black lives as white. According to Hoffman, the reason for the lessened resistance was moral decline; Hoffman even maintained that the high rate of pneumonia deaths of Blacks correlated with the high rate of black illegitimacy. Thus, Whites were healthier because they were more moral, although, curiously, Hoffman found them to have higher rates of alcoholism (a fact he blamed largely on the Irish), insanity, and suicide. From his data, Hoffman generalized that Blacks were declining in population in the North, were dying faster in southern cities than on southern farms, had a higher mortality rate before age 30, had a life expectancy of from 12.5 to 17.11 years less than Whites, and were losing ground to Whites in terms of mortality rates.

The problem of Negrophobia, fear of Blacks, continued in the North and South during and after the Civil War. The Democrats argued during the war that the Blacks would not benefit from freedom and that the freedmen would surge to the Northwest and demoralize white residents. The Republicans countered by blaming slavery for the Blacks' desire to leave the South. The Republicans claimed that since the South was the natural region for Blacks, the removal of slavery would mean the return of free Blacks to the South—if social institutions did not drive them away. The official policy of President Lincoln was colonization, and—over the objection of New England representatives—Congress wrote this policy into both the Confiscation Act of July 17, 1862, and the Emancipation Act for slaves in the District of Columbia and other federally supervised territories. The Northern states did not repeal their anti-Black laws during the Civil War. A referendum in Illinois in 1862 to permit both black suffrage and office-holding lost by a five to one majority. At the close of the Civil War, sentiment existed supporting the creation of areas reserved especially for Blacks. General Sherman in 1865 proposed two such areas, in the Sea Islands off the Georgia coast and on a strip thirty miles inland.

After the war, the basic Republican position on black rights was for equality before the law. Given this equality, Blacks would have to compete economically with Whites but would not have suffrage. Despite the federal guarantee of civil rights, even the most radical of the abolitionists—such as Thaddeus Stevens and Wendell Phillips—had no consistent idea of how to reconcile local control with federal action to protect Blacks. Military rule did not continue long; civilian governments existed in all the southern states by 1870. Radical Reconstruction was forced, in the end, to rely on local self-government by the Blacks rather than on long-term federal control of the Blacks. Thus, black suffrage assumed a conservative cast; Blacks could protect their rights at the local level through their own votes. Black suffrage became a reality mainly because of southern intransigence and resistance to Presidential Reconstruction and only through the device of constitutional amendments.

National organizations did not help black civil rights much. Women's rights, which had been connected with black rights prior to the Civil War, moved in a new direction, and the women's movement split in 1869 over the question of support of black rights. Some conservative advocates of women's suffrage, Henry Blackwell among them, wanted women's suffrage in order to bolster white supremacy. Blackwell said that southern white women outnumbered Blacks by two to one and that this voting majority could mean securer white control. On the other hand, the radical wing of the Women's Rights movement alienated the majority of the membership by combining the issue of free love with that of black rights and by backing Victoria Woodhull and Frederick Douglass who were running for office on the Equal Rights ticket. The Equal Rights ticket provided a historic first: the first woman candidate for president running with a black candidate for vice-president. However, the Equal Rights party failed to develop mass support.

Some of the white officers who commanded black soldiers during the Civil War doubted the ability of blacks to survive as free men. Charles Francis Adams, Jr., grandson of John Quincy Adams, was an example. Adams originally opposed the enlistment of black troops because he felt that slave conditioning would be difficult, if not impossible, to reverse. Later, he commanded black troops and took a less pessimistic view of their abilities. He still felt, however, that Blacks could not survive after the war without some transitional stage between slavery and freedom to prepare the ex-slave for free life. Adams believed this preparation might be provided by the army and advocated the forcible retention of Blacks in the army until they had learned habits of industry.

The Army Reorganization Bill of July 26, 1866, provided an opportunity for voluntary black army service and was passed partly because of the pressure applied by abolitionists. The Bill created two black cavalry and four black infantry regiments and provided that white chaplains be assigned to army posts to provide education for illiterate black soldiers. The black regiments were used in the West and served with distinction, but were segregated from local communities and isolated from urban areas. In 1878, Senator Ambrose E. Burnside of Rhode Island, a former Union General, introduced a bill which, on the face of it, would have ended all racial discrimination in the army by eliminating all black regiments and by permitting recruiting sergeants to enlist Blacks as well as Whites into the remaining regiments. Critics of the bill observed that the recruiting sergeants would not enlist Blacks if not required to and the bill was defeated. The army at least provided some opportunity for blacks, although it was not to be a school for freedom as Adams had proposed.

Other observers, American and foreign, were no more optimistic than Adams about the ability of Blacks to compete in a white world. Georges Clemenceau, later to become a famous French statesman, taught in the United States after the Civil War and publicly questioned whether Blacks could survive the struggle for existence. His conclusion was shared by John W. De Forest, an army and Freedman's Bureau officer, who said that in spite of the education provided in the Freedman's Bureau Schools, the black race could not compete with the "vigorous and terrible" Caucasian one and would be driven back to the lowlands of the South where tropical diseases constituted a barrier to Whites.

There were actual attempts made to displace black labor in the South. As early as 1865, Southern leaders proposed bringing in Chinese laborers to work on plantations because of their supposed advantages. The Chinese were cheaper, had been trained to work (evidently the Southern defense of slavery as a successful school for industry had been a lie), had a different biblical destiny, and were available since the railroads on which they had previously labored were completed. However, the movement for Chinese laborers never gained momentum, and by the mid-1870's, counterarguments based upon the supposed moral evils of Chinese homes and the assumed proclivity of the Chinese to physical and mental illness diminished the enthusiasm of planters. Attempts made to attract northern white laborers to the South were equally unsuccessful. In 1870, Alabama brought in migratory workers for harvesting, and in 1873, Beauregard and other Louisiana spokesmen tried, without great success, to induce northerners to go to Louisiana. Southerners attempted to tap European labor sources as well. In 1880, Louisiana contracted for Portuguese workers, and in 1881, South Carolina encouraged Italian miners to emigrate. None of the labor substitution projects proved profitable and black labor remained the key to agricultural production in the South.

White Southerners accepted Blacks provided they were under stringent social control, were segregated, and were disfranchised. Segregation was informal at first, but states and cities placed increasing legal restrictions upon Black use of public facilities. From the end of Reconstruction, southern politicians had permitted black political participation, albeit under the paternal direction of Conservative Democratic leadership. But the rise of Populism in the South, a movement by poor farmers to achieve some political control which threatened to split the Democratic party, led to Negro baiting by political candidates and vote restrictions. Devices such as poll taxes, literacy tests, and understanding clauses all served to limit black suffrage; from 1890 to 1910, southern states successfully used these devices to eliminate black voters from any significant participation in the electoral process. The Supreme Court seemingly placed its seal of approval on both the segregation of public facilities and the disfranchisement of Negroes through its decisions in *Plessey vs. Ferguson* (1896), which accepted separate-but-equal facilities on railroads, in *Cumming vs. County Board of Education* (1899), which held that a Georgia county did not deny equal protection of the laws by failing to have a high school for sixty black children although it supported a white high school, and in *Williams vs. Mississippi* (1898), which upheld Mississippi's constitutional disfranchisement plan. By 1900, the establishment of a caste system had been accomplished and legitimatized.

At the same time, the legal definition of a Negro was broadened, discouraging miscegenation. South Carolina provided a good example of the process. In 1879, South Carolina law said that anyone with one-quarter Negro blood was a Negro; in 1895, the South Carolina constitution defined a Negro as anyone with one-eighth Negro blood. The mulatto safety hatch—the hope for integration through miscegenation—which was never open, was nailed down.

Increasing racial violence was a serious problem in both the rural South and the urban North. From 1882 to 1903, the number of lynchings, which occurred mostly in the South, usually exceeded the number of lawful executions for capital crimes. The lynchings had common characteristics: the leaders came from the top levels of society, the followers were middle class, and the participants used informal trials. The lynchings became increasingly sadistic as time went on. In the South, those lynched were usually Negro males who were accused of sexual offenses, customarily involving white women. In the urban North, the issues were more often economic ones, although sexual overtones often added to the problem.

Robert H. Wiebe's seminal work, *The Search for Order, 1877–1920,* suggests a reason for increased racial friction, a reason that lay deep in the structure of American society. Prior to 1877, Americans had lived in isolated communities, with few complex social organizations, and with a low regard for governmental action. As the isolation decreased, white Americans became increasingly disturbed. Urbanization and industrialization brought black and white immigrants to the cities and fostered a concomitant distrust of urban areas as places where aliens lived. In the late-nineteenth century, the ruling elites of separate communities attempted to tighten social control over the cities and grew increasingly suspicious of other groups of differing classes or races. As Wiebe says:

In place of communication, antagonists confronted each other behind sets of stereotypes, frozen images that were specifically intended to exclude discussion. Reinforcing the faithful's feeling of separateness, the rhetoric of antithetical absolutes denied even the desirability of any interchange. If as so many substantial citizens maintained the issue was civilization versus anarchy, who would negotiate with chaos?

The analogy used by the antagonists, the controlling elites, was of a war against the enemies of society, a war to win back control of social organizations. The war metaphor fostered conflict, and all participants got angrier and angrier. The Populists in the South, as described by Wiebe, illustrated the anger:

The viciousness with which Southern farmers and townsmen attacked the Negro after 1896 told a story of the community's failure. Its members in the South and elsewhere suddenly felt stripped before their enemies.

Social thinkers worried about increasing antagonisms and proposed that Americans might prevent social conflict by excluding immigrants and by rigidly controlling immigrants and Blacks. Few suggested greater freedom for all.

I

In the controversy in the United States over the origins, abilities, and future of the Black, debaters used any evidence they could find from any paradigm. These debaters made statements that were inconsistent and contradictory and that were in keeping with their lack of training in the increasingly sophisticated sciences and social sciences.

Abolitionists attacked the idea of the innate racial inferiority of the Black, realizing that this idea was the cornerstone of the justification for slavery. Their reliance upon both the biblical account of creation and the environmental explanation for the supposed backwardness of the black man in America had been shaken by the American school of ethnology. As a result, they moved during and after the Civil War to bolster their arguments with newer historical and biological findings while retaining the belief that slavery caused black degradation.

Proponents of black inferiority based their belief in part on the claim that both ancient and contemporary black Africa had lacked civilization. This claim was countered in two ways: the old paradigm of degeneracy was applied in arguing that Africa had once been a center of learning and culture but had retrogressed. This argument—combined with that of romantic racism, which said in part that the black man's destiny was to Christianize Africa—led to a cyclical view of African history. It was believed that Africa, depressed because of paganism, would once again rise after Christianity won the continent to lead the world. The second rebuttal of the contention of African inferiority looked more closely at African history. One such rebuttal was that of Mrs. Mary Putnam, a sister of James Russell Lowell, who wrote *Record of an Obscure Man* (1861), a fictional account of a white man who visits the South in 1842 and becomes involved in a discussion of black capabilities. In his defense of black equality, the hero argued that there were contemporary civilizations in Africa that were quite sophisticated; he supported his position by using an argument that was to become basic to twentieth-century anthropology, that of cultural relativism. He argued that Africa had been measured by Western standards but that African standards were different and equally valid. He also maintained that white contact had perverted African societies, referring to the accounts of trips to the interior of Africa for support. He quoted Mungo Park, Hugh Clapperton, and Dixon Denham—all early nineteenth-century explorers—who described the natives of the interior as enlightened, intelligent, and as progressing toward a higher civilization, which progress had unfortunately been stunted by the European presence.

The romantic or humanitarian racialism of many abolitionists persisted. Moncure Conway, the abolitionist son of a Virginia slave-owner, said that the Blacks gave warmth and radiance to southern life with their innate qualities of exuberance, hope, and childlike wonder. Theodore Tilton echoed these views in a speech given at the American Anti-Slavery convention in 1863 and published as *The Negro*. According to Tilton, the Negro race surpassed the white in its religious nature. He considered the morality of the Negro race as a whole to equal that of white women; "the Negro race is the feminine race of the world." said Tilton. Hence, he argued that the presence of the black race in America was as necessary as that of the white woman; both were needed in America to civilize the white man, to curb his aggressiveness and drive. The romantic racialism of Conway and Tilton, which persisted in some circles in white America, emerged later in the black community.

In 1863, Charles Loring Brace, a philanthropist who had founded the New York Children's Aid Society, became the first reformer to utilize Darwinian ideas to attack the polygenetic argument of the American school of ethnology in a book entitled *The Races of the Old World: A Manual of Ethnology*. Brace took evidence from Darwin to support the ideas that humans had originated in one place, migrated to different climates, adapted to these climates through natural selection, and become permanent racial types. In addition, Brace used linguistic evidence to show that humans were related through common language patterns. Brace's idea of naturalized monogenesis omitted the equalitarianism of the biblical account, for Brace held that each racial type had peculiar characteristics and that intermarriage between members of different racial types resulted in inferior offspring.

Samuel Gridley Howe also cast doubt on the possibility of racial equality. Howe was a liberal reformer who was a member of the Freedman's Inquiry Commission created by Lincoln in 1863 to investigate the conditions and needs of the freed slaves. Howe studied black ex-slaves living in Canada and reported his findings in *The Refugees from Slavery in Canada West* (1864). Howe, who was also a doctor, examined the physical conditions of black Canadians as well as their intellectual achievements. He was disappointed in both; the Blacks failed to match the Whites in either case. This lack could not be attributed to slavery as some of the persons studied had never been slaves. Howe attributed the failure of the black community to produce as many outstanding individuals as the white and the failure of black students to approach white levels in higher grades of school to racial differences, to the alleged fact that Blacks were knowing rather than thinking people. Howe's acceptance of racial differences did not alter his antislavery stance but, since it relied on the best science of the day, augered ill for future beliefs in racial equality.

Southerners often relied on the literal truth of the Bible in their defense of black racial inferiority. An example of this defense was the work of the Reverend Buckner H. Payne who wrote under the psuedonym of "Ariel." In a booklet entitled *The Negro: What is His Ethnological Status?* (1867) and in *Ariel's Reply to the Rev. John A. Seiss, D.D., of Philadelphia; Also His Reply to the Scientific Geologist and Other Learned Men in Their Attack on the Credibility of the Mosaic Account of the Creation and of the Flood* (1876), Payne returned to an earlier pre-Adamic conception of black origin, with the addition of a virulent racism, and defended the Bible against the inroads of science and the South's social arrangements against northern critics. Payne claimed that the Black was a beast, a higher ape, who was created prior to Adam and who, therefore, was denied a human soul and immortality. The Black was the tempter in the Garden of Eden who caused Eve to fall. According to Payne, miscegenation was the reason for the destruction of Sodom and Gomorrah and mulattoes had crucified Christ. For Payne, every villain in the Bible was black.

Others were quick to follow Payne's lead. Robert Buchanan's *Caliban: A Sequel to Ariel* (1868) continued the argument. Buchanan also said that the Black was created prior to Adam, was related to the chimpanzee, and, since the name for black meant serpent, was the tempter of Eve. Buchanan maintained that Cain had lived with Blacks and had married one after he killed Abel. The resulting miscegenation caused God to send the flood which destroyed all mixed races. Only pure races survived—the Caucasian and the black pre-Adamite; the former remained in the Near East, the latter was driven into Africa. Buchanan also saw the hand of God in the happenings of his day. The white South suffered under black rule, he said, because Caucasians in the South had violated God's ordinance against miscegenation and were being punished by God. This experience paralleled that of the Jews in the Old Testament.

The ultimate expression of the biblical theme came from Charles Carroll, a native of St. Louis, at the end of the nineteenth century. In three books, *The Negro not the Son of Ham* (1890), *The Negro a Beast* (1900), and *The Tempter of Eve* (1902), Carroll strove hard to prove that only Whites were humans and that the biblical account of Creation referred specifically to them. The black man was an animal; one evidence of this, according to Carroll, was that the black man required twice as much medicine to be relieved as did a white man. Carroll added little that was new to the already formed biblical explanation except to change the sex of the black person in the Garden of Eden. The serpent was a black maidservant of Adam, Carroll claimed, thus implying a relationship between the tempter and Adam as well as Eve. Carroll also maintained that all races save the white were hybrid and lacked souls and that any attempt to Christianize them was doomed to failure.

Carroll's defense of the Bible was more sophisticated than that of Payne or Buchanan in that it incorporated the scientific ideas of the time. Carroll offered his readers a choice between the scriptural school of Divine Creation and the atheistic school of natural development. There could be no doubt that in Carroll's mind the former was preferable, although the latter was considered supportive of creationism. The Bible recorded, according to Carroll, three creations: heaven and earth in the first day, animals the fifth day, and man in the sixth day. The days of creation were not human days; they were geological epochs. Matter was created first and then mind; mind was shared by men and animals. Carroll claimed that the Black was created as an animal on the fifth day while the White was created on the sixth. God created a single pair of humans at the beginning; He did not create races. The terms "species" and "races" were human terms first used by Plato in his history of Atlantis and revived by Linnaeus, Lamarck, and Blumenbach in the eighteenth century. Christian writers, said Carroll, should abjure the use of race as a secular term and use the terms tribes, nations, and empires instead because these words appear in the King James version of the Bible. Carroll's attempt to renounce the nineteenth century was futile; but he shows how it was possible to use the older religious paradigm of Divine Creation to claim original black inequality.

Carroll attacked the legend of Noah as an explanation of origin by pointing to certain anomalies in the biblical account. Carroll denied that Blacks were descendents of Ham. The Bible stated that Noah cursed Canaan, the son of Ham, but Canaan had done nothing. Since God was fair, He would not have permitted Canaan to suffer, so the curse of Noah lacked God's sanction. It did not turn Canaan black, and Canaan went on to develop a high civilization (this furnished further proof that he was not black). The descendants of Canaan later sinned; they lost their land to the Jews because of wickedness, not because of blackness. Carroll had other arguments that Blacks were not descendants of Ham. If Noah's curse had turned Canaan black, Canaan would have had no one to marry but a white woman. If he had married a White, his offspring would have been mulattoes who would have become extinct (Carroll accepted the idea of the lack of fertility of the mulatto). Thus Carroll disposed of the legend of Noah.

His most important argument in *The Negro a Beast* (1890) was that the Negro was an ape; "he simply stands at the head of the ape family as the lion stands at the head of the cat family." He believed that Blacks came from the twenty-fourth stage of the anthropoid apes, the apeman. White persons had supposedly amalgamated with Blacks to create new races, contrary to God's will. Carroll denied the "atheistic" view that humans and beasts were sexually incompatible. Cain married a beast, a black woman, and was cursed for this. Carroll interpreted the biblical passage that told of Angels who lusted after strange flesh as meaning Whites who had sexual relations with Blacks; he interpreted the passage that told of the beasts of the fields eating olives and grapes as meaning black field hands, since cows and horses did not eat fruit. Carroll then claimed that miscegenation between the white humans and the black animals, which formed the brown, yellow and red races, did not give these new races souls or intellectual capability. All civilizations have been built by Whites, according to Carroll; the cities of the Indians were no exception. The Indians were a product of White-Black intermixing and the white Indians had built the cities. As proof of this thesis, Carroll quoted Prichard on the origin of human colors and pointed to the variations in color in contemporary Indians. Carroll believed that continued miscegenation in the South would result in a mixed race and a degenerate civilization. Carroll concluded his book with a prediction, taken from the French anthropologist Quatrefage's *The Human Species,* which said that Americans were becoming Indians. When this happened, America would revert to savagery.

Carroll's attempt to retain a biblical account of creation by incorporating recent biological ideas, by restricting evolutionary change only to animals or to animal crosses, by shedding as cumbersome the legend of Noah, and by trying to return to pre–eighteenth-century racial terminology underscored the dilemma of the religious southern racist. The pre-Adamic paradigm had many anomalies and the evolutionist one was unacceptable. A shaky compromise between the two had to be made.

Most Americans, in the North and the South, did not accept the idea that the Negro was a beast since this meant interpreting biblical passages in peculiar ways and since acceptance encouraged interracial aggression. Refutations of the idea, such as William G. Schell's *Is the Negro a Beast?* (1901), pointed out that Adam did not name Blacks, that Blacks had a moral faculty, and that in Africa Blacks worshipped a Supreme Being. Schell also rejected the notion that Cain had married a black woman or that God was white, saying that humans had lost their resemblance to God in the Fall. Schell attacked Carroll's scientism, although agreeing with him that humans had a common origin. Schell divided humans into races for purposes of convenience, but the variations were said to be the result of natural causes.

Another facet of the southern argument for black inequality was a historical one and was advanced in its most rabid form by Hinton Rowan Helper. Helper, a native North Carolinian, was a southern antislavery, anti-Black author. His *The Impending Crisis of the South* (1857) attacked slaveowners for bringing Blacks into American society and for perverting American democracy. Helper called himself a "rational" Republican and served as U.S. Consul to Buenos Aires during the Civil War. Following the war, he wrote two books which proposed an exclusionist answer to the Negro question.

In the first book, *Nojoque: A Question for a Continent* (1867), Helper discounted the possibility of Black and White living together in peace in the United States and proposed a deadline

(July 4, 1876, the Centennial of American Independence) for the expulsion of all Blacks. In the second book, *The Negroes in Negroland; The Negroes in America; and Negroes Generally* (1868), Helper presented an edited collection of writings on Blacks in Africa and in the United States. These writings perpetuated the current vicious stereotypes of Blacks: Blacks had hard, thick skulls, the sutures of which closed sooner than those of the whites; they smelled bad and had flat noses and thick lips; they had strange, high pitched voices and tough, insensitive skins; they were dishonest thieves and were immoral and sexually promiscuous. The writers included such explorers of Africa as Mungo Park, Richard Burton, and David Livingstone and such American leaders as John Adams, Daniel Webster, Horace Mann, William Henry Seward, Theodore Parker, Abraham Lincoln, Joseph Nott and Samuel George Morton. The descriptions of Africa drawn from these sources revealed societies full of superstition and barbarism, where black natives themselves regarded white ways as better. Helper's evaluation of Africa was the complete antithesis of that of Mrs. Putnam. Africa was backward and primitive according to Helper.

In his section on American views of the Black, Helper indicated, quite accurately, that the belief in the inferiority of Blacks was held by many prominent leaders. Included were such leading Republicans as William Henry Seward who in 1860 opposed slavery extension in order to protect the welfare of the white man, and President Lincoln who, in his campaign of 1858, spoke against black suffrage, citizenship, social equality, and intermarriage with Whites. Helper predicted that the natural defects of the Blacks in America would lead to their eventual demise. He also predicted that Blacks would be preceded to extinction, however, by the mulattoes, whose lack of physical stamina and fertility doomed them to a quicker end. Helper believed that Blacks should be legally removed from the United States but that, failing that, they would be removed by the superior drive of Whites.

Ironically, southern writers who had been unable to convince northerners of the benevolence of the slave system before the war succeeded afterwards as a new literature romanticized the pre-war plantation and Black-White relations. One of the most significant authors of this new literature was Thomas Nelson Page, a Virginian who was born on a plantation in 1853. Page attempted poetry in black dialect with little success but achieved literary recognition with his short stories, published in *In Ole Virginia* in 1887. He wrote several novels, including *Meh Lady* (1893), *The Old Gentleman of the Black Stock* (1896), *Red Rock* (1898)—his most famous book which sold 100,000 copies, and *Gordon Keith* (1903).

The themes in his novels and short stories were similar: there was a love interest, frequently intersectional; and there was reference to the benevolence of slavery, which had civilized Blacks. In *Red Rock,* a southern man and northern woman fell in love, and the heroine's equalitarian principles gave way to the hero's racist ones. According to Page, the Black had become a faithful servant under his white master's guidance; but, the Civil War had destroyed racial harmony and, in conjunction with Radical Reconstruction, had led to a loss of social control by the White and a loss of self-discipline by some Blacks. These Blacks' sexual appetites raged out of control and caused them to desire white women and to rape them. Whites then lynched black rapists, rightly according to Page. Page's novels, like the pronouncements of such "New South" spokesmen as Henry Watterson and Henry Grady, pleaded for continued control of the unruly Black through the leadership of the enlightened southern white man.

A few demurrers were entered by southerners against the conservative paternalism of the South; two of the men who protested were George Washington Cable and Lewis H. Blair. Blair, in *A Southern Prophecy* (1881), pointed to the economic difficulties incumbent on a society where the black level of attainment was kept low. Cable's books, *Old Creole Days* (1879), *The Grandissimes* (1880), *Madame Delphine* (1881), *The Creoles of Louisiana* (1884), *The Silent South* (1885), and *The Negro Question* (1888), pointed to the social difficulties in a differentially segregated society. Cable had disliked slavery because of its physical cruelty and encouragement of miscegenation; he did not, however, believe in the equality of the black race, which he felt was still basically savage. If the black race were permitted to achieve a higher status, the white race would not be polluted by miscegenation; integration supposedly meant less miscegenation rather than more. Cable attacked segregationist Southerners as irrational, ignorant, and barbaric; these people refused to recognize mulattoes, the tragic figures in Cable's works, because that would mean recognizing their own fornication. Although Cable was no equalitarian, his portrayal of the tragic mulatto, his attack on Southern

Whites, and his advocacy of elevating the Blacks caused him to be forced out of the South.

The romantic view of the Black in the novels of Cable and Page remained unchallenged in the other literature of the period. Albion W. Tourgee's first novel, *'Toinette* (1876), recounted the story of a slave girl who demanded that her white lover marry her after the Civil War. The lover refused, despite the knowledge that the slave girl had had his child, and she was left without support. Interracial sex also appeared in Mark Twain's *The Tragedy of Puddin' head Wilson* (1894), which began with the seduction of Roxanna, a mulatto woman, by a white man. The resultant child was raised as white after being switched for a white child by Roxanna. Twain showed little sympathy for the substitute boy, whom he portrayed as being heartless. Nor did other Blacks receive empathetic treatment from Twain. Negro Jim in *The Adventures of Huckleberry Finn* (1884) was a Sambo; he was superstitious and ignorant, and he was also trusting and loyal. (Since *The Adventures of Huckleberry Finn* has become an American classic, critics have differed on the intended meaning of the Black-White encounter that occurred on the raft. Did it indicate homosexual love, a return of Whites to primitivism, or utopian equalitarianism?) The Black was portrayed in Twain's work either as a seductive Roxanna or a simple Negro Jim. Both lacked greater human dimension.

Neither the portrayal of the Negro as a simpleton or a beast nor the call for his expulsion from the United States met the needs of southern society, dependent as it was on both black labor and white supremacy. A compromise position emerged, which Lawrence J. Friedman, a contemporary historian, calls the "Brownlow Tradition" and which attempted differential segregation of Blacks. Friedman insists that the main question in the South during and after Reconstruction was not segregation but rather how to control the Blacks. He says in *The White Savage: Racial Fantasies in the Post-Bellum South* (1870):

Like Baldwin, I argue that segregation and integration are not the vital issues—that white Southern efforts at segregation have been no more than manifestations of a deeper Southern abhorrence of "uppity niggers."

A solution for controling the "uppity niggers" came from Governor William Gannaway Brownlow, Reconstruction governor of

Tennessee. Brownlow had been an antislavery politician before the War, but his antislavery had been a function of his failure to become a slaveowner. He was no advocate of black rights. After the war, he envisioned an integrated society. He believed that interracial association had been one of the better features of the slave system, and could be continued in free society; only "good Negroes," however, should be integrated; "bad" ones should migrate to the segregated North.

Brownlow's position became popular among many white southerners since it fitted their racial assumptions. They believed that the American Blacks were more advanced than the African, that slavery had begun to civilize them. But the process was not yet considered complete. Blacks in the American South, they said, failed to improve their land but roamed around, hunting and fishing and engaging in emotional outbursts in taverns on Saturday nights and churches on Sunday mornings. With proper white supervision, Blacks could be restrained from such behavior. These white southerners believed that Blacks would accept the relationship of inferior to superior since they were docile, humble, obedient, and trustful by nature. Those who were not would be killed. The "Brownlow tradition" provided a psychic reward for southern "nervous Americans" who never possessed enough wealth, power, or popularity, who displaced their frustration by characterizing Blacks as inferior, but who also interacted with Blacks with a certain amount of pleasure and rationalized the interaction with the excuse that they were improving the black race.

While Brownlow lost the governorship of Tennessee in 1869, others propagated his ideas; among them was Henry Watterson, who had become editor of the *Louisville Journal* in 1868. Watterson seemed liberal on racial matters, urging the repeal of a Kentucky law prohibiting black testimony in state courts, attacking the Ku Klux Klan, and supporting the Fifteenth Amendment. Watterson supported these measures, however, in the belief that limited state action in racial matters would prevent massive federal intervention. This position was shared, to a greater or lesser degree, by other spokesmen of the "New South." Following Brownlow, these spokesmen urged a differential segregation where bad Negroes would be segregated but good ones would not.

A typical "New South" spokesman for differential segregation was the Reverend Atticus G. Haygood, President of Emory University from 1875 to 1884, who was an agent of the Slater Fund, begun by John Fox Slater, a northern industrialist, in 1882 to provide funds for industrial education of the freed slave. Haygood said that he was glad slavery had been abolished, although the slaves had benefited from the system which had given them the English language, republican institutions, habits of industry, and Christ. According to Haygood, the black race was naturally submissive, humble, and trustworthy and had misbehaved during Reconstruction because of outside agitators. Now, he said, Blacks were in trouble and the southern white leader could only offer them moral guidance and education; to do more would run the risk of appearing to restore the plantation. This meant that the major responsibilities for the lack of black progress were placed on the black race itself.

The southern solution of differential segregation had many problems, the major one of which was that segregation of the "bad Negro" removed him from both the direct control and close contact with Whites. If the black race benefited only from close contact with the white, what happened to those who had no opportunity for such experience? The fear of the bad Negro grew because of the growing physical isolation of Black and White. This fear coincided in the 1880's with the fear of the diseased Negro. Pasteur's bacterial theory of disease, which connected disease to filth, had become widely accepted by this time. Since the Black was poor and had inadequate sanitary facilities, southern Whites claimed that the Negro was a carrier of diseases and defended segregation as a physical necessity for white safety. In 1889, a South Carolina rice planter and physician, Dr. James R. Sparks, said that his practice revealed that the black man was peculiarly susceptible to contagious diseases, including those affecting the lungs, and venereal diseases. He argued that the prevention of tuberculosis and venereal diseases in Whites involved isolation from Blacks.

The discovery of both bacteria and the extent of contagious diseases also led to the myth that the Black had not suffered venereal diseases during slavery. Freedom had meant greater sexual promiscuity, a promiscuity which threatened Whites as well as Blacks. To counter this presumed threat, southerners launched a campaign for separate water fountains and toilet facilities. Thus, despite the fear of the consequences of losing contact with Blacks, the differential segregation proposed in the 1860's gave way to a complete segregation of the 1890's.

Complete segregation was not accomplished easily nor without fear for the future. In 1901, George T. Winston's "The Relations of

Whites to Negroes," an article in *America's Race Problems: Addresses at the Annual Meeting of the American Academy of Political and Social Science,* typified this fear. Winston claimed that the lessening Black-White contact caused by segregation had had pernicious effects; that Blacks were reverting to idleness, ignorance, and might eventually become extinct; and that black men had raped more white women in the last 20 years than during two centuries of slavery. The future of the South looked grim to Winston; white men were resorting to violence to restrain the "uppity Negro," who had supposedly degenerated since the removal of the social control of slavery and the white example of civilization. For southerners like Winston, the older idea of degeneracy had not been replaced by the new Darwinian notion of evolutionary progress, at least as far as Blacks were concerned.

II

In the scientific community, two trends in the 1890's modified the idea of evolutionary progress. These were an increased emphasis upon the effect of natural zoological provinces, an idea taken from Agassiz, and a continued use of Lamarckian ideas of the inheritance of acquired characteristics. Both were used to predict the future of the black man in America and were encouraged by the 1893 publication of Charles H. Pearson's book, *National Life and Character.* The Englishman Pearson succeeded in convincing many Americans of the validity of his thesis, which was that races had natural climatic zones. Black men could not survive and advance in temperate climates but conversely, white men could not survive and advance in tropical ones. Pearson debunked the idea that the higher races were triumphing over the lower, saying that that idea was based on deceptive experiences with the Indians in the United States and with the Maoris in Australia. According to Pearson, the Indians and the Maoris disappeared because they were originally few in number and because they were too primitive to resist white social influences (not racial influences). However, Pearson argued that this was not true of the colored races of his day; they had both a large population and a strong cultural base and thus were socially capable of resisting white society. Pearson went on to point out that the Chinese and Hindus were spreading in Asia and elsewhere, while the European was failing in the tropics. Thus, at the high tide of

British imperialism, Pearson cast doubt on the possibility of holding the Empire.

The future was obvious to Pearson: the Indian would reclaim Central and South America; the Chinese and Hindu would reclaim Asia; and the Black would reclaim Africa and the American South. Pearson believed that the higher black reproduction rate indicated by the census of 1880, would result in a black majority in the South; Whites would leave the area because they could not stand black rule, (Pearson accepted the population projection of an American statistician, Edward Gilliam, who predicted a population of 17,400,000 Blacks and 9,390,000 Whites in the South by 1920.) To prevent a black South, Pearson advocated the colonization of Blacks in Central Africa. But he acknowledged that such a policy was unlikely for three reasons: a lack of White interest in the American North and West in colonization, a foolish belief that the Black was an indispensable economic necessity, and a conviction that transporting 8,000,000 people across the Atlantic was impossible. Because of the failure to deport the Black, Pearson predicted that Americans would soon conclude that their continent was full and would stop European immigration, thus preventing the expansion of white Europeans into climatic areas suited to them.

Benjamin Kidd, another Englishman and a social Darwinist, echoed the theme of climatic zones in *Social Evolution* (1894) and *The Control of the Tropics* (1898). He said that while both the United States and England needed tropical areas for trade, white men could never be acclimatized to the tropics. Further, he believed that the natives of the tropics were at a lower stage of social development, which meant that they could survive on less money than Whites. Thus white men could not compete economically or physically. Kidd offered no short-range solution to the dilemma; in the long-run, he believed, Caucasians should elevate native races to the social level of Anglo-Americans and should cultivate their friendship. Thus, the necessary raw materials could be had without necessitating white settlements in tropical areas.

The questions of climatic adaption and differential reproduction rates had concerned white Americans ever since their first census. The census of 1880 proved quite alarming to Whites because it showed a significant increase in the black population.

As we have seen, one of those persons concerned was Hoffman, who believed that few pure African types remained in the United States, that the American Negro was a mixture of Black and

White. Hoffman maintained that the highest proportion of racial. mixing resulted from black concubinage to white men in cities. The resulting offspring he believed to be physically inferior to both Black and White but intellectually superior to Blacks, an assumption Hoffman derived from Nott. As proof of mulatto inferiority, Hoffman cited a study of a group of ex-slaves who had been imported from Dahomey, Africa in 1859 to Mobile, Alabama, and who had intermarried with Whites. The descendents of these individuals were found to be less healthy than their parents. Hoffman correlated the supposed intellectual superiority of the mulatto with brain size; he borrowed Civil War data from Dr. Stanford Hunt's "The Negro as a Soldier," which compared brain weights of various racial crosses (Table 7.4).

TABLE 7.4

Racial Cross	Weight in Grams
White	1424
3/4 white	1390
1/2 white	1334
1/4 white	1319
1/8 white	1308
1/16 white	1230
Negro	1331

Hoffman failed to explain why Hunt's data contradicted his assumption, why the full-blooded Black possessed a heavier brain than any of the crosses where black blood was supposed to predominate. Nor did he question the facile assumption, inherited from the phrenologists, that brain size and mental capacity were correlated. In the end, Hoffman concluded that racial interbreeding, which hurt both races involved, was on the decrease. For proof, Hoffman cited evidence from Lord Bryce's *The American Commonwealth* and Philip A. Bruce's *The Plantation Negro as Freeman,* both of which claimed that there was less illicit interracial sex in the South after slavery than during it, and statistics from northern states—which permitted interracial marriages—that showed decreases in the number of legal unions. Hoffman did not believe that the Black would or should be amalgamated into the white race.

Hoffman foresaw the gradual extinction of the Black in the United States. His conclusion was derived from the physical inferiority he supposedly found and from worsening social and economic conditions as shown by statistics on increased crime, pauperism, and illegitimacy in the black population. He admitted that the high black crime rate might reflect merely the higher apprehension rate of black criminals than white (he blamed this not on the biased law enforcement but on black inability to conceal crimes). Hoffman manipulated statistics to deny the worth of the Black as an agricultural laborer. Using Bruce's study of plantation labor, Hoffman showed that in tobacco, rice, and cotton areas where black population was concentrated, the value of harvested crops was the least. Black labor in the city had proved unreliable, according to Hoffman. Hoffman tried to suggest that the elimination of the Black would not harm southern society. He concluded that unless the Blacks learned to be moral and improved their physical constitutions, or became thrifty and hard working and bettered their social and economic conditions, they would vanish. He also concluded that the Indians, who had supposedly been physically superior to the Blacks originally were dying, killed by whiskey and immorality. According to Hoffman, the lower races, relentlessly pressed by higher ones, had to become self-reliant and chaste to survive. Thus did Hoffman incorporate Morgan's view that social evolution necessitated a change in moral behavior.

Despite Hoffman's spurious correlations and obvious biases, his seeming scientism, his protestations of neutrality, and his German origin convinced many of his veracity. Other scientists used both the data of Hoffman and his thesis that the Black had reverted to a primitive stage of slave behavior. Among these scientists were Paul B. Barringer, a professor of medicine and chairman of the faculty at the University of Virginia; and Joseph A. Tillinghast who, in a book entitled *The Negro in Africa and America* (1902), asserted that the Black was becoming less morally and less physically fit.

Hoffman believed in polygenesis, following the lead of nineteenth-century comparative anthropologists. However, his polygenesis was different from the usual nineteenth-century version that had as an underlying principle the belief that races were created for specific environments and were unable to survive in others. Most other advocates of polygenesis denied Hoffman's belief in the possibility of acclimatization; among those holding this position was William Z. Ripley. Although Ripley was not a physical anthropologist —he had studied economics and ethnology and had taught political economy at M.I.T. and Harvard—the one book that won him academic fame was a summary of the findings of European physical anthropology from 1860 to 1895, *Races of Europe: A Sociological Study* (1900). Ripley, like Gliddon, used the term types for races; he provided statistical evidence of racial differences through maps of trait frequencies and frequency distribution curves. Ripley claimed that there were only three original races, that the formation of race had occurred in the past and was complete, and that races had natural habitats for which they were best suited. He denied that race, language, and culture were connected.

It was still possible to be both a monogenesist and a racist, and to argue that acclimatization of races was impossible. Such was the position of Daniel Garrison Brinton in the 1890's. In his *Races and People* (1890), a compilation of lectures given at the Academy of Natural Sciences, Brinton asserted that racial traits outweighed other variables—such as family character, sex, and individuality—in predicting behavior and were the cornerstone of the science of ethnography. Brinton accepted the thesis that skull shape could be altered by external circumstance, quoting Darwin's contention in *The Descent of Man* that rabbit's skulls changed shape when the rabbits were trained; but he also believed that the Black had less mental ability than the White because of a smaller head. Brinton accepted Peter Camper's idea that facial angle varied directly with intelligence. Brinton also supported the idea of prognathous races, an idea based on a revision of Camper by John Beddoe. Beddoe, an Englishman, devised an index of Nigrescence, which appeared in *The Races of Britain* in 1885. Basically, the index of Nigrescence included color of skin, hair, and eyes and prognathism—the extent to which the jaw protruded beyond the upper part of the face. Beddoe used his index to prove that the Irish and the Africans were related to the anthropoid apes. The index became popular in Victorian times, and stereotyped Irishmen and Negroes appeared in cartoons and newspapers with sloping faces. (The caricature still persists in comic books of today.) Brinton also stressed other anatomical differences among races—differences in arm length, pelvic index, and teeth—which led him to conclude that Blacks were in a lower stage of physical development than Whites. He attributed Blacks' color to elements of carbon in the mucous membranes, muscles, and the grey substances of the brain; this was supposedly the residue from carbon dioxide left in Blacks because of their smaller lungs. Brinton believed that the physical traits and vital powers of each race were best fitted to particular climates and, unlike Hoffman, that the white race had inferior viability in the tropics.

According to Brinton, man originally evolved from a single anthropoid ape, and his original home was in Europe, where fossil remains of apes had been found. (Brinton incorrectly said that no fossil apes had been found in Africa.) At the same time, Brinton believed that while humans were affected by natural selection, the major changes in man occurred by means of conscious, sexual selection. Individuals varied because of the effects of climate, migration, and atavisms—reversions to remote ancestral traits; specific variations attracted other persons who were looking for mates. This sexual selection supposedly resulted in races whose traits became fixed. Brinton dated the process of changing into fixed races from the years 100,000 to 20,000 B.C.; he cited, as proof of his dating scheme, the fact that racial differences could be found 6,000 years ago in Egyptian representations. (Brinton here used data from the American school of ethnology.) Once races had developed traits that suited them to particular climates, according to Brinton, the process ended and no new races could emerge.

Brinton believed in white racial superiority. Believing that Morgan's evolutionary scheme was too simple, Brinton proposed one of his own. He argued that all races had culture; all possessed social instincts—sexual impulses, parental affection, and fraternal affection—as well as language, religion, and art. He believed the white race to have a more advanced social organization than the other races and to have progressed from a simple political form to more complex ones, from family to gens to totem to tribe to nation. The Black in Africa demonstrated intellectual inferiority, Brinton claimed, by his failure to conquer other lands, to domesticate animals, to develop food plants, to build with stone, achieve democratic government, and to have monogamous marriage. In America, the Black supposedly kept pace with the White up to age 13 or 14 years and then fell behind. Brinton maintained that Blacks could not compete physically with Whites; that north of 40° N latitude Blacks could not flourish. He also claimed that mulattoes were less fertile than pure races (he based his claim on infant mortality rates rather than on birth rates). While he thought that mulattoes possessed more intelligence than Blacks, he also believed that they probably were not as physically stable as Whites, judging from White-Polynesian mixtures that had died out in the third generation. Could the lower races be civilized? Brinton believed that none had, although he blamed the methods used by European nations for this. These methods eliminated native religions that should have been tolerated and neglected secular improvements that should have been made. Were the lower races dying out? Brinton claimed that the Indians were, but he was unsure about the Blacks as the census indicated otherwise.

In later books, *An Ethnologist's View of History* (1896) and *The Factors of Heredity and Environment in Man* (1898), Brinton denied that evolution was teleological, leading toward some predetermined end, or that there was continuity in history. He explained human change in terms of secular history, without recourse to a Providential explanation. Nor did he consider the past a product solely of human response to environmental stimuli: any history which left out the effect of conscious intelligence was wrong. Brinton trod the middle ground between two anthropological traditions —the American, English, and Russian environmental tradition and the French and German tradition that was hereditarian and racial. The extreme racial positions of the latter tradition claimed that only the Aryan with a dolichocephalic skull (a long, oval skull) and fair complexion could survive the stress and strain of city life; the extreme environmental tradition said that a colony of Germans placed in Australia and subject to the same conditions as the aborigines would become as black and degraded within three generations. Brinton compromised, saying that there were both zoological provinces (agreeing with Agassiz) and racial traits. His zoological provinces supposedly created racial traits, which then became fixed and could not be changed environmentally.

The best scientific opinions, proffered by statisticians like Hoffman and anthropologists like Brinton and Morgan, confirmed popular opinion about racial inferiority. Differences over origins, over the possibility of progress, and over definitions of various levels of civilization did not obscure the basic agreement that the Black was inferior to the White physically, mentally, and morally. Racism was full-blown.

III

Black resistance to scientific and popular racism in the late nineteenth century took at least three forms. One form accepted the division (made by Whites) of Blacks into good and bad on the basis of social development; a second still clung to the legend of

Noah and used historical evidence to deny that Blacks were on the level of savagery; and a third used the concept of the bad Negro to deny the primacy of white social values.

An advocate of the first position was Martin R. Delany. Delany, who had supported colonization prior to the Civil War, served during the war as a major in the 104th United States Colored Troops Regiment, attaining the highest rank of any black person in the Union Army. During Reconstruction Delany worked in the Freedman's Bureau and as customs house inspector in Charleston, South Carolina. He supported the white redeemer Wade Hampton in 1876 when Hampton successfully won South Carolina back from Radical Reconstruction. Delany's was a surprising position for a black leader, although not a unique one, and he was rewarded for it by an appointment as a trial justice in Charleston. He continued to promote colonization and participated in the unsuccessful Liberian Exodus Association project of 1878. Delany was no believer in social equality nor was he a friend of carpetbaggers and Reconstructionists, whom he regarded as mendacious. His southern experiences convinced him that white people would not tolerate black government; the only alternative he could envision was white, bourbon paternalism rule by the "better," richer white classes in the South. His *Principles of Ethnology: The Origin of Races and Color, with an Archeological Compendium of Ethiopian and Egyptian Civilization* (1879) supported a polygenetic explanation of racial differences, said that there were three original races, and told Americans not to confuse the native African with the debased American Black. The African race was described by Delany as noble and fully equal to the Anglo-Saxon race. Delany agreed with Hoffman that the reason for the debasement of the American Black was miscegenation. His opposition to miscegenation and his belief in black superiority to the mulatto can be found in *Blake, or the Huts of America* (1859), where the black field hands—rather than the mulatto house servants in earlier works—were the heroes. Delany also blamed environmental conditions for the low estate of the American Black; he placed part of the blame on drinking (and advocated temperance), part on a lack of self-reliance (and opposed the transferring of white planter's land to Blacks); and part on the lack of black pride in race (and therefore wore a dashiki in America). This contradictory man, often called the father of black nationalism, had a curious mixture of white middle-class ideas and black pride, a mixture illustrated by his feeling deep offense at the sight of bare-breasted African women while still maintaining his great faith in African accomplishments.

Another colonizer, Bishop Henry M. Turner, had views that contradicted Delany's on many points but that arrived at the same conclusions. Turner, like Delany, came from the South and was a free Negro. He served in the Civil War as a chaplain and achieved recognition as a Bishop in the African Methodist Episcopal church in 1880. Turner became lifetime honorary vice-president of the American Colonization Society in 1876.

Unlike Delany, Turner believed in racial equality and interracial marriage. However, he realized the latter policy to be impractical and he did not publicly advocate it. Since he felt that the miscegenation escape hatch was closed to Blacks and since he felt that increased segregation would lead to war and anarchy, he advocated that Blacks return to Africa. Echoing the romantic racialism of the pre–Civil War abolitionists, Bishop Turner said that God had permitted the Whites to enslave the Blacks in order to test the Blacks' patience as well as to provide for civilizing and Christianizing Africa. Turner did not desire that all Blacks return to Africa; in the first place, he believed that Africa could only assimilate a total of two or three million people in all at the rate of five or ten thousand per year. In the second place, he felt that two-thirds of the American Blacks were not "good enough" to return, being descendants of the supposedly weak Congo people who had been slaves even in Africa. (Turner excepted himself from this group, claiming noble ancestry.) Although Turner believed in fundamental black and white equality, he did not believe that all Blacks were equal. He called his northern opponents "northern coons" and his southern ones "scullion coons." He is even quoted by Claude H. Nolen, in *The Negro's Image in the South* (1895), as suggesting enslaving Africans for their own benefit:

Millions and millions of Africans, who are now running around in a state of nudity, fighting, necromancing, masquerading, and doing everything that God disapproves of, would be working and benefiting the world.

He was equally scornful of middle-class American Blacks who did "nothing day or night but cry: Glory, honor, dominion, and greatness to White," and he berated all Blacks in America for their lack of self-respect due to their religious indoctrination. According to Edwin S. Redkey, a noted authority on the Bishop, in "Bishop Turner's African Dream," *Journal of American History* (1967), Turner said:

God is a Negro: Even the heathens in Africa believe they were "created in God's image." But American Negroes believe they resemble the devil and hence the contempt they have for themselves and each other.

Turner combined an American, middle-class belief in self-respect gained through achievement with a belief in Black-White equality and Christianity. He eventually lost faith in America altogether; in 1906, in Macon, Georgia, he said, "hell is an improvement over the United States where the Negro is involved."

William Wells Brown continued to write after the Civil War and believe in the older paradigm of monogenesis. In 1874, he published *The Rising Son*, which was an updated version of his *The Black Man* (1863), including additional material on African history and the institution of slavery. Brown's basic contention was still that humans came from one original pair, that this pair was black, and that racial differences were environmentally produced by climate and social conditions. He also claimed that African civilizations had been the original ones and had served as the basis for Western civilization.

Brown also wrote about the current problems of the day. His last book, *My Southern Home: Or, the South and Its People* (1880) was based on his observations during a trip to the South between 1879 and 1880. Brown devoted the major part of the book to slavery and admitted that the institution had had a benevolent side, although he still called it evil. He was no longer as optimistic about the future of the Blacks in America; he thought that the indolence and the extravagances in dress and manners learned in slavery persisted. Brown admonished Blacks to work harder, to organize, and to educate themselves; he also enjoined them to emigrate to the North if not treated well in the South. Brown combined a belief in monogenesis and original equality with middle-class disapproval of a failure in self-improvement.

Brown's successor as the leading American black historian, George Washington Williams, held similar views. Williams was born in Bedford Springs, Pennsylvania. He became a Baptist minister after graduating from Howard University and Newton Theological Seminary and after serving in the Civil War. (Williams, though underage for the army, had lied and was enlisted.) He became a lawyer and was elected to the Ohio legislature, as well as to the office of Judge Advocate of the Grand Army of the Republic. Williams worked in his spare time on a book entitled *A History of the Negro Race in America from 1619 to 1880* (1883). In this book, Williams relied upon the eighteenth-century orthodoxy of monogenesis and degeneracy, accepting the truth of the book of Genesis, opposing the idea that blackness was the result of Noah's curse on the sons of Ham, and denying that the black race was a distinct species. Williams believed that the Creator had given all nations arts and sciences, but that some, like the Africans, had turned to false gods and had lost their early civilizations. According to Williams, Africa's brightest day had been when she was an infant.

Now, the Negro is the lowest strata in Africa, his blood infected with the poison of his low habitation, his body shrouded by diseases, his nature abandoned to sensuality, and his soul strangled at birth.

Williams's effort gained him considerable fame as a writer and almost won him a diplomatic post as American minister to Haiti.

Three other, lesser known works by black historians also echoed the themes of monogenesis and degeneracy. William T. Alexander's *History of the Colored Race in America* (1888) claimed that Atlantis was the cradle of all civilization and that Blacks had controlled Atlantis. Edward A. Johnson's *A Short History of the Negro Race in America* (1891) concentrated upon the idea of Noah's curse and debated the accepted interpretations of it. In the first place, Johnson said, Noah was drunk, which negated the curse. In the second, Ham fathered the Canaanites, the Cushites, Babylonians, and Egyptians; if he were cursed, then the white race, which traced its history back to these civilizations, should also be cursed. Rufus L. Perry's *The Cushite, or the Descendants of Ham* (1893) argued that Blacks were morally superior to whites, while accepting the idea that Blacks originated from Ham.

The black historians of the time refused the evolutionary paradigm and relied upon an older biblical explanation of racial differences based upon the effects of environment and sin. Degeneracy rather than progress was the key to their history; they believed that mankind was equal at his physical beginning. Africa began well and ended badly, these scholars said, but could rise again.

The leading black spokesman of the day agreed with his colleagues on the necessary goal of equality in American society but disagreed about means. Frederick Douglass continued to lead the black community after the Civil War, demanding civil rights, political rights, and equality before the law and advocating agitation, political action, morality, thrift, self-help, and racial cooperation. As he grew older, Douglass became less convinced of the effectiveness of self-help and more suspicious of segregation in the South. He moved toward supporting interracial assimilation instead, saying that America's racial problems were not solely black problems and that individual self-reliance could not solve them. Accommodation to segregation meant an acceptance of white attitudes that characterized Blacks as immoral, ignorant, lazy, and shiftless—a characterization that Douglass could not accept.

Douglass's anthropological views harked back to Prichard. (Douglass related in his autobiography that he once accepted a request to deliver a commencement address at Western Reserve University and chose as his topic, "Ethnology with special reference to Africa." Researching the speech in Prichard he discovered a picture which so resembled his mother that he regarded it as others regard pictures of dead relatives.) From Prichard, he took the idea that while men had originated from one pair, there had been certain climatic conditions following that creation that had helped create races. Douglass did not believe that the blacks should leave the South as they could withstand the climate there better than white men. Therefore, Douglass opposed a scheme for migration to Kansas and predicted that the people of the South would eventually recognize the worth of black labor and would seek to keep the Blacks there. Douglass also denied the idea that the Blacks would become extinct. In a speech commemorating emancipation of the West Indies in 1880, Douglass refuted ethnological speculation that the Black was going the way of the Indian. Douglass believed that the black man was in this country to stay and would finally achieve equality.

Booker T. Washington, who succeeded Douglass as the most recognized black spokesman in the United States, was less radical than Douglass. He, in fact, accepted accommodation to white laws and attitudes and pressed for the education of the Blacks. His ideas on industrial education fit into the prevailing ethos of white southerners who saw two kinds of Negroes, good and bad. These southerners insisted that the Negro could and should not be taught white man's skills or values beyond what were necessary for survival;

further education spoiled the worker and created a surplus of use-less educated black people. Industrial education solved the problem of Black and White alike; it gave the black man self-respect and taught him the habits of society and hard work. Washington empha-sized middle-class values at his industrial school for Blacks at Tuske-gee, Alabama, as much as mechanical skills. Children learned to keep clean, to have correct manners, to behave properly, and to fit into the pattern of behavior expected of the better class of Blacks. Washington believed that once this had happened, Blacks would eventually achieve the respect of Whites and would enter into full participation in American life. Blacks would not die out nor would they move to the North; they would remain in the South as valued partners of Whites, according to Washington.

While Washington spoke for most Southern Negroes as well as for many Northern ones, others denied both his emphasis on indus-trial education and his vision for America. Among these gainsayers was T. Thomas Fortune, black editor of the New York magazine *Age*. Fortune, like Douglass, believed that certain races were best suited to particular climates; in a speech to an 1895 Congress on Africa, he predicted that the white minority in Africa would even-tually be swallowed up by the black. He also believed that Amer-ica would become white as the black minority was assimilated into the white population through the agency of miscegenation. Fortune advocated the use of the word Afro-American to describe American Blacks; he believed that the word Negro failed to describe the racially mixed persons of African descent. Fortune also tried to pre-vent a social division between Black and mulatto. If the American Negro was to disappear as a racial entity, he needed the mulatto to make the process possible.

The black novelists of the time reflected Fortune's preoccupa-tion with the problem of racial mixture as well as the southern division of the Black into good and bad. According to Robert A. Bone, a leading authority on the black novel, the black novelists of the period came from the rising middle class and had all the char-acteristics of that class. They were Protestant ascetics, who de-nounced smoking, dancing, ragtime, gambling, card-playing, and drinking and praised neatness, good manners, and gentility. Their novels contained both a sense of repressed guilt over the lower-class behavior of some Blacks and a sense of duty to elevate the race. They attacked the black masses because the bad Black sup-posedly hindered the good Black. They argued that segregation failed to take into account the fact that all Blacks were not alike, that mulattoes were superior because of their white blood and their greater degree of cultural assimilation.

The best writer in this tradition was Charles W. Chesnutt. Chesnutt was born in Cleveland but was taken to North Carolina as a boy where, after being educated, he became principal of a state normal school. Tiring of that, he migrated to New York City and became a journalist, then moved back to Cleveland and became a lawyer. He began to write fiction and, in 1889, published *The Conjure Woman*. This was followed by a collection of short stories entitled *The Wife of His Youth and Other Stories* (1899), and novels such as *The House Behind the Cedars* (1900), *The Morrow of Tradition* (1901), and *The Colonel's Dream* (1905).

The House Behind the Cedars is typical of Chesnutt's work. The story involved a mulatto girl who passed for White and who met a cultivated white man who wanted to marry her. Before the ceremony, however, her past became known and the marriage was cancelled. She then dedicated her life to human service, school-teaching, and to the goal of uplifting poor, uneducated black children. Other novelists echoed the same theme.

An exception to this formula was the first novel, *Imperium of Imperio* (1899), of Sutton Griggs, who was a popular Negro minister and lecturer on racial problems. This first of five novels was both anti-mulatto and anti-White; its hero was a black man who led a secret student society in revolt and then joined a revolutionary movement whose goal was to seize Texas for the creation of an independent black nation. Griggs' last novel reversed the theme of the first completely. In *Pointing the Way* (1908), Griggs advocated racial accommodation and paternalism as Washington had, and said that the good Whites will take care of the Blacks.

In the white theater, the black man had become the comic "coon" instead of the docile slave. Negro writers used this stock figure also. The minstrel shows utilized a character called Zip Coon, who was an urban dandy. However, in the late nineteenth century, there appeared "coon songs," ragtime songs about black, watermelon-eating buffoons. An example of the latter is James Bland whose "Carry Me Back to Old Virginny" (1878), and "Oh Dem Golden Slippers" were written in the coon tradition. Sam Jack, a black burlesque performer, formed a company in New York in 1890 called "The Creole Show of New York." The cast went to California, the Chicago's World Fair of 1893, and to London, performing songs and dances. Another Black, John W. Isham, combined song, dance, and the minstrel tradition in the "The Octaroon" (1895), a play derived from Dion Boucicault's effort of the same name. Isham first introduced the cakewalk in the play and later tried to produce a show, "Oriental America," based upon excerpts from Italian operatic favorites. The first all-Black dramatic production was Bob Cole's "A Trip to Coontown" (1898). Black writers and producers were using white stereotypes to describe Blacks; they accepted the view that lower-class Blacks were silly and stupid.

There was, however, a tradition that reversed the values and taboos of white society and that not only accepted the bad Black but praised his badness. This undertone can be found in black folklore and may be disguised enough so as to be unrecognizable. Bernard Wolfe, who writes about black folklore, has discovered a reversal of white racial taboos in the Uncle Remus stories written by Joel Chandler Harris, a white journalist and editor of the *Atlanta Constitution*. Harris collected black legends and presented them in the format of stories being told by an old Black called Uncle Remus. *Uncle Remus, His Songs and Sayings* (1880), *Nights with Uncle Remus* (1883), *Uncle Remus and His Friends* (1892), and *Uncle Remus and Brer Rabbit* (1909) enjoyed tremendous success in the North and South. While Uncle Remus fit the stereotype of the coon, the docile, funny, and stupid Black, the hidden themes in his stories did not support white middle-class goals, those of achieving self-respect through work and sexual purity through chastity. Neither did they support the popular social Darwinian view that the physically strong would supplant the physically weak. The hero of the stories was Brer Rabbit, who had no use for manners and etiquette and who, though physically unprepossessing, almost always defeated his larger enemies. In addition, Brer Rabbit got the girls, all of them, and may even have married the wife of his archenemy, Brer Fox, a barely concealed case of miscegenation. If Brer Rabbit represented the black man in a hostile white society, his message for success was not that of Booker T. Washington.

A less veiled picture of the bad black man as hero can be seen in the folklore characters of Stackalee and John Henry. Stackalee was a killer, born with a caul over his face. A gypsy predicted that he would come to no good end (and she was right). He sold his soul to the Devil in order to gain power; he wore no shoes and his bare feet left tracks indistinguishable from those of horses or mules. Stackalee possessed a magic oxblood stetson, which contained his powers, and a girl friend, Stack o'Dollars, who had two diamond teeth with gold fillings and the strength and toughness to whip Stackalee. Stackalee had many adventures—sexual, alcoholic, and criminal—before he fought the Devil, who had assumed the form of Billy Lyons. In the melee, the Devil seized Stackalee's hat, but Stackalee killed him and was sent to jail.

John Henry was not as violent or as criminal as Stackalee. He was born in Tennessee and was a full-blooded Black who drove steel on the C & O railway line. He was, however, a bad man in that he was a great eater and lover, given over to sensual excesses. Unlike Stackalee, he was also a great worker and died competing with a machine at the age of 34.

Both the legends of Stackalee and John Henry memorialized black men whom whites had stigmatized as bad. Instead of accepting a white middle-class definition of what life should be, these men represented a countermodel, one which glorified blackness, sensuality, and which downgraded temperance, restraint, and chastity. This counter-model was an underground one that was not, as yet, supported publicly by black leaders but that was to emerge later in the twentieth century as a significant one.

The nineteenth century ended with the white majority believing that the black presence in America would be terminated by extinction, either through physical elimination or physical or cultural assimilation. Blacks could not compete on equal terms with Whites unless they adopted the behavior and values of that race. It was believed that the disabilities that Blacks suffered originated in racial inadequacies and deficiencies, which led to physical weakness and intellectual poverty. Only the most idealistic hoped for a society where equal rights prevailed, and where individuals could reach the highest levels to which their talents and efforts led them.

Chapter 8

The Indian's Past Remembered and Culture Enters the Scene

For the majority of white Americans, the drive for group uniformity based on white, middle-class behavior continued into the twentieth century. Nowhere was this more apparent than in Indian affairs. As Theodore Roosevelt expressed it in a patronizing letter to the Indian No Shirt (quoted by Roger Daniels in *Politics of Protest* [1962]):

The earth is occupied by the white people and the red people . . . If the red people would prosper, they must follow the mode of life which has made the white people so strong, and that it is only right that the white people should show the red people what to do and how to live right. . . . I wish to be a father to the red people as to the white.

President Roosevelt's statement was not out of keeping with his general attitude toward the Indians. He had attacked Helen Hunt Jackson's *A Century of Dishonor* for romanticizing the Indian and had recommended, as the best books on the Indians, Colonel Richard I. Dodge's *Our Wild Indians* (1882) and J. P. Dunn's *Massacre of the Mountains* (1886), both of which had a less sympathetic view of the Indian. During Roosevelt's second administration, the Burke Act of 1906 was passed, removing the 25-year restriction on the Indian's receipt of title for land. This acted to speed up the transformation of Indian to farmer and to increase the alienation of Indian lands.

The succeeding administrations of Taft and Wilson continued the policy of converting the Indian to European-style farmer. Not until the 1920's was Indian policy examined and found wanting. The precipitating cause of this reexamination was the introduction of the Indian Omnibus Bill of 1922 by President Harding's Secretary of the Interior, Albert Fall. Fall's bill proposed to end government wardship of the Indians and to sell or distribute the remaining Indian lands. It also proposed to prohibit the practice of native religions, which would have eliminated the Native American Church—a peyote cult. While his Indian Omnibus Bill was defeated in the Senate through the efforts of Senator LaFollette, Fall had succeeded in focusing attention on Indian issues.

Public response to the Indian Omnibus Act lasted for a decade. Indian protest, led by the Pueblo Indians, presented a more united front than had ever been achieved before. There were white voices raised as well. John Collier, who became executive secretary of the American Indian Defense Association in 1923, attacked corruption in land-grabbing inci lents in Oklahoma as well as corruption in the Bureau of Indian Affairs. Collier continued his offensive through the magazine *American Indian Life*, of which he became editor in 1926. As a result of such agitation, Congress passed two measures designed to help the Indians, the Lands Board Act of 1924 and the Osage Guardianship Act of 1925, both of which attempted to prevent the further alienation of Indian land. Moreover, the need for further legislation prompted President Coolidge's Secretary of the Interior, Hubert Work, to commission the Brookings Institution to study the Indian question. The report of the Brookings Institution, *The Problem of Indian Administration* (1928), written by Lewis Meriam and associates, coincided with the Preston-Engle Irrigation Report on the use of water resources in the West. Both reports criticized the Indian land management of the federal government and showed that the forty years under the Dawes Act had impoverished the Indian. The Indians' land had dwindled from a total 138,000,000 to 48,000,000 acres through the sale by the government of so-called surplus tribal lands to white purchasers and through the sale of Indian-owned lands by the Indians themselves. In addition, the subdivision of Indian land as it was passed from father to sons, had reduced acreages below the profitability level. The Indians appeared to be becoming poorer and poorer.

President Hoover took action early in his administration to reverse the policy of assimilation, which now seemed counter-productive. He appointed two Quaker humanitarians, Charles J. Rhoads and J. Henry Scattergood, to important positions in Indian affairs. These men questioned the value of attempts to civilize and Christianize the Indians by sending their children to boarding schools and moved to deemphasize that policy. However, Rhoads and Scattergood were equally unconvinced of the value of tribal life and made no attempts toward re-tribalization.

Meanwhile, the eastern Noble Savage image in fiction was being replaced by a western degraded savage. The first significant twentieth-century western was Owen Wister's *The Virginian* (1902). Wister, a friend of Theodore Roosevelt, completed his book while living in Charleston, South Carolina; he made the code of the West a southern apology for personal violence, emphasizing the centrality of the gunfight. Like a fellow Southerner, Thomas Dixon, who portrayed the Black as a savage, Wister saw the Indians as a primitive inferior race. The hero of his Western was a white Anglo-Saxon who fought lesser breeds, Indians and Mexicans. Wister was succeeded by the master of the popular Western, Zane Grey, whose *Riders of the Purple Sage* (1912) became one of the most famous of all such stories. Another best-selling book, Harold Bell Wright's *The Winning of Barbara Worth* (1911), followed Wister's formula of an Anglo-Saxon hero wooing a pretty white girl, although the locale was California's Salton Sea and the villain was a Mexican. Wright's book sold more than two million copies and was one of the most successful books of the decade.

More serious writers also reflected the same kind of popular beliefs about the Indians and their future. Hamlin Garland wrote fiction from an Indian point of view in *The Captain of the Gray Horse Troop* (1902), but he ended with the proposition that the Indian should be civilized. The same moral appeared in his *The Book of the American Indian* (1923), a collection of short stories. Garland told of Little Big Horn from the viewpoint of Sitting Bull's partisans; he depicted the Messiah movement sympathetically; but he ended by predicting white triumph and Indian civilizing.

Other American authors showed more sympathy toward the Indian position. One such was Mary Austin, who became interested in the Indians of the Southwest and who portrayed their ways of life in an understanding way in the novel, *The Land of Little Rain*

(1903), and in the play, *The Arrow Maker* (1911). A more famous interpreter of the Indians was John G. Neihardt, who worked in Nebraska as an assistant in the office of an Indian trader. He later served as the director of information of the Office of Indian Affairs. Neihardt's fame, however, rests on his literary efforts; he began by writing short stories with a western theme that appeared in a volume called *The Lonesome Trail* (1907). The descriptions of the Indians in these stories neither romanticized nor attacked the red man's style of life. Neiharat next turned to poetry to write an epic of the West. His epic, *Cycle of the West,* consisted of five narrative poems which were published over a span of years. These five were *The Song of Hugh Glass* (1915), *The Song of Three Friends* (1919), *The Song of the Indian Wars* (1925), *The Song of the Messiah* (1935), and *The Song of Jeb Smith* (1941).

The *Cycle of the West* traced racial conflict in the fur-trading trans-Mississippi West from the early nineteenth century to the end of the Indian wars. In *The Song of Three Friends,* and in *The Song of Hugh Glass,* Niehardt depicted conflicts among white men in the West. The longest and most important poem in the cycle was *The Song of the Indian Wars,* which, with *The Song of the Messiah,* recounted the story of the White/Indian conflict on the western plains. An Indian, Crazy Horse, was the hero of *The Song of the Indian Wars,* but the Indians lost the inevitable clash between the Indians and the white men because of the single-minded intent of the Whites to dispossess them. *The Song of the Messiah* described various Indian religions with sympathy. Neihardt failed to achieve critical acclaim outside of Nebraska—where he became poet laureate—and outside of the late night television shows in the early 1970's.

Another view of Indian life, this time a nostalgic one, came from the pen of Charles A. Eastman, whose Indian name was Ohiyesa. Eastman was born in Minnesota of Sioux parents and lived as an Indian in the upper Missouri River territory until he was fifteen, at which time his father put him in school. Eastman proved to be an excellent student, graduating from Dartmouth College in 1887, and from Boston University School of Medicine in 1890. He served as a physician at the Sioux Pine Ridge Agency, as a representative for Indian work of the Y.M.C.A., and as an attorney for the Santee Sioux. Eastman wrote a number of books, including *Indian Boyhood* (1902), *Old Indian Days* (1907), and his most famous, *The Soul of the Indian* (1911). In these books, Eastman asserted that the primitive Indian days were over and that civilization and Christianity were to be the Indian's future. He advised other Indians to follow his example in becoming competent in white men's ways.

More revealing of the problems of Indian life was *Crashing Thunder: The Autobiography of an American Indian* (1926), written by the anthropologist Paul Radin, who had gone to study the Winnebago Indians in 1909. The Indians, who lived twenty-five miles south of Sioux City, Iowa, were impervious to white ways; the Presbyterian mission in the area had converted one family in 17 years. Radin obtained informants from one family, the Blow Snakes. Although Radin became quite close to the two Winnebago informants, he grew to be dissatisfied with the standard anthropological technique of asking questions of informants since he felt that informants told him only what he wanted to hear. Radin decided to change his methods and to permit one of the informants, Crashing Thunder, to tell his story in his own way. The result was the autobiography of Crashing Thunder.

In his introduction, Radin made several claims about his book. It was, he said, the first account ever obtained from a so-called "primitive" man. It supposedly showed a man who was absolutely honest, who never confused reputation with reality, who never apologized for his behavior, who interpreted dreams like a Jungian, who never dramatized his life interest, who never asked questions of good and bad, but who always searched for religious experience. In the book, Crashing Thunder began life with great expectations; his uncle had told his mother that her child would not be ordinary. Despite this prophecy, Crashing Thunder failed to experience a vision, a crucial stage in the development of an Indian into a man. He consulted his brother-in-law, Thunder Cloud, who belonged to the Medicine Dance society, but to no avail.

Radin described Indian tribal lore as Crashing Thunder learned it from his father. The way of an Indian man was simple, according to Crashing Thunder's father; it consisted of fasting—to inspire beneficial visions—of being blessed by the war chiefs (spirits), of leading men, of giving to the needy, of dying on the warpath (instead of in a village), and of being aware while dying so as to choose a desirable form for the next life. Even if it was impossible to get the blessing of a war chief, fasting was necessary and so was getting a good wife. A wife should not be idolized nor, on the other hand, maltreated. A husband should not be jealous nor should he wrong their children.

After his grandfather died, Crashing Thunder inherited a place in the Medicine Dance. Crashing Thunder entered the Medicine Dance with high hopes of finding the religious experience he so desired, but he was again disappointed. What was worse, he discovered that the other members only pretended to be involved in their dancing, desiring only the money derived from membership and dancing fees. After the murder of his brother, he started on a downward path. He drank heavily; he learned to box; he married four wives in quick succession without bothering to divorce any; he pretended to be a holy man and tried to cure the sick; and he stole from his many women friends. In the course of his downward path, Crashing Thunder killed a deer out of season and was sent to jail. After his release, he joined a fair as a bicycle rider and cowboy; he quit and became destitute, a drunk, and a pimp; he was convicted of killing a Pottawatami for his horses; and he spent a winter in jail. Crashing Thunder seemed destined to either die an early death or to spend the rest of his life in penal institutions.

However, his luck changed after his release from jail when he found that his father and mother were members of a peyote cult, having been recently converted by the Native American church. His parents pressured Crashing Thunder to convert and he did so when he finally had a vision (of God, an eagle, a lion, and a little man in uniform). As a result, he gave up the Medicine Dance and decided to marry a good Indian woman. The autobiography ends on an upbeat note as Crashing Thunder proclaimed his reformation; he had stopped drinking, had cut his hair, had a fine wife and child, and had good future prospects.

The autobiography contained the traditional appeal of the reformed man who was saved by religion and a good woman, although in this case, the woman was Indian and the religion was peyote-oriented. This tradition goes as far back as *The Autobiography of Benjamin Franklin* and anticipates *The Autobiography of Malcolm X*.

By the 1930's, the image of the Indian was largely a reflection of earlier white assumptions. The cowboy and Indian story had fixed upon a particular stereotype of the red man, that of the wild Plains Indian who resisted white advances, but both Whites and Indians were attempting to portray Indians in ways that more nearly reflected historical complexity.

I

At the beginning of the twentieth century, the first generations of psychologists, sociologists, and anthropologists were becoming self-conscious professionals and were differentiating themselves from amateurs and from other disciplines. These new social scientists also incorporated evolutionary ideas and patterned themselves after natural scientists. Priding themselves upon their objectivity, their hard-nosed attitude toward facts, and their revulsion against sentiment and idealism, these scholars attempted to make their disciplines empirical, relying upon experiment rather than reason. However, they failed in the latter, partly because they retained certain implicit assumptions about race and partly because they continued to believe that human development showed progress.

As psychology struggled to free itself from philosophical and metaphysical foundations, much interest was focused on how evolution affected the development of the brain. G. Stanley Hall, an American psychologist who was president of Clark University, typifies this interest. Hall, who worked to develop a professional anthropology department at Clark University, derived his famous capitulation hypothesis, which applied the concept of evolution to mental development. According to this hypothesis, the mind of civilized man recapitulated the prior mental history of the human race. The child's developing mind supposedly duplicated the progressive stages of mental evolution through which the human race had gone, just as the human embryo was supposed to duplicate the various stages of physical evolution. The average mind was supposedly childlike, relying upon instinct rather than reason and responding automatically to outside stimuli. Instinct was thought to have been superior to reason at this stage because instinct worked for the preservation of the species rather than that of the individual. However, as humans evolved, the brain changed and reason supposedly replaced instinct by degrees. Civilized man was believe to have developed to the point where reason had almost complete dominance. Hall looked for support of the existence of various stages of mental evolution by searching for evidence of the primitive mind in literature and folklore, employing a comparative method not unlike that of the seventeenth-century anthropologists or that of Tylor in the nineteenth century. Although an hereditarian, believing that physical inheritance had the most profound effect on human behavior, Hall conceded that one's environment had some influence on the growth of human rationality and that education speeded the growth of reason. Thus, primitive peoples who followed the dictates of civilized Whites could advance. However, in Hall's view, this advance had to be earned by a race's own efforts; social reform and philanthropy would not help.

Hall's ideas were not particularly new; others had also argued that the mind of primitive man was different from that of civilized man. Nineteenth-century American anthropologists, such as David Brinton and John Wesley Powell, had said that races were prisoners of their mental processes. Hall's stages of mind theory, however, carried more authority because he was a psychologist and was more widely circulated because it was specifically evolutionary. It influenced men like John Dewey, the most notable educational theorist of the twentieth century. Hall provided an explanation for black and Indian behavior; the reason that members of these races acted like children was that they were in an early stage of mental development, a stage where the behavior was adaptive.

Perhaps an even more influential psychologist than Hall was William McDougall. McDougall was an Englishman who became a naturalized American and who taught at Harvard and Duke. McDougall had trained to be a doctor before becoming a psychologist and was a pioneer in the study of social and abnormal psychology; he attempted to divorce the concept of mind, which he considered metaphysical, from the physical reality of the brain. McDougall claimed that all behavior was purposive, or goal-directed, and was the product of instincts that were possessed by man and animal alike. According to McDougall, man's behavior varied little from that of other animals. Relating instinct, emotion, and observable response, McDougall advocated an experimental psychology based upon the behavior of the subject rather than on a rationalization of that behavior. In works like *Physiological Psychology* (1905) and *Social Psychology* (1908), McDougall set the theoretical framework for an instinct psychology, which reduced man from an autonomous being motivated by reason and values to a reactive being motivated by instincts and emotions over which he had little or no control.

By 1925, however, McDougall's idea of instinct was under attack. L. L. Bernard, in *Instinct, A Study of Social Psychology* (1924), summed up the objections to the theory, which had increased as psychologists had failed to find any demonstrable likeness between emotions and observable responses. Theories based on instinct fell into increasing disfavor among psychologists in the 1930's (but were resurrected by ethologists in the 1960's).

Psychological interest shifted to psychometrics, a theory of mental measurements. By 1916, a number of versions of Binet's Intelligence Quotience (I.Q.) test were being used to compare relative intelligence. Binet's I.Q. test was first devised in France in 1905 and expressed an individual's intelligence by dividing his mental age by his chronological age and multiplying the quotient by 100. Lewis M. Terman used his own Stanford version of the I.Q. test on army recruits in World War I. (W.W.I was a source of data for racial arguments just as the Civil War had been earlier.) Terman believed that I.Q. tests reflected innate ability, not environment. He believed that I.Q.'s could not be improved, that language disabilities did not limit test performances, that cultural factors affected results only to a limited extent, and that home environments were not significant. Terman also thought that mental retardation always resulted from inferior mental endowment and that schools should increase vocational training for the poorly endowed who could not pass academic courses.

The prevailing paradigm in American psychology down to the 1920's was both evolutionary and hereditarian. From Hall's primitive mind to McDougall's instincts and Terman's I.Q., the assumption was that the primitive mind was childlike, that behavior was a product of innate factors, and that the capacity for intelligence was transmitted genetically. Primitive man and inferior races supposedly relied more on instinct and less on reason than civilized man. Because of these assumptions, psychological studies reinforced racial prejudices until the end of the 1920's.

In a sister behavioral science, sociology, the picture seemed a little brighter. The first generation of professionally trained American sociologists were Darwinian in a special sense. They reacted against the conservative laissez-faire social principles of William Graham Sumner, the leading American social Darwinist. They questioned the importance of competition and advocated the use of cooperation to effect social evolution. While they denied the validity of a human struggle for existence, they believed in innate instincts and in acquired instincts—social habits that, practiced over a period of time, became subject to racial inheritance. Thus, moral behavior was believed to become a part of genetic inheritance, influencing race formation.

Such was the position of Charles Horton Cooley, a University of Michigan sociologist and President of the American Sociological Society in 1918. Cooley, in *Human Nature and the Social Order* (1902) and *Social Organization* (1909), emphasized reciprocal relationships between the individual and society and showed how each could determine the other. For example, Cooley believed that the caste system of the South had entered into the racial heritage of Blacks; if they were not originally inferior, they had been subservient so long that they had become inferior.

Franklin H. Giddings, a New England–born sociologist and evolutionist author of *Principles of Sociology* (1896) and *Democracy and Empire* (1900), placed various races on a scale derived from historical achievement. The Indians were on the bottom of his scale, next to the Tasmanians, and the Blacks were on a level just above these two more primitive races. Giddings believed that racial prejudice was instinctive and that there existed a "consciousness of kind" that had become a part of each race's inheritance. Giddings constructed graphs that purported to represent degrees of kinship feeling between various groups.

Charles Ellwood, professor of sociology at the universities of Missouri and Duke and author of *Sociology and Modern Problems* (1910), took a more extreme position on racial inheritance. This position argued that inheritance decided not only the mental potential but also the physical and moral capabilities of an individual. Ellwood claimed that a black child raised in a white family would be constitutionally unable to take on either the mental or the moral characteristics of the Caucasian race, let alone the physical ones.

E. A. Ross, who taught sociology at Stanford University and the University of Wisconsin, was an academic liberal, but he also believed in racial differences. In books like *Changing America* (1912), Ross delineated the inferiority of yellow and black people and maintained that only those races that had lived for long periods of time in great cities had developed a moral sense as part of their racial heritage. Ross believed that a moral sense was adaptive, its development was governed by natural selection, and its possession led to the institution of private property. Since only Whites qualified under this description, as shown by historical experience, they were considered the superior race.

The University of Chicago became one of the leaders in the field of sociology in the early twentieth century. Among the members of the sociology department was Robert Park, who encouraged his students to study races objectively. Several of Park's students took his advice; one such student was Edward Byron Reuter whose interest centered on the mulatto. In his book, *The Mulatto in the United States* (1918), Reuter analyzed the racial mixture of both Indians and Negroes in the United States. His findings were not particularly startling. In the Indian case, Reuter found a high percentage of mixture in areas where the Indian population was interspersed with white Americans. The Indians in these areas were more white than red; the leaders were almost always half-breeds. Reuter's study indicated that the hybrid was more vigorous than the pure blood, a conclusion contrary to that of nineteenth-century anthropologists.

By 1900, anthropologists faced dilemmas similar to other social sciences. Physical anthropologists defended polygenesis, holding that the various races had descended from original ideal types. But these anthropologists had not found an ideal type, nor had they proven that combinations of traits could be transmitted or that races were continuous through time. Some physical anthropologists had begun to define racial likeness as a similarity of a statistical combination of certain traits, but they failed to agree on which combinations most characterized a race. Until agreement could be reached or new materials or models discovered, physical anthropology was at an impasse.

In cultural anthropology, the comparative method of Tylor was maintained in the search for survivals and Morgan's theory of unilinear evolution was accepted. But both the concept of survivals and unilinear evolution contained anomalies. The theory of survivals, for example, said that ideas that were adaptive in one situation had survived only to become useless in a contemporary situation. But as Antonio Machado y Alvarez, a noted anthropological theorist, said, survivals had to be of some use to even exist and historical continuity ought to provide some justification of their persistence. In addition, the age of a survival was difficult to determine; was it recent and only seemed old or was it old and seemed recent? Further, a so-called survival usually appeared abnormal—this was usually why it was discovered—and may have been abnormal in its own time. Survivals and the comparative method were interrelated; Tylor used survivals to compare civilizations. The comparative method was based on survivals and survivals were based on the comparative method. Belief in unilinear evolution, the idea that each society moved toward civilization through certain stages of development (such as savagery to barbarism to civilization), became more and more difficult to sustain as evidence of more and more varying societies mounted. The theory of the unilinear evolution of societies had as its base the concept of cultural diffusion, which assumed that ideas and artifacts began in one place and then spread to others. This helped explain why societies were alike and why survivals in one society resembled those in another. But the theory of diffusion suffered from a paucity of evidence of a firm link between traits of any but contemporary societies.

Both physical and cultural anthropology were affected by a new paradigm, one developed in large part by the anthropologist Franz Boas and his students. Boas helped form a generation of trained academic anthropologists who attacked the connection of race with behavior, who emphasized the primacy of culture, and who denied the possibility of the comparison of cultures.

Boas was born in Westphalia, Germany, of a prosperous business family; he obtained his Ph.D. in physics at the University of Keil at the age of 23. In 1883, Boas went on an expedition to Baffinland to study Eskimos. Originally a geographical expedition to determine the influence of the climate on human behavior, the experience served instead to persuade Boas that climatic factors were unimportant. In 1886, Boas joined an expedition to British Columbia to study the Bella Coola Indians. Afterward, he visited the United States and became the assistant editor of *Science*. He decided to settle permanently in the United States because of its more liberal political climate, its lack of religious tests, and its professional opportunity. In 1888, Boas went to teach anthropology at Clark University; under his direction, Clark University produced the first Ph.D. in anthropology in the United States in 1892. Boas served as the chief assistant to the Department of Anthropology at the Chicago World's Fair and became curator of the Field Museum in the same city. Boas later returned to New York City as curator of the American Museum of Natural History and lecturer in anthropology at Columbia University.

From the start, Boas questioned the prior assumptions of other anthropologists. In 1888, his article, "On Alternating Sounds," implicitly undercut the comparative method of anthropology by explaining how observers derived linguistic similarities between Indian dialects and many European languages. According to Boas, the similarities did not lie in the languages but in the ears of the philologist, who recognized sounds only in reference to his native tongue. This linguistic thesis presaged the idea that culture imposed meaning on what an individual heard, that one could not compare cultures objectively but only in terms of one's own culture. He eventually supported historical particularism, which became anthropological orthodoxy and which denied that any theoretical synthesis could make possible the comparison of one society with another.

Boas saw no correlation between language and race. The American Blacks were African in race but European in culture, although their culture was "essentially that of the uneducated classes of people among whom they live." While the Indians were all of the same race, they had many differing languages, which were as complex as European ones. The latter fact disproved to Boas the evolutionary contention that languages, like institutions, developed from the simple to the complex.

Boas refuted the accepted anthropological axiom that the physical structure of an individual reflected racial adaptation to a particular environment and that these racial features had become permanent. In a study for the Chicago World's Fair published in 1894 in *Popular Science Monthly* as "The Half-Blood Indian," Boas showed that the offspring of Indian mothers and white fathers tended to be taller than either parent, although they had a face width nearer that of the Indian parent than the white. Both of these findings caused Boas to question prevailing hereditarian assumptions, which were based on a belief in the fixed size and shape of the skull and a theory that said that offspring of unlike parents would grow to a height between that of each parent. He began to study the rate of human growth and development and the impact of the environment in modifying individual physical inheritance.

Influenced by the theorist Edward Hahn, who had denied the theory that said that there was a succession of stages of social evolution and who emphasized the nineteenth-century idea that man was a self-domesticated animal, Boas modified his position on racial heredity to say that the significant differences between primitive and civilized persons were the differences between wild and domstic animals, caused by differences in social selection and nutrition. He believed that human physical changes were mainly caused by changes in nutrition and in the care of the body. People supposedly married people with preferred qualities (beauty, intelligence, etc.) and passed these qualities on to their offspring. Both nutrition and care supposedly affected the development of the potential inherited by the individual through the operation of social selection. Boas downgraded the idea that natural selection was a significant feature of modern life. However, he denied that the environment could cancel out hereditary factors entirely. In 1909, for example, Boas refused to support the thesis, which was a new version of an older environmental position, that the descendants of Europeans in America were approaching the physical type of the Indian because of the American environment.

Between 1908 and 1910, Boas studied a select group of immigrant children for the United States Immigration Commission; this study resembled one he had made on children's growth rates while at Clark University. From both studies, Boas discovered that the period of physical growth—whether short or long, late or early—had little effect on the final size or development of an individual. This finding refuted the assumption of racial theorists that the rapid maturation of the Negro meant mental inferiority. In his studies of immigrants' descendants, Boas found that the head shapes of children were changing toward a mean shape. The children of long-headed parents were more round-headed and vice-versa. The extent of the changes, which were statistically significant, surprised Boas and the Commission. The Immigration Commission hesitated to accept these findings as they were contrary to the prevailing racial assumptions in the Commission's report, that racial features were fixed and could no longer be affected by environment. The Commission was not alone; critics attacked Boas's results and even went so far as to insinuate that those children who had differently shaped heads than their immigrant parents were really illegitimate offspring of native white Americans. Despite this criticism, Boas had cast doubt upon the thesis of the fixity of skull shapes as well as on the correlation between cranial capacity and intelligence.

R. R. Bean made such a correlation in "Some Racial Peculiarities of the Negro Brain" published in the *American Journal of Anatomy* (1906). Bean was an anatomist who said that Negro brains were depressed in the frontal areas and bulging in the posterior ones. Bean made a study of the 152 brains collected by the Johns Hopkins Hospital and claimed that the differences in form signaled differences in the mental abilities of different races. Boas disposed of Bean's study with the statement that there was no correlation among the shape of the skull, the size of the brain, and intelligence. For proof that the size of the brain had no effect upon intelligence, Boas quoted the studies of Karl Pearson, who showed that famous intellects had had brains of various sizes and that while women had smaller brains than men, women were not inferior in intelligence.

Boas's position on race and culture was summarized in the preface to the 1938 edition of his first book, *The Mind of Primitive Man.*

There is no fundamental difference in the ways of thinking of primitive and civilized man. A close connection between race and personality has never been established. The concept of racial type as commonly used even in scientific literature is misleading and requires a logical, as well as a biological definition.

Boas reacted against the claims of psychological and anatomical inferiority of the primitive and the Negro; he attributed group differences to differences in culture. In so doing, he changed Tylor's definition of culture, removing its implicit evolutionary assumptions. Tylor had defined culture as civilization; he had believed that all people possessed culture to some degree but that higher societies had more. Thus, according to Tylor, there were no separate cultures; there was only one culture manifest to greater or lesser degrees in different societies. Boas, however, distinguished between civilization and culture and said that all groups had cultures and that each culture was unique, a product of neither innate faculties nor racial abilities but of historical events.

Boas extended the definition of culture, insisting on the plurality of cultures, on cultural relativity (the necessity not to derive any absolute standard to judge cultures), on the integrative nature of cultures, and on their behavioral determinism (that cultures dictate and determine proper standards of behavior). He admitted that there seemed to be some cultural universals—certain ideas, metaphysical notions, laws, and customs—but argued that these were few in number and could be explained first by the fact that human minds were everywhere basically the same and second by cultural diffusion—the borrowing of traits from nearby societies. Boas offered no theory as to why similar minds did not lead to common development. He did admit the existence of technological evolution in such areas as inventions and improved agricultural methods but denied that any scheme of social development paralleled that of technological development. He also accepted the idea of human biological development, but beyond these two areas—technology and biology—Boas would not go.

Thus Boas mounted a strong attack on white European notions of cultural superiority. He maintained that white standards were used to judge other peoples, that civilization was not a product of any single group, and that the reasons for the seeming superiority of white cultures were both accidental and historical. One of the reasons Boas gave for their seeming superiority was that all members of the white race participated in civilization while few members of other races participated. Why did white Europeans seem to dominate in their cultural contacts with other peoples in the past? Boas said part of the answer was chance; the Spanish, for example, had been seen as a fulfillment of Indian religious beliefs. Another part of the answer was physical; the introduction of new diseases had decimated native populations.

To questions regarding the natural ability of the American Indians to inhibit impulse, to pay attention, and to think originally, Boas answered that their ability was equal to that of Whites. For support, he relied on historical evidence of Indian endurance under torture, on logical analysis that showed how trifling and boring were the questions of the anthropologist (to answer the anthropologist's complaint that the Indian did not pay attention to him), and on an aesthetic judgment of the Indian ghost dances.

In 1917, in an article entitled "Modern Populations of America," Boas described the social position of mixed-blood Indians in the United States and projected their future. He thought that pure-blood Indian men would disappear because of intermarriage and that pure-blood Indian women already had. He denied that racially mixed Indians were physically and mentally inferior to their parents and said that any variance in intelligence could easily be explained by differences in environment. Boas did not see any deterioration in this American population.

Boas attacked the prevailing ideas of both physical and cultural anthropology without replacing these ideas with a well-thought-out paradigm of his own. In particular, he attacked Spencerian social evolution, which contained three major tenets—biological reductionism (that all behavior can be explained in terms of instinct), the belief that parallel evolution was a better explanation of social development than divergent (all societies originate the same and evolve in different directions) or convergent evolution (all societies are different at their origin but evolve towards a common end), and the conviction that social-cultural phenomena were best explained in terms of natural processes. Spencer had presumed a biological corollary for all social phenomena. Boas, however, turned American anthropology from a study of man to a study of customs. Boas, like Tylor, insisted that the proper subject of the anthropologist was the mental life of man and that mental life was not a product of race but of culture.

However, Boas never really solved the inherent theoretical problems of his own position. While Boas was a precursor of functionalism, the belief that cultural traits can only be understood in context of the culture in which they appear, he did not clearly demonstrate why cultural traits could not be compared; while he insisted on the importance of individual variability and nonconformity, he did not explain how these traits could originate without the influence of heredity. The thrust of his anthropology was that the origins and causes of human development could not be known, that there could not be a science of history. Yet in America, the search for origins and causes had motivated and would continue to motivate the study of anthropology and history for many years.

At best, Boas's emphasis on culture and deemphasis of race ended the use of the romantic concept of racial essence, genius, or soul among serious anthropologists. His lack of interest in human taxonomy and his refusal to consider race in terms of types described by arbitrarily selected physical traits reoriented anthropological thinking away from these interests. His views on race were not based on extensive study but rather on several propositions that he took as given, that a race was a population derived from a common ancestry and that the genetic types of which races were composed had originated so long in the past that their origin was obscure. Boas rejected the idea of polygenesis that pure races existed. He thought that variations within races were greater than variations between races. His demonstration of the fertility and physical vigor of racial hybrids helped to demolish the polygenetic belief that races were species, which could not successfully interbreed. While Boas had not answered all of the questions about racial differences, he had changed the emphasis of the discipline of anthropology.

In 1918, Charles Davenport and Madison Grant formed the Galton Society of New York; the Galton Society's stated purpose was to promote the study of racial anthropology by native Americans whose views were anthropologically and politically sound, that is to say, racial determinists. The Galton Society members criticized cultural anthropologists such as Boas for displaying too much interest in the American Indian and for neglecting both the biological aspects of anthropology and the problem of the differential racial composition of the contemporary American population. The Galton Society was not alone in its views. By 1923, the National Research Council, which originally began as an organization to coordinate moneys for faculty research and for the training of graduate students, had set up a Division of Anthropology and Psychology whose mission was to encourage the study of racial groups in the American population. Boas and his students failed to receive much research money from the Division until 1926. At that time, Boas persuaded the Council to establish a Committee on the American Negro; and, in 1928, he helped initiate the Conference on Racial Differences under the joint sponsorship of the National Research and the Social Science Research councils. The National Research Council began giving fellowships to Boas's students; these fellowships subsidized a whole decade of research. Among the projects funded by the Council were Melville Herskovits's study of the American Negro, Margaret Mead's study of adolescence in Samoa, and Otto Klineberg's study of American racial differences. These studies were to complete the Boasian revolution in anthropology, and, by 1934, the Boasian paradigm had swept the field.

Chapter 9

Eugenics and Racial Soul

In the years from 1900 to 1930, white Americans lost interest in the Indians, but the continuing problems of Black-White relations did not permit such forgetfulness of the Black. The attack on racism by anthropologists had only begun and the consequences of a new Mendelian genetics had not yet fully penetrated the social sciences. Indeed, there were psychologists and sociologists who reinforced the older idea of racial inferiority at the very time the idea was being severely challenged.

The Censuses showed a continuing declining percentage of black Americans in the population of the United States (Table 9.1).

TABLE 9.1

Year	% of Blacks	Total Numbers
1900	11.6	8,830,000
1910	10.7	9,830,000
1920	9.9	10,460,000
1930	9.7	11,890,000

The black percentage of the population reached its nadir in 1930. While Whites had increased between 1900 and 1910 at a rate twice that of Blacks (a fact that confirmed racial supremacists in their belief in black physical inferiorities), as immigration to America slowed because of World War I and the restrictive legislation of the 1920's, the white rate of increase had also slackened.

The succeeding Censuses revealed other trends, which were soon to be significant. The first such trend was the beginning of a significant black migration to northern cities. By 1930, fully 10 percent of the black population had moved North; most of these migrants had migrated in the last two decades of the period. Chicago, Detroit, and New York had large black populations by 1930; New York's Harlem contained 200,000 Negroes, over twice the number to be found in any southern city. Another trend evident in the Censuses was the declining economic status of Blacks remaining in the South. In 1910, there were 220,000 black landowners, but by 1930 there were only 183,000. Another significant feature was the continued rural character of Blacks while the white population had become predominantly urban. The failure of southern Blacks to become as urban as Whites did not go unnoticed; racists argued that Blacks were incapable of adjusting to the urban experience.

Racial unrest in both North and South characterized the period. The Blacks' struggle with segregation led to boycotts of streetcars in the South and to boycotts of schools in the North. These boycotts were uniformly unsuccessful, unlike later ones, and resulted in increased tension, repression, and white violence against Blacks. Lynchings persisted, mainly in the South, on a lesser scale than in the 1890's, but urban riots became commonplace. These urban riots were not confined to the South but spread to the North. The period between 1915 and 1919 was one of the worst for urban riots with 22 major disturbances, the result of white resentment against the increasing black population. The situation appeared so serious that even level-headed observers predicted all-out racial war.

The urban riots contained elements of indiscriminate violence directed against any Black unlucky enough to encounter a white mob. This indiscriminacy ignored the earlier division of Blacks into good and bad; blanket condemnation of Blacks by Whites became more commonplace. A. J. McKelway, one of two assistant secretaries of the National Child Labor Committee, in justifying the Atlanta Riot of 1906, admitted that the white mob had attacked both reputable and disreputable Blacks but excused this action on the grounds that the black leaders had failed to control the black masses and that "the Negroes are our criminal class." The white population, according to her, was stirred by the numerous reported cases and rumors of black assaults on white women and took extreme action because of extreme provocation. Black reaction to the Atlanta riot clung to the older division of good and bad Negroes. Carrie W. Clifford, honorary president of the Ohio Federation of Colored Women's Clubs, responded to McKelway by stating that Whites did not act on their religious principles in black-white relations and that the mob and police could not distinguish between black criminals and black leaders. (Dr. J. W. E. Bowen of the Gammon Theological Seminary and President Coogman of Clark University had both suffered at the hands of the mob.) Clifford defended black leaders from charges of not controling the black masses, saying that the real reason for black unrest in Atlanta was lack of job opportunity. She denied black interest in interracial sex and said that while she was part white, her whiteness was a result of white male aggression on one of her black female ancestors.

The response to the racial riots in period before the First World War, the Progressive Era, was mixed. Ray Stannard Baker, a Progressive and a close friend of Woodrow Wilson, wrote *Following the Color Line* (1908) and exposed the race problem using the sensational journalism of the muckraking tradition. Black intellectuals, among them W. E. B. DuBois, organized the Niagara Movement in 1905; this movement, supported by white progressives like Mary White Ovington and Oswald Garrison Villard, became in 1908 the National Association for the Advancement of Colored People. The NAACP began a program of education, propaganda, and legal action to end segregation and to win equal rights. The Urban League appeared a few years later and concentrated upon the plight of the Black in the cities, particularly in the areas of housing and employment. Liberal Whites and concerned Blacks looked for a society that was best described by Walter Lippmann in his introduction to Carl Sandburg's *The Chicago Race Riot* (1919), a society where

no Negro need dream of a white heaven and of bleached angels. Pride of race will come to the Negro when a dark skin is no longer associated with poverty, ignorance, misery, terror, and insult. When this pride arises, every white man in America will be the happier for it. He will be able then, as he is not now, to enjoy the finest quality of civilized living —the fellowship of different men.

Lippmann's vision was not shared by the majority of Americans, however, nor even by a majority of northern Progressives. Southern Progressives were still racists. James K. Vardaman of Mississippi combined a liberal stance on state and national issues with a demand that no money be spent on black education in Mississippi and with virulent attacks on the Blacks. Rebecca Felton, elected in Georgia in 1922 as the first woman to serve in the United States Senate, fought for equal rights for women, prohibition, and for penal reform; but, in *My Memoirs of Georgia Politics* (1911), *Country Life in Georgia* (1919), and various speeches, she predicted the eventual extinction of Blacks, advocated their disfranchisement, and justified lynchings.

On balance, conditions seemed to grow worse rather than better for the Blacks in the period from 1900 to the first World War. Southern states continued to limit black suffrage and to increase segregation of public and private facilities. Federal leadership, rather than discouraging segregation, encouraged it. Theodore Roosevelt appeared to take a liberal position in racial matters when he invited Booker T. Washington to dinner in the White House. But this occurred early in Roosevelt's administration when he was working to gain control of the Republican party. Later he professed his sorrow at having dined with Washington and, against the wishes of the black community, upheld the dishonorable discharge of black troops accused of shooting up the town of Brownsville, Texas. Nor were succeeding Presidents any better. Taft did little to further black rights. While Wilson indicated in his campaign of 1912 that he would support black goals, after his election, he began the policy of legal segregation in federal employment. Wilson's successor, Warren G. Harding, was little better. Despite his rumored part-black ancestry, Harding denounced racial amalgamation and social equality, although maintaining that he would enforce civil rights. In a speech in Birmingham, Alabama, in October, 1921, he concluded that "racial amalgamation there cannot be." While Presidents Coolidge and Hoover were not so outspoken, neither moved to place the federal government in a position of leadership in the area of civil rights.

The Supreme Court, on the other hand, proved more liberal. In *Guinn vs. United States* (1915), the Court ruled that a "grandfather clause"—an exemption from the literacy requirement for voters who had an ancestor who had voted prior to January 1, 1866

—was unconstitutional. The suit, begun under the auspices of the NAACP, was the first to successfully question the legality of barriers to black suffrage. In 1925, the Court commenced hearing a series of cases that, although not dealing directly with Blacks, were to have profound significance for them. These cases were the first to oppose state actions that limited civil rights. The first decision, *Gitlow vs. New York* (1925), specifically stated that the First Amendment, guaranteeing freedom of speech and the press, bound states as well as the federal government. In 1931, the Court declared two state laws unconstitutional in *Stromberg vs. California* and *Near vs. Minnesota*. In the first case, the court said that a California law that prohibited the display of an anarchist flag violated free speech; in the second, the Court ruled that a Minnesota law that suppressed a libelous newspaper was an unconstitutional violation of freedom of the press. These decisions, liberal as they seemed, were written by a judicial conservative, Chief Justice Charles Evans Hughes.

The Supreme Court did not reflect public opinion. Even the churches seemed unable to crack the segregation barrier. Less than one-tenth of one percent of all black Protestants worshipped in integrated congregations; the rest were either in separate Negro denominations or in segregated congregations of white denominations. The Federal Council of Churches labored hard, but unsuccessfully, for racial justice. Southern denominational journals claimed that racial harmony existed in the South and that God's order of things gave each race a separate place. Northern white denominations, like the Presbyterians, Methodists, and Baptists, tried to break down barriers but were unable to overcome general prejudice.

The Ku Klux Klan, which was originally a secret society begun after the Civil War and advocating white supremacy, was revived in the twentieth century. The Klan's primary enemies were aliens—the immigrant Jew and Catholic. The Klan feared the falling birth rate of native Americans of Nordic stock and the loss of political control by the native Americans in the cities; it deplored "the lost sacredness of the Sabbath, chastity, and the right to teach children in our schools fundamental facts and truths." According to the Klan, Jews and Catholics lived on less than native Americans; they lacked moral standards; they bred faster; and, in the case of the Catholics, they supported a religion which dabbled in politics and whose leaders lacked American principles. The

Black presented another problem to the Klan according to Hiram Wesley Evan's "The Klan's Fight for Americanism":

The Negro, the Klan considers a special duty and problem of the white American. He is among us through no wish of his; we owe it to him and to ourselves to give him full protection and opportunity. But his limitations are evident; we will not permit him to gain sufficient power to control our civilization. Neither will we delude him with promises of social equality which we know can never be realized. The Klan looks forward to the day when the Negro problem will have been solved on some much saner basis than miscegenation, and when every state will enforce laws making any sex relations between a white and colored person a crime.

The Klan probably reflected a view not unlike that of the majority of Americans. There existed, however, a minority northern opinion that became significant and that represented the thinking of such intellectuals as Randolph Bourne and Horace Kallen. Bourne, descended from a pioneering New England family, spoke in 1916 for a transnational America, an America that would take the best of European culture in preference to the popular and vulgar elements of the culture he felt was then dominating America. Despite his cultural elitism, Bourne wanted a heterogeneous America rather than the homogenized one he saw developing and applauded cultural diversity instead of conformity. Horace Kallen, a German-born Jew, opted for cultural pluralism and considered all cultures to be equal. Kallen, a philosopher who taught at Clark University, the University of Wisconsin, and the New School for Social Research, detailed his view of a culturally diverse America in *Culture and Democracy in the United States* (1924). Kallen believed that Jews in America should retain their cultural heritage, as should other ethnic groups, and that this cultural pluralism would benefit both the groups and the country as a whole. While Bourne and Kallen wanted specifically to retain European cultural traits in the United States, their pleas for tolerance of the historical heritage of European peoples could be applied as well to the heritage and tradition of black Americans.

William McDougall, an English psychologist who became a naturalized American, wrote a number of books advocating cultural and political elitism, including *World Problems* (1924) and *The Indestructible Union: Rudiments of Political Science for the American Citizen* (1925). In the latter work, a volume in the *American*

Nationalism series, McDougall advocated a racial political attitude. McDougall declared the United States to be God's country
because of its natural bounty and because of the racial stock of the
original English settlers who had produced a population supposedly second to none in physical and moral vigor. However, said
McDougall, this population had been diluted by the immigrant
and the Black. The arrival of these "inferior" persons supposedly
coincided with an attitude change. Originally, according to Mc-
Dougall, Americans did not believe in racial equality; not until the
nineteenth century did belief in equality become a common error.
McDougall claimed, "In those days there was no science of anthropology to reveal that in the most intimate structure and composition of his tissues, or his blood and bone and brain, the Negro was
distinct and different."

America had a grim future, according to McDougall. The melting pot would not work; racial mixing resulted in a lowering of
the intellectual level of the population. Blacks by their very presence supposedly displaced white Americans who would have been
born if Blacks had not been in the United States. To remedy this
difficult situation, McDougall examined three possible alternatives
—laissez-faire, melting-pot, and segregation policies. The first policy
would eliminate all laws pertaining to Blacks; this would abolish
lynching and give Blacks equal rights. McDougall believed that
this policy would result either in the physical elimination of the
Black because of an inability to compete in the economic arena or,
more likely, in a predominantly colored population in America because of the fertility of the Black. The melting-pot solution involved intermarriage and had several virtues. It would be kind, it
was believed to be achievable (through southeastern Europeans who
had less color prejudice than northern ones and who would marry
blacks), and it was consistent with American ideals. Its disadvantages outweighed the advantages, however; there was strong opposition from the white majority and an unfortunate mongrelization
of the population would result. The third solution, segregation, was
considered best by McDougall if it could be made rigid and absolute. Legal separation of populations in the same area in the past
had not prevented racial mixture; therefore geographical segregation was the only answer; the Black should be required to live in
the southern United States, Africa, or New Guinea. In other words,
McDougall wanted a separate black nation. He suggested encouraging black and white citizens to support colonization and using

European war debt money to pay the costs. McDougall concluded his advocacy of colonization in his *The Indestructible Union* (1925) as follows:

These suggestions may seem preposterous to many minds. But the American citizen should reflect on these facts: in justice, a large part of the territory of the United States, perhaps one-tenth part, must be held to the property of the colored people: the founders of the American Nation committed a tremendous act of gross injustice in bringing the Negroes to America; an equally tremendous act of reparation has long been due, and the bill grows steadily larger. Would it not benefit a nation that boldly claims the moral leadership of the world to clean its own slate, and to wipe out the stain from its record by a great national effort which would at the same time solve finally and gloriously its most distressing problem, one that, if not boldly dealt with, many prove a lasting and increasing danger to the health and even to the very life of the nation?

His statement would not seem inappropriate to a black nationalist in the 1970's (although the ideas behind it would, of course).

In the South, the question of the destiny of Blacks in America was also under discussion. The fear of a racial war persisted; so also did the fear that the South could not survive without Blacks. The dilemma, as seen by white and black Southerners, was discussed in W. B. Parks' collection, *The Possibilities of the Negro in Symposium: A Solution of the Negro Problem Psychologically Considered, The Negro Not "A Beast"* (1904). One contributor to the collection, Charles E. Dowman, the ex-president of Emory University, believed that the black position in the South was critical because southern Whites saw Blacks in terms of increased crime rates, educational failures, divorce of religion from morality, and a menace to the safety of the white home and the sanctity of white women. In addition, the northern white businessman had supposedly become unsympathetic to Blacks because of lack of return on his investments in the South in railroads, industry, and land. If Blacks would only behave themselves, Dowman maintained, they could have a promising future in the South; they had civil liberty, education at white expense, a fair field in industry, and a monopoly on domestic service. Dowman hoped Blacks would take advantage of their opportunities because he did not want to live in a South where there were no Blacks. But he believed that if they did not take up their advantages, they would disappear.

Other contributors to the collection echoed Dowman. Three speeches of Henry W. Grady, a Georgia spokesman for the "New South," a movement to accept Reconstruction and build industry in the South, emphasized the need for racial harmony under white leadership. Grady claimed that the two races had lived in peace and harmony under slavery. As evidence, he cited the record of safety of southern white women and children on slave plantations during the Civil War when white men were away fighting (Grady failed to note the apprehensions of these women or the number of individuals who were secretly murdered). Despite the interracial peace he thought slavery brought, Grady admitted that it was a bad institution and was deservedly gone. Grady acknowledged the heavy financial burden caused by a segregated society but maintained that segregation was both necessary and desirable. Both the South and the Black were gaining economically and politically and both were satisfied according to Grady; neither wished black suffrage. Thus, given white leadership, the black race could flourish.

The ex-governor of Georgia, W. J. Norton, in a speech called "Races in Harmony: South Safe as Home," claimed that racial peace existed in the South but contradicted himself by advocating severer penalties for rape (he was unable to say what would be more severe than the existing death penalty). Norton also held that the Black was not only necessary, but desirable, in the South. He also said that he would not want to live where there were no Blacks. Richard H. Edmonds, the editor of *Manufacturer's Record*, agreed, but opted with the majority for keeping the Black in the South under white control.

According to Dr. Willis B. Parks' *A Solution of the Negro Problem Psychologically Considered*, the enslaved Black had been docile, trustworthy, and loyal, a person who loved his white master and who never raped his mistress. The ex-slave, however, supposedly corrupted by alien agitators who visited his cabin at night, demanded political rights and social equality and engaged in racial mixing. The result of intermixing was the New Negro, who was morally and physically inferior to the old one. Because of this supposed degeneration, both black men and women suffered according to Parks. Southerners refused to use live-in black women as domestics; they insisted instead on separate quarters to diminish the dangers of social contact. Parks approved of this social distance and advocated further racial separation. Since field hands, said Parks, were the rapists, they must be kept in rural isolation; vagrancy laws must be enforced, and good Blacks must expose the errant ones. Only by these measures would white women be assured of safety. Parks's analysis was merely a continuation of the Brownlow tradition; the Black had been moral under slavery but freedom had meant separation from the example of white civilization and subsequent degeneration.

Three other *Symposium* participants disagreed with the solution of intensification of white control over Blacks and argued instead for greater racial separation. John Temple Graves, a leading white spokesman for sending Blacks back to Africa, began his argument by proposing that the Civil War had been a mistake, that the North had spent 12 billion dollars and the lives of a million men to free the slaves but had succeeded only in setting two opposite, unequal, and antagonistic races side by side. The white race was proud, free, progressive, and civilized according to Graves; the black race was dependent and savage. Because of the war, women were unsafe, race prejudice was rampant, and the black population had increased from four to nine million in the South. Graves questioned the usual proposed solutions to the problem. He believed that education had failed, repeal of the Fifteenth Amendment would not help, religion would not help. Miscegenation would help, but he was opposed to it. The only realistic answer to Graves was black removal, a solution that he claimed President Roosevelt was seriously considering (because Roosevelt was sending the black editor T. Thomas Fortune to the Philippines).

Graves had answers for every objection to migration. He said that it could be financially managed; the English had spent $500,000,000 to buy out Irish landlords; the United States was twice as rich and could afford much more. Graves considered several locations—the Philippines, the desert lands west of Texas in the United States, lower California (under Mexican control), and Africa. If Blacks migrated to an area under United States sovereignty, Graves advocated that they be allowed to control this area as a territory but that they be restricted to it. Graves based his argument for migration on Carl McKinley's *An Appeal to Pharaoh*, which estimated that the black population of the United States could be removed in 40 years if 12,500 females of childbearing age were taken each year. McKinley estimated that this removal would cost only $200 per person. Graves projected an annual cost of $10,000,000 per year, or a total of $400,000,000 for the total period. Graves said that the migration could be hastened if those ships that brought European immigrants to the United States were used to take Blacks back to Africa. He said that Blacks wished to leave the South, that the South would permit them to go, that white immigrants would replace them, and that, if not removed, Blacks would become as much a concern to Whites in the North as in the South (an accurate prediction). Although Graves's position was a minority one, it was shared by others. Senators J. T. Morgan of Alabama and Mathew C. Butler of South Carolina initiated federal legislation to provide for deportation and the novelist Thomas Dixon propagandized for removal.

White southern leaders continued to cling to what George Frederickson has called accommodationist racism. This racism emphasized the docility of the Black and deemphasized the extent of racial conflict. A good example of an accommodationist was Edgar Gardner Murphy, who began his adult life an an Episcopal minister and ended as a full time secular reformer. Murphy was a southern liberal who organized the Montgomery Conference on Race Problems to improve the black position in the South in 1900. He maintained, in his *Problems of the Present South* (1904), that Blacks did not want a race war, that they should not be lynched, that they were peaceful, and that a reservoir of good will toward Whites still existed.

Other southern liberals uttered similar sentiments. Charles T. Hopkins, after the Atlanta Riot of 1906, said that the black race was a child race, that black rapists were few in number; he concluded that "social christianity" was the answer to racial problems. It was true, other liberals said, that there had been a deterioration of black morality since the Civil War, but they blamed this on social isolation from the better classes of Whites. Miscegenation was thought to continue only between predatory white men and lower-class black women. If black women became middle class, the liberals maintained, miscegenation would cease and black sexual purity would emerge. These liberals attacked peonage, reducing free Blacks to semi-free farm laborers, and unequal suffrage restrictions, as well as advocating industrial education of the type proposed by Booker T. Washington. However, they failed to convert the South because they were few in number and because they lacked power—they were clergymen and intellectuals rather than policy makers. In the South, they made racial extremism a little less respectable; but in the North, they converted opinion leaders.

The Southern conservative racial position remained a curious amalgam of pre-Darwinian science, religious orthodoxy, and evolutionary social theory, an amalgam which was both contradictory and inconsistent. Such an admixture can be found in H. A. Eastman's *The Negro* (1905). Eastman's thinking represented a compromise position, one which accepted the idea of black inferiority but rejected the supposedly scientific explanation made by Carroll in *The Negro A Beast.* Although a biblical literalist, Eastman began by asserting that Adam was a red man. His proof was curious; he claimed that the word Adam meant red in Hebrew and that, in their pure racial states, both Jews and Arabs were red. Thus, the three races—red, black, and white—originated with Noah who was red. The three sons of Noah were, according to Eastman, three different colors; Shem was red, Japheth was white, and Ham was black. All of Noah's sons married red women but since Eastman believed that the genetic power of the male overwhelmed that of the female, the children assumed the color of the father. (Eastman distinguished two kinds of Negroes, the straight-haired ones were supposedly descended from Ham's antediluvian wife, and the woolly-haired ones from his post-flood wife.) The other so-called contemporary races came from amalgamation; the brown was a cross between red and black while the yellow was a mixture of red and white. Like other advocates of racial purity, Eastman condemned this amalgamation.

Eastman took pains to reject Carroll's contention that Blacks were beasts who lacked souls. His rejection centered on both Carroll's scientific theory, which Eastman called atheistic, and on the logic of Carroll's arguments. Eastman's rebuttal made the startling claim that all animals possess souls. He also claimed that some animals eat grapes (a key link in Carroll's explanation of the biblical passage "beasts of the field"), and that snakes did have legs and did walk upright at the beginning of time. Using the injunction of St. Paul to preach to the Ethiopians for support, Eastman concluded that God believed that Blacks possessed souls. Eastman even offered a $100 reward for proof that fertile offspring could result from the union of man and beast and for any passage in the Bible where the ape was identified as a beast.

Despite this contention that the Black was not a beast but a human being possessing an immortal soul, Eastman implicitly accepted the developmental model of human history that proved that Whites were most civilized and Blacks were least. Black meant moral depravity; the Sodomites were black, as were the Canaanites,

Jezebel, and the priests of Baal. Black destiny was slavery because of the African environment, which fostered slavery. Despite this destiny, Eastman believed that slavery was a curse on both the South and the Blacks; slavery was cruel to the slave and injurious to the social structure of the South; it drew class lines and encouraged the miscegenation of white slave owners with black slave women. Though the cost to the South and the Black was high, Eastman felt this cost was to be borne because it was part of God's plan for the world, which was for Christian Blacks to return to Africa to spread God's word there.

A more respected southern view was that of Alfred Hart Stone; his view appeared in his influential book *Studies in the American Race Problem* (1908). Stone owned a plantation in Mississippi but was also an economist who produced a number of scholarly papers. Stone's economic studies purported to be scientific and he specifically disclaimed racial extremism. Both of these claims added weight to his findings. *Studies in the American Race Problem* began with the propositions that the goal of southern Whites was to control the Black in the same fashion as white South Africans did, and that the white population in the North differed little from that of the South in regard to prejudice. Using these propositions, Stone analyzed four possible models for a biracial society: a racially amalgamated society such as Mexico, a black controlled society such as Haiti, a society with limited black participation such as the British West Indies, and a completely segregated society such as South Africa. He concluded that the majority opinion in the United States, North and South, wanted the limited participation solution.

Why did the North seem more liberal on race than the South? Stone gave several reasons. One was that the Northerner encountered mulattoes while the Southerner encountered Blacks. Since Stone believed that all great Blacks were mulattoes, he claimed the North saw only the best. Another factor was the low proportion of Blacks in the North and their concentration in cities, which made their control easier. Stone predicted that as Blacks moved North, racial conflict would increase and Northerners would accept Southern solutions. Stone documented his thesis by citing the creation of segregated schools in Kansas City after racial incidents in integrated ones in 1902.

Southerners had a heavier burden than Northerners, according to Stone; they had to control Blacks with a judicial system designed for Whites. Hence, Southerners resorted to lynching in frustration. Stone lacked enthusiasm for black labor. While he believed that the Black had economically contributed much to the South as a farmer and plantation laborer, Stone thought that the Black was unsuited to industry where he would come into intimate contact with Whites. Intimate contact led to rape. Stone claimed that the rape of white women happened only in areas where slavery had not been significant and where white women had a tradition of working in the fields. Finally, Stone said that the economic lot of Blacks was improving but that they still could not save money nor shed the habits of immorality, gambling, and drinking, making more white control and management necessary.

Stone projected past experiences into the future. He had tried a rent system on his plantation which failed, according to his analysis, because of the restless nature of the black worker. This experience, combined with admittedly unreliable economic data, led Stone to predict the gradual displacement of the black laborer. Even before the Civil War, Stone claimed, the Black had lost ground to the white worker and now the process was accelerated because of black inefficiency, unreliability, and lack of thrift. The South was not dependent upon the Black for labor according to Stone; Italians migrating into Mississippi proved much superior to Blacks. The Italian phenomenon presaged the future to Stone; the Black would slowly disappear under the pressure of superior white groups. Black inferiority was not attributed to color, descent, or lack of intellectual ability; rather it was supposedly a deficiency of character and of what Benjamin Kidd, a noted social Darwinist, called "social efficiency." Black home life was immoral and chaotic, according to Stone, while white strength lay in domestic institutions. Like many nineteenth-century white Americans, Stone was a social evolutionist who held that defects in moral character, as well as physical strength, could be transmitted and that moral traits signaled success in racial adaptation.

Stone carefully discussed race, acknowledging that the concept was not scientifically valid but claiming, at the same time, that natural racial antipathy existed. This racial rejection supposedly emerged from the desire to control society. The South had greater racial antipathy than the North because it had been exacerbated by the mulatto who supposedly exercised a pernicious influence upon the total black community. Stone believed that while the full-blooded Black was happy, content, idle, given to petty crime but not to racial hate, and without the desire for suffrage and integration, the mulatto was ambitious, discontented, and able to effectively arouse the more passive Blacks. As proof, Stone quoted a prominent mulatto editor as saying that he was "tired of hearing about good Niggers, that what he wanted was to see bad Niggers, with guns in their hands." Stone believed that if the mulatto influence could be eliminated, the South would have peace.

Stone's *Studies in the American Race Problem* also included three papers written by Professor Walter J. Willcox, a Massachusetts statistician who had been the racial expert for the 1906 Bureau of the Census "Supplementary Analysis and Derivative Tables." Willcox contributed statistical data about the extent of racial crime, racial intermixing, and black population increase to the Census study. He concluded that black crime was on the increase in the North and South and that the increase resulted from a number of historic and racial factors—defective family training in slavery, an inability to earn a living, too strong competition from superior Whites (Willcox's major point), class separation among Blacks, and friction created by increased black racial pride. Since racial friction was believed to originate from Blacks and since white attitudes seemed unlikely to change, Willcox predicted increased racial tension. Whether the South could avoid a racial war depended upon the relative numbers of White and Black in the future, upon which race outnumbered the other. In order to find an answer, Willcox turned to the Census of 1900. This Census differed from earlier ones in that it had no separate category for mulattoes. Congress had mandated the Census Bureau to enumerate quadroons and octaroons in 1890 but the Bureau encountered so many problems that it omitted the category in 1900. Willcox assumed the number of mulattoes in 1900 to be about the same as in 1890. Starting with this assumption, he described the changes in the black population. It was more urban, more female, more widowed and divorced, and less illiterate than before; but, because of a death rate twice that of Whites and because of a declining birth rate, the black population had failed to keep pace with the white. The rate of natural increase of Blacks was only three-fifths that of Whites.

Willcox projected the probable increase of Blacks in the United States and criticized the erroneous projections of earlier writers. E. W. Gilliam in articles in *Popular Science Quarterly* (1883) and *North American Review* (1884) had estimated that the black population would reach 200,000,000 in 1980 with 192,000,000 of this population in the South. Gilliam had based his prediction on black increase between 1870 and 1880 but had been led astray. Others had been equally misled. Thomas Nelson Page had predicted a black population of 60,000,000 to 80,000,000 in the United States in 2000; Booker T. Washington had said that the black population would reach 10,000,000 in 1900. All of these projections erred because of an overestimation of the rate of natural increase. Willcox read the population data differently and said that, despite the errors in the 1890 census, which numbered as many as those in the one of 1870 and which overlooked many Blacks in the South, a pattern could be discerned. In each decade since the Civil War, the rate of increase of the black population was one-half that of the decade earlier. This resulted in a population of 8,850,000 in 1900 instead of the 10,000,000 Washington had predicted and a probable population of 24,000,000 in 2000 instead of the 60,000,000 to 80,000,000 Page had projected. Since white population was growing much faster, Willcox believed that the percentage of Blacks in the South would decline from 32.4 percent in 1900 to 17.6 in 2000. Willcox said that the inability of the Blacks to compete with Whites was the reason for a failing birth rate and an almost stationary death rate. Like Stone, Willcox saw a process of natural selection at work, a process which would gradually displace the Black.

II

Franz Boas's cultural relativism slipped somewhat in his attitude toward Blacks. His views appeared in a title article in *The Southern Workman* in 1909 ("Industries of the African Negroes"). While encouraging the study of African art and industry in order to determine the nature of African culture, Boas said the black experience in America had been characterized by a lack of genius and by "backwardness, inertia, and lack of initiative, of the great masses in the South." The Black in America, Boas thought, was capable of fulfilling the duties of citizenship but was not capable of rising as high as the majority of Whites (Boas said in *The Mind of Primitive Man* [1911] that he preferred Blacks to the mentally and physically retarded defectives "we permit to drag down and retard healthy children"). The Negro's "theomorphisms," or supposed primitive traits, Boas said, may have been caused by chance genetic inheritances in local populations and may not have been characteristic of all members of the race. Boas claimed in *The Mind of Man* to see evidence of evolutionary retardation in the face of the Black.

The alveolar arch is pushed forward, and thus gains an appearance which reminds us of the higher apes. There is no denying that this feature is a most constant character of black races, and that it represents a type slightly nearer the animal than the European type. The same may be said of the broadness and flatness of the noses of the Negro and the Mongol.

Boas believed that black genetic inheritance would be modified by social selection, that interracial mixture was on the increase, and that southeastern Europeans would intermarry more with Negroes than other groups because they had less prejudice. By 1921, Boas felt that intermarriage was necessary to solving America's race problem.

Nathanal Shaler, unlike Boaz, was much influenced by the evolutionism of his time. Kentucky-born, Shaler went to Harvard to study under Agassiz and remained there as professor of paleontology before becoming professor of geology. He achieved scholarly recognition in both fields, attaining the presidency of the Geological Society of America in 1895. His racial views took on the air of authority even when these views lacked any empirical base. Like Boaz, Shaler assumed a position of objectivity on race. He admitted that Blacks were not savages in Africa; they had domesticated many plants and were excellent farmers. However, showing ignorance of African history, Shaler said that Blacks had not reached a stage of civilization and had never developed a sophisticated political or social structure, literature, art, or law. Supposedly, they were no more advanced now than at the dawn of history. Physically, the Black was not considered inferior by Shaler. The higher death rate of the Black was believed to be a product of living conditions, not racial weakness; indeed, the black was the only race, according to Shaler, that could accomodate itself to different climates than the one from which it came, for the Black could live in areas beyond 40° North and South latitudes. In character and ability, however, the Black was considered inferior. He could not progress without outside help; here, Shaler cited the examples of Haiti and the American South after Reconstruction for evidence.

The Black was said to possess several admirable traits; he was friendly—unlike the hostile Indian—he loved children, and he loved Whites, as proven historically by the relatively small number of slave revolts. Shaler said that the Black lacked a sense of form but had an aptitude for color and music. On the other hand, his rational powers were described as low; he supposedly had no talents for history, physical science, or mathematics, despite the attainments of individuals like Benjamin Banneker. The Black, according to Shaler, tended toward thievery, sexual brutality, and drunkenness (the low-class White he considered to be even worse). The sexual brutality commonly associated with the Black was not held to be a universal trait by Shaler, but was probably limited to no more than five percent of the population, the same percentage as in the white. However, Shaler said that the bad black man had not been weeded out by natural selection as had the bad white man. Given these characteristics of the Black, what was the answer for America? Shaler considered miscegenation and rejected it. Only one percent of the American population, said Shaler, was an admixture and this one percent showed that race mixing was not successful. His father, whom Shaler quoted, had said that he had never seen a mulatto who lived to be over 60 years old and that younger ones were often sterile. Shaler, despite his denial of the physical benefit of miscegenation, still insisted that almost all of the Blacks of merit in the United States were mulattoes. Instead of miscegenation, Shaler opted for intensification of improvement efforts, for more white help for Blacks through industrial education, for the encouragement of black acquisitiveness, for the setting up of self-help programs, and for the providing of state and federal aid for racial improvement. The Black, although a "relatively simple species of our genus," could with care be placed in a modern state and might even add to it. Shaler believed, however, that only about one-half of the black population would ever reach a level of full participation in society; the rest would remain laborers, segregated and inferior.

Shaler's ideas were echoed by Edward Eggleston in *The Ultimate Solution of the American Negro Problem* (1913). Eggleston denied the creationist explanation for man's origin and differences and accepted naturalistic ones instead. Thus, man was the highest animal, but he had evolved from the apes. Each race, according to Eggleston, had evolved at different times; Javanese man was the first to have done so. The four main racial varieties had developed through slow adaptation to special environments; each race was best suited to a particular climatic area, and each climatic area produced different intellectual qualities. The temperate zones were supposedly the civilized zones, and the tropics were the primitive ones. The black race was considered most primitive, followed by the Indian; the former, said Eggleston, had always been savage and barbaric while the latter had developed a high civilization in Mexico.

To prove black racial inferiority, Eggleston used evidence derived from nineteenth-century physical anthropology. The cephalic index (ratio of breadth to length of head) of the black was 15 percent smaller than that of Orientals and 20 percent smaller than that of Caucasians. Eggleston's explanation for the smaller skull size (and thus smaller brain) of the Black was that the sutures in the black skull closed sooner than those in Whites. In addition, he claimed that Blacks had a more limited blood supply to the brain, fewer brain cells, and less lung capacity. These physical limitations supposedly resulted from laziness and consequent lack of exercise, which culminated in the long run in mental and physical inferiority. Thus, Eggleston used an essentially Lamarckian explanation, in which physical changes were brought out by character traits.

In his book Eggleston essayed to write a history of Blacks in America. In his version, the first Blacks in the colonies may not have been slaves but probably had a more circumscribed servitude than Whites. But slavery became a fixed institution with built in cruelty and immorality. During colonial days, miscegenation was more common than later, said Eggleston, and treatment of slaves less humane than in the nineteenth century, when slaves had accepted their lot and showed their contentment through "doglike" devotion. Reconstruction had taught the ex-slave to hate and had started racial difficulties. Eggleston thought that the racial problem was almost solved, although not through the conventional answers of miscegenation, extermination, deportation, colonization, and segregation. Eggleston's final solution was to be natural extermination as Blacks lost the struggle for existence; unable to find jobs because of southern prejudice, white skilled competition, and trade union intransigence, Blacks would starve.

According to Eggleston, the Black was in a retrogressive position. He had not understood freedom, mistaking it for license; education had hurt rather than helped. The black population was described by Eggleston as divided into several classes: a small frugal and moral middle class, a lower class composed of hardworking farmers and laborers, and a still lower class that was shiftless and that comprised half the Black population. Because of this stratification, Eggleston proposed that shiftless Blacks be given enough education to read, write, and count, as well as 10 acres on which to eke out a subsistence living. These Blacks, according to Eggleston, should remain marginal farmers as that was the extent of their capabilities. Those who had risen above this station had done so because of racial mixture, according to Eggleston; he also claimed that half of the graduates of Hampton's Institute had some white ancestors.

Subsistence farming was not to save Blacks from extinction; using Stone's data, Eggleston concluded that the percentage of Blacks to Whites in America was declining because of high infant mortality and death from T.B., pneumonia, and venereal diseases. Black immorality, a racial trait according to Eggleston, meant black extinction. This was again a Lamarckian position. Eggleston believed that eventually the black birthrate would fail to replace those who died, and the black population would decrease absolutely. Quoting Stone, Eggleston cited the supposed replacement of Blacks by Italians as proof that the displacement of Blacks already had begun. Eggleston proposed this scenario: segregation would intensify as Blacks moved to cities, they would be further disadvantaged because of segregation, and they would die faster. The natural end was certain to Eggleston. "No house is large enough for two families. No nation is large enough for two races."

Not all sociologists were so convinced that the Black would disappear. Edward Byron Reuter, a student of Robert Parks, had the opposite view. He produced a historical critique of the American racial experience called *The Mulatto in the United States* (1918). He based his views on what was perhaps the only serious study of racial intermixture of the time, Dr. Eugen Fischer's *Die Rehobother Bastards und das Bastardierungsproblem beim Menschen* (1913). Fischer believed that miscegenation in South Africa had resulted not in the creation of a new race, but rather in endless new combinations of the traits of the two parent races. The combinations, Fischer claimed, proved superior in intellectual ability to the black parents but inferior to the white. Reuter believed that there had been a great amount of miscegenation in the seventeenth century between indentured servants and Blacks and in the nineteenth century when Union soldiers sought out black women, infecting them with venereal diseases.

Reuter claimed that the mulattoes, who formed the cutting edge of a new class, were descendants of house servants favored because of lighter skins and white ancestry. Although hated by the pure-blooded Black, the mulatto was the principal achiever in black society as Reuter saw it. Using data from Kelly Miller and W. E B. DuBois, two pioneer black sociologists, Reuter estimated that 20 percent of the black population, the mulattoes, constituted 85 percent of the superior individuals. Despite their achievements, however, the mulattoes were rejected by the white community. The southern black community also rejected them because so many mulattoes resided in the North and because they lacked sympathy and understanding for the southern rural Black. The rise of the middle class, the increase of agricultural and industrial education, and the development of segregation were all pushing the mulatto to the forefront, and Reuter envisaged the beginning of a separate caste, at least in the North, which would constitute an intermediate step between White and Black. Reuter indicated that America was solving its racial problems as Latin American countries had in the past, by the creation of a mulatto escape hatch and by the transformation of race discrimination into class discrimination. He, however, admitted that he was not certain of this trend and identified certain other trends that might have negated caste formation. For example, white prejudice and segregation forced the black community to be more isolated, and this racial isolation helped create a black language, religion, manner, and history, all of which previously had not existed. As a result, the drive toward becoming part of white America slowed and racial mixture lessened.

In the 1920's, physical anthropology had almost completely separated from cultural anthropology; individuals had become specialists in one area or another. While cultural anthropologists emphasized racial inheritance, physical anthropologists turned to anthropometrics. The most significant figure in physical anthropology next to Boas, was Aleš Hrdlička, a native of Bohemia who came to America at the age of 13. Hrdlička joined the staff of the National Museum in Washington in 1903; he eventually became curator. His interest in physical anthropology led him to found the *American Journal of Physical Anthropology* in 1918.

Hrdlička wrote many scholarly works in the tradition of Topinard, one of the leading French anthropologists of the late 1800's. In 1911, Hrdlička commented on Indian origins by claiming that the Indian and the Eskimo were anthropometrically (physically) alike, that they were of the same *homotype* as the yellow-brown race, and that they had come to the New World from Asia in the Holocene period. In 1919, he published *Physical Anthropology: Its Scope and Aims: Its History and Present Status in the United States.* In this work and in an essay in *Human Biology and Racial Welfare* (1930), Hrdlička still argued that behavioral characteristics could be correlated with different races. In 1925, Hrdlička made the first professional anthropological study of the native American; he defined a native American as a white person possessed of four native-born grandparents. The study appeared as *The Old Americans* (1924) and contained data on 900 individuals. Hrdlička concluded from these data that the native white Americans never had been predominantly blond and that they were becoming gradually darker-haired and skinned. He predicted, as well, that future Americans would be taller and heavier, with a wide range of physical variations. This meant that old Americans and new ones were becoming indistinguishable, that immigrants were approaching the physical norm of nonimmigrants, and that a new American race, judged by a set of physical measurements, was evolving.

Melville J. Herskovits used Hrdlička's study as a benchmark and made an anthropometric study of the American Negro which appeared as *The American Negro: A Study in Racial Crossing* (1928). Herskovits did his research at Howard University under the direction of Boas (who had influenced Columbia University's Council for Research to subsidize the effort). Herskovits's major problem was to explain why the Census of 1910 showed that 20.9 percent of Blacks were mulattoes while the Census of 1920 showed that only 15.9 percent were. He concluded that both Censuses had erred and that the "pure" Negro was actually in a minority, a conclusion derived from both anthropometric and genealogical data.

Here is how Herskovits arrived at his conclusion. He first researched the family histories of 538 black males and then measured their lip size, leg length, breadth of nostril, skin color, finger length, interpupillary distance, stature, and hip width. He compared the physical measurements with the genealogies and found correlation that seemed to prove that the term Negro included people of different mixtures (Table 9.2).

Herskovits concluded that the use of the term Negro was too broad to cover the American Black, who constituted a new race. Compared with the white Americans studied by Hrdlička, the Blacks had less variability in length of face, height of ear, and

TABLE 9.2

Percent of Total Population Called Negro

Negro 22%
Negro and Indian 6.3%
More Negro than White 24.8%
Half Negro and Half White 16.7%
Half Negro and Half White and Indian 8.5%
More White than Negro 9.3%
More White than Negro plus Indian 5.5%
Total mixed 78%
Total with Indian 27.3%

height while sitting. On the other hand, they varied more in cephalic index (size of head). Compared with African tribes, the American Black was more homogeneous. This stability indicated to Herskovits that a new group had been created. Herskovits compared the results of his studies with those obtained by scholars from 6,000 American Negro soldiers in World War I and from results obtained from Negro women at Tuskegee and Nashville. The studies produced similar data and showed that while American Blacks resembled all of their ancestors, they were the same as none of them.

Herskovits speculated on the reasons for the growing physical homogeneity of the American Black and decided that the causes were social rather than biological. He argued that the prime element was the operation of white values on the black community, values which had economic and social consequences. The belief that white was best resulted in a social selection of the lighter-skinned Blacks for mates and for better jobs. Herskovits tried to find a correlation between skin color and I.Q., but could not; he concluded that the relative advantage of the lighter-skinned Negro was historical in origin. This explained both why the Negro professional classes were lighter-skinned and why upwardly-mobile black men preferred lighter women.

His demonstration of the desirability of a light skin in the Negro community seemed confirmed by another analysis of the Census of 1920 made by a black scholar, Charles S. Johnson. Johnson's study showed a disparity between black and mulatto sex ratios. In the black population, there were 1,018 men for each 1,000 women; in the mulatto, there were 886 men for every 1,000 women. From Johnson's data, Herskovits concluded that it was more advantageous for mulatto men to pass for White, while remaining mulatto was more advantageous for women. To be White gave the man an employment advantage; to be mulatto gave the woman a marriage advantage.

The results of Herskovits' study pointed out ambiguities in the concept of race. A mixture of different racial groups did not necessarily lead to great physical variability. The study also showed that American Blacks were a homogenous population descended from a mixed variety of groups. Herskovits concluded that the concept of race was only confused by his measurements. While American Blacks fit two of the accepted criteria of race—having a physical type and low physical variability—Herskovits claimed that American Blacks were not a separate race but a homogeneous population group in the process of stabilizing.

His study of black physical types had a significant consequence in that it seemed to end the search for a mulatto solution to the American race problem. Earlier thinkers had suggested that as the black population became mixed with the white, a separate mulatto class would emerge. Now Herskovits had showed that physical mixing had already occurred without a completely rigid social class stratification.

Around 1900, a new science called genetics emerged, inspired by discovery of the work of the botanists Gregor Mendel and Hugo DeVries. Mendel established in experiments with peas that biological units (genes) controlled plant characteristics, that these units were transmitted independently, and that inheritance of characteristics could be described mathematically. This science emphasized the compelling aspects of heredity, attributed physical change to mutation, and encouraged the development of eugenics, which was an attempt to apply genetic principles to human societies. The Eugenics Movement had the status of a new science, but it reinforced old prevailing notions of racial inferiority.

The Eugenics Movement was founded by an Englishman, Francis Galton. Galton, a cousin of Charles Darwin, believed that genius ran in families, and he developed instruments to test this thesis. He used the questionnaire method to collect social data and was the first person, with J. D. H. Dickson, to develop a method of statistical correlation to make the data meaningful. In 1869, he published *Hereditary Genius, An Inquiry into Its Laws and Consequences* in which he claimed that inheritance was the key to evolution, that the distribution of mental capabilities in individuals followed a bell-shaped curve, that races were unequal but natural selection developed individual fitness for living, and that man's instinctive nature did not keep pace with his physical and psychic progress. (Men were animals whose instincts failed them in new social circumstances, and cultural changes occurred too rapidly for most races to respond morally to these new situations.) The nonwhite races, Galton maintained, were moral fossils in terms of human evolution (an opinion that became an integral part of the racial argument in America in the early twentieth century).

Galton proposed a law of ancestral inheritance in *Human Faculty and Its Development* (1883), which law said that the hereditary influence of an individual ancestor diminished in geometrical ratio through succeeding generations. He also supported Darwin's idea of pangenesis, a hereditarian hypothesis that held that a fertilized ovum contained genes from the cells of both parents, and ideas on inheritance of acquired characteristics, and advocated the control of human evolution by selective breeding. This selective breeding would be accomplished by encouraging healthy couples to have more children through such social policies as subsidized housing. Galton considered birth control dangerous because he believed it to be most attractive to intelligent people and least attractive to less intelligent ones; the latter already had higher differential fertility. In 1901, Galton, along with the famous statistician Karl Pearson, began a quarterly journal, *Biometrika*, devoted to a statistical analysis of biological problems. In 1906, he founded the Eugenics Education Society, which published the *Eugenics Review*. The journals became the leaders in the field; and Galton began to achieve a reputation in Edwardian England matching that of his cousin Darwin.

Americans early became interested in eugenics; the Eugenics Movement in America was established in 1904 when the Carnegie Institution of Washington built a Station for Experimental Evolution at Cold Harbor Spring, Long Island, with Charles B. Davenport as director. In 1910, Davenport created a Eugenics Record Office, which, combined with the Station for Experimental Evolution, became the Department of Genetics in 1921. The Association of American Agricultural Colleges and Experimental Stations also supported the eugenics idea, forming the American Breeders Association in 1903, an organization that became the American Genetic Association in 1914 and whose official organ was *The Journal of Heredity*.

The ideas of the Eugenics Movement were best expressed by

four men: Charles Davenport, David Starr Jordan, Edward M. East and Harry H. Laughlin. Davenport was a native New Yorker who graduated from Harvard and taught biology at the University of Chicago prior to becoming director of the Station for Experimental Evolution. His ideas can be found in two books, *Eugenics* (1910) and *Race Improvement by Eugenics* (1911). Davenport combined the newly rediscovered Mendelian inheritance laws with the poly-genetic idea that races were different elementary species and with an instinct psychology that postulated innate racial differences. He advocated sterilization of inmates of state institutions and felt that the pernicious environments of cities destroyed the quality of the nation's germ plasm thus leading to the corruption of American society. He favored both racial segregation and immigrant restric-tion to prevent the sexual contact of inferior races with superior ones, but supported women's rights as long as the women involved were biologically superior. He believed human hybrids to be in-ferior to pure races and, with M. Steggerda, published *Race Cross-ing in Jamaica* (1929), which purported to show the pernicious physical results of black and white mixtures. According to the study, racially mixed individuals had such physical anomalies as arms and legs that were disproportionate in size to the rest of the body and such mental anomalies as a greater proportion of "mud-dled and wuzzle-headed." Davenport believed that American suc-cess depended upon the country's ability to remain racially pure.

David Starr Jordan was an ichthyologist (a fish biologist) and the first President of Stanford University (1891), as well as a paci-fist and anti-imperialist. In works such as *Care and Culture of Men* (1896) and *Imperial Democracy* (1899), Jordan argued that while all men were brothers, they were not equal: that certain climates suited certain races best so that Anglo-Saxons degenerated in the tropics; that war was counter-productive because it killed the brave and good; and that Blacks in America should be left alone to sink to their natural level.

Edward M. East was a botanist and geneticist who was born in Illinois and did research at the University of Illinois Agricul-tural Experiment Station prior to going to Harvard. In *Mankind at the Crossroads* (1923) and *Heredity and Human Affairs* (1927), East emphasized racial differences less than other eugenicists but, like them, believed racial mixture to be bad.

The last member of the group, Harry H. Laughlin, taught biol-ogy at North Missouri Normal School before going to the Eugenics Record Office. Laughlin also served as consulting eugenicist for the Municipal Court in Chicago and as an expert for the Committee on Immigration and Naturalization in the House of Representatives, the committee that originated the immigration restriction acts of the period from 1921 to 1931. Laughlin believed that immigration restrictions would preserve the biological superiority of the Anglo-Saxon race. He thought that American political superiority had resulted from the unwillingness of American pioneers to mix with the Indians, that Anglo-Saxon women had saved and would continue to save the moral order of America. Laughlin, like all the eugenicists, wanted the best persons to have the most children, wanted to limit the number of children of inferior races, and wanted to prevent racial mixing. Davenport, Jordan, East, and Laughlin formed a formidable quartet who shared the respect given to natural scientists and, with the exception of Laughlin, shared the respect associated with the most prestigious universities of the day.

The Eugenics Movement had many offshoots and many persons shared its ideas. The birth control advocates of the early twentieth century, individuals such as William J. Robinson, Winfred Scott Hall, and Margaret Sanger, wanted to modify the operation of natural selection in urban life and to exercise social control over lower groups. Margaret Sanger, the most famous birth control advocate, believed that birth control would save American society by lowering the reproductive rate of working-class families and by increasing selective mating. While she accepted many of Davenport's ideas, she categorized the unfit on the basis of class rather than race.

Sterilization had fewer advocates among eugenicists than did birth control, although a vocal minority pushed this solution. Among these was Paul Popenoe, a student of David Starr Jordan and the first editor of *The Journal of Heredity.* Popenoe shared the anti-city bias of Sanger and felt a general return to the farm would improve the quality of the American population. He proposed that feebleminded individuals be sterilized and claimed that the laboring class produced 46 percent of all such individuals. He defended antimiscegenation laws because he was convinced the Black's genes (bearers of heredity) were inferior; the caste system of the South supposedly reflected this inferiority. Both birth controllers and sterilizers popularized the ideas of the hereditarian eugenicists as they publicized the need for a planned American population.

The major proponents of the idea of racial heredity, however, were Madison Grant and Lathrop Stoddard. Grant was a New Yorker, an amateur zoologist and a trustee of the American Museum of Natural History, whose *The Passing of the Great Race* (1916) had a significant impact upon American thinkers of his era. Stoddard, a native of Massachusetts and a professional writer, had two almost equally influential books, *The Rising Tide of Color Against White World-Supremacy* (1920) and *The Revolt Against Civilization: The Menace of the Under-Man* (1922).

According to the preface by Henry Fairfield Osborn, Grant's purpose was to write a history in terms of race, a pioneering effort since Grant utilized the modern ideas of Galton and Wiesmann on the primacy of heredity in human affairs and denied Spencerian environmentalism. Osborn also indicated that Grant's goal was to save America by keeping her racially pure.

Grant laid out his beliefs in his first few chapters, saying that race was not synonymous with national or linguistic groupings but consisted of immutable hereditary characters, unaffected by environment. These racial elements, unit characters in Mendelian terms, did not change over time. For proof, Grant argued that the present Egyptian fellaheen (peasant) resembled persons of 6,000 years ago, at the beginning of recorded time. (This was the same example used by Gliddon and Nott about Blacks a hundred years earlier.) Grant discounted the research findings of Boas that indicated significant environmental influences on skull shapes. These shapes were determined by heredity and were fixed according to Grant. Because they were fixed, the best method of classifying races was by cephalic index. The yellow and black races were separate species, Grant asserted, and in any racial cross the lower race prevailed. Thus a cross with a Black always produced a Black.

Grant tied his racism to an antidemocratic ethos. Democracy supposedly encouraged the lower types; an aristocracy of the wisest and best was to be preferred. America had begun with an aristocracy based on birth; the aristocracy of wealth, which had followed, was under attack. Even slavery and serfdom had advantages according to Grant; Indians had supposedly been in better social and economic circumstances under the paternalistic Hudson Bay Company than they had been ever since. Grant preferred a hierarchical society and deplored the democratic changes that had ensued since the beginning of the Republic. He was a true conservative.

As far as the United States was concerned, said Grant, the future was unsure. The melting pot idea was a mistake because it resulted in mongrel races, as in Mexico, a true melting pot society. In the United States, Grant believed there had been, fortunately, little intermixture with the dominant race because most miscegenation involved white men and black women and did not put "negro blood into the American stock." Instead, it put white blood into black stock, displacing black children who might have been born. Grant, unlike other eugenists, saw little evidence of increased racial mixture. Believing in Aggassiz's natural zoological provinces, Grant said that the Black was displacing the White throughout the coastal regions and the Black Belt of the South. Grant was not unhappy with this development, for although he believed Blacks had no potential for progress, he also believed they were willing followers of white leaders and obeyed without question unless, as in Reconstruction, they possessed social equality. Echoing Booker T. Washington, Grant insisted that Blacks never became socialists or trade unionists, and thus they constituted a tractable labor force. In addition, the South supposedly knew how to control Blacks by insisting upon no social mixing and no intermarriage, rules difficult to enforce in the North where the races lived side by side. Grant did give some advice to the South; Blacks should be given birth control information in order to reduce reproduction. In the end, Grant predicted there would be separate societies of White and Black located in different climatic zones in the United States. This potential development concerned him very little when compared to the dilemma created by immigrants to America.

Little of what Grant said was new. Indeed, his ideas would have been quite acceptable to the American school of anthropology in 1850, containing as they did elements of polygenesis, climatic zones, and racial types. What was new was his hereditarianism derived from the newest genetic theory and his pessimism about the future of the white race in America under pressure from Europe.

Grant's pessimism was mild compared to Lothrop Stoddard's, whose *The Rising Tide of Color Against White World-Supremacy* (1920) reflected the rampant American disillusion after World War I. Stoddard, like Grant, analyzed global developments and said little about domestic problems in the United States. His main thesis was that World War I was a white civil war that had enabled the brown, black, and yellow races to gain strength. Outnumbered by other races and faced with a declining birthrate, Whites were threatened by more primitive races who resented white control. While the white race doubled every 80 years, the yellow and brown races doubled every 60 and the black race doubled every 40. The fact of differential population growth throughout the world meant the end of white world supremacy to Stoddard.

Stoddard divided the world into white man's land, yellow man's land, brown man's land, and black man's land. In black man's land, sub-Saharan Africa, the native population possessed great fecundity and animal vitality but lacked a historic past or civilizations of their own. As with all primitive races, black genes supposedly became dominant in any racial mixing. "Black blood, once entering a human stock, seems never really bred out again." Crossing with Blacks was considered inevitably fatal to the white, yellow, or brown races. As far as control was concerned, although the brown man was penetrating Africa from the Near East and black men were claiming Africa as their own, the white man probably would be supreme in Africa for some time.

In red man's land, America from the Rio Grande to the tropic of Capricorn, the evil of racial mixture appeared most obvious. The Indian had genuine virtues and had developed civilizations, but conquest had perverted these virtues and destroyed the civilizations so that the race had stagnated and decayed. Later, the mongrel population of Mexico and Latin America had caused political instability and cultural backwardness.

The supposed ebbing of white world power was correlated with the supposed decline of racial quality. According to Stoddard, colonialism had failed in the early twentieth century because of low birth rate and intelligence in Whites; the nationalism that led to World War I had also contributed by killing off many of the best young white men. Stoddard posited a white minority under siege; the outer dikes of white control were crumbling and could not hold; the areas of white settlement were threatened. In order to survive, America must prevent the influx of new persons from Europe and Asia and improve her racial stock.

Stoddard's Spenglerian (Oswald Spengler was a German who wrote *The Decline of the West*) pessimism continued unrelieved in his next book, *The Revolt Against Civilization: The Menace of the Under-Man* (1922). In this work, his theme was that the revolutionary unrest of the postwar world had originated in racial impoverishment similar to that which destroyed the great civilizations of the past. Stoddard questioned the implicit progressive model of history assumed in the nineteenth century. Rather, he said, civilization was recent and fragile; history showed many lost civilizations.

Stoddard tried to recover the reasons for these failures of the past. Although he accepted an evolutionary scheme that traced development from savagery to barbarism to civilization, Stoddard claimed that two necessary factors—race and civilization—had to be present in order to achieve and maintain high culture. Stoddard conceived of race as the soul of a culture and civilization as the body. Some cultures had fixated at certain levels because of racial inadequacies; Bushmen and African "black-fellows" supposedly remained in savagery while Asians, American Indians, and African Negroes stopped at barbarism. The inability to become civilized was connected with both high fertility and extraordinary physical vigor. The fecund lower races, attracted by civilized amenities, migrated to white societies, according to Stoddard. As they entered these societies, they supposedly upset the living standard, "socially sterilized" the higher native stocks through a higher reproductive rate, and if intermarriage occurred (as it usually did), mongrelized the total population. Stoddard said that all of this resulted in the decay of white civilization.

Unlike Brooks Adams, a descendant of John Adams and a noted turn-of-the-century writer who in *The Law of Civilization and Decay* (1896), posited the natural end of every civilization, Stoddard believed a civilization could last forever if the genetic quality of the populace could be sustained. Supposedly, this rarely happened, leaving white societies with three insurmountable problems—structural overloading, biological regression, and atavistic revolt. According to Stoddard, the first was a product of the increasing burden of civilization, which was transmitted by "social heredity," learned behavior. While the quantity of learning was said to increase exponentially through each generation, man's brain had not grown in size in historic time (Stoddard relied on archeology here for confirmation) and so was incapable of incorporating all new learning. Biological regression was attributed to the tendency of the worst people to have the most children. Thus, while each generation had to learn more, each had a lower potential for learning. The concept of atavistic revolt held that persons who were uncivilizable could not and would not assume the burden of civilization. Because of their own inadequacies, uncivilizable people hated the social order, which relegated them to an inferior place, and plotted revolt. Led by superior people, who were also disillusioned with society, they demanded equality. But equality supposedly became less and less attainable as evolution continued;

Stoddard here developed what he called an iron law of inequality. Ability was a function of heredity, and since like married like, the span between most able and the least able widened. Although he believed that equality of ability was unattainable, Stoddard feared revolutionists might achieve social equality through either covert or overt subversion of the natural aristocracy. Stoddard countered revolutionary arguments with an advocacy of the status quo and an isolationist or fortress America.

Stoddard's evidence included a new input, one which was to become more significant in the 1920's and 1930's. This was the so-called Intelligence Quotient test. The I.Q. test provided a means for eugenicists to prove their theses in an assumed scientific fashion, despite the fact that the original test was designed only to predict success in school and was standardized on those who succeeded. Stoddard included one I.Q. study in his *The Revolt Against Civilization*. This was conducted by Miss A. H. Arlett of Bryn Mawr, who tested several hundred elementary children in 1913 and discovered that the I.Q.'s of these children correlated with the socioeconomic status of their fathers (Table 9.3).

TABLE 9.3

I.Q. Scores of White Americans		*I.Q. Scores of Others*	
professional	125	Italians	84
business	118	Colored	83
skilled labor	107		
unskilled labor	92		
all	106		

From this study, Stoddard argued that foreigners and Blacks were a danger to the American society and that white persons with better I.Q.'s should be encouraged to have more children, perhaps through tax incentives. In the long run, if American society were to survive, Stoddard felt, Whites must reproduce faster than Blacks.

By 1916, various versions of the Binet I.Q. test, which had originated in France in 1905, had been devised, including the Stanford version. Lewis Terman used this version on recruits in World War I (World War I was a source of data for racial arguments just as the Civil War had been earlier). Terman's army tests, which were administered to prospective soldiers, showed significant mental differences between Blacks and Whites, with Blacks averaging a mental age of 10.14 years and Whites averaging 13.1 years. Another version of the Binet test had been used to test Blacks before the War; Alice C. Strong had tested 125 Negroes in 1913, B. A. Phillips had tested 85 Negro schoolchildren in 1914, and W. H. Pyle had tested 408 Negro children in 1915. But the new army tests included greater numbers of Blacks, included Whites in the same age categories, and were assumed to be more scientifically accurate.

In April, 1917, the American Psychological Association appointed a committee of psychologists to aid the war effort; the National Research Council did the same. The two committees combined at the behest of psychologists to form one new committee to advise the Medical Department of the Army in the construction and administration of tests with the goal of eliminating the mentally incompetent and selecting the ablest recruits for officer training. The committee recommended the use of the Binet I.Q. test, with the new Goddard, Stanford, and Yerkes-Bridge Point Scales as variants. The tests gave I.Q. scores of black and white soldiers, which could be compared with those of civilian counterparts (Table 9.4).

TABLE 9.4

Colleges	Median Score	Lower Quartile	Upper Quartile
(Negro) Lincoln Memorial	86	56	121
(Negro) Atlantic South Dental	80	57	95
All White Officers	139	116	161
Massachusetts Agricultural	150	135	164
Dartmouth	147	132	165
Women's Normal (Sam Houston, Texas)	88	71	105

To the testers, the poorer performances of Blacks indicated a hereditary deficiency.

Terman's coworker in some of his studies, Robert M. Yerkes, had more pronounced racial assumptions. Yerkes, a professor of psychology at Yale, organized and directed the Yale Laboratories of Primate Behavior. Yerkes's study of primates led him to write such books as *The Mental Life of Monkeys and Apes* (1916) and *The Mind of a Gorilla* (1927). In these books, Yerkes claimed that monkeys and apes showed such emotions as fear, rage, affection, and sympathy and advocated the continuing scientific psychological study of anthropoid apes (prior to World War I, no one had done this). Despite his empirical efforts, Yerkes retained an eighteenth-century belief in the close connection between the Black and the ape. He said in *The Mind of the Gorilla* (1927):

It is an odd fact that Africa, a continent rich in relatively primitive varieties of the human species, is also the home of the highest types of anthropoid apes and of endless varieties of monkeys. Negro and chimpanzee seem to recognize in each other similarities which attract and differences which repel. The feelings of the Negro are pretty generally shared by mankind, for the appearance and behavior of monkeys and apes offend while they fascinate most of us.

A final book in the hereditarian genre was Samuel J. Holmes's *The Trend of the Race* (1921). Holmes, a zoologist at the University of California, wrote his book as a result of an invitation to give a series of lectures on eugenics. He then went on to write *Studies in Evolution and Eugenics* (1923) and *The Negro's Struggle for Survival* (1937). Holmes, unlike Grant and Stoddard, was more concerned over American domestic problems and less concerned with global issues. He used Baldwin's idea of social heredity, the transmission of unit characters such as arm length, to prove his case. Holmes, in addition, utilized census data to a greater extent than did Grant and Stoddard. From these, he discerned another cause for alarm in the declining white American birth rate. A study made by the statistician Willcox of census returns from 1800 to 1910 had totalled the number of children, aged 5 and under, born per woman in the age group of 16 to 24 and showed a reduction from 976 to 508 children per 1000 women in this group. Holmes facetiously projected the trend forward for 150 years and arrived at a future figure of no births at all. While he could not accept this as happening, he did see evidence that the more prosperous middle-class women would have fewer children and that the less able, poorer women still had high birth rates. He also hypothesized that another reason for the decline in birth rate was urbanization. Using the census of 1910, Holmes found the data in Table 9.5.

TABLE 9.5

Number of Children per 1,000 Women (25–45 yrs.)			
urban white	252	rural white	603
urban Negro	290	rural Negro	652

Holmes attributed the difference between birth rates of city and country women to fewer marriages, more divorces, higher venereal disesase, more contraception, and more abortion in the latter. Like Sanger and Popenoe, he felt that rural life was better for America's genetic future but that rural life had become less typical.

Although the birth rate of Blacks exceeded that of Whites, Holmes believed that natural selection would intervene to limit black population expansion. Because of climatic and socioeconomic conditions, black life expectancy was shorter than white. Lacking natural resistance to diseases, particularly to those found in cities, Blacks failed to keep pace with the urban white population. Holmes even thought that if the Black had not been immune to malaria, he would have been eliminated from Africa. Although Blacks supposedly lacked the physical essentials for survival in America and although their increasing urbanization supposedly meant an acceleration of decline, Holmes felt that the race might survive in diluted form through increased miscegenation. As the Black went North and to cities, the rate of intermixture multiplied. Again using census data, Holmes presented the figures in Table 9.6.

TABLE 9.6

Percentage of Mulattoes in Total Negro Population			
1850	11.2	1890	15.2
1860	13.3	1900	census did not specify
1870	12.0	1910	20.9

Since the Black was not considered intellectually equal to the White and the mulatto was considered superior to the Negro, it was thought that the mulatto might survive as the Black died out and mulatto children might be born instead of white children. Holmes denied Grant's view, which argued that a mulatto child would be born in the place of a Negro child. The believed end result of racial mixing, however, was the same for both Grant and Holmes, a population with a lowered genetic capability.

The hereditarian evolutionists viewed twentieth-century society with alarm. As natural scientists impressed with the importance of genetic transmission of human traits, they saw the United States as besieged in a world of color and envisaged a fortress

America where Whites of an older stock fought against the influx of inferior races. If immigration ended, the native white, Anglo-Saxon American could survive providing he had more children than the poorer, immigrant population. In this view, however, Blacks would probably not survive in America unless they remained in the rural tropical South or somehow intermarried with Whites. The eugenics movement was anti-Black but was even more anti-lower class and anti-immigrant; the movement for genetic improvement focused as often upon the responsibilities of better white Americans to have more children as upon the high birth rate of black Americans.

III

By the 1930's, the black community had changed, but the leaders of that community had failed to fully recognize the change. These leaders were trying to answer imputations of biological inferiority, racial immorality, and physical degeneration of the black race. Their defense responses varied; none was fully satisfying because of a heavy reliance upon nineteenth-century, pre-Darwinian, anti-slavery assumptions. Often these assumptions were accompanied by the argument that pure Blacks were inferior but the racially mixed were not.

One such proponent of this position was William Hannibal Thomas, a member of a northern racially mixed family, which had been free for three generations prior to the Civil War. Thomas had achieved moderate success as a carpetbagger in South Carolina in 1871 when he had vigorously campaigned for black rights. By 1901, he became disillusioned and in *The American Negro* (1901) he stigmatized southern Blacks as stupid and lazy persons who only wanted to attack white women. He urged more stringent segregation as both necessary and desirable. Thomas claimed that the mulatto had the some moral standards as the White and that the American social system ought to have three categories—Blacks, Whites, and mulattoes.

The mixed opinions in the black community can be found in *The Negro Problem,* a collection of articles by black scholars, published in 1903. Booker T. Washington's essay "Industrial Education for the Negro" still advocated self-help through vocational training. By hard work and the resultant pride in accomplishment, Blacks would reap the psychic rewards of self-esteem and respect from the white community. Charles W. Chesnutt's "The Disfranchisement of the Negro" was less optimistic. The author proposed eliminating the word Negro since that term of convenience was imprecise and failed to describe the 1,000,000 persons who were over half-White. The word Negro evoked the image of "the low-browed, man-eating savage whom the southern white likes to set upon a black and contrast with Shakespeare and Newton and Washington and Lincoln." Chesnutt argued for a restoration of black rights. He decried the loss of the black franchise, which had had economic repercussions and had resulted in peonage, loss of jobs, taxation without representation, and bad education. He felt that the Negroes of his time were making a mistake, that they "decry [their] own race, approve [their] own degradation, and laud [their] oppressors." According to Chesnutt, only northerners believed industrial education had made Negroes so valuable that Whites would protect them from insult or injury. Further, he said, black acquiescence in both slavery and disfranchisement had reinforced a Southern belief in black inferiority. To demand was to gain respect, Chesnutt argued.

Chesnutt's argument for more vigorous black demands was not supported by H. T. Kealing's "The Characteristics of the Negro People." Kealing combined a support of industrial education with a romantic racialism, claiming that Blacks had both inborn and inbred traits that fitted them to that kind of education. Inborn traits supposedly made the Black religious, imaginative, affectionate (without vindictiveness toward white people as shown by behavior in the Civil War), enduring, courageous, and cheerful. The inbred traits were supposedly learned in slavery and made the Black shiftless, incontinent, indolent, improvident, extravagant, unreliable, and ignorant. Since inbred traits were learned, Kealing argued that industrial education could reverse the learning process and permit the inherent inborn goodness to emerge.

T. Thomas Fortune offered still another solution in "The Negro's Place in American Life at the Present Day." Fortune felt that the Afro-American had no pride of ancestry because of slavery and lacked unity because of a lack of leadership in the past; but through the direction of the mulatto, he thought that the "alleged race characteristics and tendencies" of the black people were changing. Unlike the Indian, who Fortune believed was doomed to extinction, the Black would be assimilated through intermarriage.

This collection shows the hesitancy and lack of agreement among black Americans. Adding to this lack of agreement were two black separationists, Bishop Henry M. Turner of the American Methodist Episcopal Church and Bishop L. H. Holsey of the Colored Methodist Episcopal Church. Turner believed that white spokesmen did not know American Blacks and, out of ignorance, assumed that Blacks were content. They were not, said Turner; they wished equality, but had been given no rights in American society except to pay taxes or to work on roads. Turner had his own views about black Americans; he believed that they were descendants of inferior Africans sold into slavery by superior ones. Like Martin Delaney, whose views he shared, Turner believed that the destiny of the American Black was to civilize and Christianize Africa.

Bishop Holsey took a separationist position because he felt that Black and White could not live together in peace and harmony and that the disfranchisement of Blacks hazarded their lives, liberty, and property. According to Holsey, Blacks were becoming Anglo-Saxonized and while racial amalgamation might create harmony, it was unthinkable. Holsey saw no practical existing alternative to the increasing black serfdom and the sexual pollution of black women by white men except the creation of a black state. Since the race problem was national and not just a southern one, said Holsey, the federal government should provide a black territory similar to the Indian one where no Whites could reside except necessary governmental officials and those married to Blacks. Any Black should be eligible to go to the territory except for criminals and other undesirables.

Romantic racialism, the belief in the Christ-like image of the Black whose destiny was to save either America or Africa, persisted, but it was modified by growing pessimism and bitterness. Romantic racialism often became coupled with increased black militancy and was used to reproach Whites for their prejudices.

The change towards pessimism and bitterness was obvious in the ideas of Archibald and Francis J. Grimké. The Grimkés were mulatto children of a white slaveholder and the nephews of Sarah Moore and Angelina Emily Grimké, noted female abolitionists. Archibald Grimké became a lawyer and publicist for the Republican party. He edited *The Hub,* a journal promoting Republican interests, from 1883 to 1885 and served as Consul to Santo Domingo from 1894 to 1898. He wrote *The Shame of America, or, The Ne-*

gro's Case Against the Republic (1924), an impassioned plea for racial justice. His brother, Francis J. Grimké, graduated from Princeton Theological Seminary and served as pastor of Washington D.C.'s 15th Street Presbyterian Church. Both the Grimkés accepted social Darwinian ideas without relinquishing romantic racialism. At the beginning of his career, Francis Grimké supported Booker T. Washington, industrial education, and character training for the Black to improve his moral condition. But by 1900, he became convinced that Whites were evil and that Washington's ideas were pernicious for failing to recognize that fact. By 1918, F. Grimké believed that white Americans were savage and that, through suffering, Blacks provided a good example for bad white Americans. Archibald Grimké concurred.

Another advocate of racial Christianity was William H. Ferris; he also combined evolutionary ideas with a faith in the superior religious nature of the Black. In his book, *The African Abroad: Or, His Evolution in Western Civilization* (1913), Ferris said that the mission of the Black was to humanize Western civilization. Ferris also held the contradictory view that since conflict was inevitable in any society, the black man should become as aggressive as the white in order to survive. It was this conviction which led him to call Booker T. Washington an "Uncle Tom" (he was supposedly the first to use that term in relation to Washington).

Black clergymen reflected growing impatience with white America while still clinging to the belief in the mission of the black Christian. Their problem was to encourage the Christ-like virtues of Blacks—patience, meekness, and humility, which admittedly came from the slave experience—while also urging greater black militancy. How they did this is instructive.

Two who tried were R. R. Wright, Jr., and Reverdy C. Ransom, both ministers and editors of denominational journals.

Wright, who knew Jane Addams and Clarence Darrow in Chicago and continued in their reformist educational tradition, began a black settlement house there. He earned a Ph.D. in sociology from the University of Pennsylvania in 1912. Ransom in turn helped begin the N.A.A.C.P. Wright and Ransom independently reached positions that were remarkably similar. Wright, who became militant after witnessing a lynching in 1915, urged Blacks to become politically active and to retaliate when attacked. While he advocated greater black aggressiveness, he clung to the faith that black religion could save white America if given a chance. Undecided as to whether religion should revolutionize society or reform it, Ransom also urged Blacks to return violence for violence while claiming that Blacks were more Christ-like than Whites. He eventually expanded his thesis to conclude that only the Black was Christian and would eventually replace the white woman as the moral arbiter of American society. Both Wright and Ransom never satisfactorily solved the paradox of how Blacks, conditioned to submission by slavery, could react violently, nor did they explain why Whites would accept a black moral example.

The dichotomy that existed in the ideas of black pastors existed in those of black scholars as well. These scholars were marginal men who were caught between two cultures, forced to choose between middle-class white and lower-class black standards and between the idea of the mission of the Black and the idea that there were no peculiar racial qualities.

Typical of these scholars were Kelly Miller, George Edmund Hayne, and W. E. B. DuBois. Kelly Miller, a pioneer Negro sociologist at Howard University said in works like *Race Adjustment* (1908) that the evils of urban life caused black backwardness and that these evils—criminality, illiteracy, and unemployment—could be eliminated by improving schools, employment, and housing. Miller believed that the black man's lag was environmentally inspired. This sociological orthodoxy alternated with his view that the Black possessed special virtues. Blacks ought to be better, judging by white standards; but Whites also ought to be better, judging by black standards. By the end of the 1920's, Miller had come to believe in the need for a pluralistic society where men had equality of opportunity but not social equality and where each race could teach the other how to survive. Blacks could give lessons in music, style of living, and social adaptability. But Miller knew that American society had not reached this goal; for most Blacks, as he said, it was either get out or get white to get along.

George Edmund Haynes, one of the founders of the National Urban League and a professor of economics and sociology at Fisk University, was more optimistic. In *The Trend of the Races* (1922), he pictured America as being torn between two forces, greed and charity, with Blacks representing charity and Whites representing greed. Unselfish white Christians, along with Blacks, would move America back to the principles of Christ, he felt, thus forming a community where Black and White would live together in peace and harmony.

The most famous Negro scholar of the twentieth century, W. E. B. DuBois, early shared the romantic racialism of his contemporaries. However his approval of it gradually eroded in the 1920's and 1930's. DuBois, who had taught economics, history and sociology at Atlanta University and who had been one of the founders of the N.A.A.C.P., held two conflicting opinions: the scholar's belief that one should be cosmopolitan and take the best from all civilized societies, and the emotional identification with black society which led to a belief in natural racial virtues. As DuBois said in *Souls of Black Folk* (1903):

It is a peculiar sensation, this double-consciousness, this sense of always looking at one's self through the eyes of others; of measuring one's soul by the tape of the world that looks on in amused contempt and pity. One ever feels his twoness—an American, a Negro; two souls, two thoughts, two unreconciled strivings; two warring ideals in one dark body, whose dogged strength alone keeps it from being torn asunder.

DuBois could not bring himself to like black music, jazz or ragtime, nor anything else associated with lower-class black behavior. He preferred classical music and the standards of a white intellectual elite, but he still clung to the mystical idea of the genius of the black race.

In *Souls of Black Folk* (1903), *Morals and Manners Among Negro Americans* (1914) and in *The Negro* (1915), DuBois described American society as a spiritual failure and proclaimed the mission of the Black to redeem America. DuBois felt this redemption was possible because the black race differed from other races in certain innate qualities and historical experiences. These qualities were evident in the black experience in the "germinal institution" of the Black, which was the church, and enabled the race to survive. Thus did DuBois marry evolution and romantic racialism. In addition, DuBois, in works like *Darkwater: Voices From Within the Veil* (1920), *The Quest of the Silver Fleece* (1911), and *Dark Princess* (1928), praised the purity of black mothers, the beauty of black women, and attacked the sexual aggression of white men against these women. According to Dubois, any miscegenation that had occurred in America had originated in white male lust. Insisting on full social equality, DuBois was an ardent integrationist as well, at least until the 1930's. In 1921, he said that the separationism implicit in President Harding's denial of the possibility of social equality for Blacks would lead to racial hatred. DuBois wanted an equalitarian America where the Black was equal, but he also wanted a society which retained intact the black racial soul and mission.

Meanwhile, a new generation of Negro sociologists had emerged. Prominent among this generation were students of Robert Park at the University of Chicago. Park conceptualized the problem of Blacks in America as a one of class and status conflict. Whites supposedly conceived of Blacks as lower-class even after Blacks acquired middle-class possessions. Prejudice, the scholars claimed, resulted from poverty, which provided the original lower-class image. While this explanation denied the biological inferiority of Blacks, it also deemphasized the ideas of racial soul and mission. The sociologists in this tradition distrusted such romantic survivals and concentrated upon objective, value-free social science.

The leading black sociologist to come from Chicago was E. Franklin Frazier, who taught for years at Howard University. His ideas appeared first in an article, "Social Equality and the Negro," in the journal of the Urban League, *Opportunity*, in 1925. Frazier blamed the inferior position of the Black on two social factors. One was the caste system in the South, which was intended to keep the Black in a subordinate role. The second was the social disorganization in the black community, created by the movement from rural areas to the cities. (The theme of social disorganization in urban areas was a favorite one of Park's and appeared in both his and his students' research.) Both of these social problems could be solved, according to Frazier, by the education and assimilation of Blacks into American life. Frazier accepted the American dream of a society where all were equal and fully accepted; he denied the value of a separate black tradition, racial soul, or mission. He believed that the urbanization of Blacks, although creating problems, provided a long-range opportunity for Negroes to exchange a rural, folk community for a better, urban one.

Charles S. Johnson, another graduate of the University of Chicago, was less optimistic. He was the author of the study *The Negro in Chicago* (1922), which analyzed the Chicago race riot of 1919, and the editor of the N.A.A.C.P. journal *Opportunity* during the 1920's. Race relations, as revealed in Chicago and on the national scene, in that era permitted few illusions. Johnson saw that the black move to an urban society merely meant a different kind of discrimination and segregation, which prevented Blacks in the cities from advancing to higher levels as effectively as the southern system had in rural areas. Indeed, urban life caused severe psychological problems, such as avoidance (social isolation), displaced aggression (transferring anger at White to Blacks); and an "oppression psychosis" (a severe reaction where the necessary fears of white dominance are exaggerated). However, Johnson believed that the increased educational opportunities in the cities would balance the destructiveness and would make black advance possible. This advance necessitated learning how to operate in two worlds, white and black, but he felt that Blacks could do this. Johnson found more to value in the black lower-class experience than Frazier had; but he agreed with Frazier that the eventual destiny of the Black was to lose racial identity and to enter the world of middle-class white America.

The ideas of a black racial soul and mission did not die. They reappeared in both political and religious movements, albeit minor ones led by self-appointed Messiahs. One such Messiah was Cyril V. Briggs, the founder of the African Blood Brotherhood. Briggs, a native of the British West Indies, advocated black separatism. In 1917, he asked that ten percent of the United States, preferably land in California and Nevada, be reserved for a black nation. By 1919, Briggs had begun to advocate the creation of a black state outside the United States, somewhere in Africa or South America or the Caribbean. Briggs joined the American Communist Party in 1921, two years after its founding, becoming one of the first black members. There he continued to propagate his separatist ideas, which were based upon belief in the innate qualities and destiny of the black race.

Two small religious sects sought unity through a belief in a common black religious heritage. These sects were the "Moorish-American Science Temple," founded in Newark, New Jersey, in 1913, and the "Black Hebrew" congregation organized in Philadelphia in 1915. The leader of the first group was Noble Drew Ali and Prophet F. S. Cherry was the leader of the second; both preached a strikingly similar doctrine. Each claimed that Blacks had lost their identity because of the white man and that this loss of identity was responsible for their problem. Ali declared that the American Negroes were not really black, but were olive-colored instead. They had supposedly come originally from the northwestern and southwestern shores of Africa and been members of the tribe of

Moabites. According to Ali, the Whites had enslaved the Moabites, had hidden their identity, and had called them Negroes, colored, black, or Ethiopian. But once believers rejected their false names, Ali said, and assumed their true identity as "Moorish-American," they could achieve freedom. After enough had taken their new identity, Ali predicted that a heavenly sign would be given for the end of white rule. Cherry, on the other hand, took his ideas from those circulating in the Carolinas in the early 1900's and claimed that Blacks were really Ethiopian Jews, descendants of the Queen of Sheba, who had been robbed of their identity by slavers. Like Ali, Cherry preached a return to a lost identity and to a lost religion in order to bring salvation.

More significant than the African Blood Brotherhood, the "Moorish-American Science Temple," or the "Black Hebrew" congregation was the Back-to-Africa Movement of Marcus Garvey, who capitalized on the interest in pan-Africanism in the twentieth century. Garvey was a black Jamaican who established the Universal Negro Improvement Association and who brought pan-Africanism ideas to the United States in 1914. He succeeded in reaching the black masses in Harlem, although he was eventually indicted by the federal government for using the mails to defraud. He was imprisoned and subsequently deported from the United States. He died impoverished in London.

Garvey's movement emphasized black racial pride and the impossibility of achieving freedom and equality in a white-dominated society. He attacked mulattoes who led the black community and called them traitors to the Negro race. He denounced their dependence upon white people and their pride in white ancestry. They contributed, Garvey claimed, to the belief that "a Negro is a person of dark complexion or race, who has not accomplished anything and to whom others are not obligated for any useful service." The mulatto would be replaced, however, said Garvey. He is quoted in E. David Cronin's *Black Moses* (1955) as saying:

The Uncle Tom nigger has got to go, and his place must be taken by the new leader of the Negro race. That man will not be a white man with a black heart, nor a black man with a white heart, but a black man with a black heart.

Garvey was unable to decide whether racial prejudice had originated as an innate instinct or had become an acquired trait;

but once begun, Garvey believed that racial prejudice was genetically transmitted and that its existence doomed any struggle for racial equality in a biracial society. Hence, Garvey preached racial separation and black removal and supported those who agreed with him regardless of their color. His newspaper advertised such books as Ernest Sevier Cox's *White America,* a white segregationist tract; he received money from John Powell, the founder of the Anglo-Saxon clubs of America; and, in 1922, he went to Atlanta to confer with Edward Young Clarke, the Imperial Giant of the Ku Klux Klan. Garvey consistently inveighed against racial intermarriage and defended his connections with white racists on the basis of a similar belief in racial purity.

Garvey, however, insisted upon the equality of the Black and upon the necessity of racial pride. He said, "I am the equal of a white man," and sponsored a version of history that claimed that Blacks had ruled the world when Whites were cave-dwelling savages. In 1919, Garvey advised black parents to buy black dolls when the Harlem firm of Berry and Ross started mass production, believing this use would help black self-identity. He encouraged his Chaplain General (the titular head of the African Orthodox Church, which was the official church of the Universal Negro Improvement Association) to urge Blacks to visualize a black Christ, a black God, and a black Madonna. The movement to conceptualize Christ as black gained little acceptance in the black community at that time, but Garvey's advocacy of a black Messiah seemed the penultimate statement of the idea of the Christ-like Negro.

Another contribution to black pride would be to establish an African nation, said Garvey, the creation and Christianizing of which was a black mission. Garvey believed that only the establishment of an independent black nation with all the apparatus of sovereignty would enable Blacks to gain both self-respect and the respect of Whites. He also wanted to uplift Africa as shown by two of the aims of his United Negro Improvement Association:

1. to assist in civilizing the backward tribes of Africa.
2. to promote conscientious Scriptural worship among native tribes of Africa.

According to W. E. B. DuBois, Garvey perverted the American values of liberty, brotherhood, and equality to mean only liberty for the black African, brotherhood among Blacks, and equality of black leaders in dealing with white ones. However, Garvey furthered American ideas, albeit minority ones, of racial soul and racial destiny. While his back-to-Africa movement failed, black pride remained.

IV

The image of the Black in the popular white culture of the twentieth century continued to be basically unfavorable and grew to be more vivid because of a new medium, motion pictures. An example of this phenomenon involved the transformation of the racist novel, *The Clansman* (1905), into a movie, *The Birth of a Nation* (1915). The book was one of a number written by Thomas Dixon, a North Carolinian who served as an American Baptist Minister in New York City from 1889 to 1899.

The Clansman, Dixon's most famous work, was more influential as a movie than a book, mainly because of the genius of D. W. Griffith, who directed the film. Griffith was a Kentuckian with southern values and agreed with the racial ideas expressed in the book. Basically, the book and the movie articulated the Brownlow tradition. The story began with the "Plantation Illusion," a view of the good life in the South with contented Negro slaves and sensitive white masters. The War and Reconstruction then changed all of this, releasing the bestial Negro from white social control. In Dixon's Reconstruction, however, the loyal Negro—the old exslave and the new servant—still existed. The bad Negroes, who attempted sexual assaults on white girls, were not southern servants; they were, instead, a northern Black and a mulatto. The mulatto was portrayed as the most dangerous of the two because he had both the sensuality of the black race and the intellectual ability of the white race. Although the plot was hackneyed and old, the cinematography of Griffith was compelling and revolutionary. The endorsement of the film by President Wilson and the subsequent furor in the black community only served to publicize the ideas more widely and to increase the movie's patronage. One film critic has said that with *The Birth of a Nation,* "significant motion picture history begins"; if so, it began with a presentation of a peculiarly southern racial view.

Griffith's effort had been preceded by earlier portrayals of the Black that were just as unflattering, though not as explicitly sexually threatening. Edison's early films, made in the 1890's, included ones with such titles as "Negro Lovers," "Chicken Thieves," and "Colored Boy Eating Watermelon." These short features of Edison's used the popular stereotypes of the Black to provide supposedly humorous fare. Other film producers were equally guilty of this kind of racial exploitation. A slapstick film series made prior to World War I was centered on "Rastus," a black man, who appeared as a primitive and a thief. Typical titles in the series were "Rastus in Zululand" and "How Rastus Got His Turkey." The tradition of the stupid, childlike Black entered into the films at their beginning and persisted through the silent era into the period of the talkies.

The Sambo stereotype also appeared in the other media of the day such as newspaper cartoons, joke books, and children's books. Whenever a waiter, a watermelon eater, or another silly comic figure was needed in cartoons and joke books, the Black was used. Inez Hogan, in her children's series, *Nicodemus,* had as her protagonist a young boy who was coal-black and apelike, who had big red lips and long arms, and who was stupid and foolish. The Sambo stereotype had gained too firm a place in American life to be easily eradicated.

In white drama, the same dreary picture emerged. The coon and minstrel shows continued, although most black actors were forced from the white stage by the beginning of World War I. Serious white playwrights, however, began to create realistic black characters. Edward Sheldon, the founder of the Harvard Dramatic Club personified such attempts in his *The Nigger* (1909). In this play, the governor of a southern state who stood on a white supremacy platform discovered that he was the grandson of a slave. While the playwright seemed more sympathetic to the supposed white man, he also attacked southern white racial assumptions. Sheldon also wrote another play with a racial theme, *Lula Belle* (1926), in which he tried to trace the social gradations in a black urban community. In *Lula Belle,* the protagonist, a dark-skinned Negro man, followed his light-skinned girl from Harlem to Paris, and strangled her when she rejected him.

In the 1920's, the black man entered serious white drama most significantly through the plays of Eugene O'Neill. In *The Dreamy Kid* (1919), a one-act play, O'Neill portrayed a black hero who killed a white man in self-defense and was captured at the deathbed of his grandmother. O'Neill's black hero was a human with emotions that could be universally understood. In 1920, in *The*

Emperor Jones, one of O'Neill's most famous plays, he tried to enter the mind of a black dictator on a Caribbean island to show the combination of fear, anxiety, ambition that made that dictator what he was. *All God's Children Got Wings* (1924) was based on the life experiences of Jack Johnson; the play concerned a black fighter who married a white lower-class woman of easy virtue. The theme of miscegenation, despite the character of the woman involved, proved so controversial that the mayor of New York City prohibited participation of child actors—black and white—in it.

Another serious dramatist of the 1920's, Paul Green, also wrote plays about Blacks and interracial mixing, among them *Lonesome Road* (1926) and *In Abraham's Bosom* (1927), which won Green a Pulitzer Prize. The latter play involved the illegitimate son of a white man and a black woman who fought his father over the construction of a school for Blacks and over the practice of lynching. The play ends with the illegitimate son dying of a beating administered by his own father.

A more famous writer about Blacks was Du Bose Heyward. Heyward, a South Carolinian, wrote a novel entitled *Porgy* in 1925; in collaboration with his wife, he turned it into a play in 1927. George Gershwin set the play to music and later based an opera on the theme. All versions told of Porgy, a handicapped Black who traveled around Catfish Row in Charleston in a goat cart, and of his love for Bess, a black woman. Through the various media, the story became widely known; for many white Americans, *Porgy* was their first introduction to the confusion and complexity of southern black urban life. While the mood was tragic, the protagnoists evoked sympathy and not a little admiration.

Success also attended Marc Connelly's play *Green Pastures* (1929). Connelly received a Pulitzer prize in 1930 for this dramatic adaptation of Roark Bradford's book, *Old Man Adam and His Chillun.* The play itself was a black account of Biblical history told from the view-point of God. Heaven was a place where watermelon feeds and catfish fries went on interminably and where both black virtues and vices abounded. The play was made into a movie with an all-black cast; although sympathetic in conception, it was condescending in tone. While *Green Pastures* was hailed as a breakthrough by white liberals, it contained many of the old Sambo stereotypes.

The revived interest in the Black in white drama in the 1920's was also reflected in novels. T. S. Stribling won a Pulitzer prize in

1933 for his *The Store*, a novel about a southern country store. He wrote realistically about Blacks in this and in one of his earlier novels, *Birthright* (1922). *Birthright* told of a Tennessee-born mulatto who graduated from Harvard and attempted to open a black school after his return home. Failing because of prejudice, the disappointed protagonist gives up on the South and goes to Chicago.

A white romantic belief that somehow the Black was more primitive and more vital than the White was emerging at about this time. There was even the beginning of an idea that Blacks somehow tapped an earthiness that Whites had either lost or never possessed. This view constituted a return to a romantic racialism, which differed from that of the nineteenth century in that it had no religious base and admired the Black for his supposed physical rather than spiritual virtues.

Meanwhile, a wave of creativity in the arts swept black Harlem. This wave also emphasized a secular romantic racialism. The racialism centered on the supposed primitive sensuality of Blacks and attracted the interest of both black and white persons. An earlier black Bohemia had existed in New York's Tenderloin District in the 1880's, but it was not until the early 1900's that Harlem became an attraction. It first attracted middle-class Blacks as a place to live and then attracted thrill-seeking Whites to visit. By 1910, when most black entertainers were effectively barred from the white stage (save for a few individuals such as Bert Williams who toured with the Ziegfeld Follies), the black community turned inward; Harlem theaters and cabarets provided the main source of employment for these displaced artists. New theaters, such as the Crescent Theater, opened to take advantage of the situation. The leading theater was the Lafayette, where the traditional kind of black review done for white audiences continued in such plays as the *Darktown Follies*. Gradually, however, the themes in the all-Black plays became more realistic and the music utilized a more Black-oriented idiom. When white theaters opened again to black performers after World War I, many of these performers remained in Harlem and those who returned to white stages insisted on vehicles that were less derogatory to Blacks. Aspects of black culture had become acceptable to white customers and artistic black innovations, particularly in the dance, became commonplace. The Charleston appears to have originated with black dancers in South Carolina in 1920, and Blacks first danced the Lindy Hop in the Savoy Ballroom in Harlem in 1928. The same acceptance occurred with popular music. In 1920, Okeh Records issued "Crazy Blues" sung by Mamie Smith, without giving any indication that she was Black. The record sold 75,000 copies in a month and encouraged further attempts to sell black music to a wider audience. At this time, live black music—ragtime, jazz, and the blues—also attracted listeners from beyond the black community. White intellectuals made a habit of going to Harlem to hear jazz in segregated theaters and clubs. Thus, black artists were encouraged to become residents of Harlem and to create black art.

The novels of black writers early in the twentieth century reflected older racial assumptions about the tragic mulatto and mulatto middle-class values. The creative product of the Harlem Renaissance, a term used to describe the flowering of literary endeavors in the 1920's, claimed to find new values in a "New Negro." The term New Negro had been used by the *Cleveland Gazette* in 1895 to describe civil rights activists and by Ray Stannard Baker in 1908 to refer to those persons who believed in Booker T. Washington's self-help doctrine. The writers of the Harlem Renaissance appropriated the term and defined it to mean a creative, aggressive, searching individual.

The image of the New Negro began to emerge in James Weldon Johnson's *The Autobiography of An Ex-Colored Man* (1912), which included the first well-rounded black character in American fiction, according to Robert Bone, an authority on the black novel. Johnson, who was educated at Atlanta University and who had been successively a public school principal in Jacksonville, Florida, a writer in New York, and U.S. Consul in Venezuela and Nicaragua, incorporated elements of his own life in his book. The hero of the novel was a light-skinned Black who was swindled out of his inheritance by another Black as he was en route to college. Unable to remain in school, the protagonist found work in a cigar factory in Jacksonville, but traveled north to Harlem after the factory closed. Supported by a white patron, the hero went to Europe to sample the best of European culture before returning to the South to collect folk songs and to document black creativity. A lynching caused him to flee the South, to return to the North, and to pass for White. Although the novel ended with the seeming triumph of white values, the book did not disparage black folk or popular culture. The hero speaks favorably of ragtime and the cakewalk and admits to nostalgia for the vitality and life he had found in the urban black experience.

Johnson continued these ideas in a later history of Harlem, which he called *Black Manhattan* (1930) and which attributed much of the social pathology in the black community to the lack of jobs, high rents, and the beginning of ghetto formation. Johnson blamed the urban church for failing to solve the problems of Blacks in the city. He lauded the fact that 200,000 people, a population twice as large as any in Southern cities, lived in Harlem without racial friction. He also reiterated his view that there were creative elements at work in the black community.

The writers of the next generation, the Harlem Renaissance, rebelled not only against the moral attitudes of American society (as did their white contemporaries) but against the belief in the Christ-like Black with a special mission. These writers denied the middle-class values of both their parents and white Americans and tried to find alternate values in the folk art of the lower-class Black. They wished to discover what was distinctively black in the complex life of the times; they found it among the black masses whose cultural distinctiveness and language had been ridiculed by prejudiced Whites and educated Blacks but whose earthiness and sensuality were considered superior to the white civilized virtues that the educated Blacks emulated.

The best novel in this tradition is generally conceded to be Jean Toomer's *Cane* (1923), a novel which failed to achieve popularity in its own time but which later earned critical approval. Toomer had discovered examples of black folk culture in Georgia in 1921, when he was a school superintendent. He wrote *Cane* to capture that culture, which he was convinced was dying. In the novel, which Robert Bone calls a southern *Winesburg, Ohio,* Toomer described the lives and characters of six black women who lived on Dixie Pike in rural Georgia as well as life on 7th Street in Washington, D.C.; Toomer contrasted rural and urban characters. Although Toomer found no ultimate meaning in the experience of being Black in America, he portrayed the sexual adventures of the Georgia women with sympathy and suggested that urban, ghetto life was fuller and richer than Whites realized. He claimed that the animal passion of black women attracted both black and white males and was superior to the often-praised cultivation of white women. Toomer's *Cane* indicated that while Negroes had no mission to save America, they did have a full life despite poverty and prejudice.

Black poets like Langston Hughes, Claude McKay, and Countee Cullen also took up similar positions, ones which praised black Americans and attacked white American prejudices, in such poems as "America" (1925), "America in Retrospect" (1926), and "A Thorn Forever in the Breast" (1927). Langston Hughes, in an article, "The Negro Artist and the Racial Mountain" published in *The Nation* in 1926, typified a new-found faith in the black folk figure. He distinguished between two kinds of Blacks, "high-class" and "low-down" folks. The former accepted white standards and wanted to be white: the latter liked gin, shouting religion, and ecstasy. These "low-down" folks expressed their life best in jazz, and Hughes admired them for this. In this essay and in a later novel, *Not Without Laughter* (1930), Hughes attempted to find a compromise position between high and low culture. The hero of *Not Without Laughter* was a true marginal man. He liked jazz but wanted a white education; he was brown and wanted to be alternately Black and White. He resolved his personal dilemma by becoming a writer, hoping to retain black instinctive gifts while utilizing white intellectual training. The novel illuminated the major problem of the writers of the Harlem Renaissance. How could educated, urban Blacks identify with uneducated, rural Blacks? On the one hand, these writers condemned the black masses as "Uncle Toms" who had a slave mentality and a slave religion; on the other, the writers admired the earthiness of the black people and their ability to survive in a hostile society.

The conflict between the educated and the uneducated Black can be seen in the novels of Claude McKay, a Jamaican-born writer who graduated from Tuskegee and the University of Kentucky prior to moving to Harlem. McKay's first novel, *Home to Harlem* (1928), juxtaposed Jake, a returned veteran of World War I whose primary interests were food and sex and who followed his appetites wherever they led, with Ray, an overcivilized Black who was an introspective intellectual. The two became rivals for the same girl, whom Jake won. The novel ended as Ray, the rejected suitor, set sail for Europe. McKay's *Banjo* (1929) began where *Home to Harlem* ended. Ray, living on the Marseilles waterfront, rejected both white civilization and its bourgeois culture. Attacking the mulatto middle class for being imitative and for lacking originality, Ray adopted "nigger music" and language under the tutelage of Banjo (who was Jake under another name). In the end, Ray fails to compromise between two ways of life.

The same dilemma occurred in Walter Thurmond's *The Blacker the Berry* (1929). The heroine, a dark-skinned daughter of light-skinned parents, developed a deep self-hate when snubbed by light-skinned people who mattered—doctors, lawyers, and other community leaders. After falling in love with a shiftless light-skinned man, the heroine became involved in Harlem's under-class world. Rejected by this world, which she found attractive, she returned to middle-class society, only to find life banal. Thurmond's message to Blacks was to accept blackness and to stop trying to be white.

The problem of the black woman was also discussed in Nella Larson's *Quicksand* (1928), whose plot was quite similar to that of *The Blacker the Berry*. The heroine, Helga Crane, was the daughter of a white Dane and an American Black. Educated by a white uncle, Helga taught in a black college in the South out of a sense of obligation to her race. Disillusioned, she moved to Harlem where she tried to become a primitive, trying to live by the senses rather than by reason, but could not. She next moved to Copenhagen, trying to become a middle-class white, and failed again. Finally, she turned to religion and married a dark-skinned black minister who served in a small Alabama town. This failed as well; she remained too white to become black and too black to become white. Like the heroine in *The Blacker the Berry*, Helga was too educated to become a primitive Black with instinctive freedom.

Alain Locke faced the same dilemma. Editor of *The New Negro* (1925), a collection of essays about the racial ideas of the times, Locke had a Ph.D. from Harvard and had been a Rhodes scholar. Like DuBois, Locke rejected the accommodation of Booker T. Washington and insisted upon full and equal rights for Blacks. He believed Blacks should be educated in integrated schools, although he also wanted black control of all-black colleges. Despite a belief in the superiority of folk art and in the creativity of the black masses, he had difficulty in identifying with those masses because of his middle-class experiences. He thought that the answer to the increasing dehumanization of white American society might be in the humanity of black spirituals (an humanity others found in jazz and the blues), but he never discovered how to change an educated Black into the believing worshipper.

The black man became more conspicuous in the period from 1900 to 1930 because of fears of racial wars in the South and increasing urban violence in both the North and South. This visibility stimulated speculation about supposed racial differences and explanations using both polygenesis and monogenesis appeared in conjunction with a defense of Scriptural literalism. The Sambo stereotype transferred easily from the old media to the new—the movies and the newsprint cartoons. In the new academic disciplines—economics, psychology, sociology, and anthropology—evolutionary theory, often modified by a neo-Lamarckian belief in the physical inheritance of acquired social characteristics, still served as the main paradigm. The hereditarian enthusiasm of the early twentieth century led to a pessimism about the future of America and a belief that American society, along with those of Western Europe, might not survive in a world of color. All of these ideas, in one way or another, contributed to an accepted view of black racial inferiority.

The concept of race still had supporters in the black community, who used it to bolster the belief that the Black had Christ-like qualities and a special mission in world history; this belief gave meaning to the slave experience and inspired black pride. Another model of racial character, however, emerged in the 1920's. The model emphasized character traits which were secular and earthy rather than religious and spiritual and portrayed the lower-class black as the authentic human whose vitality contrasted favorably with the sterility of white and black middle-class life. This model was not fully accepted even by the intellectual minority who encouraged it; indeed, black scholars vacillated between the desire for full equality in a homogeneous American society and the wish to return to the emotional fullness of the black masses. The conflict was not to be easily resolved; it persists to this day.

Chapter 10

Indians Up, Race Down

The decades of the '30's and '40's saw a new approach to the Indian problem; after 150 years of trying to civilize the Indian, the United States government gave up. The results of trying to make the Indian into a white farmer had been landlessness and pauperism; the allotment system had failed. The Indian Reorganization Act, or the Wheeler-Howard Act of 1934, attempted to turn Indian affairs back to the Indians by permitting them to organize for self-government. Under the law, tribes could write a charter or constitution and elect a tribal council and tribal court. They could revive their native religions, including the Peyote Cult, and develop handicraft industries. While the purpose of the Reorganization Act was to restore tribalism, it had severe limitations. It did not counteract the Dawes Act, individuals' allotments did not revert to tribal holding, nor did the growing fragmentation of Indian land cease. Further, the Act assumed there to be one standard form of Indian government and forced some tribes to create governments alien to their traditions. Although federal citizenship had been granted to Indians in 1924, the Wheeler-Howard Act allowed some Indians to be exempt from state laws while on the reservation. Approximately 75 percent of the Indians organized immediately after passage of the act while others, including the Navahoes, waited for a decade. Under the Act, tribes were organized within state lines, which meant that new tribes did not replicate historic ones. Some tribes were fragmented; out of the old Sioux came five different tribes. New tribes were composed of members of several tribes.

Reaction to the Indian Reorganization Act varied sharply. Many traditional Christian churches opposed the act, saying that the Indians wanted to be assimilated into the larger society and that tribalism meant paganism. These churches particularly feared the encouragement of native religions. On the other hand, John Collier, who became the New Deal Commissioner of Indian Affairs in 1933, campaigned vigorously for the right of Indian self-determination, praising the vitality and worth of Indian culture. In 1945, Collier became director of the National Indian Institute and President of the Institute of Ethnic Affairs. His defense of the ability of the Indians to rule themselves appeared in his most famous book *Indians of the Americas* (1947), which waxed poetic in its evocation of the values of Indian life. The pressure exerted by Collier and other Indian defenders finally bore fruit as Congress passed the Indian Claims Commission Act in 1946, which specifically allowed Indians to sue the United States and which provided for the reconsideration of many old Indian treaties.

Another defender of the Indian was Ruth Benedict, whose *Patterns of Culture* (1934) has been called the most widely read anthropological work ever written. Benedict earned her Ph.D. at Columbia under Boas in 1923, doing the fieldwork for her dissertation among the Serrano Indians in California. She later studied the Zuni, Cochiti, Pima, Mescalero Apaches, and Blackfeet. During World War II, she worked for the Office of War Information (OWI) as Head of the Basic Analysis Section, Bureau of Overseas Intelligence, which studied Asiatic and European cultures.

Benedict borrowed from Neitzsche the idea (which he had taken from Greek tragedy) of the existence of two kinds of contrasting cultures, Dionysian and Apolonian—the first representing an inwardly repressive but outwardly aggressive society, and the second representing a passive, nonaggressive one. In her *Patterns of Culture*, Benedict applied these ideas to three societies, the Zuni Indians in the American Southwest, the Dobu Islanders off New Guinea, and the Kwakiutl Indians in the American Northwest. Benedict indicated a preference for the Apollonian synthesis of the Zuni society. The Zunis appeared gracious and calm under difficult circumstances; their culture deemphasized emotional behavior. They were cooperative and noncompetitive, sharing goods in common and not striving for personal success. They lacked a sense of sin and were sexually permissive. They were in a minority, however; according to Benedict, most other American Indians—the Sioux, Crow, Dakota, and the Blackfoot—were Dionysian. These Indians fasted, tortured themselves, used drugs and alcohol to attain religious ecstasy, punished adultery severely, cried loudly at funerals, and competed vigorously for personal prestige. The Kwakiut Indians carried Dionysian elements to their logical extreme through committing murder to appropriate another person's honors and through their frenzied, cannibalistic dances.

While the patterns of culture Benedict saw were based on Greek cultures and appeared to describe Indians' behavior, they caught the spirit of neither the Indians nor the Greeks. Indian behavior was far more complex than Benedict indicated, and the Greeks defined Dionysian and Apollonian exactly the opposite of Benedict in *Patterns of Culture*. For the Greeks, Dionysian excesses were used to integrate society by merging individual differences and Apollonian rites served to accentuate individual differences.

Benedict compared the Dionysian Indians with the white citizens of Muncie, Indiana. The Indians, although admittedly not the most desirable ones in her view, came out best. Benedict felt that both Indian and white American societies had zest and vigor obtained at a cost to the individual. Both were warlike. However, the Indians permitted a variety of unorthodox behavior in their societies and tolerated "unstable human types." For example, the Indians regarded homosexuals as being exceptionally able and welcomed trances and epileptic seizures as signs of religious revelation. Muncie mores demanded conformity, on the other hand, and eccentricity was greatly feared. Benedict blamed white American traits of conformity and rigidity on the Puritans, whom she did not understand and whom she called psychopathic.

The Indians continued to interest poets and novelists as well as politicians, churchmen, and anthropologists. In Faulkner's short story, "Red Leaves," Chickasaw chief Issetibbeba was bitten by a snake, whom Issetibbeba addressed as his grandfather. In "The Bear," Sam Fathers, who was half-Indian and half-Negro, also called a snake his grandfather. Thus, the image of the Indian as the snake in the Garden of Eden persisted in American literature. There were other literary attempts, which tried to go beyond the stereotypes of the day and which claimed to catch the character of the Indians. Among these efforts, the works of two white novelists stand out—Oliver La Farge's *Laughing Boy* (1929) and Edwin Carle's *Fig Tree John* (1935).

Olive La Farge was a novelist with a side interest in Indians and Indian reform. He participated in several archeological expeditions in Arizona, Mexico, and Guatemala, was Director of the Eastern Association on Indian Affairs from 1930 to 1932, and was President of the National Association on Indian Affairs from 1937 to 1942. La Farge won a Pulitzer prize for *Laughing Boy;* his other novels, including *Sparks Fly Upward* (1931), *Long Pennant* (1933), *All the Young Men* (1935), *The Enemy Gods* (1937), and *The Copper Pot* (1942) were also well received.

Laughing Boy was a love story in which the titular Indian hero fell in love with an Indian called Slim Girl who agreed to marry him. Encountering the opposition of his family, Laughing Boy left them. Slim Girl had had a checkered past; she was an orphan girl educated in a Christian Indian school. After leaving school, she worked for a time for a missionary family and became pregnant by a white rancher. Thrown out of the missionary home, she became a prostitute and a mistress of another rancher. Determined to reform after marriage, Slim Girl became a model Indian wife who cared for all her husband's wants and whose efforts even won over her husband's family. However, in order to establish Laughing Boy in the silver shop he craved, she once again became the mistress of a rancher, deceiving Laughing Boy into believing she was working as a domestic servant in a white minister's home. Discovering the deception, Laughing Boy wounded both Slim Girl and her lover before being persuaded to forgive them. The reconciled duo, however, met tragedy when another Indian, jealous of Slim Girl, killed her. The story ends with Laughing Boy returning to his Indian home, resolved to live for the memory of Slim Girl.

Edwin Carle was born in New Jersey and educated at Harvard but settled in California to write radio and movie scripts. While there, Carle visited the Salton Sea and discovered a legend about an Indian named Fig Tree John. Carle incorporated the legend in a book that was the first of sixteen he was to write. *Fig Tree John* begins with the arrival of an Apache brave and his wife to the Salton Sea where his son was born and where his wife planted the fig trees that gave Fig Tree John his white name. There the Indians lived in peace and harmony with nature, subsisting off the natural bounty of the land. Renegade whites, in search of loot, broke the peace and killed Fig Tree John's wife. Alone, Fig Tree John proved incapable of teaching his son, Johnny, the fullness of Apache culture. As a result his son became a hired man for a white rancher and wanted white tools and a car. Johnny married a Mexican girl, whom he took back to Fig Tree John's shack. Fig Tree John, acting on an old Apache custom, tried to share his son's wife but was deterred by both his son and his son's wife. Fig Tree John then attempted to kill his daughter-in-law. As a result of the assault, she fled the area and urged Johnny to join her because she was pregnant. When Johnny attempted to leave, his father demolished Johnny's car and attacked him. In the fight, Johnny killed his father. The story ends with Johnny going to his wife, determined to live as a white man.

Although the plots of *Laughing Boy* and *Fig Tree John* are dissimilar, the two books share many common features. Both show the tragic nature of Indian life, with protagonists caught between two cultures, red and white. Both contain themes of interracial sex. While the books present Indian life as peaceful and harmonious, they also show it as primitive, ugly, and full of squalor. While *Laughing Boy* and *Fig Tree John* were acclaimed by white audiences, their supposedly realistic picture of Indian life did little to dispel the image of the Indian as the corrupted primitive.

The poet John G. Neihardt, while working on his *Cycle of the West,* encountered an Indian in 1930 who exerted a profound influence upon him. The Indian was Black Elk and his life story appeared in a book that, little noticed at the time, became a significant part of the Indian revival of the 1960's. That book was *Black Elk Speaks: Being the Life Story of a Holy Man of the Oglala Sioux* (1932). (The original edition lists Neihardt as the author, but the 1961 reissue lists Black Elk as the author and Neihardt as the voice of Black Elk.)

Black Elk began his story with "The Offering of the Pipe," a statement of the theme of his life. Declaring all life holy and good, Black Elk described his story as that of a "man with a vision too weak to use, a holy tree that is withered and a people's dream that died in bloody snow." He recounted how the Sioux had received their sacred relic, a red willow bark pipe, from the spirit bison woman; the pipe had a picture of a bison on one side, representing the earth that fed the Indians, and twelve feathers attached to it, which represented the twelve moons of the year. Black Elk was told by his father of a Lakota prophecy—that the four legs (bison) would go back to the earth and that a strong race would weave a spider's net that would entrap the Indian, who would then go to live in square grey houses in a barren land. Now, Black Elk said, it had all come true.

The story of Black Elk encompassed the story of the Indian Wars. Black Elk's first memory was of his wounded father returning from the Battle of the Hundred Slain (Fetterman fight), when Black Elk was but three, and of the fear of all the Indians that the Whites would come and attack them. In 1874 when he was eleven, Black Elk heard a medicine man warn that Whites were coming to seek gold in the Black Hills. Black Elk joined Crazy Horse when he was thirteen, armed with a six shooter his aunt had given him. Even at this age he was contemptuous of the advice of those who wished to sell Indian land to the Whites. He experienced the Sun Dance that June as warriors prepared for the battle of Little Big Horn by touching the holy tree, by purifying themselves, and by dancing with rawhide thongs inserted in cuts in their backs or chests and connected to the holy tree. Black Elk's experiences at Little Big Horn were gruesome; in the fight, he tried to take his first scalp, but the wounded soldier to whom the scalp belonged ground his teeth so much that Black Elk shot him instead. After the battle, the moment of triumph was short-lived and succeeded by pursuit by soldiers, the death of Crazy Horse, flight to Canada, and final return in desperation to the Powder River country.

Much of Black Elk's story concerned his attempts to obtain and interpret religious visions. His first vision, which he experienced when he was five, consisted of birds talking to him; this vision was small compared to another he had when he was nine and very ill in which two men with lightening flashing off their spears came to take him to his grandfathers in the sky. There he saw many marvelous sights, including twelve horses standing at each of four compass points, who changed into other animals at will, and six old men who represented the powers of these same compass points and of the sky and earth. The old men gave him a cup of water and a bow as tangible tokens of his visit. After the vision passed, Black Elk woke to find himself back home. His parents said that he had been lying as if he were dead for twelve days. The vision influenced him throughout his lifetime but was not the last he was to have. Black Elk's next vision came eight years later, when he was seventeen. He felt sick and called on his grandfathers to help him.

They warned him that the Blackfeet were plotting trouble. They also instructed him to perform a Horse Dance, which he did; everyone supposedly benefited. Another vision followed this one almost immediately; this one was of dogs whose heads appeared out of the dust to be transformed into the heads of white men. These visions helped Black Elk to become a successful medicine man who healed with sacred herbs and demonstrated the mysteries of the universe with a Bison Dance and an Elk Ceremony.

Black Elk also became a world traveler. In 1886, he and other Oglalas joined Buffalo Bill's Wild West Show and went to New York, London, and Paris. These metropolitan areas failed to impress Black Elk; he felt instead the insensitivity of Whites who refused to help each other, who had forgotten the earth was their mother, and who resorted to jails to punish criminals. The last significant experience for Black Elk was his Ghost Dance; he danced at Wounded Knee Creek and had a vision that the Whites would disappear and the bison and the dead Indians would return. By chance, he missed the massacre at Wounded Knee; looking at the dead women and children afterwards, he felt no sorrow because he believed that they were happy in a better land. He did want revenge, however. The next day he attacked the soldiers and was severely wounded, through achieving neither revenge nor honorable death. He buried his heart at Wounded Knee; the rest of his life was an anticlimax.

Black Elk Speaks is really an Indian history of the West in the years between 1860 and 1890. It precedes *Bury My Heart at Wounded Knee* by about thirty years, but the theme is the same—the unsuccessful struggle to keep white intruders from the land of the Great Plains Indians. The relative lack of success in its own time of *Black Elk Speaks* as compared to that of the works of La Farge, Carle, and Collier suggests the kinds of Indian experiences that most attracted white audiences. The ability to view the epic of the West from the Indian point of view had yet to be developed.

The movies of the thirties and forties continued the theme of cowboys and Indians fighting in the West, although other issues intruded. With the advent of the singing cowboy—such as Gene Autry and Roy Rogers—and the updating of the Western setting to contemporary times the banker sometimes superseded the Indian as villain. (The Indians were no longer a threat, but the bankers were.) There were even movies made that tried to portray the exploitation of the Indian, the most noticeable of which was *Massacre*

(1934). For the most part, however, the image of the vanishing degenerate American persisted.

I

The idea of race changed drastically in the 1930's with the appearance of a mathematical basis for population genetics in such works as Sewell Wright's "Evolution in Mendelian Populations" in *Genetics*, R. A. Fisher's, *The Genetical Theory of Natural Selection* (1930), and J. B. Haldane's, *The Causes of Evolution* (1932). From these beginnings, the study of population genetics mushroomed, and a number of important books on the subject were published by the time of the Second World War. These included Theodosius Dobzhansky, *Genetics and the Origin of Species* (1941); E. Mayr, *Systematics and the Origin of Species* (1942); and Bentley Glass, *Genes and the Man* (1943). These studies completed the Mendelian revolution, adapted it to Darwinian evolution, and, in the process, demolished the older definitions of race that were based upon outward physical characteristics.

Starting with Theodosius Dobzhansky's definition of a "human race as a population which differs significantly from other human populations in regard to the frequency of one or more of the genes it possesses" (*Genetics and the Origin of Species*), these geneticists claimed that human evolution consisted of changes in gene frequency through mixture, mutation, natural selection, and genetic or random drift (the possibility that some genes had become either lost or more significant in a small, isolated population). These thinkers criticized the looseness of the earlier definitions of race and said that the term race referred to a population that was continuously interbreeding and exchanging common genes. This meant race was a dynamic rather than a static concept; with the constant recombination and mutation of genes, there was continuous change.

Certain problems appeared in the new genetic definition. Like earlier definitions of race, there was no agreement as to how large a population must be to constitute a race. Did the American Blacks make up a race; would the black population of the Mississippi Delta be a race? In the second place, since the definition of race was a statistical one dependent upon data from a large number of individuals, race as a historical concept was almost completely eliminated. In any given population, the original strains could not be recognized; in a population of mulattoes, the exact skin color of the forebears could not be deduced. Since the size of the human population in the past was relatively small and since fossil remains were few, the evidence from which to deduce race was quite limited. This led geneticists like Dobzhansky to claim that a person's heredity was not a status but a process, that a person inherits a potentiality, not an actuality. What was inherited was not a unit character (a fully developed personal attribute) but a manner of reacting to one's environment. Also, the geneticists concluded that the overall genetic differences among human groups was small. Bentley Glass, for example, postulated that there were only six pairs of genes that distinguished white individuals from black ones. (Skin color in man probably resulted from several pairs of genes acting together, as evidenced by the fact that there were no significant number of throwbacks in interracial marriages; whereas in a classical Mendelian population, where a single pair of genes determined traits, the proportion should be 25 percent.)

Thus, the relation of heredity to environment was a dynamic one, according to the geneticists of the 1930's and 1940's. H. L. Shapiro's study of the Japanese in Hawaii and Japan, *Migration and Environment* (1939), showed that the Japanese who migrated to Hawaii had increased in sitting height and greater head broadness; from this, thinkers concluded that Boas had been right to argue the plasticity of the human organism. While not going as far as Agassiz, the geneticists conceded the influence of geography on group differences. Geographic features might act as a barrier that trapped a population and caused genetic drift, emphasizing a formerly insignificant gene; exposure to intense ultraviolet light would affect pigmentation over a long period of time, turning skin dark. Since difference in skin pigmentation appeared to be adaptive, darker peoples would be found in the tropical areas and the lighter ones in the polar regions. To the question as to why the Eskimos of the North and the Indians of Tierra del Fuego were dark, the answer was that these two populations had not lived in these regions long enough to have become light-skinned.

The concept of man's origin also changed. The discovery of *Pithecanthropus* (extinct man) skeletal remains in Java in 1894 and later fossil discoveries in North China led paleontologists to shift their search for man's original home to the Far East. There, they theorized, *Homo erectus* had walked upright but had resembled a chimpanzee in that he had no chin. Succeeding expeditions to the Far East by investigators like Ray Chapman Andrews proved unproductive, however, and attention switched as early as 1924 to Africa where Broom, Dart, Robinson, and Leakey had found fossil remains of *Australopithecus*. These hominids had smaller brains than *Homo sapiens* but had skulls shaped like later men; *Australopithecine* remains were found in sites containing tools and were dated to as far back as 2,000,000 years ago. The success of the search for fossil man in Africa restored the idea that humans had originated there.

These discoveries in no way ended the controversy between monogenesis and polygenesis. As early as 1910, a German named Klaatsch claimed different primate ancestry for different races—Whites supposedly came from a chimpanzee-like ancestor, Blacks from a gorilla-like one, and the Orientals from an orangutan-like one. Klaatsch's idea revived the eighteenth-century conviction that different geographic locations corresponded with different anthropoid apes and different-colored peoples. Klaatsch's ideas were spread to America through the works of R. R. Gates, *Human Genetics* (1946) and *Human Ancestry from a Genetic Point of View* (1948). Gates also maintained that different races derived from different primate ancestors and that only Whites were *Homo sapiens*. Klaatsch and Gates displayed a nineteenth-century polygenesis existing side by side with a genetic theory of race.

The more orthodox genetic view of race offered less certainty about polygenesis and monogenesis. At the beginning of the century, scholars connected *Homo sapiens* in a direct line with each newly discovered fossil man. As time wore on, however, too many anomalies arose and an alternate explanation, which said that it was impossible to tell whether modern humans came from one ancient race or several, gained popularity. Human development was said to have been long and complex, involving a number of progressive human subforms and influenced by two antagonistic forces—speciation, which produced human subspecific types (variations, races), and aggregation, which tended to blend human types through interbreeding and socialization. Human evolution was considered irreversible, thus untraceable, because of its complexity. (It could be reversed in the microevolutionary state, before the formation of races, species, and perhaps genera had occurred; but in the macroevolutionary stage, where the formation of genera, families, and ordinal took place, the alteration of genes had been so great that the probability of retracing the steps became almost impossible.) Species such as *Homo sapiens,* which geneticists held to encompass all living humans, had evolved slowly, through the interaction of diverging populations, breeding communities, and races which occupied extensive areas. It was said that the species *Homo sapiens* may have begun as a race, for races were considered incipient species; but at present, the species had developed to contain several races. Each fossil man had features that were absent from other fossil men and from contemporary man. The result, many geneticists held, was that it was impossible to regard one fossil man as an ancestor of another or to find *the* ancestor of *Homo sapiens.*

The difference between a species and a race indicated the openness of the genetic system. Races could interbreed, but species could not. The common ancestor of apes and humans was probably of a separate species from either. In the end, the genetic paradigm held that race was a statistical phenomenon, that no pure races existed or would exist, that man was of one species, and that races were geotypes (defined by geographic location) but not ecotypes (defined by ecological environment).

In an effort to find those human elements that were least modified by evolution, physical anthropologists turned to the analysis of blood groups. William C. Boyd, one such anthropologist, has explained why. According to Boyd, there were two physical characteristics in humans that had changed little through time, these were sex organs and genes. However, because of prudery, sex organs had been ignored by scientists. Genes had become the subject of study because of the belief that they were unaffected by evolution and because of the belief that they were nonadaptive (beliefs that were to prove erroneous). The most advantageous genes to study seemed to be those of blood groups; the genes that determined physical characteristics took longer to find and, in the 1930's, were not even known. The genes that determined blood groups had the advantage of not affecting physical appearance, of being common, and of being understood in genetic terms. Further, testing could be easily done by technicians with minimal training.

Karl Landsteiner, a German bacteriologist, and his students discovered the four classical blood groups between 1900 and 1902. The realization that different populations had varying proportions of blood groups came during the First World War through the work of two Polish doctors on the Macedonian front, who published their result in 1919. Another German, F. Berstein, demonstrated in 1925 how blood types were inherited. Finally, in 1940, Dr. Landsteiner, along with A. S. Wiener, discovered the existence of the Rh factor. Because of the extreme difficulties created by incompatibility of blood cells of different Rh factors (an Rh negative mother can develop antibodies against her fetus's blood), the use of blood groups for hereditary study became even more valuable.

Early advocates of racial typing with blood groups made over 1500 observations of humans and anthropoid apes by 1950. Physical anthropologists tried to derive "serological races," based on blood groups, which were more accurate than physical measurements. One such researcher, Boyd, identified six races by blood groups—Eastern European, European, African, Asiatic, American Indian, and Australoid. However, it soon became apparent that blood types were adaptive—sickle shaped blood cells, for example, were more common in malarial areas where they were more useful —and that race typing by blood groups was as arbitrary as race typing by external physical features.

Not all physical anthropologists converted to a serological concept of race. Blood typing of dead individuals was difficult, while fossil skeletons could be found and used as hard physical evidence. In addition, older anthropologists had found genetics difficult to understand and resisted the overly enthusiastic claims of the advocates of "serological races." But genetics had to be acknowledged by all physical anthropologists, and they did modify their ideas in line with the ideas of the population geneticists. This modification, however, took time.

An example of this was E. A. Hooton, who was unsure whether there were behavioral traits characteristic of different races and in his works showed the dilemma of an older scholar attempting to cope with a new paradigm. In *Up From the Ape* (1931), Hooton maintained that human races could be categorized by multiple physical characteristics, most of which were nonadaptive (he was to change his mind about this in his second edition in 1946). These characteristics consisted of primary traits (such as skin color and head shape), modified only by evolution, and secondary ones, which were intermixtures of two or more primary features. Hooton, like the geneticists, rejected the idea of the existence of any pure race and maintained that any social intercourse between groups always implied sexual intercourse. "Man is the most promiscuous animal ever evolved in the matter of indiscriminate interbreeding." Not that

Hooton disapproved of this; in general, he favored racial intermixture. He believed that, historically, civilizations had risen from the mixture of two races not too physically dissimilar from each other. He quoted with approbation the 1910 study of R. B. Dixon that showed that half-White Indians had a larger number of children and greater vitality than full-blooded ones. But Hooton had not abandoned the belief in a connection between race and culture. He denied that a link had been proven but was willing to keep the question open.

Hooton's midway position between the older physical anthropology and the newer cultural anthropology could be seen in his *Apes, Men and Morons* (1938). In this collection of lectures, Hooton still insisted that race was a physical subdivision that could be determined. While admitting that most persons were a mixture of racial stocks, Hooton claimed that gross physical features, including color, correlated to character and behavior. In primitive human society, where humans adapted physically to their environment, natural selection supposedly operated freely and, with interbreeding, led to the preservation of the highest types. However, in all present civilized societies, social restrictions permitted the survival of the physically inferior, the antisocial, and the mentally ineffective. What America needed, according to Hooton, was a purge of these defectives by using selective breeding. At the same time that he said this, Hooton also pointed out problems with the Eugenics Movement and attacked the Nordic theory of pure races as advocated by the Germans. Hooton urged a modified eugenics position, one based not on race but on desirable and undesirable physical qualities. With his mixed views, Hooton was an interesting example of how a eugenics proponent could assimilate a genetic theory of race, could react against German racial theory, and still believe that inherited physical characteristics influenced behavior.

The 1930's saw the full-blown development of a new belief in racial equality, which affected psychology. The most typical statement of this belief appeared in Thomas Russell Garth's *Race Psychology: A Study of Racial Mental Differences* (1931). Garth had begun his study convinced that he would find clear-cut racial differences in mental ability but was unable to do so.

Garth criticized the position of the earlier proponents of the existence of racial mental differences—Grant, Stoddard, and Mc-Dougall—as well as their belief that races had become fixed through time. Garth accepted, instead, the ideas of Boas, Ward, and Dixon that races were fluid and were, in fact, descriptive of a process rather than a status. The process of change that was called race was only a concept, a shorthand term for describing group differences. Human physical differences were, Garth claimed, a product of the geographic isolation of some populations and probably were a late development in human evolution.

In order to prove racial differences, Garth stated that four testing conditions must be achieved: mental processes must be correctly measured, standard conditions must be maintained for test and control groups, subjects must represent racial groups, and results must be interpreted in light of all the facts. All but natural variables must be eliminated from test situations; cultural differences such as education, behavior modification, ideals, and the attitude of the experimenters should be filtered out. In other words, race must be approached scientifically and empirically. Using these standards, Garth analyzed the mental studies done before 1930, beginning with those that tested individuals who were racially mixed.

The first example Garth examined was a test administered by C. O. Ferguson at Camp Lee, Virginia, in 1919, which purported to find a direct correlation between light-skinned blacks and high I.Q. scores. Another study examined was one that Garth himself had administered to Indians in 1921 and that he had reported in the *Journal of Applied Psychology*. He had concluded that mixed-blood Indians scored 11 percent higher on the average than full-blood Indians because of the presence of white blood. However, when Garth closely scrutinized both studies, he discovered that differences in education provided an alternate explanation that reduced racial differences to insignificance. This discovery, combined with Klineberg's finding, published in *Archives of Psychology* (1928), that there was no significant correlation of nose width, lip thickness, ear height, interpupillary span, or a composite of all racial traits to the results of I.Q. tests in the black subjects Klineberg tested, led Garth to conclude that "no device for measuring mental traits has been sufficiently refined so that in its operation it could produce results conforming to the accepted principles of Mendelian inheritance." Thus, he concluded that all of the I.Q. tests made on mixed populations, White-Black and White-Indian, up to 1930 were invalid. Table 10.1 contains Garth's summary of I.Q. findings which he considered wrong.

In individual tests of Blacks, the I.Q. ranged from 78 to 103;

TABLE 10.1

Year	Median I.Q.	Test Group
1922	75	247 Negroes in Arkansas
1925	75	1,272 Negroes in Texas
1926	76.5	613 Southern Negroes (nonlanguage)
1928	78	222 Negroes in Secondary Schools in Texas
1929	75	734 Negroes in Tennessee
1925	70.4	1,000 full-blood Indians
1925	68.6	1,050 full-blood Indians
1927		765 subjects
	77	quarter-blood Indians
	75	half-blood Indians
	74	three-quarter bloods

(brace for last four rows: all done in Indian school)

there were no individual tests given the Indians. The results yielded these median figures: white Americans—100, northern Blacks—85, southern Blacks—75, and Indians—70.

Garth next reviewed the early studies on supposed racial differences in sensory traits, beginning with R. S. Woodworth's study of primitive people at the World's Congress of Races in 1904. Woodworth tested 300 individuals, including American Indians, Negritoes from the Philippines, Malays, Ainus, Africans, Eskimos, and Patagonians, for sensitivity of sight, hearing, smell, touch, and color discrimination. The results showed little difference among groups, although all these individuals had slightly better sight and slightly inferior hearing than their supposedly more civilized brothers. Woodworth concluded that the better sight was not the consequence of natural ability but was rather a function of superior use of visual cues and, hence, was a learned response produced by environmental necessity. Woodworth also tried a form of board test to determine intelligence but failed to obtain valid results. Garth agreed with Woodworth's conclusions from the study, which were that there was no basis for the myth of primitive superiority in elementary psychological processes and that all humans were about equal in sensory abilities.

Turning to other studies of racial mental traits, Garth found the same results. Beginning in 1881, 104 such tests had been administered, 40 to the American Black (25,000 individuals). The interest in America's racial problems made the Blacks and the Indians the most popular groups to study. The first studies involved psychophysical measurements of reaction time and sensory processes and showed no significant racial differences. Intelligence tests superseded the earlier studies because I.Q. tests could be administered to groups as well as individuals, unlike sensory tests, and were faster and easier to administer. Group tests of rote memory, abstract memory, logical memory, ingenuity, and the ability to do sustained work indicated that all races were inferior to the White, except for the Chinese who ranked higher in rote memory. In 1913, Aline C. Strong used the Binet I.Q. test on South Carolina Blacks to confirm their racial inferiority. By World War I, I.Q. tests had driven out sensory ones both because I.Q. tests were easy to use and because they confirmed the existence of racial differences.

These early mental testers had tested without a clear idea of what they were testing. Garth pointed out that the concept of intelligence appeared only indirectly in psychology. Nineteenth-century theorists had not even used the term, which first emerged in controlled experiments as a description of animal talents. When referring to humans, intelligence originally alluded to the negative quantity possessed by feebleminded individuals. The concept of intelligence was neither defined nor mentioned in the majority of psychology textbooks before 1927. Even when defined, the word had several meanings for educational psychologists. Thorndike defined intelligence as the combination of an individual's special abilities, while Spearman defined it as one unit. Despite the lack of a generally accepted definition of intelligence and despite the lack of thought about what was being tested, I.Q. tests became a necessary part of the psychological apparatus.

Garth criticized the testers for overlooking the influence of education and the fact that Indians and Blacks did not share a common cultural environment with Whites. He (accurately) predicted that someday it would be shown that the skin color of the Black handicapped him in a testing situation, that the Indian deliberately chose not to take the white man's tests seriously, and that both nurture and environment altered I.Q. While Garth questioned the validity of the I.Q. tests, he continued to use them, attributing differences in scores to environmental and not racial differences. He also tried to measure the effects of education on the I.Q.'s of white, Indian, and black children. His results showed that the white I.Q. scores went up rapidly until age 15 before leveling off. The black scores resembled the white except that they ascended more slowly. The black median I.Q., according to Garth, began to decline at grade seven, a phenomenon he attributed to the dropping out from school of superior students, who sensed the lack of relevance of education. Education raised all scores. The median

I.Q. of Indians never matched that of the Whites. Mixed-blood Indians surpassed white students in Indian schools but fell behind in white public schools. This provided further evidence to Garth that the I.Q. was questionable and that there was no culture-free test for non-Whites. (This did not prevent him from hoping that such a test might be constructed.)

Garth also evaluated tests for color preference, musical talent, personality, mental fatigue, and the comprehensiveness of a community of ideas. He found few significant differences among Indian, black, and white subjects. The Indians saw more colors; white children performed a little better on the Seashore Test for Musical Talent (which incidentally was standardized on white children); Indians seemed slower in decision making than Whites while Blacks fell in between the two; there was no real difference in the time it took to become mentally fatigued; and the black community of ideas seemed slightly more limited than the white. But none of these findings were significant or conclusive.

Garth's conclusions sound surprisingly contemporary. He stated that races were mutable, that the concept of race was an artificial one, that mental traits were difficult to isolate, that I.Q. tests showed differences that probably resulted from unequal environments, and that I.Q. could be changed by manipulation of the environment. Racial differences in sensory traits appeared either insignificant or nonexistent; the same was true of personality, musical talent, color preferences, and mental fatigue. In the end, Garth expressed the belief that the poor showing of Blacks and Indians on I.Q. tests was a function of inferior schools and social environment and would be only temporary.

Otto Klineberg followed Garth's salvo with added explanation of poorer black scores on I.Q. tests in his *Negro Intelligence and Selective Migration* (1935). Klineberg was a follower of Boas and dedicated his *Race Differences* (1935), which was the most significant statement of the newer anthropological view of race, to Boas.

In *Negro Intelligence and Selective Migration*, Klineberg indicated that testers had neglected to take into account regional differences in scores, although these differences were obvious in the data. For example, the tests showed Northern Blacks often scoring higher than southern Whites. Northern Blacks also had a median I.Q. of 86.3 compared to a median of 79.6 for Southern Blacks. The reasons for the difference could have been a better social environment in the North or the location of superior individuals there, which he called selective migration. Klineberg determined to find out the explanations.

Klineberg studied the black migrations to the North of 1916 to 1917 and 1923 to 1924. According to both northern and southern white newspapers, the first black migration had consisted of inferior people; on the other hand, northern and southern black newspapers had said that the bright Blacks had moved North. By 1924, northern white newspapers had accepted the black explanation; only the southern white newspapers said otherwise. Klineberg then examined the school records of black students who had lived in Nashville, Birmingham, and Charleston prior to moving to New York City as well as the school records of black students who had always been resident in the city. He tried to correlate test scores with the number of years of residence in the North.

Klineberg found no evidence that the Blacks who moved to the North were originally superior to those who stayed in the South, but he discovered a gradual raising of test scores of migrants over a period of time. The scores in both group and individual Stanford-Binet tests of Blacks improved in direct ratio to their length of residence in the North while performance tests remained the same. Klineberg concluded that the changes reflected no difference in intellectual capability but, instead, showed improvement in linguistic ability because of the superiority of the New York City school system. To demonstrate that race was not the basis for raised test scores, Klineberg tested the hypothesis that there was a correlation between skin color and I.Q. results and, like Herskovits, found that such a relationship did not exist. There was no doubt in Klineberg's mind that the superior northern environment had raised the Black's test scores and that if an equal environment could be provided for southern Blacks, equal test scores would ensure.

In his *Race Differences* (1935), Klineberg mounted a major attack on all areas of the racial front. He criticized the ideas of Gobineau (a European racial theorist in the nineteenth century), Madison Grant (whom he called America's Gobineau), and R. B. Dixon and pointed to the difficulties of identifying race. Any definition of race, to be scientifically valid, had to include physical characteristics that were determined by heredity and the statistical distribution of these traits in different populations. But the characteristics and traits said to be racial were shared by many populations and, as Boas had shown, physical types changed because of environmental circumstance. Even if races could be definitely established, there was no connection between race and nation or race and language. Klineberg denied the theory of polygenesis and denounced Klaastsch in particular; he believed in monogenesis and that humans were of a single species. Nor did Klineberg accept the idea of serological races; he said that the serological division of people bore little relation to the usual racial one. More difficult for Klineberg to challenge was a side attempt of physical anthropologists to classify races on the basis of endocrine glands.

In the 1920's, some explanations of racial differences exploited the new discovery of the functions of hormones. Sir Arthur Keith, a Scottish anthropologist, was perhaps the leading figure in the movement, although German theorists such as Baur, Fischer, and Linz also were prominent. In an article, "The Evolution of Human Races in the Light of Hormone Theory," which appeared in the *Bulletin of Johns Hopkins Hospital* in 1922, Keith postulated that different races had different glandular balances that produce physical and behavioral differences. The Mongoloid race supposedly had an over-large thymus and were hypothyroid. The steatopygia of the African Hottentots (excessive fat on the buttocks) was attributed to a pituitary enlargement, and the Nile blacks supposedly had gonads which were deficient in cells. Keith's major thesis was that white racial supremacy came from superior adrenal development. Like Prichard, Keith argued that humans were originally black but, because certain individuals had more adrenal development, they became white. Those who remained dark supposedly suffered from an adrenal insufficiency, which also operated to retard them culturally. Keith tied twentieth-century medical discoveries to nineteenth-century evolutionism to develop a hormonal theory of race.

Klineberg revealed part of the problem with the hormonal approach to racial classification. Attacking Keith and L. Berman—another of the hormone racists whose article in the *Scientific Monthly,* "Anthropology and the Endocrine Glands" (1925), circulated widely—Klineberg showed how both men had ascribed a hormonal deficiency to all members of a race without finding evidence of all the symptoms of the hormonal deficiency. For example, adrenal insufficiency produced passive, physically weak individuals, but Blacks were not passive or physically weak. Neither the Nilotic Black nor the Hottentot showed loss of sexual powers, as they should have if their gonads or pituitary glands had been abnormal.

Further, the Chinese should have shown physical and mental retardation if they were hypothyroid, but they did not.

The old claims of racial inferiority because of a lower facial angle, physical differences, lower cranial capacity, and a different kind of brain still persisted, and Klineberg attacked these as well. To D. G. Patterson's contention in *Physique and Intellect* (1930) that cranial volume correlated directly with the extent of cultural evolution, Klineberg countered by questioning why the Eskimoes, who had the largest heads, had remained primitive. To studies that found mental differences to be products of variations in brain size and structure, Klineberg opposed studies that found just the opposite. He scoffed at the possibility of determining mental differences from outward physical features. To those who claimed to find a connection between late physical maturation and superior intelligence (and, like Nott, attributed black inferiority to the early closing of skull sutures), Klineberg showed that different rates of growth had little impact on final intelligence. Nor did physiological differences count for much. Klineberg found little evidence to show that the lower vital capacity and higher blood pressure discovered among Blacks and the lower respiration rate and poorer circulation among Indians came from hereditary factors, suggesting instead that these might be environmentally induced.

The last half of *Race Differences* contained a psychological approach to the problem of race. As in *Negro Intelligence and Selective Migration*, Klineberg insisted that there were no demonstrable variations in sensory reactions among members of different races. Klineberg claimed that I.Q. tests did not measure intelligence, but reflected such extrinsic factors as motivation (which was lacking in Indians), rapport between the person being tested and tester, culture, socioeconomic status, language (Blacks did not speak standard English), education, and sampling errors. He showed again that place of residence made a large difference to test scores, that city children achieved higher scores than rural ones and that northern children tested higher than southern ones, regardless of race. On differences in nonintellectual traits, Klineberg consistently denied both the reliability of tests and the significance of the minor variations they showed.

Klineberg also refuted eugenicists, such as R. R. Gates and C. B. Davenport, who maintained that racial intermixture was bad. Gates disliked miscegenation because he believed Blacks and

Whites had evolved separately from different anthropoid apes; Davenport supposed that mixed inheritance resulted in physical anomalies. Klineberg denied both these theories; he believed that humans came from one origin and that racially mixed persons had proved as healthy and physically able as anyone. Klineberg, in addition, defended Blacks against the charge of being social and mental misfits; he attributed the amount of black crime to social and economic deprivation rather than to race. He discounted the idea of mental abnormalities in Blacks, an idea that had originated in the nineteenth-century South and had been perpetuated by early twentieth century psychiatrists. M. O'Malley, for example, in an article "Psychoses in the Colored Races" in the *American Journal of Insanity* (1914), said that freedom from slavery had caused black animal appetites to be released, that all Blacks feared the dark, and that Blacks did not suffer from involutional melancholia because they lacked moral standards. (Involutional melancholia was the name for a psychosis that usually occurs during female menopause or male climacteric and is characterized by agitated depression.) W. M. Bevis, in his "Psychological Traits of the Southern Negro, with Observations as to Some of His Psychoses," in the *American Journal of Psychiatry* (1921) echoed these ideas. Klineberg argued that there was no racial foundation for these supposed psychological characteristics, which themselves had no basis in fact.

Klineberg concluded his book with a reemphasis upon the primacy of culture. Culture, according to Klineberg, modified physical drives such as sex and hunger, determined normal and abnormal behavior, defined childhood and adolescence, and controlled the expression of emotions. (He disagreed with McDougall and Darwin who believed emotions to be natural and connected to instinct.) Klineberg argued that all human minds resembled each other, that race had no connection with culture, and that the belief in racial differences only served to rationalize ill treatment of others.

Klineberg's book was probably the most complete refutation of his time of the idea of a racial basis for group differences. Certainly, his explanation became the standard one for group variations to be found in anthropology, sociology, and psychology textbooks. The new psychological orthodoxy spread; it appeared in a highly regarded textbook of the period, Anne Anastasi's *Differential Psychology: Individual and Group Differences in Behavior* (1937). Anastasi, who was a professor of psychology at Barnard, defined race as common traits transmitted by heredity but found racial classification based on skin color, head size or shape, blood groups, endocrine systems, or physique to be quite dubious. Anastasi claimed that race had no connection with nation or language and that there were no pure races. She accepted the concept that racial mixture might be pernicious but admitted the cause of this perniciousness might be prejudice rather than physical difficulties. She attributed the poorer showing of Indians and Blacks on I.Q. tests to language handicaps, difficulties with testing situations (the testers who gave the Army Beta test to Blacks could not keep them interested), educational differences (the American Indian attended schools irregularly), and differences in cultural milieu, traditions, customs, and interests. The supposed criteria for intellectual superiority, she attested, was related too closely to white society and school achievement to apply to non-Whites. Comparisons of the achievements of races could not be made because of different environments and histories and shifts in status; at the time of its ascendance, Benin (Nigeria) was superior to Europe. Like Klineberg, Anastasi accepted the idea of cultural causality; culture determined differences, not race.

In the realm of ethnology and cultural anthropology, the attack on race as an explanation of behavior continued the elaboration of the counter-explanation of culture. By 1948, the culture concept had become firmly fixed as the cornerstone of anthropological studies. However, no sooner was it accepted than it was modified.

An example of this was one of the leading ethnologists of the 1930's, Robert H. Lowie. Lowie was an Austrian who came to the United States as a child. Although originally intending to become a psychologist, Lowie decided to major in anthropology at Columbia because of the influence of Boas. After graduation, he volunteered to work for Clark Wissler, the head of the Department of Anthropology at the American Museum of Natural History. Wissler was a member of the Galton Society and his major works *Man and Culture* (1922) and *Social Anthropology* (1929) showed the influence of the eugenics movement. In addition, Wissler had achieved a reputation as an expert on the American Indian because of his *North American Indians of the Plains* (1912) and *The American Indian* (1917). Wissler's ideas combined biological and cultural explanations. He was an evolutionist and claimed that mental abilities of individuals representing different races could be compared and that psychology dealt with the innate, original nature of humans. In describing societies, Wissler used biological analogies, one of which was the "age-area" concept, which said that societies developed in the same ways as human beings. At the same time, Wissler was a cultural determinist who claimed that the shape of a society resulted from learned human behavior.

Lowie respected Morgan's evolutionism; he had personally verified Morgan's description of the Crows' kinship relationship and had been much impressed by W. H. Rivers's *Kinship and Social Organization* (1914), which he felt vindicated Morgan's theory that the terms used by persons to describe their religion had an intimate connection with their own social structure and matrimonial customs. Although he accepted a moderate Morgan-like theory of cultural evolution, he attacked other ideas of Morgan. Morgan, Lowie said, should not have equated ironmaking with civilization, for the pyramids of both Mexico and Egypt were built by peoples with only bronze tools. Nor should he have used domestication of plants or animals as an infallible correlate to cultural development.

Lowie also found fault with *Human Heredity* (1931), a book written by three Germans, Eugen Fischer, E. Baur, and F. Linz, who had abandoned the thesis that human races differed significantly in average mental ability but who insisted that there were important racial differences in the range of intelligence. They argued that an inborn supremacy of the white race was shown by the extreme deviations of some of its individuals from the norm; only Whites were geniuses, they claimed. The Germans believed that a genius required a certain number of genetic units and that the absence of even one unit was fatal. Other races supposedly lacked the genetic strength of Whites. Lowie used history to refute the Germans, pointing out that there had been great Indians—Tecumseh and Chief Joseph—and great Africans—the kings of Benin and Zulu states. Thus Lowie assumed the practice of using the cultural achievements of different civilizations to measure their relative intelligence.

Lowie's best known work was *The History of Ethnological Theory* (1937), which defined ethnography as that part of anthropology that dealt with the culture of human groups and not with race or psychology. Insisting that cultural anthropology was a science, Lowie attacked the newly formed union between psychoanalysis and anthropology, which he thought added uncertainty to the latter discipline. Lowie never abandoned the possibility of comparing cultures. Further Lowie believed that elements from one culture should be studied in relation to those from other cultures and that perhaps the study would "justify a greatly tempered parallelism or neo-evolutionism." He denied that societies could be categorized by patterns of cultures as Benedict had done. Indeed, he had harsh words for her efforts. "White visitors to the Hopi, including some justly esteemed ethnologists, have voiced veritable paeans of praise of the Hopi way of life and their attitude toward the universe. I was never able to share this enthusiasm." In summary, Lowie denied that race contributed to cultural growth but claimed that heredity did and that cross-cultural comparisons might be made.

Meanwhile, Boas and his students also continued the attack on the last remaining defenses of the older paradigm of cultural evolution based upon racial differences. In 1940, Boas questioned the validity of I.Q. tests in a speech before the American Educational Research Association, revealing the failure of scientists to define intelligence adequately. Boas assaulted Hitlerism and the Nordic racial theory in articles and speeches compiled in *Race, Language, and Culture* (1940). Included in the collection was an essay, "Aims of Anthropological Research," written in 1932, which advocated the study of racial functions, attacked I.Q. tests, and said that the proper object of psychological study was the individual under cultural stress. However, Boas was not consistent in his thinking and, by 1940, was no longer in the vanguard of the critique of racism; he still retained elements of an older conceptual framework.

Ruth Benedict, Boas' student, had admired Boas greatly, but her anthropology varied considerably from his; she had a poetic touch that he lacked (she wrote poetry under the name of Anne Singleton). She became an influential teacher at Columbia University, although the Faculty of Political Science, in which anthropology resided, had never before included a woman member. Her intellectual interests ranged widely; she showed the influence of the German theorists Nietzsche, Spengler, and Dilthey. From Dilthey she acquired historicism, the idea that a society can only be understood in terms of its own history, a historical concept parallel to the anthropological one of cultural relativism. From Spengler she took the idea of a group ethos, the idea that each society possessed a unique spirit.

In 1940, she essayed a popularly written account of racism in *Race, Science and Politics,* which reacted mainly to overseas events. Benedict began by saying that:

Race is a matter for careful scientific study; racism is an unproved assumption of the biological and perpetual superiority of one human group over another.

Benedict denounced German racial ideas and defined race as determined by those traits that were transmitted genetically; she denied the connection between language and culture or between race and civilization. She attacked the theory of polygenesis and the attempt of physical anthropologists to classify people by either outward forms—skin and eye color, hair, nose and head shape—or internal ones—blood groups or hormones. She claimed that all humans were now racially intermixed because of mobility and urbanization, although curiously, she maintained that racial intermixture between disparate racial groups was socially unfortunate:

The evils of these prohibited mixtures in Germany and in India are unquestionable; they are apparent to any observer. Those who have themselves made mixed marriages and the children of such unions are the first to testify to the unsatisfactory situation in which they find themselves.

While Benedict did not consider racial mixture biologically pernicious, she felt that its social costs were high for those involved. Benedict denied white racial superiority in mental ability and repeated the already popular criticisms of I.Q. tests, contending that Blacks and Indians had cultural handicaps. She believed that the Indian and the Black had developed high civilizations that had been subverted by white pressures; one could not, however, derive a law of cultural progress by comparing these civilizations with white ones.

Benedict traced the history of racism from primitive tribes to the present time. Her history of racism was superficial and full of errors; she claimed, for example, that racist ideas originated in Germany, coming to the United States only in 1890, and that American racist literature did not discuss America's great national racial problem. Her attempts to explain universal racial prejudice were equally superficial; she maintained that prejudice reflected either a class or national interest or the need to justify social conflict. Turning to the United States, Benedict castigated the South for failing to end racial discrimination and stated her position on Blacks:

Granted that great numbers of Negroes are not ready for full citizenship, the social conditions which perpetuate their poverty and ignorance must be remedied before anyone can judge what kind of citizens they might be in other, more favorable circumstances.

Race, Science and Politics is a curious book, for while Benedict saw European racism clearly, she failed to recognize the strength of American racial prejudice. While her data on newer ideas of race were up-to-date, her history and analysis of racism was weak.

Benedict believed that culture appeared in patterns. These patterns could be compared so that patterns of patterns could be constructed; the patterns of patterns would then correspond to certain inner psychological states of the members of the culture. She proposed to study primitive people who had had more time to elaborate cultural themes and whose problems were couched in simpler terms than those of Western civilization. Benedict denied that primitive people were racially inferior; she claimed that humans were infinitely plastic and that hereditary inheritance could not be determined except in geographically isolated communities. Nor would she accept the idea that primitive people represented human primordial origins. She was, in other words, anti-evolutionary and accepted the Boasian ideas about culture and race. However, despite her belief in cultural relativism, she compared cultures; as a contemporary anthropologist, Victor Barnouw, says in "Ruth Benedict: Apollonian and Dionysian," *University of Toronto Quarterly* (1949), she "passed out value-judgments right and left on the culture of her day."

Benedict attacked the acquisitive American society of the 1930's, with its sexual repression and its excessive competition. The Zuni Indians represented, for Benedict, cultural values sorely needed in American civilization. Because of her desire to improve America, she romanticized the Indians, despite her denials of the fact. She committed all the errors of the nineteenth-century armchair anthropologists whom she condemned for not going into the field. Victor Barnouw accused her of making facile generalizations, ignoring evidence, relying on little data, and misinterpreting reasons for cultural development. She failed to see the Dionysian elements in the drinking, scalp dances, and initiation whippings of the Zuni culture. Her categorization of the Indians distorted them into ideal types and oversimplified complex social reality. She failed to explain why individuals were socialized into one kind of behavior and not another, nor did she reflect much on the origin of behavior in general.

More crucial than her errors of oversight or evidence, however, was Benedict's insistence upon cultural relativism (that all patterns of culture were equally valid for the people who possessed them) set alongside her suggestions that some cultures were to be preferred over others. This dilemma was not hers alone; it was implicit in the formulation of the concept of cultural relativism and rendered very difficult the counterattack on racism. As a critic, Elgin Williams has said the idea of cultural relativism carried to its ultimate conclusion would lead to an acceptance of Jim Crow in the South. If a pattern of prejudice was functional in a society, by what standards could it be called bad?

Margaret Mead, a student of Benedict and Boas whose field work in the Pacific had resulted in her classic *Coming of Age in Samoa* (1928), also turned her attention to American racism. Mead, one of four anthropologists commissioned by the Committee for National Morale in 1939 to analyze American society, applied field techniques to research *And Keep Your Powder Dry* (1942). Although Mead claimed she could see America better because she had been to the South Seas, she missed the import of American racism almost entirely. She said:

A twenty-one-year-old boy born of Chinese-American parents in a small upstate New York town who has just graduated *summa cum laude* from Harvard and a tenth-generation Boston-born deaf mute of United Kingdom stock are equally perfect examples of American national character.

However, she did not mention Blacks or Indian-Americans among her examples. She justified Indian removal: "When the Indians and other European nations interfered with the job which we had decided to do on this continent, we pushed them aside without scruples." Apparently, white Americans only did what needed to be done. Her orientation was toward winning World War II; her fear was that Americans were not aggressive enough to do so; she attacked pacifism. Her basic premise was that American behavior was best understood through the immigrant experience, thus again overlooking Indians and Blacks. Mead unconsciously reflected the prevailing assumptions of the time, that all Americans had similar pasts and behaved in similar fashions.

Another student of Boas, however, expanded the paradigm of culture to its utmost limit, an effort that revealed some of the problems in the model. This was Alfred Louis Kroeber, who studied the culture, languages, and religions of the North American Indians as well as the archeology of Mexico and Peru and who had been sent by Wissler to study the Ute Indians. Unlike Lowie, Kroeber used psychology and tried, in conjunction with Terman, to design a "culture-free" I.Q. test in 1920. His major contribution to anthropological theory, however, was the doctrine of cultural determinism, most completely articulated in *Anthropology* (1948). As David Bidney, a historian and critic of anthropological theory, says, "He [Kroeber] was the first to formulate a theory of emergent evolution of cultural development and a deterministic philosophy of cultural history which Boas and his other students did not share."

Kroeber, unlike Boas, attempted to resolve the questions implicit in the concept of cultural differences. Did the culture of an area completely determine the actions of all its members or did an individual in a culture possess some limited freedom to influence his own development? One position conceived of culture, like race, as an independent and natural entity, which determined human destiny and rendered any possibility of individual change difficult. A second position denied the total influence of culture and provided space for explanations of individual change. Boas had not chosen between the two alternatives, but Kroeber did. He opted for cultural determinism; he conceived of culture as a natural phenomenon. He ignored history and regarded cultures as constant and unchanging through time. He equated cultural areas with natural, ecological ones. What Kroeber did was to substitute culture for race as the determining condition of man's social development. What he failed to do was to account for social change and for different kinds of cultural development in societies. He reified culture, he tried to transform an abstract idea into an almost physical reality.

Another influence in American cultural anthropology of the period was that of a Polish-born, English-trained anthropologist, Bronislaw Kasper Malinowski, who ended his teaching career at Yale University. Malinowski had lived among the Trobriand Islanders from 1914 to 1918 and had published the results of his studies in such works as *The Natives of Mailu* (1915), *Argonauts of the Western Pacific* (1923), *Sex and Repression in Savage Society* (1926), and *The Sexual Life of Savages in Northwest Melanesia* (1929). His theoretical ideas appeared in two posthumously published books, *A Scientific Theory of Culture and Other Essays* (1944) and *The Dynamics of Culture Change* (1945), where he articulated the concept of functionalism. Functionalism was a kind of instrumentalism which argued that the usefulness of an idea determined its truth. According to the idea of functionalism, as Malinowski defined it, the nature of a cultural entity was described by its effect in a given social context. For example, an Indian spear has a special meaning in Indian society that does not correspond to the meaning of an African spear to an African. No cultural entity could be studied in isolation from the cultural whole, nor could aggregates of cultural traits or forms from one culture be compared with those of another culture. Instead of trying to formulate general historical or cultural laws, functionalists like Malinowski strove to discover psychological or sociological laws within a culture. As David Bidney has said, anthropology, which began as a study of the evolution of the culture of mankind, had become the science of particular cultures conceived of as functional wholes. Although Boas himself did not accept functionalism, he had helped contribute to it; and the addition of functionalism completed cultural relativism.

The impending war did not divert scholarly attention from domestic problems. The Catholic University of America Press published a compendium entitled *Scientific Aspects of the Race Problem* in 1941, which included essays by Hrdlička, Robert Lowie, and Otto Klineberg. Hrdlička, who had become the Curator of the Division of Physical Anthropology at the National Museum in Washington, had changed his racial views. He had redefined a race as encompassing the physical characteristics of the differing but more or less persistent strains shown by a group within a single species. Hrdlička maintained there was no connection between race and culture, but he still clung to the idea of racial differences. He believed that all men had evolved from the same primate ancestor (a monogenetic position) but that races had differentiated since. Races supposedly differed mentally, morphologically, and physiologically in proportion to the length of their separation from the original primate stem and the extent of their total experiences and activities. Hrdlička, however, predicted a future world where racial differences would disappear.

The argument for culture and against the use of the concept of race received its penultimate expression in M. F. Ashley Montagu's *Man's Most Dangerous Myth: The Fallacy of Race* (1942). Montagu defined a race as a subdivision of a species which had inherited physical characteristics distinguishing it from other populations of the same species. He traced a history of the idea of race, dating its origins in the 1760's and saying that the concept reached its zenith in the writings of Gobineau. Montagu recapitulated the genetic theory of race, which had, according to Montagu, four postulates—monogenetic origin, human dispersal through migration, race formation through geographic isolation, and further differentiation of isolated populations through genetic drift and mutation. (Montagu did not realize that his explanation of the origin of races paralleled that of the sixteenth and nineteenth centuries with the added mechanism of genetic change.) Montagu repeated the findings of his time, denying that physical characteristics of various people could be ranked, that a correlation existed between brain size and intelligence, or that there was a connection between race and culture. His most startling, though logical, proposal was to eliminate the word race in favor of a new term, ethnic group, which he defined as a population in the process of undergoing genetic differentiation. Montagu evidently believed that the elimination of the concept of race would help end racial prejudice; he denied that there was any original American prejudice because of color.

Montagu relied on a psychological explanation for prejudice. He said that it originated as frustration caused by the socialization process; it was a sign of undeveloped personality; and it could be eliminated by education. He did not, it seems, realize the strength of the racial idea nor the extent of historical forces.

By World War II, American social scientists had accepted a new paradigm centered upon the concept of culture. The concept of culture replaced the concept of race, which increasingly came under attack. Although the war is often cited as the beginning of this attack, the evidence seems to indicate that the attack originated much earlier.

Chapter 11

Lingering Doubts

The assumption that the black man, like the Indian, was a vanishing American seemed confirmed by the Census of 1930. The percentage of Blacks in the total American population reached its lowest point since the seventeenth century. The Census of 1940, however, showed a black increase while the Census of 1950 revealed that Blacks were holding their own. The figures are in Table 11.1.

TABLE 11.1

Year	Black Population	Percent of Total American Population
1930	11,890,000	9.7
1940	12,870,000	9.9
1950	15,050,000	9.9

The 1930 census, like earlier ones, probably underestimated the number of Blacks, and the 1940 increase may have been the result of this underestimation. In any case, the virtual end of European immigration to the United States provided, for the first time, the opportunity for an accurate comparison of black and white natural increase rates in the United States. Since the black death rate remained higher than the white, the increase in the number of blacks from 1930 to 1950 indicated that the birth rate was probably higher among Blacks than Whites.

The censuses also spelled out the increasing urbanization of Blacks and their migration to the North. By 1940, only 75 percent of the total black population was left in the South. The proportion of the black population that lived in the North resided almost entirely in cities, which included nearly three million black inhabitants of urban ghettoes. The migration was, in part, a result of both World War II and a heightened demand for labor in industrial areas. Nowhere had Blacks become the dominant urban population. The Blacks in central cities were a minority; the day of black majorities in these areas was yet to come.

By the 1950's, conditions in the black community had improved somewhat, although the improvement was more symbolic than realistic. Caught in an economic pinch early in the 1920's, the misery of black farmers and workers had intensified in the depression of the 1930's. Although the New Deal has been commonly identified with the growth of civil rights, the movement in that direction was slow and uncertain. Franklin Roosevelt made little commitment to the cause of the American Negro, balancing off his debts to the Blacks who had supported him (and who were the first Blacks to desert the Republican party for the Democratic party since Woodrow Wilson) with his debts to the traditionally Democratic white South. When Walter White, black Secretary of the NAACP in the 1930's, called on Roosevelt to support a federal antilynching bill, Roosevelt refused because he knew that the South would oppose such legislation and he did not wish to lose southern white votes. Roosevelt did not publicly associate himself with black projects or leaders until 1935, but his wife Eleanor did. In a sense, she became a symbol of the racial liberality of the New Deal; by such acts as encouraging Marian Anderson to sing in Washington after the DAR (Daughters of the American Revolution) had refused to hear her and by intercession with the President, she gave Roosevelt's administration the appearance of civil rights progressivism.

The New Deal record was insubstantial. Relief programs were segregated; although the amount of federal money sent to areas was in direct proportion to their total population regardless of race, black families received less than their fair share of the money as apportioned by local authorities. In Jacksonville, Florida, for example, 15,000 black families received 45 percent of the total relief funds while 5,000 white families got 55 percent. The National Recovery Act codes, which set minimum wages and hours, failed to cover agricultural workers, domestic servants, those engaged in the service trades, and unskilled workers. This meant that black wage-earners, who fell mainly into these categories, lacked a federal floor under their wages. The TVA (Tennessee Valley Association) discriminated against Blacks in housing practices in the Tennessee Valley, building separate homes for white workers but putting black ones in barracks. The Agricultural Adjustment Administration paid benefits to white landlords, but few black tenants or sharecroppers received any of the money. Additionally, the soil conservation provisions of the AAA, designed to remove arable land from crop production, actually speeded up the displacement of black tenants and sharecroppers as white landlords took their land out of use.

The NAACP tried hard to improve the conditions of Blacks in the 1930's but lacked money and support. In 1932, the organization attacked the concept of "separate but equal" by showing that segregation was essentially unequal; however, legal support for the attack was not really established for another decade. Abram L. Harris, a spokesman for the younger, more radical elements of the NAACP, urged black alliance with white workers, trade unions, cooperatives, and workers' councils in order to provide a common class tie instead of separate racial ones, but this failed to gain majority approval of the controlling element of the organization. There was some progress on the legal front, however. In *Missouri ex rel Gaines* v. *Canada* (1938), the Supreme Court ruled that Gaines, who was black and who wished to go to law school in Missouri (a state that had no black law schools and that refused admission of Blacks to the University of Missouri law school), had to be provided with legal training in the state and not be shunted off to a northern state with transportation and tuition costs paid, as was the common practice of Southern states. The Court required that the state of Missouri provide legal education for Gaines either in a separate law school or in a desegregated University of Missouri law school. The decision was the first in a series leading to the 1954 school desegregation cases.

The group that had the most successful impact on President Roosevelt was not the NAACP, which Roosevelt disliked, but the March-on-Washington Movement, which, because of its mass appeal, has been called the first of the new civil rights movements.

Led by A. Philip Randolph, the founder and president of the black union called the Brotherhood of Sleeping Car Porters, the movement threatened a mass black protest march to Washington unless its demands were met. These demands included a Fair Employment Practices Commission (FEPC), which would forbid: discrimination in hiring or firing in industry, the awarding of governmental contracts to discriminating employers, the supplying of workers by the U.S. Employment Service to businesses on a racial basis, discrimination and segregation in the armed services and the federal government, and providing government benefits to unions that denied membership to black workers. Randolph mobilized many Blacks behind him and, for the first time since Garvey, the nation faced the possibility of major mass action by Blacks. The march did not occur as Roosevelt, fearful of the impact of the demonstrators, capitulated by signing Executive Order 8802, which established the FEPC in June, 1941. The Commission proved less than effective during the second World War and died in 1946. Other demands made by the March-on-Washington Movement were not met. Even a request of Edwin R. Embree, a black consultant to the Julius Rosenwald Fund, for a commission of experts on race relations to advise Roosevelt during the war went unheeded.

World War II elicited a different reaction from the American black community than had World War I. Blacks had greeted the first World War as a test of their ability to fight and of their patriotism; they were less enthusiastic about the second World War. Capitalizing on propaganda aimed at totalitarianism and racism abroad, Blacks reacted against racism at home and pushed for an end to discrimination in the armed services, draft boards, blood banks, and employment. Black resistance to the war puzzled white Americans who could not understand black demands and who often blamed them on the radical black press and leaders. Even Secretary of War Stimson, who was usually well informed, said that the racial tension in the United States was deliberately caused by black radicals to obtain "racial equality and interracial marriage" (as quoted by Richard M. Dalfuime in "The Forgotten Years of Negro Revolution," *Journal of American History* [1968]).

There were attempts to placate Blacks. The Selective Service Act of 1940 contained an anti-discrimination clause; ROTC units were created in Negro colleges. (Although the second Morrill Act of 1890 had provided for officer training in Negro colleges, this provision had been honored more in the breach than the practice.)

Benjamin O. Davis became the first black general in the army's history; and another Black became an aide to the Secretary of War. After much pressure, an aviation school to train black fliers was located at Tuskegee. But the treatment of black soldiers in Army bases in the South and in the North negated token advances. Segregation on and off military bases led to racial tension, and the attempts of white commanders to make black soldiers conform with local customs and laws depressed the morale of black G.I.'s even further. As a result, there was rioting at almost every southern base —including Fort Bragg, North Carolina, and Fort Benning, Georgia, two of the largest infantry training facilities in the United States. One of the major eruptions occurred in Alexandria, Louisiana, in 1942 when an M.P. tried to arrest a black soldier. The riot resulted in the shooting of 28 persons and the arrests of 3,000. In the same year, the governor of Mississippi formally requested that all Negro regiments be removed from the state, a request that was refused by the War Department. The racial situation looked ominous.

An explosion came in 1943 when there were 242 racial incidents in 47 cities, the worst being the Zoot Suit riots (which involved Mexican-Americans) in Los Angeles and the race riot (which involved Blacks) in Detroit. The latter occurred in a city overcrowded with war workers, black and white, and started at Belle Isle amusement park when tempers flared on a hot June day. Another riot developed in Harlem in New York City two months later, with considerable personal and property damage. The Roosevelt administration did little to eliminate the roots of the problem. Roosevelt did consider broadcasting a fireside chat on race relations, but his aides successfully dissuaded him from taking this action and from asking Congress to investigate the problem. Roosevelt took two steps to preserve civil order. Procedures for introducing federal troops into riot areas were clarified, and J. Edgar Hoover's advice, to grant armed service deferments to policemen, was followed.

Racial difficulties stimulated interest in race relations. During World War II, the membership of the NAACP increased ten times over pre-war membership, and a new civil rights organization, the Congress of Racial Equality, emerged in 1942. CORE was a spin-off of a pacifist organization, the Fellowship of Reconciliation (FOR); led by black pacifists like James Farmer and Bayard Rustin, it attempted to use tactics of civil disobedience to gain racial equality. White social scientists also became more involved in the civil rights cause, as did white liberals. These interested individuals founded committees and study groups; civil rights became increasingly respectable. By the war's end, the racial situation had cooled, the March-on-Washington Movement had declined, and Blacks seemed less militant.

The induction of Truman to the presidency on the death of Roosevelt did not seem to augur well for civil rights advocates. Truman hailed from a border state and had a southern background. His uncle had served in the Confederate Army; his mother had always condemned the Republicans for being abolitionists. Bess, his wife, never championed the black cause as Eleanor Roosevelt had; when the DAR refused to rent Constitution Hall to Hazel Scott, a black woman, Bess retained her membership and even attended a tea given in her honor by the DAR. Truman, however, proved to be a civil rights supporter, largely because of extrinsic circumstances. Believing that lynching and discrimination in hiring were wrong, Truman became convinced that the racial discrimination he had seen in the army and in defense plants was wrong. He stated that the black soldiers and workers only wanted equal facilities, not integrated ones. Truman's early record was unimpressive. When the federal government assumed the operation of the Capital Transit System in Washington during Truman's first administration, the FEPC asked Truman to use this opportunity to end discrimination in hiring of operatives and seating of patrons. Truman refused. He did, however, establish a Committee for Civil Rights on December 5, 1946. This committee recommended that the Civil Rights section in the Department of Justice be made a division, that discrimination in the Armed Forces be ended, that the FEPC be made permanent, and that discrimination in the public schools in Washing, D.C., be ended. Eventually all but a permanent FEPC became actuality, although not all during Truman's administration.

Legal pressure on segregated institutions increased after World War II, encouraged by favorable Supreme Court decisions and by the actions of "freedom-riders," who were CORE workers and sympathizers. In *Morgan v. Commonwealth of Virginia* (1946), the Supreme Court invalidated a Virginia statute that assigned passengers to different seats on public transportation according to race; the Court argued that this assignment interferred with interstate commerce. In *Bob-Lo Excursion Company v. Michigan* (1947), the Court ruled that the Michigan Civil Rights Act, which prohibited racial discrimination, applied to the Bob-Lo Company, which carried passengers on lake excursions to Canada. By dint of much effort, the iceberg of legal segregation was being chipped away.

The campaign of 1948 moved Truman in the direction of greater sympathy for civil rights. Dissident southern Democrats, called Dixiecrats, left the Democratic party because of the inclusion of such planks in the Democratic platform as a permanent Federal Commission on Civil Rights, a federal anti-lynching law, and anti-segregation laws relating to public accommodations. Having lost the support of white Southerners before the election, Truman asked the Secretary of Defense to end discrimination (but not segregation) in the army as soon as possible. The Secretary of the Army, Kenneth Royall, and the Chief of Staff, General Bradley, refused to take action. Truman publicly rebuked them, issued an order barring discrimination in government employment, and created a committee to advise him on ending discrimination in the Armed Services. Truman began to speak for civil rights in his campaign and to openly court the urban black vote. He was the first President to speak in Harlem, which tactic helped win him the election.

Truman's second administration resulted in little significant civil rights legislation. Bills outlawing the poll tax, making lynching a federal crime, establishing a permanent FEPC, and prohibiting segregation and discrimination in interstate transport failed; the public housing bill of 1948 passed without a provision prohibiting segregation. In 1949, Truman, by executive order, desegregated the Armed Forces, a process which took four years to complete. The Korean War intervened, complicating the procedure. Thurgood Marshall, who investigated the behavior of the army in Korea, found evidence of continued segregation and, in "Summary Justice —The Negro G.I. in Korea," *Crisis* (May, 1951), quoted one white officer of the 24th Infantry Regiment as saying:

I despise nigger troops, I don't want to command you or any other nigger. This division is no good and you are lousy, you don't know how to fight.

Meanwhile the Supreme Court continued its actions, questioning segregation in education. In *Sipuel v. Board of Regents of the University of Oklahoma* (1948), the Court directed the School of Law of the University of Oklahoma to admit the black woman Sipuel since there was no other law school in the state that she could attend. In *McLaurin v. Oklahoma State Regents* (1950), the Court held that the University of Oklahoma could not, once a black student had been admitted to graduate study in education, segregate him from the other students in his class. Finally, in *Sweatt v. Painter* (1950), the Court decided that the black law school established for the plaintiff Sweatt after he was denied admission to the University of Texas Law School was inferior and was thus a denial of the equal protection clause of the 14th Amendment. In this decision, the court insisted that even if the black school had an equivalent faculty, budget, and facilities, it would still be unequal because of the weight of tradition that the white school possessed. This decision, if universally applied, struck deep at the principle of separate but equal since no black professional school supported by the state was as old as its white counterpart.

By 1950, an impartial observer might have said that the racial problems of the United States were being solved. Slowly, the legal handicaps on Blacks were ending and progress in white attitudes was being made. The lack of racial incidents after the second World War was a hopeful sign, as was the growing respectability of white support of blacks' civil rights. Most Americans, occupied with the presumed external threat of Communism, viewed racial problems as less pressing and looked toward their peaceful resolution.

I

The black image in movies reflected the changing white American attitudes. The criticism that Hollywood was lowering the morality of America had resulted in efforts at self-regulation through voluntarily accepted codes in the 1920's. These codes drastically limited the portrayal of sexual activities, but also included the prohibition of interracial romance or miscegenation in talking pictures. Producers had to concern themselves with state and local censorship rulings as well, as shown by reception of a Russian film, *Of Greater Promise,* which was censored in Ohio because "the picture encourages social and racial equality, thereby stirring up racial hatred . . . all the above doctrines are contrary to accepted codes of American life."

While themes of interracial sex were muted in the 1930's, the stereotype of the Sambo persisted. In *Our Gang* comedies, the Negro character Farina displayed all of the characteristics of the

Sambo—superstition, cowardice, and ignorance. The advent of talkies added to the stereotype as black dialects appeared on the sound tracks and seemed to confirm racial stereotypes. The first all-sound film, *Hallelujah* (1929), was an all-black production shot on location in the South. The poverty of the area and the often incomprehensible dialect of the nonprofessional actors detracted from the director's (King Vidor) goal of presenting the humanity of the American Blacks. His efforts were not much imitated. In 1939, *Gone With the Wind* perpetuated the plantation legend seen in *Birth of a Nation*. Negroes were either loyal servants, silly and infantile like Scarlett's maid or bossy like the housekeeper, or else treacherous freedmen who had been corrupted by northern carpet-baggers and mulattoes.

Stepin Fetchit, a ranking Negro actor, was a standby in the comedies of the time and served as a foil to humorists like Will Rogers and Irwin S. Cobb. Fetchit's portrayal of the frightened, stupid, shuffling Sambo in such movies as *Steamboat Round the Bend* (1935) confirmed Americans in their stereotyping of the Negro. The Sambo character took other forms in the movies of the time; in the Charlie Chan series, he was a Negro chauffeur whose cowardice contrasted unfavorably with the cool skill of the Oriental detective.

Not all Blacks were cast as Sambos. Paul Robeson could be seen in a number of roles; he was the protagonist in O'Neill's *The Emperor Jones* (1923), and he played an important part in the 1936 version of *King Solomon's Mines* as well. Robeson conveyed a sense of strength whenever he was given roles that permitted him the opportunity.

Topical films of the 1930's began to portray the black man as victim. In *I Am a Fugitive from a Chain Gang* (1932), the hero Paul Muni had his shackles struck off by a Negro convict; the movie stirred sympathy for the plight of all prisoners, whatever their color. In *Fury* (1936) and *They Won't Forget* (1937), the horror of lynching in the South was the subject, but neither film investigated the conditions leading to the practice. It was not until *The Ox Bow Incident* (1943) that an anti-lynching film combined artistic excellence with a message; this movie, however, took place in the West not in the South, and the victims were white. The only Black in the movie played the minor role of a minister.

There were attempts to make low-budget, all-black films in the thirties. Two of the more interesting ones in this genre were *Bar-*

gain with Bullets (1937), which was a gangster picture typical of the era, located, however, in Harlem's underworld. The success of this film, which was shown mainly in black theaters, led in 1938 to *Harlem on the Prairie,* a sequel that had a Western format and moved black players to the range.

During World War II, the film industry turned to themes supportive of the war effort, with token Blacks in conventional roles. Typical of these films was the sentimental *Since You Went Away* (1944), where the ubiquitous Hattie McDaniel filled a mammy role as the Negro cook. The war did encourage several significant documentaries, including one entitled *The Negro Soldier.* Filmed late in the war (1944), this orientation film purported to take a balanced look at the problems of the black man in uniform, and while failing to advocate full equality, it did show considerable understanding of the black dilemma. The nature of the film, however, limited its distribution and, hence, its audience.

World War II carried American racial problems to Europe where they were reflected in films, notably in Italian ones. The acclaimed Italian movie *To Live in Peace* (1947) centered on a peasant family in Italy during World War II. This family sheltered two American soldiers, one white and the other black, at the risk of being put to death. Hidden in the cellar, the black soldier became drunk and was responsible for the death of both his white buddy and of the German soldier visiting the family in the house above. A number of critics believed the action of the black soldier to be detrimental to the image of an American fighting man, but the noted essayist and critic, James Agee, said in *Agee on Film* (1963), "it is the only pure presentation of a man of his race that I have ever seen in a movie." Agee argued that the film was honest, that it portrayed the black soldier as a human being, and that it showed both his weaknesses and his strengths.

Post-war Hollywood movies discovered prejudice as an American social phenomena. The solution they offered, according to Parker Tyler, a noted film critic, was only a disguised variant of their usual theme of material success. Any American—Jew or Black —could become a full member of society by getting rich. Hollywood dealt with prejudice by having a WASP masquerade as a Jew or by having a light-skinned Negro pass as a White. In Hollywood, Jews and Blacks were always at least middle-class; these individuals could not be poor or dark. Tyler says in his perceptive article, "Hollywood as a Universal Church," *American Quarterly*

(1950), that Hollywood showed only a homogeneous personality, one which was "socially crass." In its version of the melting pot, Hollywood created "the cult of the Divine Robot, in which the mixing of all the racial colors is supposed to produce, not a depressing grey, but a glowing pink, and in which an undesirable religion may be overcome by changing one's nose or taking a course in diction." If only the Black or the Jew looked and acted like WASPs, everything would be all right.

From 1946 to 1950, five major films dealing with racial prejudice—three concerning anti-Negro prejudice and two concerning anti-Semitism—were made. These were *Crossfire, Gentleman's Agreement, Home of the Brave, Lost Boundaries,* and *Pinky.* The first two were about Jews; the last three about Blacks. *Home of the Brave,* which starred Sidney Poitier, was a war movie whose plot concerned a black G.I., a man of dignity and natural gentility, who suffered because of the continuing prejudice of white soldiers and who was thrown into shock by the horrible death of a white friend. Unable to walk because of a psychosomatic reaction, the black soldier learned from a white psychiatrist that black skin was not a fatal curse and that some persons did not regard skin color as significant. Cured of his ailment, the Black left the Army to enter into the restaurant business with another exsoldier, a white amputee. The moral of the movie, according to Tyler, was that a one-armed White equalled a two-armed Black and that an individual's race and character were surface phenomena.

Lost Boundaries and *Pinky* both involved the dilemma of the light-skinned Black who could pass for White. In the first movie, a doctor and his wife, resident in a northern town, passed for white but were discovered and were about to be run out of town. A white pastor, however, saved the couple by a passionate recital of their good deeds, all of which were eminently middle-class. Because they were so white, inside and out, they were permitted to stay. *Lost Boundaries* also taught that the answer to racial prejudice was to become white. *Pinky,* on the other hand, had an opposite message, to remain black. The heroine, a light-skinned black woman, abandoned her role as a white doctor's wife in the North to open a nursing clinic for black children in the South. Her altruism was rewarded when a white woman bequeathed the heroine property for a new clinic. Prejudiced and greedy relatives of the dead woman contested the will on racial grounds but failed to break it. Although Pinky chose to be a Black, her reward was also money and success. The moral in both films was clear; act middle class and have money. Although both movies were shallow treatments of the racial problem, they signaled one change in attitude. The mulatto was no longer a villain, as he was in *The Birth of a Nation*, but was now a hero. Also, miscegenation could be mentioned.

Two other films of the era also were notable in their portrayal of black life. One was a prize-winning documentary, *The Quiet One* (1948), which described the work of the Wiltwyck School for Boys through the eyes of a delinquent black child. The film treated the boy and his mother with sensitivity and understanding, as well as showing both black and white social workers possessed of compassion, strength, and insight. The second was the film version of Faulkner's *Intruder in the Dust* (1950). In *The Film Till Now* (1967), Paul Rotha claims that this was the first film to show the dilemma of Negro-White relations in an honest way. The black hero, as conceived by Faulkner, had enormous dignity; though poor, he placed a white boy in his debt. The white liberal lawyer who defended the Black in a murder trial, however, echoed an older kind of racial view. The Black would survive because he had patience, said the lawyer Gavin Stevens, echoing the romantic racialism of the abolitionists. Both of these films showed the halting progress made by the medium of films.

Older racial stereotypes continued in both feature films and short subjects. Among the last of the refuges of the black stereotypes were cartoons. From animation's origins, cartoons portrayed the Sambo image. Negroes were drawn with exaggerated kinky hair, wide grins, and toothy smiles; they acted silly and had inconsequential fears as well as an insatiable desire for watermelon and fried chicken. The Tom and Jerry cartoon series, which MGM first released in 1947, contained a Negro maid whose face was never seen but whose dialect, dress, and irrational fears made her readily identifiable. In one cartoon, "Old Rocking Chair Tom," Tom was Old Black Joe and had white whiskers and a fondness for watermelons and sloth. In "Mouse Cleaning" Tom portrayed a Sambo when he fell into some coal and was blackened. The series did not drop the Negro maid until 1963; the producers dubbed a new voice into some of the older episodes at the same time. Because of the reruns on children's programs, however, the cartoons of the 1930's and 1940's still appear with most of their racial stereotypes intact.

The radio was also guilty of perpetuating certain images of

Blacks. Probably the most popular radio program of the 1930's was *Amos 'n Andy*. Created by two white men who broadcast from Chicago, it was expanded from a local program, *Sam 'n Henry*, to a network success. *Amos 'n Andy* became a fifteen-minute serial that was on the air daily from 1929 to 1942. *Amos 'n Andy* concerned the various plights of two southern Negroes who had moved to the urban North and their encounters with confidence men and with conniving women in their struggle to survive the Depression. Andy, the most exaggerated of the two figures, possessed all of the assumed Negro faults, a heavy dialect combined with malapropisms and mispronounced words, laziness to the point of no movement at all, and the simple-minded acceptance of the schemes of the confidence man, Kingfish. A taxi company founded by the two characters carried the imposing title of "The Fresh Air Taxicab Company, Incorpulated"; their other enterprises had the absurd names of the Okek Hotel and the Fresh Air Garage. Charles Correll and Freeman Gosden, who played Amos 'n Andy, never felt they were maligning Blacks and retired from radio broadcasting unable to understand what had caused their loss of favor in the black community. The series served as a basis for a movie, performed by Whites in blackface, as well as for a television series, acted in by Blacks, which lasted until 1961 when pressure from the black community helped to terminate it.

Another famous radio comedian, Jack Benny, had a Negro foil called "Rochester." Rochester, played by Eddie Anderson, called Benny "Boss" and was often shown successfully getting money from the tightwad Benny. Rochester also illustrated the supposed Negro vices of laziness, gambling, and general silliness, although the Sambo caricature was less pronounced than it was in *Amos 'n Andy*. Anderson appeared in the less-than-successful films Benny made, playing the same role with an added touch of cowardice.

Black entertainers, particularly those with musical reputations, could also be heard on the radio. Cab Calloway and Duke Ellington broadcast as early as 1930, while Ethel Waters sang the blues for Texaco in 1935. Lionel Hampton and Teddy Wilson were regulars on Benny Goodman's *Camel Caravan*, and Slim and Slam, a song and dance team, had their own show on the Mutual network in 1939. While these shows gave white listeners an appreciation of black musical talent, they also served to confirm the assumption that artistic talents were the only talents Blacks possessed.

The image of the Black in white literature was not much improved, although it was more common. Part of the reason for its commonness was the emerging creativity of southern writers who, for the first time, achieved primary literary eminence. Since these writers used southern settings and southern themes, the rural Black was a figure seen more and more in the American novel at the same time that he was leaving the South in vast numbers.

Perhaps the most famous southern writer of the 1930's was William Faulkner. Faulkner had published four novels in the 1920's, *Soldiers' Pay, Mosquitoes, Sartoris,* and *The Sound and the Fury.* The latter work, along with *As I Lay Dying* (1930), had established his literary reputation. In succeeding works such as *Light in August* (1932), *Absalom, Absalom!* (1936), *The Hamlet* (1940), and *Intruder in the Dust* (1948), Faulkner elaborated his view of southern life, which was an essentially tragic view. The white man had sinned, according to Faulkner, by cheating the Indian of his land and depriving the Black of his freedom. The white man had compounded his sins through racial mixing, by imposing his sexual will on the black slave woman. The results supposedly were racial contamination and continued sexual threat. In Faulkner's view, the mulatto, through no fault of his own but through his father's sin, became a feared figure as well as a tragic one, doomed to a violent death. Charles Bon, the mulatto in *Absalom, Absalom!,* was such a man. Desirous of his white half-sister, he was shot by his white half-brother to prevent an incestuous union. Joe Christmas, a mulatto character in *Light in August,* also attempted to possess a white woman and died at the hands of a white man who castrated him. The all-black characters in Faulkner's novels did not share the sexual lust of the mulatto but had strength and patience as well as the willingness to remain in their places. Faulkner's image of the Negro was essentially a nineteenth century one. As conceived by the Southerner in the Brownlow tradition, there were two kinds of Blacks, the bad mulatto and the good Negro; both were products of their racial heritage.

More popular although less critically acclaimed than Faulkner was Erskine Caldwell, a native Georgian. His novels showed the squalor, misery, ignorance, and vitality of the lives of poor Southern whites and shed light upon the racial mores of the South. Without editorializing about race relations, Caldwell showed the low esteem in which the Negro was held by Whites and revealed the symbiotic relationships that existed between Blacks and Whites in both economic and sexual matters. Dude Lester, the leading character in

Tobacco Road (1932), a best-seller that was also made into one of Broadway's longest running plays, commented on the death of a Black by saying, "Niggers will get killed." Clary Harey, in *Journeyman* (1935), professed in similar circumstances that he did not mind seeing a dead darkey now and then as long as it was not planting time. If it were planting time, the death might inconvenience the White, and he might have to work his fields himself. In *Trouble in July* (1940), a white girl accused a Negro of rape. The sheriff, Jeff McCurtain, escaped the duty of protecting his Negro prisoner by locking himself in a cell and throwing out his keys. As a result, the mob took the accused prisoner and lynched him. When the sheriff showed remorse over failing his duty, another man told him, "Hell, if there wasn't no more niggers in the country, I'd feel lost without them . . . . Besides, who'd do all the work, if the niggers was sent away?" Caldwell's Whites were barely human, and they viewed Blacks as beasts to be used as sexual objects or as work animals. Both images had the unfortunate effect of adding to a sense of northern white moral superiority over the South and to the self-deception of these Whites as to their own racial liberality.

Another southern writer, the romantic Thomas Wolfe, portrayed Negroes unfavorably in his works. While Blacks were not as prominent in his novels as the Irish Catholics or the Jews, Negroes were shown in the southern environment, and their presence was felt. In *The Web and the Rock* (1939), a Negro war veteran, Dick Prosser, went beserk and murdered nine men before he himself was caught and killed, after which his body was displayed in an undertaker's window. This portrayal of the Negro was not typical of Wolfe's novels, however; for the most part, Wolfe's racial attitude can best be summarized by the statement of one of the characters in *The Web and the Rock* (1939) about Negroes, "It was proper to cuff these people kindly, curse them cheerfully, feed them magnaminously."

The early novels of Truman Capote, *Other Voices, Other Rooms* (1948) and *The Grass Harp* (1951), utilized another tradition that was an integral part of southern regionalism, the Negro as a grotesque figure. Grotesqueness in Capote was not confined to Negroes but permeated all of the disintegrating southern society. In *Other Voices, Other Rooms*, a wizened Negro hermit, called Little Sunshine, acted as a father figure to Joel, the white hero. Joel tried unsuccessfully to run away with his girl friend, Idabel, to escape his homosexual past. In the same story, Zoo, a white girl who tried to go to Washington when her father died, was raped by three Whites and two Negroes. The image of Negro in Capote's works was an old one and combined child-like actions with sexual aggression. Negroes aroused the fear of heterosexual relations but also elicited the emotions of filial love and sisterly affection. The conception Capote used dated back to at least the nineteenth-century defenders of slavery.

The southern preoccupation with the Negro as a sexual threat was brilliantly explored by a Southern journalist, W. J. Cash, in his book *The Mind of the South* (1937). Cash, a North Carolinian, argued that the crux of the racial problem in the South was sexual, was the fear of black male attack on white women; he traced this fear to psychological factors created by historical circumstances. In the era of slavery, the white slave owner had two families, one in the big house and the other in the slave quarters. The black mistress in the slave quarters had seemed to possess a sexual prowess superior to that of the white wife, who was limited by the repressions of white civilization. In order to compensate for his sexual philandering, the white man insisted upon the absolute purity of the white woman, thereby deriving the cult of Southern Womanhood. According to Cash, emancipation did not change the situation; the white man continued to seek out black women. The guilt the White felt over his interracial affairs was displaced onto the black man, said Cash. After all, if the white man wanted the black woman, must not the black man lust after the white woman? If black women were superior sexually, were not black men also? According to Cash, this displacement was the underlying reason for the accusations of black rape and for the high incidence of lynching in the South. Cash clamied that the racial problem was really a white sexual one and explained why prejudice was so difficult to eliminate. While he liked the South, he offered no solution to the racial problem and the prospects of further miscegenation concerned him. He was not able to demolish the popular myth of superior black sexuality.

The myth of black sexuality was sometimes used as evidence of racial superiority. This tradition continued in the 1930's and 1940's in the work of the writer, Henry Miller. Miller, who spent the 1930's in Europe writing novels that were considered so pornographic that they were banned from the United States, considered himself the spiritual heir of D. H. Lawrence. In *Tropic of Cancer* (1934), *Black Spring* (1936), and *Tropic of Capricorn*

(1939), Miller depicted himself as a declassed, alienated man roaming the streets of Paris and New York, seeking physical pleasure in women and food, and revealing the social and cultural disorder of the time. In *The Colossus of Maroussi* (1941), Miller's account of a stay in Greece, the values of Western civilization—progress and technological growth—were questioned; and in one passage, Miller juxtaposed the sensuality to be found in the black music of Louis Armstrong with the sterility of white European civilization. The theme of the supposed lack of repression in the more primitive black man persisted in the works of Henry Miller and provided a bridge between the literary views of the 1930's and the 1960's.

II

Unfavorable depiction of the Black was not confined to novels. The hereditarian arguments of the early twentieth century continued in the works of Madison Grant and Lothrop Stoddard. In 1933, Grant turned from global preoccupations to write a social history of the United States. He called it *The Conquest of a Continent, or the Expansion of Races in America.* In the introduction, Henry Fairfield Osborn, a biologist and paleontologist and president of the American Museum of Natural History, denied that Grant believed in racial superiority. Grant believed, as Osborn did, that racial superiority and equality were equally erroneous. The truth, according to Osborn, was that races were unlike because they were suited to particular climates; the black man was physically superior to the white at the equator while the white was superior in temperate zones. Therefore, they could not be compared. Osborn claimed a racial relativity as Boas had a cultural one and, like Grant, clung to Agassiz's ideas of zoological provinces.

Grant based his work on the immigration studies of Marcus S. Hansen and the research of Paul Popenoe, the eugenicist. Grant attacked the melting pot idea and praised the National Origins Act of 1924, which limited the number of immigrants from Southeast Europe in relation to those from Northwest Europe, as "a new Declaration of Independence." He faulted Catholics for pushing for racial unity and criticized President Wilson for advocating self-determination of national states rather than colonialism. Grant declared that the abolition of slavery had been a mistake since it meant loss of white control over Blacks; that the Civil War had killed too many good Nordic men; and that a better solution would have been to restrict slavery to the South and to have left it alone. Two hundreds years of American slavery had, according to Grant, made possible more progress for the Black than 2,000 years of freedom in Africa.

Grant's ideas on race had changed between 1910 and 1930. He still was a polygenesist, believing that not all men were members of *Homo sapiens* but that the Negro and the Mongol were members of separate species. On the other hand, he admitted that race was difficult to define, and his definition in the *Conquest of a Continent* (1933)—"a collection of hereditary characters common to a great majority of individuals in a given group"—was not far from the scientific orthodoxy of the day. He said that the belief in pure races was a mistaken one. Thirty years earlier people had assumed that there was an Aryan race; now it was only possible to use the term Aryan in connection with a linguistic group. Finally, he stated that "it is unsafe to attribute the inception of any cultural feature to a given race." The winds of change in genetics and anthropology had blown some of his earlier ideas away.

However, Grant demonstrated that an accommodation could be made between a genetic definition of race, which avoided racial comparisons on the one hand, and a continued belief in hereditarianism, which relegated the Negro and Indian to an inferior status on the other. Grant said that the South understood how to treat Negroes, firmly but kindly keeping them in their place. However, the Negro was moving into cities of the North and was presenting a serious problem. Grant thought that while the Negro lacked the qualities necessary for civilization (self control and cooperation) and had a lower vital capacity (as shown by susceptibility to tuberculosis and pneumonia), he was holding his own in the city because of certain physical advantages—a tough skin, which made it hard for germs to penetrate, and a higher birth rate. Black migration to the cities created an additional problem, Grant believed, because Negroes wanted to marry light-skinned persons. This encouraged miscegenation as Jews and Italians were supposedly willing to marry Negroes and to have mulatto children. Like most Southerners, Grant regarded the influence of the mulatto as pernicious. He felt that the mulatto was the most likely American to become a Communist and that, if present trends continued, America would be flooded with mulatto Communists living in cities. Grant's fears of miscegenation were extreme, and were based on an assumption common to the period—that much racial mixing occurred in the cities.

What could be done about this? Grant considered three possibilities, all of which were unsatisfactory. Amalgamation led to racial ruin, he felt; deportation was impossible because the European powers which controlled Africa would not accept American Negroes; and segregation would only work if it were complete. In lieu of these solutions, Grant advocated passing stronger miscegenation laws, deemphasizing mulatto achievement, encouraging the Negro to respect his own race, providing birth control information to all Negroes, and taking away Negro citizenship—thus reverting to the political circumstances he thought had prevailed at the beginning of the Republic. (Grant's history was as shaky as his genetics; some states had black citizens by 1790.)

Lothrop Stoddard did not limit his views on racism to the problems of the United States as Madison Grant did. In *Lonely America* (1932) and *Clashing Tides of Color* (1935), Stoddard attacked pacifism and depicted an America alone in a hostile world. Stoddard, however, was less pessimistic about the future than Grant. He also had modified his racial views; he had come to admit that there were no pure races and that race and nationality were not the same. However, he still held that racial diversity in a society meant less political stability, that racial diversity had mongrelized Latin America, and that France was becoming degenerate because of her attempts to admit colonists on an equal footing with native Frenchmen.

Stoddard's *Into the Darkness* (1940), was a curious book. Traveling as a special correspondent for the North American Newspaper Alliance, Stoddard visited wartime Germany to observe the operations of Nazi society. Among his stops was a eugenics court, which decided on sterilization of persons. As might have been expected, he was not sympathetic to the Hitlerian regime, commented unfavorably upon the bad treatment of the Jews, and concluded that he would be glad to get home "among my own kind who are not worried and harrassed and ulcerated by nationalistic hatreds."

Both Grant and Stoddard showed how complex hereditarian racial ideas were and how firmly they were held. Each had assimilated the genetic theory of race without really changing his ideas; each man proclaimed his patriotism and nationalism. Stoddard attacked a nation which put ideas parallel to his into practice. Both

Grant and Stoddard, finally, retained a desire for an America dominated by the "better" white groups.

Another hereditarian whose ideas combined the older paradigm of race with newer scientism, the belief that the methods of science provided the best tools for understanding society, was S. J. Holmes, a professor of zoology at the University of California. In his *The Negro's Struggle for Survival: A Study in Human Ecology* (1937), Holmes tried to update Hoffman's *Race Traits and Tendencies of the American Negro* (1896).

Holmes' basic ecological premise was that "when two species occupy the same territory and depend on the same means of subsistence, each tends to supplant the other. Human beings are no exception to this rule." Believing that Blacks and Whites were of different species, Holmes projected population trends from census data to postulate a condition of unstable equilibrium in the American population. Holmes believed that this instability would result in one of four outcomes—an all-black America, an all-white America, an America of hybrid stock, or a permanently biracial America.

In his study of the census, Holmes included data on black immigration into the United States; others had ignored this as insignificant. His figures on Negro immigration to the United States can be found in Table 11.2.

TABLE 11.2

Year	Number	Percent of Total Negro Population
1850	4.067	0.1
1860	4,363	0.1
1870	9,645	0.2
1880	14,017	0.2
1890	19,979	0.3
1900	20,336	0.2
1910	40,339	0.4
1920	73,803	0.7
1930	98,620	0.8

Holmes claimed that this immigration disguised the fact that the Negro was being displaced. Using other census data, Holmes claimed that the rate of growth of the Negro population had slowed since 1880. The reasons for this were greater white immigration, a declining birth rate for Negroes, and a continuing high death rate. Holmes admitted that the censuses were inaccurate, agreeing with Kelly Miller, a black sociologist. Miller claimed in an article in the *Scientific Monthly* (1922) that the 1920 Census had undercounted Negroes because the census takers had either failed to enter black districts or, having entered them, had not counted all residents of crowded tenements. Miller admitted an undercount of 100,000 Blacks in the 1920 Census. Holmes adjusted the Census figures to show a total black population increase of 8.5 percent from 1910 to 1920 instead of the 6.5 percent shown in the Census and an increase of 13.6 percent from 1920 to 1930 instead of 11.5 percent.

Despite these corrections, the rate of increase per thousand Blacks was still lower than the rate of increase of Whites. From this fact, Holmes projected four trends—that the black rate of increase would not maintain the black population in northern states; that the rate of white and black increase would stabilize; that in the large cities in the North and South, the black rate of increase would be insufficient for permanent maintenance; and that in the South, the black rate of increase would mean a slow growth. These trends meant Blacks would eventually be found only on southern farms.

For an explanation of the lower black rate of increase, Holmes turned to black mortality rates. It was obvious that Blacks had always had a higher death rate than Whites, although there were no reliable statistics on this subject until 1900. Prior to 1900, Holmes estimated, 30 percent of black deaths went unrecorded. Even with his uncertain data, Holmes believed that the black death rate had risen from 1865 to 1890 and then declined, with the rate of decline increasing after 1910. The supposed decline reflected a reduction of mortality in birth and childhood and would have been greater if it were not for the urban environment, which supposedly shortened black life expectancy at every age level. Holmes, using army physicals from the years 1906 to 1910, concluded that the Black was not weak; fewer Blacks were rejected because of physical defects than Whites—104.8 per thousand compared to 136.2 per thousand—but Blacks had special susceptibility to certain debilitating diseases.

Holmes scrutinized the diseases that he claimed were more prevalent among Blacks. Syphilis was widespread among Blacks; some authorities estimated that 50 percent of the black population were infected, but Holmes reduced this estimate to between 10 and

15 percent. Syphilis caused a higher rate of abortion, stillbirths, and other reproductive complications and significantly lowered black ability to compete in the biological struggle for survival. Holmes next turned to tuberculosis, utilizing post-Civil War army studies that showed a lower lung capacity in black soldiers and a public health study from 1876 to 1920 in Baltimore that showed higher black mortality from T.B. Holmes concluded that, despite the admitted influence of poorer physical living conditions, the greater susceptibility to T.B. was racial in origin and affected the black survival rate. Holmes also felt that other factors besides syphilis and T.B. were lowering the ability of the Black to compete reproductively. Infant mortality was still high among blacks, particularly in rural areas of the South. In addition, the number of black children per each one thousand women of child bearing age in 1920 had fallen below the number of whites for the first time, revealing the consequences on the birth rate of the harsh environment of northern cities.

In his consideration of the ultimate fate of the black man in white America, Holmes rejected the ideas of Boas and Herskovits, who said that miscegenation would lead to a new, racially mixed population. Holmes claimed instead that racial intermixing was decreasing because it was becoming less respectable. For proof Holmes again used census data. Table 11.3 contains the data Holmes found (he excluded the faulty 1880 Census and the 1900 Census that did not count mulattoes):

TABLE 11.3

Year	Percent of Mulattoes to Negroes
1850	11.2
1860	13.2
1870	12.0
1890	15.2
1910	20.9
1920	15.9

Holmes believed that the indicated decrease in mulattoes between 1910 and 1920 was caused by lower mulatto fertility and the northern environment. He denied Kelly Miller's explanation that mulattoes were either passing for Whites or calling themselves

Negroes in 1920. Holmes predicted a continued decrease in racial assimilation and a greater absorption of mulattoes back into the Negro community. This did not necessarily mean an increase in that community since Holmes believed that white men cohabited with black women and that the mulatto child substituted for a black child for the black mother. Thus, miscegenation supposedly occurred at the expense of the Negro population.

Holmes attempted to refute Herskovits's study of the Negro by saying that American Negroes were not homogeneous, that American Negroes varied more than African tribes, more than European peoples, and more than the old Americans. Finally, he believed that despite the hindrances of city life, of the northern climate, and of a higher mortality rate, Blacks could outstrip the Whites if white birthrates decreased. If this happened, Holmes predicted that the white majority would impose some kind of population control on the black minority.

Holmes's work can be considered the last gasp of the early twentieth-century hereditarians. Using an older description of race, one based on physical differences, and using data from eighty years of censuses, Holmes tried to do in 1937 what Hoffman had done in 1896. However, the interest of physical anthropology had shifted away from comparative physical measurements of individuals, and the genetic theory of race had replaced the theory of physical racial types. Both shifts in emphasis made Holmes's book seem antiquated, from another era.

Scientists of the new era had moved away from the study of racial measurements to the study of culture. They had moved to a new paradigm—racial equality. Illustrative of this change was E. B. Reuter's *Race Mixture* (1931). Reuter's study was a sequel to his *The Mulatto in the United States* (1918), but his tone had changed. The biological emphasis in the earlier book remained but was overshadowed by a sociological one in the second. Reuter denied that racial mixture was necessarily pernicious, as the hereditarians had said, but he did not regard it as necessarily good. He believed that the benefit of racial mixture depended on culture; mixtures of homogeneous races supposedly improved them by offsetting their isolation and primitiveness. On the other hand, racial amalgamation brought about, Reuter thought, social disorganization. Whether racial mixture was, in the long run, advantageous, he did not say. Reuter retained an evolutionary standard of cultural measurement; he believed Africans to have low but uniform cultures, inferior to European ones. This inferiority, however, he attributed to cultural isolation and not race. In America, the supposed superiority of the mulatto was considered by Reuter a product of the attitudes of Whites and Blacks, both of whom assumed that lighter skins were preferable. Because of this social selection, mulattoes were supposedly unable to decide whether they were white or black and became unadjusted persons with divided loyalties. Reuter called for the mulatto to provide greater leadership for the black population; only then could the Black "find a tolerable life and develop a wholesome personality." Reuter had changed his position from hereditarian determinism to cultural determinism without changing his prediction of the ultimate destiny of the mulatto. He originally had believed that the mulatto would save the Black through superior inherited qualities; now he believed that the mulatto would do so through his superior (white-oriented) cultural values. Reuter showed how an argument for racial superiority could be easily transformed into one for cultural superiority.

Reuter did not belong to the new generation of sociologists, however, although this generation shared his view of the role of the mulatto and of the ultimate destiny of the American Black. Beginning in about 1930, a sociological theory of assimilation emerged; it received its best formulation in Robert E. Park's *Race and Culture* (1949). Park stated in this book that contact between racial groups led successively and irreversibly to conflict to accommodation to assimilation; according to Park, no innate racial traits would bar this process. Like other assimilationists, Park maintained that a growing segment of the black community possessed both the value orientation and behavioral attributes of middle-class white society. He believed that lower-class Blacks were victims of racial injustice that isolated and impoverished them and created values that needed to be changed. The first step in the transformation of values was to discover what the barriers to the eventual absorption of the black man into white society were. Once these were found, Park felt that they could be eliminated.

At the same time, Park still clung to an older view of natural racial traits, articulated by his generation of sociologists and inherited from the nineteenth century. This view persisted despite Park's seven-year connection with Tuskegee Institute and his service as secretary to Booker T. Washington. In *Race and Culture,*

Park attacked biological racism and insisted on the primacy of culture but he also insisted that there was a black temperament and that the Black was:

by natural disposition, neither an intellectual nor an idealist, like the Jew; nor a brooding introspective, like the East African; nor a pioneer and frontiersman, like the Anglo-Saxon. He is primarily an artist, loving life for its own sake. His *métier* is expression rather than action. He is, so to speak, the lady among races.

Thus did Park echo the sentiments of the abolitionists of the 1840's, and his romantic racialism was easily reconcilable with Harriet Beecher Stowe's *Uncle Tom's Cabin.*

The anthropologist M. F. Ashley Montagu, however, argued that racial mixture was not harmful and tried to dispel myths about the American Black. These myths included statements about the inferior size of the brain, the different shape of the pelvis, the bad smell (Montagu said that his family had had twelve maids; only one had smelled badly and she did because she was fat), and the different size of the black penis. Montagu said that there were no racial differences of this sort. Relying upon Herskovits's early study of the American Black, Montagu said that the American Black was a blend of Indian, African, and European ethnic groups. He believed that education, reduction of aggression and frustration, and elimination of the word race would bring about the assimilation of the Black.

In the late 1930's and early 1940's, a plethora of books on the social problems of Blacks in white southern society appeared. These included John Dollard's *Caste and Class in a Southern Town* (1937); John Dollard and Alison Davis' *Children of Bondage* (1941); Hortense Powdermaker's *After Freedom* (1939); Alison Davis, Burleigh B. Gardner, and Mary R. Gardner's *Deep South* (1941); Charles S. Johnson's *Growing Up in the Black Belt* (1941); and E. Franklin Frazier's *Negro Youth at the Crossroads* (1941). With the exception of the last two books, these studies were the works of white Northerners influenced by anthropological insights.

Hortense Powdermaker was one such observer. Powdermaker began her anthropological studies in Melanesia and continued in Cottonville, Mississippi, where she studied that community as she had studied Melanesian ones. The result of her studies was *After Freedom.* John Dollard was a psychologist who studied under the aegis of the Yale Institute of Human Relations, producing *Caste and Class in a Southern Town.* Both books showed similar findings. They indicated that the South had a rigid caste system in which sex was symbolically very important. Both authors tried hard to be objective and to resist premature conclusions, especially Dollard who admitted having biases against the South.

Caste and Class in a Southern Town opened with a brief history of Blacks in America, a history that was conventional but inaccurate. Dollard correctly insisted that the African societies from which slaves had come had been culturally significant if technologically retarded. He erred in claiming that the North had idealized and identified with the slave during the Civil War, that Reconstruction had placed the Black on the top level in Southern society, and that emancipation had weakened the black family and ended aristocratic domination of the South. Unconsciously, perhaps, Dollard accepted a southern white view of the past. His most important conclusion about the contemporary social scene was that the South had moved to a caste system based on race, which denied social mobility to the Black. This caste system, according to Dollard, was exclusively southern and resulted in diminished black role possibilities, in social isolation, and in distinctive psychological problems for Blacks.

White gains from this caste system were not inconsiderable, said Dollard. Middle-class Whites gained economic, sexual, and status advantages from the caste system. They avoided manual labor, had relatively high purchasing power, and access to black women as well as to white ones. Dollard said that the realm of sexuality was one of fantasy and counter-fantasy for White and Black. Black women appeared in white male conversation as seductive and accessible, while white women represented purity. Although popular sentiment among middle-class Whites was that lower-class Whites engaged in interracial sexual activities, Blacks claimed that middle-class Whites also indulged. Typically, white boys obtained their sexual experience from black women. Despite the continued sexual relations, Dollard thought there was less racial mixture now than in the past probably because of more sophisticated contraceptive devices and because white women were supposedly more promiscuous than before and, thus, more available to white men.

The psychological problems of the Black came from an aspiration to be white, Dollard claimed, basing his thesis on Mary O'Malley's "Psychoses in the Colored Race" (which, as we have seen, was rejected by Klineberg). O'Malley maintained that black psychotics commonly had delusions of being White as shown by constant references to lightness. In non-psychotics, the aspiration manifested itself in the practice of marrying lighter-skinned individuals. Dollard felt that while some Blacks did not internalize whiteness and did not try to achieve white values, these were mostly lower-class agricultural workers who represented the stereotype of the Black to both northern and southern Whites. According to Dollard, the middle-class Black, who was typically either a teacher or minister, tried hard to escape identification with the lower-class Black by emphasizing a high standard of sexual behavior, by rejecting spirituals and jazz in favor of classical music, and by discouraging his wife from working. But his struggle proved fruitless; he was still considered black.

Negro servility, a necessary element of the caste system, contributed to a sense of white security but led to repressed antagonism on the part of the Black. This servility, combined with black errors of speech, furthered Whites' belief in their superiority. It also convinced many Blacks. The result, Dollard felt, was that "most Negroes accept the superiority of white characteristics and the inferiority of their own, and attempt to edge over toward the white model."

Because of the demands of the caste system, middle-class Blacks suffered psychological damage in varying degrees. According to Dollard, Blacks could respond in five ways to the aggression evoked by the caste system. They could aim their aggression at Whites; they could suppress all aggression; they could displace their aggression on other Blacks; they could surrender white middle-class values and backslide into the lower class; or they could restrain aggression while still striving for white values. Displacing of aggression onto Blacks was shown through sexual jealousy, the carrying of weapons, the weakness of family ties, hatred between husbands and wives, gossip, and mutual insults. Since the expression of aggression against Whites carried the highest risk, it was done covertly, mainly by black women. Both sexes, however, used gossip and humor as a verbal assault on Whites. Most middle-class Blacks supposedly chose the last alternative. Opting for white values required great skill to fulfill, as it involved both repression and competition. But Dollard believed that this course had the most future promise.

Resulting from existing social isolation, there were gains to be derived from lower-class behavior. The lower-class Black supposedly had a greater ability to enjoy sexuality, and Dollard noted less sexual perversion in lower-class individuals, greater freedom from resentment of Whites, and the luxury of a dependency relationship with Whites. Thus, Dollard concluded that the lower-class Blacks were happy persons with great impulse freedom and without the "noxious barriers of conscience and restrictive social patterns" to hinder that freedom. They supposedly had the ability to do what they wanted to do without inner repression, to eat when hungry, to make love when feeling like it, etc. These Blacks supposedly had a "natural relationship" with each other; they lived directly rather than vicariously. Their families were less stable than middle-class families but put fewer restrictions upon the members. However, these patterns had a social cost. "The permissive character form of the Negro unfits him in one sense for widespread *immediate* participation in our society." Because of this, Dollard said, the lower-class Black had to be changed through the agency of technical training and improved work habits since the dominant goal of American society was middle-class behavior.

Dollard inadvertently lent scientific respectability to the Sambo image by describing black lower-class behavior as child-like and socially pathological. However, he assigned the responsibility for the behavior to white prejudice. With the removal of this prejudice, Dollard thought that the lower-class patterns would disappear and the Black would be fully assimilated into American life. Dollard hoped his book would speed up the process by changing white American values through education about the caste system.

In 1938, the president of the Carnegie Corporation called for a general study of the Negro in America. Gunnar Myrdal, a Swede, came to the United States in September of that same year to begin the research. He recruited twenty American scholars, among them Otto Klineberg, to aid him, and on his return to Sweden in May, 1940, he asked these individuals to prepare memos on important aspects of the study. The memos and the study based on the memos were published. The study was Myrdal's book, *An American Dilemma: The Negro Problem and Modern Democracy* (1944), an exhaustive report that became justifiably famous. It had little that was creative but rather summarized the work of several decades. Its basic thesis was:

In practically all its divergences, American Negro culture is not something independent of general American culture. It is a distorted development, or a pathological condition, of the general American culture.

Basically, the authors agreed that African culture and tradition had been completely destroyed by enslavement, that there was no distinctive black culture, and that such phenomena as emotionalism in the black church, the proliferation of black social organizations, and the supposed instability of the black family were visible evidence of social breakdown. They also concluded that American Blacks should be assimilated into the mainstream of white American culture as quickly as possible.

Otto Klineberg's memo appeared in *Characteristics of the American Negro* (1944). His chapter on black intelligence merely repeated many of his findings in *Race Differences* in abbreviated form. Other chapters were newer. Guy B. Johnson, for example, studied black stereotypes. Taking the traits attributed to Blacks by other Blacks and those attributed to them by Whites, Johnson showed the areas of agreement. Both groups of respondents suggested that Blacks were more emotional and had greater sexuality; both agreed that the black aesthetic sense appeared to best advantage in music and the dance. Johnson, as a result of his findings, asked two questions. Did racial stereotypes have some validity? Why did Blacks believe the same things as Whites? He answered that stereotypes reflected caste conditioning, which influenced both Blacks and Whites.

A chapter by Eugene Horowitz of City College of New York concluded that racial prejudice originated in the frustration-aggression syndrome. The frustrated individual vents his frustration by behaving aggressively toward a minority group even though he has not had contact with the group before. Louis Wirth, the pioneer Chicago sociologist, and Herbert Goldhamer contributed a significant essay that, for the last time, treated racial mixture as a serious problem worthy of scholarly attention. The question of racial mixture had lost meaning since, by definition, there were no racial hybrids if there were no fixed races. Although genetics had emptied the question of meaning, Wirth and Goldhamer still tried to frame the question in terms of the history of Black-White mixture in the United States. Starting with the principles that neither the African Black nor the American White was a homogeneous racial type and that both had complex cultural endowments, Wirth and Goldhamer attributed most racial mixture to slave days. Basing their views on Caroline Bond Day's *A Study of Some Negro-White Families in the United States* (1932), a volume in Howard University's African study projects, they claimed that there were few Black-White marriages. Most Black-White marriages were supposedly between black men and white women; the black men involved were upwardly mobile; black women supposedly married black men in their search for social status. In addition, Wirth and Goldhamer maintained that increasing numbers of mulatto men were passing for white. The authors also accepted Herskovits's idea of the existence of a new type of American Black, whose uniqueness sprang from environmental factors and social selection rather than from genetic inheritance. The authors thought, contrary to the white majority opinion, that the mulatto would play a decreasingly important role in the affairs of black America, partly because of increasing incidence of state laws against interracial marriage. Perhaps Wirth and Goldhamer were right, but, if so, for the wrong reasons. In any case, with the study by Wirth and Goldhamer, the issue of racial mixture faded from the attention of American sociologists.

Another, and more important, book connected with the Myrdal study was *The Myth of the Negro Past* (1941) written by the anthropologist Melville J. Herskovits, who had switched his interest from the American Black to the African past. Much attacked in its own day, the book was to become the Bible of black scholars in the 1960's. Herskovits denied the conventional wisdom of the assimilationist sociologists, such as Robert E. Park and E. B. Reuter who were white and E. Franklin Frazier and Charles S. Johnson who were black. Sociologists' insistence that the Black was culturally an American whose African past was almost completely eradicated was severely challenged by Herskovits who maintained that the African past was real and still very much present in the culture of the contemporary American Black.

Herskovits contradicted the commonly held myths about the Black—the beliefs that the Black was childlike, that only the poorer African stocks had been enslaved, that slaves had lost their tribal identity in America, that African cultures were primitive, and that the American Black lacked a past. In so doing, he resurrected the method of cross-cultural comparison, which cultural anthropologists had avoided, and the theory of historical development, which functionalist anthropologists had discarded. He also went against the grain of the work of black scholars who had discarded the African past as savage. Believing that primitive cultures inevitably succumbed to technologically superior ones, these scholars doubted the existence of African survivals in America.

Herskovits began by reemphasizing the point that most American slaves had originated in the heavily populated coastal areas of West Africa. This fact, once known, made the quest for African beginnings easier and the study more manageable. Looking at West African societies, Herskovits affirmed their cultural integrity and denied that European intervention had disorganized them during the Age of Discovery. Herskovits showed that European influences had been minimal until the Europeans penetrated into the interior in the nineteenth century. He outlined African social forms—polygamous families, kinship groups, funeral rites, religions, secret societies, and music, art, and dance.

Herskovits argued that these forms had survived enslavement, despite pressures on the African to become acculturated. Blacks in South America had supposedly retained more of the African heritage because more Blacks had been imported there over a longer period of time and there had been less black and white cultural contact. In North America, according to Herskovits, musical and dancing traditions had persisted while other traditions had faded. Traditional family unity supposedly remained, centering around the cult of the dead, as did a number of other cultural traits. While Herskovits believed that many social values of the slaves had changed from African to American ones, he felt that others had continued, although slightly modified. The American Black was not a complete African in Herskovits's view, but he was vitally African in part of his being.

Herskovits criticized the sociological studies of black Southerners in the 1930's for failing to understand this fact. In particular, he singled out Hortense Powdermaker for her lack of historical insight in *After Freedom* (1939) and John Dollard for his psychological preoccupation, which caused him to overlook other reasons for black behavior in *Caste and Class in a Southern Town* (1937). Herskovits listed a number of African survivals that he had discovered in American Blacks and that included kinds of motor behavior—in planting and harvesting rhythms—as well as cultural practices—such as wrapping heads with handkerchiefs, membership in lodges and benevolent groups, mother-dominated families, and funerary rites. Herskovits also explained the attraction of the Baptist faith for the American Black in African terms; the faith permitted shouting, display of emotions, possession by spirits, and a submerged magic, all of which were part of African religions. In language and the arts, African remnants could be found. Black music was African music; black dance was African dance; black folklore was African folklore; and black language reflected both the structure and the grammar of African languages, said Herskovits.

The conclusion of Herskovits was the same as his departure point. Blacks had an African past; much African culture supposedly remained in the New World in the inner values retained by the Black. Since the belief that the Black had no past led to prejudice, according to Herskovits, the study of Africa was a step toward the achievement of equality.

Herskovits's conclusion barely dented assimilationist orthodoxy of the 1930's and 1940's, which explained prejudice as a function of class rather than race and which saw lower-class black behavior as indicative of social disorganization. For every phenomena that Herskovits claimed was African in origin, assimilationist scholars found an American source. The Black was a Baptist, Frazier claimed, because the Baptist church appealed to the lower-class emotionalism of black Americans. Black music was said to resemble white folk music of the Appalachians, which supposedly showed cultural retardation. Black language, in addition, showed the effects of poor education and caste lines, which reinforced linguistic errors. According to sociological orthodoxy, the black family was unstable, largely caused by missing fathers and illegitimate children, because of lower-class values and not because of the African polygamous family. Herskovits's position led to pessimism about the future; if African cultural survivals had endured 300 years of suppression, could they ever be eliminated? However, the concept of cultural survivals was suspect; the doctrine had been first developed by seventeenth and eighteenth century amateurs and revived by Tylor in the nineteenth century. Now it was discredited.

Herskovits's work ended with a logical contradiction. He claimed that cultural forms were unique, defined by a particular historical sequence of events, while also claiming that there were universal cultural patterns. He also relied on generalizations that David Bidney described in *Theoretical Anthropology* (New York, 1953) as ones "which no anthropologist had considered worthy of being designated as 'laws.'" Although of the cultural-relativist school, Herskovits applied universal categories of culture—social organization, magic, art, folklore, and language—to particular African societies. Herskovits did not lack inconsistencies.

III

The black reaction to their situation in the 1930's and 1940's varied. Articulate middle-class spokesmen agreed that assimilation was the desired goal, that the problem of prejudice was a psychological one, and that the elimination of racial prejudice would ease the transition from an outcaste status to a middle-class one. Typical of this group was Robert Russa Moton, who succeeded Booker T. Washington as President of Tuskegee and who wrote *What the Negro Thinks* (1929). Born and educated in the South, Moton denied that Whites understood Negroes, although he insisted that Negroes understood Whites. Segregation had diminished contact between the two groups and had helped conceal the Negro's true feelings. Moton maintained that the Negro accepted white standards of behavior (to too great a degree, Moton thought) and suffered from not being able to associate with Whites who had demonstrated ability in the areas of science, art, government, and business. Moton still held to the Brownlow tradition, believing that better Negroes should associate with better Whites and that bad Negroes suffered from lack of white contact. He, like Herskovits, said that the physical appearance of Negroes was changing, that they no longer resembled the caricatures found on Gold Dust and Cream of Wheat boxes. Negro girls no longer had pigtails; Negro women were supposedly prettier than before. Moton claimed that Negroes had cleaner homes, that their manners were better, and that they were better educated and richer. Moton's major argument was that Booker T. Washington's goal was being achieved; Negroes were acting and even beginning to look like middle-class Whites.

Moton, however, did not ask for total integration. He wanted the end of racial separation in schools and the return of suffrage to Negroes, but he also wanted Negroes to retain their recently developed pride in their folk music and art. He insisted that Negroes did not want to mix socially with Whites if they were not wanted. What Negroes wanted instead was a sense of dignity—to be addressed as Mr. and Mrs.—and an end to the condescension of lower-class Whites, to segregation, to cheating landlords, and to white male predatation on Negro women. Moton tried to predict the future; he conceived of an America where the two races would live in harmony, socially separate but with some contact. He discounted the feasibility of either Negro emigration to another land or of the complete physical demise of the Negro and thought that the present social arrangement would be continued but be improved.

Two of the most prominent black sociologists in the 1930's conceived of the American Black as solely American. Charles S. Johnson, who was head of the Social Science Department at Fisk University, interviewed 612 black families in Macon county, Alabama, and published his results in *Shadow of the Plantation* (1934). Johnson's results were curious as he made no reference in describing the black rural life to political disenfranchisement, unequal educational opportunities, unfair job discrimination, or prejudice. His basic premise was that the Black in the South possessed a lower-class life style. In a later study, sponsored by the American Council on Education and entitled *Growing Up in the Black Belt* (1941), Johnson interviewed ten southern Negroes from rural areas in order to determine their attitudes. His findings were not surprising. Blacks feared Whites who cheated them commercially and who attacked them physically when they protested. While Blacks in general liked their own color, some expressed a desire to either be lighter-skinned or to have longer hair. Those with dark skins disliked mulattoes, and the mulattoes described the blacker individuals as difficult to live with and naturally mean. All of these attitudes reflected a basic white orientation of the black population, according to Johnson.

E. Franklin Frazier, in such works as *The Negro Family* (1939) and *Negro Youth at the Crossroads* (1941), saw the roots of Negro difficulties in cultural lag and geographic isolation. The high illegitimacy rates, the large number of marriages and divorces without legal or religious sanction, and the extended nuclear family supposed typical of the Negro were attributed to failures of socialization in America rather than to survivals from the dimly remembered African past. Frazier held out hope for the Negro masses; with education, he said, they could escape into the middle class. Not that this escape was without a price; in *Black Bourgeosie* (1957), Frazier pointed to the overemphasis on middle-class standards in black families.

Johnson and Frazier accepted the majority black position in the 1930's, which said that the white American society was not perfect, but that its imperfections could be overlooked in the drive for integration. Their studies were aimed at identifying those elements in black behavior that blocked acceptance in white society, at showing those elements to be products of a century of poverty and discrimination, and at finding ways to overcome them. W. E. B. DuBois was the major black scholar who rejected this assimilationist philosophy in this era; his argument, that the Black should turn more inward, cost him his leadership position with the NAACP in 1938. DuBois was the outstanding advocate of extralegal tactics, arguing against alignment with white labor and liberals in using traditional economic and political measures.

The drive for middle-class respectability also entered into black literature. Walter Thurmond, who had preached the acceptance of blackness in his *The Blacker the Berry* (1928), attacked the Harlem Renaissance and the concept of black elemental virtues in *Infants of Spring* (1932). In this novel, Thurmond found nothing good in the movement he had previously praised; the literature of the Harlem Renaissance was bad, the foundation laid for future literature was shifting sand, and the presumed creativity of black artists was a delusion, he said.

The 1930's, however, did not see the end of the black literary efforts. The Federal Writers Project, an offshoot of the WPA, gave encouragement to black as well as white writers and fostered a whole generation of significant authors. Led by Sterling Brown, editor of *Negro Affairs,* the Federal Writers Project created a community where black intellectuals came together to share their works and to refine them. One of those so encouraged was Arna Bontemps, who turned from a Harlem renaissance theme of black sensuality versus white civilization in *God Sends Sunday* (1931) to a historical theme in *Black Thunder* (1936), a story of the Prosser Rebellion, and in *Drums at Dusk* (1939), an account of the Haitian rebellion of Toussaint L'Ouverture.

While sociologists were calling black lower-class ways pathological, some novelists were writing of these ways with sympathy for those caught in a system not of their own making. A new appreciation for earlier generations emerged, which, though tinged with reproach for past "Uncle Toms," still included respect for these individuals for surviving. Typical of the novels with this point of view was *Jonah's Gourd Vine* by Zora Neale Hurston, a black woman who trained in anthropology under Boas. This was the story of Jonah, the black son of a Virginia sharecropper; Jonah became an itinerant minister who roamed from place to place preaching and engaging in numerous illicit love affairs. Although he constantly hurt his family and was, in many ways, disreputable, Jonah emerged as a human being trying desperately to come to grips with life, hampered by exceedingly difficult circumstances.

The most famous fictional portrayals of the black lower class were the works of Richard Wright. Wright was born on a plantation near Natchez, Mississippi, and like many of his generation, migrated to Chicago. There he joined the Federal Writers Project. He won first prize for the best story by a WPA writer in a contest sponsored by *Story* in 1938. He had earlier published *Uncle Tom's Children* in 1936, but his reputation as a major writer was not established until the publication of *Native Son* (1940), which became a Book-of-the-Month Club selection, a play staged by Orson Welles, and a movie directed by himself. Wright was to write a number of other works, including *Black Boy* (1945), an autobiographical account of his life, but he was never again to achieve as much artistic acclaim as he had with *Native Son*.

Native Son told the story of Bigger Thomas, a black boy caught in a Chicago slum, and was based on Wright's own experiences. The hero, Bigger Thomas, influenced by an evil environment, went from one bad situation to another. His short life of freedom ended when, afraid of being discovered in a white girl's room, he killed the girl in a fit of panic. Despite the horrible nature of his deed, he was fulfilled by it and had, he felt, achieved something in his life. He was later hunted down, captured, tried, and sentenced to death, a casualty in the everyday war in the urban ghetto.

Although Bigger was portrayed as a kind of walking dead person, a monster, he was a monster created by a white society that lacked spiritual values, and he still was human. There was a community described that did possess spiritual values; Wright conceived of a moral black community in opposition to white society. This black community was a secular one, whose aim was not the redemption of all men in the next world but the redemption of some men in this world.

The secular romantic racialism of Wright had a religious counterpart, although not a conventional Christian one. It was declaimed by the many sects stimulated in the urban ghetto by the depression. Lacking the resources and the will to deal with the black situation, traditional Christian churches lost ground before storefront churches established and run by persons such as Father Divine and Daddy Grace.

One of the new sects, the Black Muslims, the Lost Found Nation of Islam, was founded by W. D. Fard, who appeared in Detroit in 1930 selling silks from door to door and claiming to be the possessor of lost information concerning the black man in America. Among the information that he revealed was the assertion that the Black had been dispossessed of his original religion, Islam. Fard converted a number of disciples to Islam, including Elijah Poole, a Georgian Black who had migrated to Detroit and who had met Fard on an automobile assembly line. Fard mysteriously disappeared in 1934, but not before he had given two works to his followers, *Teaching for the Lost Found Nation of Islam in a Mathematical Way* (a written manual), and *Secret Ritual of the Nation of Islam* (an orally transmitted report).

In his teachings Fard presented a new history of the black man, one that was a curious amalgam of nineteenth-century anthropological ideas and one which turned the orthodox biblical paradigm upside down. The original people, said Fard, were members of the tribe of Shabazz, who came to the earth 60 trillion years ago when a great explosion separated the earth from the moon. The tribe of Shabazz supposedly inhabited an area bounded by the Nile Valley and Mecca and made up the Black Nation of Asia. Approximately 50,000 years ago, scientists of the tribe of Shabazz bred a people with kinky hair who were sent to Africa to tame the wild beasts there. A more significant deviation among men had been created through the agency of an amoral genius named Yakub who was born 6,600 years ago. Yakub, who graduated from all the colleges and universities of the Black Nation before he was eighteen, began to experiment with the genetic makeup of black persons. As a result, the authorities exiled him along with 59,999 of his followers to the island of Patmos in the Aegean Sea. There, over a period of years, Yakub developed a white man through the selective breeding of light-skinned individuals and through the selective elimination of Blacks. The result was a white man whom he called Adam. The descendants of Adam proliferated and spread from Patmos, creating so much difficulty with their devilishness that they were exiled to Europe. From there they managed to enslave some of the lost members of the tribe of Shabazz in Africa 379 years ago. Such was the history of the Lost Found Nation of Islam.

Fard went on to predict the future. The coming of World War I signaled to him the beginning of the end of white civilization; by 1955, the white man would be gone from the Western hemisphere, and the Black would be free, Fard said. When the fall of America, which was to equal the biblical fall of Babylon, failed to happen, the Black Muslims changed Fard's prophecy to a more ambiguous one—the Black would either return to Africa or set up a separate state in North America. (In 1959, the Black Muslims asked for three or four states in the South for this purpose.)

Fard included elements of polygenesis and pre-Adamic ideas in his history. He argued, as had Carroll in *The Negro a Beast,* that the black man had existed before Adam. However, the white man in Fard's history was created by a black man instead of by God and was an agent of the Devil (the last thesis was a neat reversal of Carroll's). Moreover, Fard's chronology nearly matched that of the traditional religious account of creation (4004 B.C., the traditional date of creation, was 6,000 years ago, about the time Yakub supposedly created Whites) and his use of the island of Patmos as the home of the exiled Yakub was ironic in that Christians believed that the prophecies of St. John, in Revelations, had been written on that same island. But most important, Fard's emphasis upon the black race as the chosen race echoed a theme used by Christian abolitionists in the past and was backed by tradition. Although the Lost Found Nation of Islam was never to become numerically very large, its emphasis upon black superiority and upon white responsibility for black troubles as well as its vision of a glorious future touched a familiar chord in Blacks and was reflected in their feelings about their experience in America. The Black Muslims only added another variation to the long tradition of romantic racialism in America.

A new kind of romantic racialism also developed in the concept of negritude in the works of black writers in Africa and French Carribean. It appeared in the writings of the Martinique poet Aimé Césaire and in the thoughts of the African Léopold Sedor Senghor. Senghor, perhaps the leading spokesman of the new attitude, combined the neo-Lamarckian ideas advanced by American social scientists in the early twentieth century with the environmental ones common to the eighteenth century. According to Senghor, the African tropical environment had produced a human being with a special type of nervous and glandular systems. These equipped Blacks to be more receptive to the physical stimuli of shapes, colors, odors, sounds, and rhythms. The inherited traits of the Black, which were in part responses to sensory stimuli, could not be destroyed by an alien white culture; according to Senghor, they persisted no matter where the Black lived and no matter where he was taken. The African inheritance was not just color; it was also the ability to live a full aesthetic life.

Jean-Paul Sartre, in his preface to Léopold Senghor's 1947 anthology of African poetry, likened the concept of negritude to an African Eurydice, recovered from Hades by the song of Orpheus. Sartre commented that "Negritude in African poetry is an antiracist racism; it is the moment of negativity in reaction to the thesis of white supremacy." The implicit dialectic obvious in Sartre should not blind one to his perceptiveness. Although the concept of negritude was not native to black America, it soon became part of the American community of ideas.

While the genetic theory of race had become scientific orthodoxy, the older concept of racial physical traits lingered on in the media of the time; left-over eugenicists still talked in terms of racial characteristics. Blacks also did not entirely give up those ideas that there were certain aspects of their lives that might be hereditary and that they might have a special destiny.

Chapter 12

Culture Questioned

The Indian question, long thought answered, reappeared with a vengeance in the 1960's. A new pride in being Indian, coupled with calls for Indian unity and power, characterized the formerly dormant Indian movements. Indian points of view became more familiar to Whites as the media reported events and gave time and space to Indian leaders.

Despite the creation in 1946 of the Indian Claims Commission, which set up a mechanism for adjudicating treaty disputes, the question of Indian rights still remained open. The government had not completely abandoned the policy of Indian assimilation. Although Congress had passed the House Concurrent Resolution of June 9, 1953, which indicated that it was the intent of Congress to end its involvement in Indian affairs, in *Tee-Hit-Ton Indians* v. *the United States* (1955), the Supreme Court held that the Fifth Amendment did not apply to Indians and that their original possession of land did not constitute ownership since they had been dispossessed of land by force. The Eisenhower administration continued the attempt to assimilate the Indians; Eisenhower's Commissioner of Indian Affairs, Dillon Meyer, proposed a plan for urbanizing the Indian. Under this plan, 50,000 Indians were moved to the cities, and such was the seeming success of the program than even such opponents of the administration as Hubert Humphrey applauded it. Philleo Nash, a noted anthropologist and the Commissioner of Indian Affairs under Kennedy, continued the project with less enthusiasm; fewer Indian were moved. The program was not promoted by President Johnson; Johnson, however, appointed in 1966 the first Indian since Ely S. Parker, Grant's Commissioner of Indian Affairs, to serve as head of the Bureau of Indian Affairs. Despite the greater involvement of Indians in the Bureau and despite the relocation program of the 1950's, there were few new solutions proposed for the Indian problem. This poverty of ideas reflected both a lack of will and a trust in a bureaucracy that had done little to deserve that trust.

The Indians themselves were becoming activists, however. In 1962, the National Indian Youth Council was formed; its program and tactics clashed sharply with those of older groups such as the National Congress of American Indians. Other new organizations emerged and employed direct action. Groups of Indians occupied Alcatraz and the Bureau of Indian Affairs as they saw the Bureau as the source of their troubles. They protested the building of dams, which deprived them of needed fishing areas, the building of power stations, which polluted their air, and the allocation of water, which limited their ability to irrigate and farm. Indian churches also showed new vitality. The Sioux Sun Dance, the Medicine Lodge religion, and the Native American Church all grew. The Native American Church, for example, doubled its membership in the 1960's to encompass 40 percent of the Sioux in South Dakota.

Anthropologists and others who wrote about the Indian continued to argue that the American social system did not permit the integration of the Indian and that Indian religions increased in reaction to this circumstance. If white families had adopted Indians as equal members, these writers claimed, the Indian might have become White (they overlooked the early attempts of some Puritans to do just that). These writers concluded that Indians became acculturated without being assimilated and described several defense mechanisms that Indians had created to combat white pressures. These included messianic religions—those of the Prophet and the Ghost Dance—which preached the recovery of lost cultures, as well as accommodationistic religions—those of the Longhouse and Peyotism—which provided cultural emancipation while preaching acceptance of the white world. Neither kind of religion helped the Indian become assimilated, but they did make his exclusion more palatable.

While the anthropologists still conceived of Indian culture as socially disorganized, other writers were more sympathetic. One of these sympathizers was the literary critic Edmund Wilson, who turned his attention to the Iroquois in the 1950's. Before this, Wilson had already expressed fears over the growing power of the federal bureaucracy; he had seen the Indian as an underdog engaged in fighting a blind, insensitive Leviathan. Wilson began *Apologies to the Iroquois* (1960) because his land was near that reserved for the Iroquois by the Treaty of Fort Stanwix in 1784 and because of his acquaintance with Standing Arrow, the leader of a band of Mohawks who lived near Amsterdam, New York. Standing Arrow claimed that the Iroquois had never been conquered by the United States and that they were the only Indians whose government was recognized as sovereign by the United States. He also pointed to a provision of the Treaty of Fort Stanwix, which said that no land assigned to the Confederation could be sold except with the consent of both the Confederation and the government of the United States. The sale of land recognized by only the federal government was invalid, according to Standing Arrow. Impressed with the argument, Wilson read Lewis Henry Morgan's *The League of the Iroquois,* which completed Wilson's conversion to the Indian cause. Wilson met Louis Papeneau, a Mohawk living in Onandaga, who was an Indian nationalist and who provided Wilson with additional data, such as the growth of Indian population from 10,000 in 1763 to twice that by 1957.

Wilson's main concern became the grievances of the Iroquois with the government of the United States. Their first grievance involved the question of citizenship. The Iroquois had obtained the right to vote, as all Indians had, from the Citizenship Act of 1924, but they had not exercised that right. In World War I, the Iroquois had officially declared war on the Germans as a separate nation but had remained neutral in World War II. However, during World War II, local New York draft boards had considered Indians draft-eligible and had either drafted them or declared them draft-evaders, despite the facts that part of the Iroquois nation lived in Canada and that all were uncertain of their American citizenship. A second grievance arose over confusion about which government, federal or state, had primary legal jurisdiction over the Iroquois. More significant than either of these two issues, however, were the claims of the federal government that the Indians should pay income taxes and that they should sell their lands so that the St. Lawrence Seaway and power project could be built. In all these issues, Wilson took the Indians' side and castigated the United States government for failing to live up to its treaty obligations and for failing to recognize Indian sovereignty.

Wilson was quite impressed with Iroquois culture and religion. In particular, he praised the psychological acumen of the Iroquois. Relying upon Anthony F. C. Wallace's "Dreams and the Wishes of the Soul: A Type of Psychoanalytic Theory Among the Seventeenth Century Iroquois," which appeared in the *American Anthropologist* in April, 1958, Wilson showed how the Iroquois used an early form of psychological therapy based upon the interpretation of dreams and upon the belief that the soul had natural desires that were made known through these dreams. If dreams were satisfied, the body of the individual would supposedly remain healthy. If not, the body would become diseased, and the individual might die. Since dreams were considered so significant, the Iroquois went to great lengths—traveling long distances and resorting to human sacrifice—to ensure dream fulfillment. The Iroquois had a form of institutionalized dream analysis in their Festival of Fools (first noted by the French in 1656), which centered on the acting out of dreams by participants who asked onlookers to guess their meaning. Wilson used these data to confirm his thesis that the Indians were eminently sensible people and were, in this case, considerably advanced in medical theory over Western society, anticipating Freud by at least 250 years.

Wilson explained that the Indians' poor physical environment, their unpainted shacks, reflected not laziness but rather a different set of values. The Iroquois traditionally believed that indifference to physical possessions was a sign of moral superiority. Further, both the process of economic competition and the value of private property were alien to the Indian conceptions of cooperation and communal property. This explained the Indians' lack of enthusiasm for becoming farmers or traders and added to their seeming strangeness. Wilson used the Indian to illustrate white faults; while Whites had described Indians as vile people, the Indians did not shoot their relatives or sit in bars watching Westerns where actors simulated killing each other. According to Wilson, the Indians shared the worldwide reaction of non-white races against the meddling and encroachment of white colonial powers. The Indian represented to Wilson the struggle to prevent the encroachment of government upon personal property. Wilson used the Indian to symbolize what Whites ought to do; white Americans ought to be,

like Indians, less materialistic and more resistant to big government. The symbol of the Indian predicament became more important than the reality; the living Indian was hidden behind the
symbol.

Indians were included in serious American literature more and
more in the 1960's. The first of a new Western genre of serious
fiction, according to Leslie Fiedler, was John Barth's *The Sot-
Weed Factor* (1960). In this novel, Barth recounted the classic
story of John Smith and Pocahontas but with a different twist.
Barth's Pocahontas was seductive and desirous of being promiscuous; in the end, Smith saved himself from execution by deflower-
ing her, a feat which no one else had been able to accomplish. After
the act, Pocahontas became a whore. Barth's plot, which was an
elaboration of an old dirty joke, created a counterparable about
Pocahontas. She was not the traditional innocent in the woods but
rather the dissolute of the forest. Barth's anti-Pocahontas image
was used again in Fat Ellen in Leslie Fiedler's, "The First Spade
in the West," Hotwater Anna, in David Markson's *The Ballad of
Dingus Magee* (1965), and Indian Jenny in Ken Kesey's *Sometimes
a Great Notion* (1971). The Indian woman in literature was still
the object of white sexual desires, but she was no longer the long-
dreamed innocent heroine. The myth of love in the woods ended,
and that of sex in the tepee replaced it.

The white hero also changed; in works like Thomas Berger's
Little Big Man (1964), he became a kind of antihero. Little Big
Man lacked physical prowess, was a victim of circumstance, but
did have considerable sexual ability. Rather than dominating a
situation, Little Big Man was dominated by it, just as he was dominated by his white wife, who resembled the anti-Pocahontas figure.

The Indian man, however, retained his traditional literary position as the companion of the white man, resisting the dominance
of white women. In Ken Kesey's novel, *One Flew Over the
Cuckoo's Nest* (1962), a 6'6" Indian chief named Bromden fulfilled
this role. Bromden and his white friend McMurphy were both psy-
chotic inmates of a mental hospital; both had escaped into madness, the ultimate retreat from civilization. When McMurphy sexually attacked his archenemy, Big Nurse, she revenged herself by
having him lobotomized. He was saved from his vegetable fate by
Bromden, who mercifully killed him. The literary critic Leslie
Fiedler draws two morals from this novel. These are that the Indian can survive the white man and that madness may be the only

true frontier left to man, the last place where man can escape into his fantasies.

In the late 1960's, Indians were used to represent the world of drugs and counter culture; the Indian entered the white pantheon of prophets. Theodore Roszak in *Where the Wasteland Ends* (1972) has said that two of the major heroes of the counter culture were Black Elk and Carlos Castaneda. Books on and by Black Elk became popular and were more successful in their revised than in their original editions. Neihardt's *Black Elk Speaks* (rev. ed., 1961) competed with Joseph Epes Brown's *The Sacred Pipe: Black Elk's Account of the Seven Rites of the Oglala Sioux* (1953) for the reader's attention.

Carlos Castaneda gained fame with his study of Don Juan, a Mexican Indian, which he chronicled in three volumes: *The Teachings of Don Juan* (1968), *A Separate Reality* (1971), and *Journey to Ixtlan* (1972). Sections of Castaneda's work also appeared in such popular magazines as *Esquire*, increasing Castaneda's audience. His story represented the triumph of the Indian's mysticism over the anthropologist's scientism. Beginning as a student working on a graduate degree in anthropology, seeking a primitive informant for his own purposes, Castaneda ended as a disciple of his Indian master, having shed his middle-class world of beliefs for one of "non-ordinary reality."

In Don Juan's world, a separate reality, there were spirits and forces that were unaccountable in Castaneda's world. At first, it was difficult for Castaneda to accept the existence of these forces; but, through patient practice of Indian rituals and through experience, Castaneda became physically aware of them. The conversion to another reality was difficult for Castaneda, he said, as Don Juan never answered questions in a straight-forward manner and frequently puzzled Castaneda by his seemingly bizarre actions. Castaneda came to realize that the problem of understanding was not in Don Juan but in himself; he felt that he was incapable of fathoming the meaning of the separate reality because of his past mind set or because of his lack of Indian experience. In the end, Don Juan became a guru, a prophet who led Castaneda, no longer interested in anthropological scientism, to new heights of awareness. This awareness was not the rational wisdom of science; it was the intuitive wisdom of the heart and the psyche obtained by sharpening the senses through the use of drugs, through spiritual exercise, and through the physical training of the body.

Don Juan symbolized another, new image of the Indian. No longer was he the pitiful object to be studied, a person lost in poverty and ignorance; he had become the subject who possessed power and knowledge in his own right, both of which overshadowed the technological achievement of the white observer. In the end, Castaneda had to scrap his learned anthropological framework as too limiting and had to accept Don Juan's structuring of reality instead.

The belief that the Indian possessed a superior truth struck deeply into the consciousness of the counter culture. William Irwin Thompson quoted, in his *At the Edge of History* (1971), the conversation of some hitch-hiking Hippies:

Most of us are reincarnated American Indians who died at the hands of the white man and his technology. Now we have returned to be on the other side of the same event, but this time it is those who have what they think is power that are to be destroyed.

Concomitant with this new idea, that the Indian was reincarnated in the Hippie, was Thompson's conception of Indian origins, which was based upon a cyclical, antiprogressive view of history and which capitalized on the anomalies in the conventional anthropological explanation of Indian migration from Asia. Thompson based his views on history on ideas of Michael D. Coe, chairman of the Department of Anthropology at Yale.

According to Coe, in his *America's First Civilization: Discovering the Olmec* (1968), the Olmecs had had the earliest civilization in Mesoamerica and had appeared at the beginning with fully developed calendrical, mathematical, and technological systems that were advanced enough to allow the building of sophisticated artificial mounds and lagoons. There was evidence of all this at San Lorenzo Tenochtitlán, which evidence persuaded Coe to accept the Olmec version of their own past. The Olmecs maintained that they had come from the East to Veracruz, bringing the "writings, the books, and the paintings." The place of supposed origin was a land where some were black and some were white, where there were persons of many tongues and classes. In support of this thesis, Coe used statues carved by the Olmecs at La Venta, some of which had faces that were obviously Negroid or Semitic.

Thompson concluded that the Olmec Indians had come from Atlantis. More important, he believed that instead of evolving a new civilization in America, the Indians had degenerated. The Indians who succeeded the Olmecs in Mesoamerica seemed to have added nothing to the original ideas; they did what the Olmecs did, but less successfully. Since this supposed regression was counter to the implicit evolutionism of historians and anthropologists, it was difficult to explain. Because it was difficult to explain, it was usually ignored in favor of evidence that supported the thesis that the Indians had come across the Bering Strait from Asia, gradually evolving a complex civilization in the New World. While Thompson certainly detected an anomaly in this latter paradigm, he did not succeed in changing it. It would be ironic, indeed, if the statues of the Olmecs helped discredit the evolutionary model of history as the paintings of Egypt had helped discredit the biblical model of history. It would be even more ironic if the accepted explanation for the origins of the Indians became that prevalent in the sixteenth century and if the paradigm of evolutionary development was replaced by a paradigm of degeneracy as conceived in the eighteenth century.

An American Indian response to events in the 1960's combined a similar view of history with an apocalyptic vision. The vision originated with "Mad Bear" Anderson, whose dream appeared in Frank Water's *Book of the Hopi* (1963), another writing popular with the counter culture. According to Anderson's dream, the Indians of the Southwest had lived at first on an island; a flood had drowned most of the population while a few had escaped through tunnels to the high mesa country of the Hopis. Here they had prospered until the white man came, bringing disaster with him. A new time of troubles had arrived, according to Anderson, signaled by the reappearance of a race of sixty-foot giants, fourteen of whom had already been seen, and by riots and demonstrations led by Blacks and Indians. These civil disturbances were to lead to general anarchy, the eventual intervention of the Chinese Communists in America, and the final destruction of white Americans. Mad Bear's vision resembled that of Fard, the founder of the Black Muslims, except it was more specific; it was part of the long tradition of Indian apocalyptic hopes for the elimination of white Americans and a return to an Indian America.

Typical of another kind of response was that of Vine Deloria, Jr., a Standing Rock Sioux. Born near the Pine Ridge Reservation in South Dakota and the son of an Episcopal minister, Deloria graduated from Iowa State University and attended the Lutheran

School of Theology before becoming Executive Director of the National Congress of American Indians. His articles first appeared in *Playboy,* and were titled "Indians Today, Real and the Unreal," and "Anthropologists and Other Friends." These, along with unpublished essays, were put together in a book, *Custer Died for Your Sins* (1969), which became a best-seller and which made Deloria a recognized Indian authority. Deloria followed this book with another, *We Talk, You Listen* (1970). Both books were opinionated and critical of both American Indian policy and white views of the Indian.

Deloria asserted in *Custer Died for Your Sins* that the Indian was unreal to Whites, even to those Whites who claimed to have Indian blood. Confirming Fiedler, Deloria found that these Whites always claimed to descend from an Indian princess who was always a grandmother. So prevalent was this belief in American society, Deloria maintained that the only Whites who did not hold it were Jews. Because of their fancied Indian grandmothers, white Americans believed that they understood Indians. However, they did not understand, said Deloria, or they would not have forced the Indian to enter into white society, a policy just the opposite from that of segregation for Blacks. Part of the white ignorance about Indians stemmed from the inaccurate portrayal of Indians in literature. According to Deloria, there were only three novels written by Whites that gave even a partially true account of Indian life. These were Hal Borland's *When Legends Die,* Thomas Berger's *Little Big Man,* and Dan Cushman's *Stay Away Joe.* Other novels purported to be about Indians really were not, said Deloria. He particularly disliked the work of Oliver La Farge, whom Deloria called the most skillful white manipulator of the Indians, a person who was only comfortable with Uncle Tomahawks and who rejected any attempts toward Indian leadership or union formation. Deloria believed that La Farge took a pro-Indian stand only in the white press and that he was really contemptuous of the Indian.

Deloria's attack on white novelists was mild compared to the one he made on the other "supposed" friends of the Indians, anthropologists and missionaries. He particularly disliked anthropologists who maintained that they had studied the Indian and knew him well. Deloria felt that they were mistaken, that they misled others because of their errors. Although anthropologists assumed an aura of scientific detachment, they were deceived, Deloria believed, by their search for quaintness. They taught that Indians were folk

people and Whites were urban, and that the cultural variation between White and Indian resulted from that distinction. They described the Indians as bicultural persons who were failing in the
struggle to live in two worlds and who, as a consequence, had lost
their identity as Indians. Deloria scoffed at these theories and
claimed that they served only to block Indian development and
to excuse Indian failure. He denied that the problem of the Sioux
lay in the conflict between their self-concepts as warriors (as anthropologists had claimed) and the pressures of white society
where warrior values were inappropriate. The real causes of the
Sioux troubles, Deloria said, were poverty and prejudice, not identity. Deloria contended that while the anthropologists encouraged
the Indian to cultivate folk arts such as dancing to maintain their
identity, dancing had a limited economic benefit and diverted Indians from their real problems. He offered as proof the example of
the Apaches who had been left alone by anthropologists and who
therefore supposedly had no identity problem; because they did not
worry about whether they had a folk or urban culture, they could
proceed with necessary economic development.

Similarly, Deloria had little use for white missionary efforts
aimed at the Indian. Despite his own seminary training, he believed that Christianity was inferior to the native Indian religions
that saw life as a whole entity. Christianity divided life into religious and secular provinces and, consequently, failed to provide
guidance in most human social relations. Indian religion, which
Deloria believed would eventually save the Indian, taught the Indian to respect all members of society, to believe that sharing with
others was the highest good, to mark the divisions of life by appropriate religious ceremonies, and to accept death as a natural good.
Rather than make the Indian a white Christian, Deloria wished to
combine Indian religion with Christianity in a syncretic way and
suggested that white denominations could do this by creating and
supporting an Indian Christian Church.

Deloria's strictures against anthropologists and missionaries
can best be understood in the context of Indian pride. Both anthropologists and missionaries wanted to save the Indian, but they had
assumed, implicitly or explicitly, a position of cultural superiority.
Both had thought that the Indians would become extinct because
they were unable to cope with the pressures of an urbanized, industrial society. Neither belief was correct, Deloria argued; there-

fore it was necessary to reject these white sympathizers as Blacks had rejected white liberals in order to declare independence.

The Indian problem had been misconstrued, according to Deloria, because white Americans regarded the problems of the Indian and Black as the same. Deloria said that Whites regarded Indians and Blacks as different kinds of animals. Whites supposedly regarded Blacks as domesticated, ex-draft animals and repressed them to disprove evolution. The Indians, on the other hand, were thought by Whites to be ex-wild animals who had to be made into Anglo-Saxons. Thus, Whites destroyed Indian culture while making Blacks create their own; they tried to integrate Indians into the mainstream of American society through agriculture while taking away the land that made such an integration possible. Whites gave Blacks civil rights, but then restricted the use of these rights. Because of differential treatment by Whites, Deloria thought that each group, red and black, should go its own way; had he been in charge of Reconstruction, Deloria would have given Blacks reservations.

In addition to analyzing past mistakes, Deloria predicted the Indian future. He ended *Custer Died for Your Sins* on this note and devoted the major part of *We Talk, You Listen* to it. Deloria, following Marshall McLuhan, argued that tribal consciousness was to be the wave of the future, that Americans must adopt the tribal-communal way of life if they wished to survive, and that the Indians provided the best models for both this consciousness and way of life. The Indians supposedly had a model society that provided security, ease, and the leadership opportunity that should be emulated by all. The Hippies tried to do so in their communities, said Deloria; they became like Indians in their free stores, their sharing of goods, and in their other common practices. However, Hippies failed to create viable communities because they had no tradition of group customs, the cement that held Indian society together. If the Hippies had somehow acquired tradition and adequate land, they would have succeeded in creating an ideal community, according to Deloria.

In 1969, according to Deloria, there was a mass rediscovery of the Indians by non-Indians; the Indians became everyone's favorites. The conservatives liked the Indians because they were less active in civil rights than the Blacks; the liberals liked the Indians because they were oppressed and because they voted Democratic. The Blacks liked them because they were anti-establishment. (Deloria maintained, however, that the Indians were not radical, quoting an Old Sioux who said he would not support the overthrow of the establishment "until we get paid for the Black Hills".) The Hippies supposedly admired the Indian style of life, and other minorities related Indians to their own problems. However, these were only surface reasons; according to Deloria the major reason that the Indian had become popular lay deeper. This major reason was a new world view that was said to be coming and that emphasized the group rather than the individual. What McLuhan called tribal consciousness had supposedly overtaken the American people, who were becoming tribalized. Deloria believed that in order to survive, white Americans were assuming the thought patterns of the Indian, rejecting their Western linear sequence of ideas for an Indian, circular, holistic one. Deloria maintained that Indian thought was always on center and always returned to where it started, a logical way of proceeding. Thus, the Indian absorbed all the information around him but was not changed by it, while the deluge of sensory information perceived by the non-Indian caused him to "think the world is going up or down" (1970). When the non-Indian accepted the fact that interior reality did not change, his development mania would end and balance rather than progress will be sought, said Deloria.

Deloria believed that a cycle of history was almost complete; Deloria foresaw an eventual Indian triumph, as Whites either became Indians or vanished. The tables had supposedly turned and the superior group had supposedly become the inferior one.

The assertion of Indian superiority served much the same function for Indians as the assertion of black superiority did for Blacks; it bolstered egoes and enhanced self-confidence. Perhaps Leslie Fiedler was correct in supposing that the Indian had triumphed in his insistence upon the ability of drugs to enhance reality and in his capturing the minds of the counter culture. Maybe Vine Deloria was right in saying that the Indian could serve as a model for other ways of thinking and living. Yet the observer is left with a lingering doubt concerning the reality of the new Indian image; it seemed that approval of the Indian was a reaction against the common pieties of white society rather than an appreciation of the Indians' own virtues.

The image of the new Indian appeared in movies in the 1950's and 1960's, which displayed greater sympathy for an Indian point of view. Many of these movies were simplistic films providing a mirror image of an older version of the Indian situation. The Indian was all good and his white oppressor was all bad; the characterization of each was on a surface level only. Such a movie was *Cheyenne Autumn* (1965), which was based on a Mari Sandoz novel and which recounted the hardships encountered by the Cheyennes on their return from a reservation in the Southwest to their ancestral home in the North. Another was *Tell Them Willie Boy Is Here* (1969), whose plot concerned the attempt of Willie Boy, an Indian, to steal a bride. The traditional tribal method backfired when the bride's father was killed by Willie and a white mob, not comprehending what had happened, gathered to lynch the culprit. During the Vietnamese war, there were movies that tried to compare the treatment of the Indians with that of the Vietnamese and had obvious moral overtones. These, like the other simplistic films, were artistic failures.

More successful were the films *Little Big Man* (1970) and *When Legends Die* (1972), both adaptations from thoughtful novels. *Little Big Man*, like *Black Elk Speaks*, was a history of the Indian Wars, but it was told by an ancient White-cum-Indian to a social worker in a ward of a mental hospital. According to this 100-year-old man, he had been orphaned early, had become an Indian, served as army scout, and had alternated between a White and an Indian world during the period of the Indian Wars. He had been a participant of both Little Big Horn and the Massacre at Wounded Knee. The Indian way of life as portrayed in the movie was dignified and attractive, but the Indian was not sentimentalized into a noble savage. *When Legends Die*, on the other hand, dealt with contemporary Indian life and described the interaction of an Indian rodeo rider with his white sponsor. This movie showed both men caught in a vicious system; the Indian, in particular, became victimized by it. Both movies were critical successes and perhaps began to raise hopes that the real Indian was being seen by white Americans.

I

By the 1960's, sociologists were in the process of reweighing the idea of the assimilation. All Americans had not become part of a homogeneous whole, Indians had not entered into white society, nor had the elimination of caste lines and the transformation of the black masses from peasants in the South to city dwellers in the North made them indistinguishable from other members of the larger society. In order to find out what had gone wrong, sociologists turned to an analysis of American society and the attitudes within that society; from that analysis, they derived new models for explaining the lack of successful assimilation. One explanation pointed to the basic structure of American society. Another indicated the lack of power in the hands of Blacks and Indians in America. The new model provided a way out of the morass provided by the earlier model, that of structural-functionalism with its view that social consensus and equilibrium were necessary conditions of American society.

The preeminent structural-functionalist in American sociology in the decade of the 1960's, as in the 1950's, was Talcott Parsons. In two essays, "Certain Primary Sources and Patterns of Aggression in the Social Structure of the Western World," and "Full Citizenship for the Negro American? A Sociological Problem," Parsons claimed that the organization of work and the family in American society produced anxieties and tensions that were directed at an out-group, primarily Blacks. Parsons' view differed from the thinking of such persons as John Dollard and Hortense Powdermaker, structural functionalists in the 1930's, in that he saw aggression in social rather than individual terms. Parsons envisioned the future not as assimilation but rather as inclusion, a situation where ethnic groups retained identity but were possessed of legal rights, political and economic rewards, and the opportunity for a decent life. He foresaw this as an evolutionary process where society changed and where Blacks and Indians acquired one freedom at a time. Such change was not considered inevitable; it might be frustrated by unforeseen forces or events.

A European sociologist, Rolf Dahrendorf, used the concept of power as an important variable in the study of social organization. In his *Class and Class Conflict in Industrial Society* (1959), he argued the seemingly obvious point that every society had an authority structure. In order to change the authority structure, those who were underlings must change from a collection of individuals to a full-fledged interest group; they must submerge their private interests into a public one. The necessary catalysts for this action were leadership and an ideological perspective around which to develop a group perspective, both of which could only be found in a society that was not totally repressive. According to Dahrendorf's theory, Indians and Blacks lacked the power to break into the white authority structure; hope for the future lay in the acquisition of that power.

The ultimate expression of the idea of social power was Gerhard E. Lenski's *Power and Privilege: A Theory of Social Stratification* (1966). In his book, Lenski utilized two major concepts that were readily applicable to the situation of an ethnic minority and specifically applicable to the black situation in America. These were "power class" and "status inconsistency." Lenski maintained that various social roles were accompanied by specific statuses in the white social structures but that these roles, when filled by Blacks, acquired different status assumptions. Blacks could achieve high status in some of the roles, but they lacked status in others because of their color. The result was status inconsistency, a clustering of statuses with contradictory elements of high and low prestige. Thus, a black person could achieve middle-class status and still not be accorded middle-class recognition. Lenski showed the weakness in the thought of earlier sociologists who had assumed that the racial problem was only one of social class; they had failed to recognize that prejudice could be racial as well as social and that assimilation into middle-class America required more than money or values. Lenski argued as well that factors affecting the socialization of Blacks differed from those affecting Whites. The black man might combine high achievement with low independence in a job, as he valued security in an occupation more than Whites did. The Black's job expectations had no association with the status he achieved, and his search for status involved different motives than the white search. Further complicating matters, according to Lenski, were the psychological and social barriers erected by the white power class to keep the Blacks out. These difficulties could also be related to the Indian position in a white society.

The assimilation theory of Park and his students, which assumed that contact led to competition, that competition led to accommodation, and that accommodation led to assimilation, had proved too simple. Not enough individuals had followed this path; only organized groups could do it with any hope of success. Some fortunate persons had achieved high status in a work role only to find they were denied status in a racial one. The net result of this realization was to cause sociologists to emphasize the need for power to break out of a social structure that was stronger and more repressive than earlier scholars had realized. This emphasis led to

a study of social structure, of the nature and extent of white prejudice, and of the impact of this prejudice upon the individual personalities of the members of a racial group.

In the 1930's, social psychologists had believed that racial
prejudice was a function of economic forces and that it was confined largely to the South. The explanations in the the 1960's had
changed to other themes. One focused on the psychological problems of the prejudiced individual. Prejudice supposedly resulted
from frustration-aggression, a need for scapegoating, and an authoritarian personality. An alternate explanation of prejudice was a
structural one that blamed the composition of society. According
to this explanation, prejudice was a function of the successful attempts of those in control to favor themselves, which resulted in
discrimination toward others. Finally, there was a cultural explanation; prejudice was simply a product of ethnocentrism in a particular culture.

Each of the explanations had inherent contradictions. The
psychological explanation of frustration-aggression, which Dollard
used in *Caste and Class in a Southern Town,* held that blocked
goals led to hostile impulses in specific individuals. These hostile
impulses were redirected toward a stereotype through displacement
or projection. Prejudice thus supposedly resulted from the psychological damage done to an individual by a socialization process that
generated hostility because of implicit sanctions and threats of punishment. The unhappy individual projected his failings on individuals from other racial groups by scapegoating, thus allaying his
own feelings of guilt and justifying his discriminatory practices.
The problem with the frustration-aggression explanation was that
it was too easy. Aggression was not necessarily negative; it could
serve beneficial social purposes. Further, the explanation failed to
suggest why the target for aggression was always the members of
particular groups. Similar problems could be found with the explanation that prejudice resulted from authoritarian personalities. The
original impetus for this explanation came from T. W. Adorno,
et al, The Authoritarian Personality (1950). Adorno studied the
phenomenon of Fascism and listed the character traits that individual Fascists possessed in order to establish a scale of authori-
tarianism. Subsequent studies, however, showed that the traits
Adorno labelled as authoritarian were also characteristic of non-
authoritarian personalities, indicating that the categories were not
discriminating enough to explain why prejudice existed. Finally,
the cultural explanation of prejudice was static; it failed to explain

the origins of prejudice. Although structuralists argued that prejudice acted as a mechanism to keep society together, there was no explanation of how the mechanism had come into being and had persisted through different time periods and different social assumptions. None of the solutions seemed adequate.

There were students of Black-White relations in America who thought that perhaps these relations were so intertwined with the way American society was integrated that they would not change. Such at least was the position of Francis L. K. Hsu, a Chinese student of American character. He argued that those who regarded racial prejudice as an aberration in American society were wrong. The ideal of equality, which Myrdal thought was in conflict with prejudice and which he thought would eventually end the American dilemma, was not the American core value according to Hsu. Hsu thought that the belief in equality was a part of a larger belief in American goodness. This latter belief was one of Myrdal's articles of faith and was shared by the psychologist Gordon Allport as demonstrated in his *The Nature of Prejudice* (1954), one of the significant analyses of prejudice in the 1950's. Because of his belief in American goodness, Allport could not bring himself to accept his own findings that church members were more prejudiced than non-church members. Since both he and Myrdal believed that Americans were good and valued equality, they also believed that the practice of discrimination had resulted from historically determined circumstances that would die as American values triumphed. Hsu did not believe this. He claimed that the core value for Americans was not equality but was, rather, self-reliance. Self-reliance meant not depending on anything or anybody, which, in turn, meant insecurity and competition. Hsu said in "American Core Values and National Character," in *Psychological Anthropology* (1961):

The individual who is enjoined to be self-reliant, unlike one who is taught to respect authority and external barriers, has no permanent place in his society. Everything is subject to change without notice.

Because of this striving for status, Americans supposedly feared most the contamination of status by human beings who were dubbed inferior by the society. Thus, Hsu believed that racial prejudice was not viewed as a contradiction of equality by most Americans and that prejudice was a natural corollary to the value that underlay a competitive, striving society.

Such was also the conclusion of Pierre van den Berghe in his *Race and Racism: A Comparative Perspective* (1967), one of the most important books on the topic of race relations in the 1960's. Van den Berghe, like Hsu, had the advantage of looking at the United States from the point of view of an outsider. Van den Berghe began with a consideration of the paradigm of the social scientists of the 1950's. These scholars, Van den Berghe said, assumed "that phenotypical or genotypical differences between sub-species of *Homo sapiens* (if they can be determined) are not significantly related to any differences in intelligence or any other socially meaningful capability," and that individual or group differences were primarily the result of differing social environments and prejudice. Van den Berghe insisted that the evidence in support of these two assumptions was tenuous and that the absence of significant group differences had not been proven nor could specific effects of prejudice be substantiated.

According to Van den Berghe, part of the difficulty in the older paradigm lay in the ambiguity of the concept of a race, which had been used to mean four different things. It was defined by physical anthropologists as one of the various sub-species of *Homo sapiens,* by more ordinary people as a human group with a shared culture, by nineteenth-century thinkers as a species, and by recent social scientists—such as himself—as a human group that defined itself and/or was defined by other groups as different from others. Van den Berghe, unlike Montagu who urged elimination of the term race, claimed that the concept could be used in a non-genetic sense as a kind of shorthand symbol for group differences. Van den Berghe accepted the social usage of the term race and took that as a basis for further investigation.

In his book, *Race and Racism: A Comparative Perspective* (1967), Van den Berghe defined racism as:

Any sets of beliefs that organic, genetically transmitted differences (real or imagined) between human groups are intrinsically associated with the presence or absence of certain socially relevant abilities or characteristics, hence that such differences are a legitimate basis of invidious distinctions between groups socially defined as races.

Racism included a belief in the inferiority or superiority of groups. But it was not, according to Van den Berghe, the unique discovery of nineteenth-century Western civilization. Racism had supposedly developed in Western countries because of the congruence of three factors—capitalism (which led to colonialism and slavery), Darwinism (which led to the invidious comparison of races), and the equalitarian ideas of the Enlightenment (which ironically led to the concept of "Herrenvolk" democracy, a political society where the dominant majority professed a belief in equality but denied participation in that society to a minority group). Van den Berghe discounted the psychological explanations of racial prejudice, pointing out that most racists in a racist society were not sick nor were their prejudices internalized. Societies became racist because of various economic factors, intellectual and political ideas, and social systems.

Van den Berghe suggested two models of racially-mixed societies, paternalistic and competitive, which are useful for understanding the dynamics of racism. The paternalistic type, found in the pre-Civil War American South, divided role and status on racial lines, thus setting maximum social distance between the races. However, the society permitted physical intimacy without perceiving a threat to the white majority, and miscegenation existed in the form of institutional concubinage. Racial prejudice was not unknown, but it was muted by "pseudo-tolerance," arising from the fiction of the existence of a contented black slave, and the belief that the subjugated minority was child-like and stupid. On the other hand, the competitive model, post-Civil War American society, reflected the economic tensions in an industrialized urban society. Class differences became more important than racial ones and the caste line slanted obliquely, rather than horizontally through society. Along with "Herrenvolk" democracy, the image of the minority race changed. Instead of being conceived of as child-like, the minority was regarded as aggressive, insolent, oversexed, and clannish. Miscegenation became less frequent and less acceptable as physical contact lessened and social segregation increased. Each of the two types of society could be pluralistic, segmented into groups, but this pluralism varied. It might be based upon cultural differences, as in South Africa, or on social differences, as in the United States. But this pluralism did not mean the end of conflict; both in South Africa and in the United States, there were conflicts between groups.

Van den Berghe applied his two models of racist societies to contemporary situations in Mexico, Brazil, South Africa, and the United States. Mexico was unique in that it had begun as a racist

society of the paternalistic type and had become a nonracist one
without ever having become a competitive one. Because there was
never a clear connection made between race and culture in Mexico,
because few Mexican social distinctions were based on race, because the brutality and arrogance of the Spaniards had led to racial
homogenization, and because racial variation was so complex, the
early system of prejudice broke down in Mexico. The same could
not be said for Brazil, which had the most problematic racial situation in Latin America, according to Van den Berghe. Brazil had
moved from a paternalistic type of racist society in the nineteenth
century to a competitive one in the twentieth century. As in the
United States, the growth of derogatory racial stereotypes, the lessening of miscegenation, and the increased consciousness of differing physical appearances signaled the change. The same situation
was believed to exist, in an attenuated form, in South Africa.

According to Van den Berghe, the United States had been
"since its birth and until World War II, a 'Herrenvolk' democracy."
From the start, America had been a racist society, said Van den
Berghe. Beginning as a paternalistic society, the United States became a competitive one after the Civil War. It was still racist;
Van den Berghe made an unpublished study of American presidents from 1790 to the 1950's, that claimed that all these presidents
were racists except for the two Adamses and James Garfield. Like
Hsu, Van den Berghe saw American racism as a function of the
values of a large society.

Many well-meaning American "liberals" mistakenly regard racism as
the underlying cause of most evils in their society, instead of viewing it
as but a fairly superficial symptom of much more widespread and basic
problems.

Van den Berghe concluded from his own comparative analysis
that, despite different kinds of attitudes and historical development,
all four societies—Mexico, Brazil, South Africa, and the United
States—showed great similarities in race relations. All had begun as
paternalistic; all had had a minority population with much physical intermixture through miscegenation; and all had converted the
subjugated race to the dominant group's culture. Van den Berghe
did hold out hope, however. Each social system supposedly contained the ideological seeds of the destruction of its own racism;
the educated elite of the minority group and the progressive ele-

ment of the majority would question racist assumptions. Finally, Van den Berghe made what was possibly his most important points, that race was a subjective concept and that it was a social reality in countries with mixed populations.

By the 1970's, conceptions of race relations had changed. No longer was there the easy optimism of the late 1940's that assimilation was an on-going process or even that assimilation would occur at all. The view that prejudice was an external manifestation of an internal psychological state had lost favor, as had the view that racial prejudice was merely a surface social problem. Theorists had become impressed both with the complexity of the phenomenon and with the magnitude of the effort required to remove it. They had come to realize that attitudes toward diverse groups were connected to other social attitudes that were basic to the operation of a society, so basic that the possibility of expunging racism seemed unlikely.

Historians, like sociologists, were finding that racial prejudice had deep roots in American values and in the structure of American society and that, in order to find these roots, they had to reexamine these values and structures. Their examination took two different, but connected, forms. The first form concerned the nature of the assimilation process in America and analyzed successes and failures. The second concerned the origins of racial prejudice and the connection between racism and slavery.

The first branch of historical effort questioned the possibility of assimilation in America. The black experience in America was not unique according to this questioning; Blacks had replicated the immigrant experience, but the immigrant experience had perhaps been misrepresented as being easier and more successful than it actually was. This argument had two sides. On the one side, it held out the hope that Blacks could eventually do what other immigrants had done. On the other, it created doubts about whether assimilation had occurred in American society at all. This argument could lead to a belief in a multinational America or to a belief that America was coming apart.

Some examinations of the immigrant experience seemed to show that the supposed assimilation of European ethnic groups had been more imagined than real. Will Herberg exemplified this in his *Protestant, Catholic and Jew* (1955), a book that maintained that there was a triple melting pot situation in America. These pots contained people of the three religious persuasions, and what mixing occurred was between members of different ethnic groups of the same religion. Thus, a Norwegian Lutheran could marry a Dutch Calvinist without difficulty but might have problems marrying an Irish Catholic. The Herberg model did not include Blacks or Indians, but it did illuminate the limited extent of assimilation even among groups of close physical and social proximity.

A similar statement on historic assimilation came, not from a historian, but rather from a sociologist, Milton M. Gordon, who in his *Assimilation in American Life* (1964) also focused upon religious ties. Gordon's conclusions were shared by E. Digby Baltzell in his book *The Protestant Establishment* (1964), which claimed that a WASP caste still existed that prevented Jewish inclusion in private clubs, the ultimate status-giving institutions, although some Jewish persons had achieved both money and power. The thrust of Baltzell's argument was clear: even white Americans had not become homogeneous. It was also ominous. If white Americans who had achieved status and power refused to share their status with other Whites, could they be expected to share this status with less powerful red or black Americans?

Nathan Glazer and Daniel Moynihan, a Jew and an Irishman, also considered this problem in a study of Negroes and Puerto Ricans in New York City in *Beyond the Melting Pot* (1964). The authors examined the inhabitants of New York City as Handlin had done earlier and tentatively suggested that ethnic groups would not amalgamate into American society but would remain separate. Glazer, a sociologist, continued to collect evidence in later studies to show that even white ethnic groups had not moved rapidly into American society; he concluded that the Italians and Poles remained poorly assimilated while the Blacks had been assimilated better than Puerto Ricans or Mexicans. This lack of general assimilation did not lead Glazer to a belief in the need for complete group separation. He attacked the idea of ethnic nationalism, that a group should have its own country within the United States. The idea of a separate nation pushed the tolerance of the majority too far, he said; white Americans have permitted revolutionary nationalism in terms of separate schools, foreign languages, diverse religions, and ethnic customs; they have never tolerated physical separation. Physical separation for Blacks was considered unnecessary because Blacks were not an internal, dependent colony in the United States but were supposedly merely experiencing the usual immigrant difficulties.

Concomitant with the growing desperation about the failure to understand that assimilation of European immigrants had been limited was the question of whether the goal of assimilation was even desirable. Such books as Peter Shrag's *The Decline of the WASP* (1971) and Michael Novak's *The Unmeltable Ethnics* (1972) argued that immigrant values were more vital, colorful, and useful than were the supposed superior values of the dominant WASP elite. The failure of Poles to be converted to WASP values was considered a blessing in disguise and, for Shrag and Novak at least, the existence of a society with divergent and undissolved ethnic groups was reason for optimism.

II

By the 1950's, the culture concept in anthropology had been fully developed and was, perhaps, at its peak. The conventional explanation for the different life patterns of various groups now involved the paradigm of cultural determinism. This explanation had two facets. The individual in society was completely subordinated to his culture and was completely determined by it. No one culture could be compared to another nor could any evolutionary scale be used to weigh the development of cultures.

The two most significant proponents of the culture concept were Melville Herskovits and A. L. Kroeber. In his general theoretical statement in *Man and His Works* (1948), Herskovits stressed the determinant force of acculturation. He claimed that it was possible to infer general laws from ethnohistory, which he defined as the cultural history of a particular people. These general laws, however, were cultural ones covering changes in processes. While Herskovits took a functionalist position, saying that cultural forms were unique to each society, he also took an uniformalist one, saying that cultural processes were universal and did not change. Herskovits glossed over the apparent contradiction by assigning the task of determining the shape of unique cultures to ethnohistorians and the formation of laws of cultural processes to comparative sociologists.

The major books in the culture tradition, however, were written by Kroeber. These include his *The Nature of Culture* (1952) and, with Clyde Kluckhohn, *Culture: A Critical Review of Concepts and Definitions* (1952). In the former, a collection of essays and papers, Kroeber argued that "the most significant accomplishment of anthropology in the first half of the twentieth century has been the extension and clarification of the concept of culture." He also said,

the outstanding consequence of this conceptual extension has been the toppling of the doctrine of racism—that bland assumption of race superiority which is so satisfying emotionally to most people and so unwarranted. We have learned that social achievements and superiorities rest overwhelmingly on cultural conditioning. The racist illusion rests on a naive failure to distinguish fixed biological processes from essentially variable cultural processes. Once the nature of the cultural process is clearly grasped, the racist illusion is bound to melt away rapidly.

In addition to this attack on racism, Kroeber denounced ethnocentrism and claimed that the culture concept could aid in psychological studies. He denied that recent genetic theory would aid the study of races; he thought that genes and chromosomes were too complex to decipher. He admitted that research on racial groups had produced a few correlations of race and physical traits but said that these traits were inconsequential ones.

Although Kroeber downgraded the influence of biological factors on human accomplishments, he still defined anthropology as a natural science. He said in *The Nature of Culture* that he believed "cultural phenomena to be part of nature and therefore a proper study for investigation by natural science." Anthropology was the recognition and description of social traits in terms of the total patterns or value systems of the culture in which they existed; thus he evolved the following definition, "culture is [a] value-laden, transmitted pattern selected from tradition, which may on the one hand be considered as products of action, on the other as conditioning elements of further action." Kroeber distinguished between his patterns of culture and those of Benedict, which he considered excessively static and impervious to change. He described his own approach as a historical one that combined nature and history and that conceived of culture as composed of superorganic elements emerging from natural phenomena. Despite his insistence upon cultural change, Kroeber failed to explain the underlying causes of historical development.

The work of Kroeber and Kluckhohn, according to the noted historian Robert F. Berkhofer Jr. in "Clio and the Culture Concept,"

Social Science Quarterly (1972), completed the establishment of the term culture. Although the word had been common in America since Taylor had popularized it in 1871, it had not assumed elements of normativeness and patterning until the 1930's when these elements became commonplace. According to Berkhofer, by 1952, culture had changed from a definition "based upon equality of physical artifacts, outer behavior, and ideation to a definition purely in terms of the latter, and causality and integration as well as the manifestations of behavior were sought in terms of patterns of ideas and values." Anthropologists had gone from counting material objects of culture and from observing behavior characteristics to the study of the ideas behind artifacts and behavior. The result was that the concept of culture came to mean mind, norms, and values. Culture had become attitude.

There were always problems with and tensions within the culture concept. Was culture common to all men or were there specific, individual cultures? The word was often used with both connotations. Anyway, could a psychic unity of humans be demonstrated empirically? Such a feat was difficult to conceive of unless there were absolute standards by which this unity could be measured. Anthropologists denied the existence of such standards, while at the same time accepting the concept of cultural universals. If cultures differed, could one culture be understood in terms of categories derived from another culture and interpreted by the anthropologist? The answer would logically be no; but, in order to study other cultures, the answer was assumed to be yes. Moreover, was not the concept of culture a nineteenth-century Western idea that might have no meaning in another time or place? Finally, could an individual culture be understood on the outside as the people inside the culture understood it? The problem of how to get inside the mind of people of another social system was not easily solved.

James Boon, a contemporary anthropological theorist, has argued that the culture concept never even approached the status of a paradigm. It was not sufficiently precise to qualify as a model or theory to be used for the analysis of human behavior. Instead, Boon says, in "Further Operations of 'Culture' in Anthropology: A Synthesis of and for Debate," *Social Science Quarterly* (1972), the culture concept was a "more or less articulate sense of the dilemma which helps prevent anthropologists from committing inadequate reductionisms when confronted with radically complex and always colorful and intriguing data." The concept of culture, then, was a historically useful device for demolishing another concept that was equally invalid, the concept of race. But the culture concept was itself fatally flawed.

The dilemmas inherent in the concepts of culture and cultural relativism were revealed at least as soon as the concepts reached their ultimate formulation. One of the leaders in this reanalysis was David Bidney, another anthropological theorist. In an essay on "The Concept of Value in Modern Anthropology" and in the book *Theoretical Anthropology* (1953), Bidney revised the revisers of anthropological theories and pointed to the misunderstandings of the Boasian generation, finding a lesson in the historical development of anthropology. Noting that thinkers of the eighteenth century had begun with a hypothetical history of man based upon biblical sources and focused on discontinuities in cultural development, Bidney claimed that the ultimate aim of these thinkers had been to draw a moral lesson. Nineteenth-century ethnologists had removed the explicit moralizing and had described and evaluated stages of cultural evolution in terms of natural laws. The early twentieth-century anthropologists had attacked the idea of cultural progress and had switched anthropology from a study of the social evolution of man in general to a study of particular cultures as functional, integrated wholes. The twentieth-century process was amply demonstrated in Boas, who admitted the possibility of technological progress but who rejected the concept of progress in art, religion, or morality. He and his students claimed to be scientific and inductive; however, said Bidney in "The Concept of Value in Modern Anthropology," *Anthropology Today* (1953):

in practice, they carried on their field investigations and applied their cultural knowledge on the romantic assumption of an irreducible plurality of types of culture, each of which had an intrinsic value of its own, and therefore made no attempt, on principle at a comparative evaluation of cultures.

This attitude reached its apex in Ruth Benedict's *Patterns of Culture,* in which there was no standard for normality or abnormality of behavior, which argued that there was a harmony between culture and human existence, and which indicated that no society lived in perpetual crisis. But, according to Bidney, these propositions were not sustained by actual study of most societies.

Despite his defects, according to Bidney, Boas had had a definition of culture that was more realistic than that of later anthropologists. Boas had held the paradoxical view that while cultures were closed systems, change and continuity existed within them. However, in order to prevent the reduction of cultural phenomena to either psychological or organic phenomena, the American School of Historical Ethnology, following the lead of Boas, "postulated the uniformity of human nature in historical times." Anthropologists claimed that all men had identical psychological processes and denied that there had been evolution in human mentality. The result of these claims was that culture was divorced from organic evolution, refuting the social evolutionists who had assumed natural laws of cultural evolution. But in refuting these evolutionists, the followers of Boas had to abandon the comparative method and, at the same time, had to explain cultural phenomena in terms of other cultural phenomena.

Bidney attempted to bring back comparative and developmental theories in anthropology; he argued that both mental and cultural evolution had existed and that culture had no existence on an autonomous level of reality. He also tried to resuscitate Morgan and Tylor, whom he felt had been misunderstood and misrepresented by twentieth-century anthropologists. Both of these scholars had seen evolution as based upon technology, as linear in the development from primitive man to Western civilization, as being equivalent to progress, and as making possible a comparison of societies. Tylor had seen evolution as the moral development of individuals, while Morgan had seen it as the progress within art and social institutions. Neither had said that societies necessarily had to develop through similar stages, despite Boas's claim to the contrary. Morgan had believed cultural evolution to be independent of biological evolution while Tylor had not. Both had postulated a law of development based upon what they thought was the natural logic of the human mind. Both, Bidney believed, had had more insight than their modern critics.

Bidney particularly attacked Melville Herskovits for his faith in the idea of cultural relativism. In *Man and His Works*, Herskovits said that the only reality was culture, that primitive people were only non-literate, that there were neither universal values nor universal progress, and that ethnocentrism was bad while cultural relativism was good. According to Bidney, in *Theoretical Anthropology* (1953), Herskovits erred in that "instead of the study of the relation and sequence of culture forms in the context of given cultures and societies, he advocated the study of particular ethnic groups in their ecological settings." Herskovits did not even follow his own advice in his study of New World Negro cultures; there he used a "scale of intensity of Africanism"—a cross-cultural comparison—and used such categories as technology, economic organizations, social structure, religion, magic, folklore, and language—all representative of cultural universals. Herskovits, like other cultural relativists, failed to realize the need for a common core of objective values with which to establish such universals or that cultural ideologies are useful because they incorporate absolute universal values.

The problems with the anthropology of the 1950's were caused, Bidney believed, by the confusion between natural and cultural history. The classical nineteenth-century evolutionists had said that these were two facets of the same thing; that the laws of cultural development paralleled those of biological development. Boas and his students had rightly attacked this concept, but had failed to develop an alternate theory of cultural history, one that included both form and process.

Bidney's proposed return to evolutionary anthropology had less success than his attack on the concept of culture. The climate of opinion among professional anthropologists in the 1950's was extremely anti-evolutionary. Leslie White was the most articulate proponent of evolutionary views of the time but had few disciples other than those students he taught at the University of Michigan. Despite his lack of following, he published *The Science of Culture* (1949), which used an evolutionary hypothesis for human history as an explanation. He conceived of social evolution as a function of increased energy levels; as societies harnessed and controlled energy, they evolved toward more complex forms of social organization.

White elaborated his ideas ten years later in *The Evolution of Culture: The Development of Civilization to the Fall of Rome* (1959). In this book, White insisted that he was an evolutionist in the tradition of Tylor and found some consolation in the fact that Julian Huxley had, in 1955, asked for a reconsideration of cultural evolution. Huxley called evolution the key to phenomenal reality and indicated that it operated on three levels—inorganic, organic, and psycho-serial (human). Inorganic evolution had supposedly ended far back in the distant past; organic evolution had supposedly lasted until the mid-Pliocene period (5,000,000 years ago) when all purely physical and material possibilities of development had been exhausted. At that point, according to Huxley, psycho-serial evolution took over as the most significant evolutionary process. Huxley said that anthropologists had failed to recognize this fact because they lacked a common definition of culture and a conclusive answer to the question of how culture was transmitted. Huxley advised anthropologists to clarify their thinking and to use the proven methods and theories of biology.

White, in *The Evolution of Culture,* deviated from nineteenth-century Darwinism by claiming that man and non-man had different kinds of brains. He admitted that primates and man shared tool use but insisted that only humans had progress. According to White, this progress could be seen in the development of a culture of mankind, which was a single system in which the so-called individual cultures were merely parts. This was White's solution to the dilemma of culture vs. cultures. He believed that this solution answered the critics of evolutionary theory, who had correctly indicated that specific cultures had not evolved in the ways early evolutionists had predicted. White felt that a science of culture could be developed (which he called culturology) that could integrate the theories of cultural diffusion and cultural evolution and that could show these processes as irreversible and non-repetitive. Like Spencer, White thought that thermodynamic laws could be applied to social systems. Unlike Boas and his followers who rejected the search for original institutions, White postulated that the family had evolved from promiscuity because of an incest taboo, a supposition not unlike Morgan's.

White was not a racist; he saw no connection between social development and ethnic groups. However, his evolution, if modified to fit specific population groups rather than a larger social system, could be used for comparative purposes. His ideas were restated in more rigorous and acceptable form by other scholars, notably by Julian Steward in *Theories of Culture Change: The Methodology of Multi-Linear Evolution* (1955) and by Marshall Shalins and Elman Service in *Evolution and Culture* (1960). White's ideas were popularized in a book by Peter Farb with a long and inaccurate title, *Man's Rise to Civilization as Shown by the Indians of North America from Primeval Times to the Coming of the Industrial State* (1969). Farb simplified the idea of multi-linear evolution, arguing that Indian societies provided a demonstration of how all humans evolved. The tribal organization of the Iroquois supposedly provided information about that of the ancient Hebrews (thus did Farb echo eighteenth-century ideas), and the institutions of the Aztecs supposedly told modern man about the Assyrians. Emulating Morgan, Farb created a taxonomy of political institutions, noting that this table of development was based on man's sociability and that every group did not go through each evolutionary stage.

I.   The Band
    a. The family
    b. The composite band
    c. The patrilocal band (centered on the father)

II.   The Tribe
    a. The lineal tribe (based on common ancestry)
    b. The composite tribe

III. The Chiefdom

IV.   The State

Farb answered none of the questions that had plagued nineteenth-century anthropologists. What caused one tribe to develop in one direction while another did not? If the explanation was technology, the question of how technology evolved remained unanswered. Reviewers rightly panned Farb's book, but the choice of his thesis signaled growing awareness on the part of the public of the evolutionism of White, Steward, Shalins, and Service.

While these scholars attempted to win acceptance of cultural evolution in the 1950's, the new physical anthropologists had almost all been converted to the comparative study of blood groups. Only the older physical anthropologists continued to compare human bones. Almost all of these new scientists had accepted culture as an explanation of group differences and had abandoned racial explanations. An exception to this consensus was Carleton S. Coon. Coon not only continued to accept racial explanations of group differences but clung to a modified version of polygenesis. In his *The History of Man* (2nd edition, 1962) and *The Origin of Races* (1962), Coon said that those who objected to the use of the term race were either religious fundamentalists, who denied the theory of evolution, or were "academic debunkers and soft-pedalers," who were social rather than physical anthropologists and who supposedly had a prevailing prudery about race that fully matched the Victorian prudery about sex. He also denounced geneticists who said that the question of racial determination of human behavior should remain open until all chromosomes were identified. Coon's own position was that human characteristics had a hereditary base but could be modified by the environment. As far as human origin was concerned, Coon maintained that humans had evolved from Miocene apes into *Homo erectus,* a primitive form of man. Raciation supposedly took place after this evolutionary step, with the development of five races, the members of which became *Homo sapiens* through standard evolutionary processes but at different times. The possession of fire, which Coon used to signal the beginning of civilized development, had supposedly come to humans in China 360,000 years ago, in Europe 250,000 years ago, and in Africa 40,000 years ago. According to Coon, all races had become one species only 35,000 years ago. When his ideas are closely examined, it becomes apparent that Coon's position was a singularly nineteenth-century one, combining the concepts of polygenesis and evolution with a comparative method that utilized technology as a standard for cross-cultural evaluation. Coon differed from the thinkers of the earlier century, however, in that he believed that races had been separate species that had become a single one.

Coon's ideas were outside the mainstream of physical anthropology, which now looked to blood groups for racial classification rather than to physical characteristics. In the 1930's, blood groups had seemed to be an ideal indicator of genetic traits because they were assumed to be impervious to environmental influences and because they could be tested easily by laboratory technicians. This early optimism, however, soon vanished as the first assumption proved to be erroneous. Blood groups were not impervious to environmental influences; they affected and were affected by natural selection. The belief that blood groups could provide a stable measurement of racial differences had been wrong.

William C. Boyd admitted as much in a chapter of Kroeber's *Anthropology Today* (1953); Boyd confessed that he had erred in the 1930's in believing that racial characteristics could be found that were nonadaptive and that could be traced from generation to generation. Boyd felt, however, that the discovery that blood groups were not selectively neutral should stimulate the study of other human genes and that, as a result of this study, a composite of all genes would be made that could be used to identify race. Boyd defined a race as "a population which differs significantly from other human populations in regard to the frequency of one or more of the genes it possesses," and he postulated the existence of six races—Early European, European, African, Asiatic, American Indian, and Australoid—of which each group had a different gene frequency distribution.

In a later book, *Races and People* (1958), written in collaboration with a popularizer of science, Isaac Asimov, Boyd tried to produce a clear and simple statement about race and racism from the vantage point of physical anthropology. Although the word race had mystic overtones, Boyd felt that it could be used if rigorously defined as a population with a certain genetic frequency. However, racism could not be retained in anthropology since it was the undemonstrated belief in inferior and superior races. Repeating the orthodoxy of the time, Boyd said that man was one species, that races were varieties of this single species, and that races were not correlated with nationality, culture, or language. Disposing of earlier attempts to categorize races by such physical differences as skin color, hair, eyes, bone size, and cephalic index as being both overly simplistic and inadequate, Boyd promoted the use of blood groups for racial determination.

This (determination of race by blood groups) reserves classification to scientists who are interested in the development and evolution of man. It keeps a person from making judgments of his own about his neighbor's race and from building up superstitions and prejudices about it.

Boyd was clearly uninformed of the fact that early scientists had been leaders in making judgments about racial capabilities. The assumption that the concept of race could somehow become value-free if only handled by scientists demonstrated both naiveté and historical ignorance; the belief that races could be identified without being compared also ignored the evidence of 200 years of comparisons.

Boyd attacked the possibility of determining intelligence through I.Q. tests, saying that the genes that control intellrgence were so little known that even the quantity still was unknown. Further, he said, intelligence depended so much on circumstance and environment that it was difficult to know what was inheritable. Thus, he felt that group I.Q.'s ought not to be compared. Boyd concluded that:

The whole notion of race is really quite useless to the average man. Except for certain unscientific and superstitious ideas, it tells him nothing. The notion of race is useful only to anthropologists and other scientists for tracing human migrations and so forth. The rest of us might just as well stop worrying about the whole thing.

The attempt to restrict the use of the word race to scientists appeared doomed to failure. Without an academy to set standards for the language, Americans would continue to use such words as race whether or not they were rigorously defined or value-free.

Other scholars in the 1960's also found a place for the concept of race. Among these was Theodosius Dobzhansky, one of the scientists who helped develop a genetic theory of race. In his *Mankind Evolving* (1962), Dobzhansky outlined the history of evolutionary theories from the discovery of the first Neanderthal skull in 1856 to his own time. He denounced both Social Darwinism and racism as untenable concepts and found the works of Galton and Pearson on the inheritance of genius to be invalid, while accepting the idea of genetic influence on intelligence. Dobzhansky believed that I.Q.'s were partially determined by heredity and that health and disease resistance could be passed from parents to children. Natural selection still operated on humans, he claimed, but only when certain conditions existed. The greater the number of offspring of a pair of parents the greater the chance of the transmission of their genes, all other factors being constant. The smaller the number of children per family in a population, the more natural selection operated and the less chance that any single inherited combination of genes would dominate.

Man belonged to one species, according to Dobzhansky, although species were not easy to define. Dobzhansky cited as evidence the fact that different races could sexually reproduce. Since races are genetically open and species were genetically closed, man must be of one species. *Homo sapiens* could not have arisen from the coalescence of several species, Coon to the contrary. Races, Dobzhansky felt, may become species if they become closed reproductively. Dobzhansky claimed that it was impossible to determine whether man's origin was monogenetic or polygenetic and attacked the theory that argued man's domestication—one Boas accepted—because domestication implied the end of the operation of natural selection on man in favor of complete social selection.

Although students of race supposedly used the wrong methods and were possessed of wrong theories, races did exist, Dobzhansky believed. They were difficult to classify; no racial taxonomy was completely satisfactory. Dobzhansky himself proposed a classification of 34 races, including four new ones that had supposedly emerged in the last 400 years. These last were North American colored (Blacks in America), South African colored, Ladino (Central and South American peoples), and Neo-Hawaiians. His divisions relied on gene frequency, upon blood groups and other similar gene clusters. Race differences were facts of nature, Dobzhansky asserted, and could be ascertained objectively, given sufficient study. He rejected Montagu's attempt to substitute the term ethnic group for race. Race was considered a superior term because it fitted into an already developed biological framework and reflected biological differences, probably the result of natural selection operating through sexual selection and/or genetic drift. Although Dobzhansky insisted that race was a valid and useful concept, he denied that there was racial evidence to justify any belief in superior or inferior races.

By the mid-1960's, the renewed emphasis upon genetic determination of group differences and the possibility of cultural evolution had made an impact upon a generation of anthropologists who had formerly attacked these ideas. This can best be seen in Margaret Mead who always functioned as a kind of anthropological weathervane, swinging to face whatever winds were blowing. In 1964, Mead's Terry Lectures appeared under the title *Continuities in Cultural Evolution.* In her introduction, she herself admitted that she had had to rethink the problem of evolution because of new ideas stimulated by the Darwin Centenary celebrated in 1959.

In 1964, Mead denied that Boas had challenged the general proposition of evolution or had even questioned the theory that human cultures had evolved from initially simpler forms (Mead's position was seemingly inconsistent with Boas's general anti-hypothetical position). Mead maintained, instead, that Boas had only attacked the hypothesis that evolution was a simple, continuous process without interruption. Regardless of Boas's position, Mead confessed that the study of cultural evolution had little attraction for her generation of anthropologists, although Elsie Clews Parsons had undertaken to investigate the Old World origins of the American Indian and Melville Herskovits was investigating the African origins of the black American. The books of Leslie White and V. Gordon Childe, a student of the origins of Near Eastern civilizations, had not aroused much interest in the anthropological community. But now, Mead conceded, cultural evolution had come back in style. As a result, Mead proclaimed herself an evolutionist, midway between Dobzhansky who emphasized individual genes as the significant natural factors in evolution and White who emphasized cultural ones. She said that she was not so biological as Dobzhansky nor so cultural as White and that she wished to avoid the determinism of either.

Although Mead repeated her earlier strictures against the spurious connections among race, language, and culture as well as her assertion that only humans had culture, she wavered on the issue of whether human behavior was a product of culture or of biology. She believed there were both behaviors that were common to apes and humans and behaviors that were useful in distinguishing between primates and other groups. Mead proposed her own version of cultural evolution, which, like White's, depended upon technology, but which could be either divergent or convergent. The direction of human evolution should only be charted, she felt, in order to show what alternatives were possible, not to indicate that the path taken by one group was in any way superior to others. In addition, Mead accepted the use of population statistics and concepts such as genetic drift, gene pools, and ecological niches in describing the process of human evolution. But Mead warned that the charting of direction in evolution and the use of genetic terms did not imply either cultural or biological determinism.

Mead's emphasis throughout her lectures was on the conscious participation of humans in the evolutionary process. She said that this might be done through understanding biology, which could lead to genetic control (raising the specter of totalitarianism), or through understanding history, which could lead to a stimulation of cultural evolution. She preferred the latter, although she recognized that problems had arisen in past attempts; historians had studied societies and eras separate from each other and social scientists who projected present data into the future had made many errors. But the need for historical understanding was there, and Mead, reversing the ideas of her mentor Boas, proposed the construction of a general cultural history of man. In addition, she suggested that cultural evolution could be stimulated by encouraging what she called evolutionary cultures. Adapting Galton's study of genius, Mead advocated the development of communities of geniuses who would use their genius to promote social change. After all, Mead claimed, it was not Christ but his disciples who originated Christianity, and it was not Hitler who formed Nazi Germany but the small group around him. Mead seemed to be impressed by hereditarian arguments, enough so that she could be fairly called a kind of elitist.

Reflecting on the study of cultural evolution by others, Mead developed a set of conclusions that, despite her disclaimers, took the form of cultural laws. The lower a society was on the scale of evolution, the greater were its chances of being caught in nonproductive cultural practices. These blind alleys increased the possibility of social disaster and placed a society in real jeopardy. To prevent extinction of marginal societies, Mead proposed that anthropologists analyze societies of the ancient and modern world to ferret out the necessary preconditions for the highest development of civilization; this knowledge could then be passed on to "the eager primitive and peasant population of the world." Her last goal, of course, duplicated that of certain nineteenth-century anthropologists, who had helped create the idea of the white man's burden. The total impression was that Mead had returned to an earlier evolutionism with greater sophistication.

In her appendix, Mead, along with Theodore Schwartz, presented the problem of developing a non-evolutionist classification of human societies. Mead and Schwartz had tried to do so and had failed; they concluded that the "typology of whole cultures is either evolutionary or trivial." Further, in her notes, Mead accepted some somatyping (classification of persons on a physical basis) and argued that American Blacks had endured both negative and positive social selection. Slavers had captured those individuals who had been too weak or stupid to escape; thus negative selection had operated. Those slaves who had been sold for political reasons, who had survived the middle passage to America because of stronger will and greater stamina, or who had been sexually attractive to white masters all reflected positive social selection. Mead's advocacy of evolution included value assumptions about higher and lower societies; implicit in these assumptions was a spirit of condescension toward primitive societies not unlike that of Tylor. The ideas of cultural determinism and cultural relativism, if not eliminated in Mead's thought, were considerably changed.

How much times had changed could be seen in a symposium on race sponsored by the American Association for the Advancement of Science and published as *Science and the Concept of Race* (1968). The book originated from a concern about the level of available information on race. The American Association for the Advancement of Science delegated a committee of the Scientist's Institute for Public Information to study the biological and social aspects of race. The results were read as papers at the 1966 meeting of the Association for the Advancement of Science and were published under a multiple editorship that included Margaret Mead and Theodosius Dobzhansky.

In the introduction, Margaret Mead offered a note of pessimism. She claimed that the American public had been better informed on matters of race in the 1930's than in the 1960's because of the work of geneticists, anthropologists, and psychologists which refuted German theories on race in the 1930's. The scholars who contradicted the Germans, however, gave up their research on race when the Second World War ended. No new research on the topic had been started, so no new findings emerged. Mead claimed that in order to test the question of hybrid vigor, which had once more arisen, she had to rely upon the study of the Bastards in Africa made in 1913 and on the study of the survivors of the Bounty made in 1923. As further evidence of the dearth of new material on race, Mead reported that a request for new findings on racial differences made by the American Anthropological Association to the American Association for the Advancement of Science had elicited a negative response. The results were published by L. C. Dunn as "Science and the Race Problem" in *Science* in 1963. This was immediately challenged by three persons who supported the idea of racial physical traits: Carleton Putnam, Henry H. Garrett, and Wesley C. George. Mead commented that the general level of the scientific articles of the 1960's on race were inferior to those of a decade earlier despite the tremendous advance in biological knowledge; Mead had no patience with the ideas of Putnam, Garrett, and George. She denounced the classification of American Blacks based on some known but often minute element of African ancestry. These classification ideas showed ignorance of genetics, treated American Blacks as an isolated population, which they were not, and failed to recognize "that the attributed cultural achievements of African populations of 50,000 years ago are irrelevant to the potential behavior of children in the United States who happen to have some ancestry of African origin." Yet, Mead concluded that anthropologists had erred in the 1930's, for however much scholars like Montagu denied the existence of race and however much anthropologists refused to discuss racial differences, the general public still used the word race and believed that racial differences existed. Therefore, she insisted, anthropologists should discuss race and racial differences seriously.

The rest of the symposium did just that. The first topic on the program was behavior-genetic analysis and its relation to the concept of race. Benson E. Ginsburg and William S. Laughlin stressed that the concept of race should be used by biologists only in the study of animal or plant levels of organization. Even that use was ambiguous for a race, or a reproductive community could be defined in different ways depending upon the size and scope of a study. Ginsburg and Laughlin did see some value in the study of non-human behavior in a reproductive community. In animals, for example, evidence seemed to show that animal perceptual systems would only respond to certain experiences. (The authors warned against drawing any human social consequences from this assumption.) In human populations, there were genetic differences in behavioral potential as well as in potential for physical and mental growth. According to Ginsburg and Laughlin in their chapter entitled "Behavior-Genetic Analysis and Their Relevance to the Construct of Race," the serious student was advised against overemphasizing environmental changes and was told to not "denigrate the biological components of these aspects of phenotype." Ginsberg and Laughlin also denied the validity of two classical anthropological objections to the earlier theories. The first objection stated that biologically based differences were superficial and that all important behavioral characteristics were so fundamental to the entire species that human subgroups shared these as a common evolutionary heritage. The second stated that animal data did not apply to man and that genetic research on the human species was premature and dangerous because it led to racism. Ginsberg and Laughlin claimed that the opposite was true, that there were genetic inequalities within different breeding populations that could be studied; that human behavior was a product of genetic inheritance and genes could be found that determined behavior; and that much behavior that seemed to be connected to human learning was in fact produced by biological factors. They did admit, however, that differences between groups were not necessarily a reflection of different genetic abilities.

Ginsburg and Laughlin attacked the psychologists Audrey M. Shuey and William Schockley, a Nobel laureate in physics who argued a hereditarian and racist position at the regional meeting of the National Academy of Sciences in 1966. Schockley regarded the question of racial differences in terms of *nature vs. nurture,* or genetic inheritance versus environmental conditioning. Ginsburg and Laughlin felt that Schockley's position failed to take into account the complexity of the heredity-environment relationship. At the same time, Ginsburg and Laughlin denied the existence of human equality; in so doing, they denied the central concept of the theories of the cultural anthropologists after Boas, the "psychic unity of mankind." This concept was a pre-Mendelian, pre-Darwinian throwback to the idea of the fixity of the species. According to Ginsburg and Laughlin, if evolution affected the behavior of different breeding populations differently, as they believed, then these populations would not have the same psychic identity.

In the section of the symposium on biological aspects of race in man, H. Bentley Glass, a noted biologist, summarized the research of the time, concluding that all human populations shared the same genes but in different proportion, that races were subdivisions of species formed through geographical isolation where mutations created new possibilities, and that these mutations had become common human possessions through intermarriage. As a result, biologists felt that separate races were disappearing and, in the distant future, would disappear. If race were used, it ought to merely represent a shorthand term for biological variations in humans. Paul I. Baker, in a chapter entitled "The Biological Race Concept as a Don't Know Research Tool," defined races as "an interim structure for dealing with genetic and phenotypic distances and should be replaced with quantitative systems." Glass and Baker considered the concept of race to be too vague; it was sometimes used to mean a breeding population and sometimes used to mean a statistical phenomenon. They also agreed that the overlap among human races was great. Thus, the biological conceptions of race had remained fairly constant in the two decades between 1950 and 1970.

The section of the symposium on social and psychological aspects of race treated such issues as the connection between intelligence and motivation. Dwight J. Ingle, a physiologist from the University of Chicago, insisted that racial inheritance ought to be studied, that the ability to reason and learn had a genetic base, that Blacks performed less well in I.Q. tests than Whites (using Shuey's data), and that the issue of racial differences was not closed. Morton H. Fried, chairman of the Department of Anthropology at Columbia, disagreed, contending that most psychologists used a pseudo-scientific concept of race. For example, Shuey defined race in terms of gross physical features rather than using the geneological techniques of the modern ethnographers, and Coleman used a social definition of race rather than an anthropological one. Neither definition approached race scientifically. Fried concluded his essay with a warning against the misuse of the "new physical anthropology," which blended somatic studies, physiology, ethnology, and genetics to reduce the explanation for behavior to one based on species-specific instincts instead of culture, and which emphasized the connection between phenotype and behavior. Fried feared that this new scientific, biological emphasis in anthropology could revive pseudo-scientific racial speculation.

Mead concluded the symposium with comments on the American historical experience; her comments reflected her changed views. The Japanese and Chinese had succeeded in America supposedly because they had migrated from older, more complex civilizations that had resisted white intrusions, while Blacks had supposedly failed because they had come from less technologically sophisticated societies that could not effectively repel white invaders. Mead attacked conventional black history by insisting that the black American had no more cultural connection with another land than any average white American whose ancestors had been in America eight to ten generations. "Invoking the history of a Central African kingdom to provide points of racial pride is as ridiculous as endowing the descendants of eastern and western Europeans with the achievements of Mediterranean history." Mead thus used history selectively to explain cultural evolution, a position that must have caused Boas to turn over in his grave.

By the end of the 1960's, the older anthropological paradigm, in which culture was regarded as a determinant of behavior and in which cultural relativism denied the validity of cross-cultural comparison, was under considerable attack. A new emphasis upon evolutionary models of history combined with a willingness to discuss concepts of race had undermined the certainty of the 1930's. The new anthropology had not yet revived the concept of race as an explanation for group differences, but the possibility of there being both genetic influences on behavior and differing racial genetic potentials were grudgingly admitted. Thus the defenses against racial explanations were lowered.

It remains to be seen whether the cultural explanation of human behavior, dominant in the 1930's and 1940's, was only a temporary aberration from a continuing naturalistic paradigm or whether it is a new paradigm still struggling to be born. Perhaps the antievolutionism of the social scientists of that time could not dent the implicit developmentalism so ingrained in American society. Perhaps the idea of competition was so entwined with other elements of social theory that an attempt to reject comparisons of societies would always fail. Or, perhaps the new naturalism of the 1960's merely reflected an older naturalism that had not yet been supplanted.

Chapter 13

The Persistence of Race

The black population of the United States, which in 1930 was at its lowest percentage of the total population, grew rapidly in the 1950's and 1960's. Based on the latest censuses, Frank Pollara has projected black population proportions for the next twenty years (Table 13.1).

TABLE 13.1

Year	Total Number of Blacks	Percent of Total Population
1950	15,050,000	9.9
1960	18,870,000	10.5
1970	25,400,000	12.3
1980	30,970,000	13.2
1990	38,140,000	14.1

If Pollara is correct, the black population will achieve the same proportion of the total population in 1990 as it had at the time of the Civil War. The decline in population percentage that began in 1860 has ended. The more rapid increase of black persons than of white persons in the last few decades has been a result of two factors —a higher black birth rate (in 1960, black births were 27 per 1,000 Blacks; white births were 18 per 1,000 Whites), and a more nearly.

equal death rate (in 1966, black deaths were 9.8 per 1,000; white deaths were 9.5 per 1,000). Because of the higher birth rate, the black population was younger than the white; in 1966, the median black age was 21.4 years while the median white age was 28.7. The lower median age, in turn, should mean the birth of more children and, Pollara estimated, would result in a lower black death rate by 1985. No longer could Whites believe that Blacks would eventually die out and leave the American population all white.

In addition, the movement of Blacks to cities has changed the population patterns in American societies; the North and the city now are the home of many black citizens. In 1940, 75 percent of all Blacks still lived in the South; in 1950, 68 percent remained in the South; in 1960, 60 percent were there; and by 1985, only 49 percent of all Blacks will live in the South if present migration patterns persist. Whether they lived in North or South, Blacks became more urban than Whites. In 1960, 72.2 percent of all Blacks lived in cities while 95.2 percent of all northern Blacks resided in metropolitan areas. Because of segregated housing patterns, the black population was concentrated in the central parts of the cities. Less able to move to the suburbs, Blacks became the dominant population in major American cities, such as Washington, D.C., and Newark, New Jersey. By 1985, according to some projections, 30 out of every 100 central city residents will be black. Already, the lower median age and the higher birth rate of the black population has meant that large city schools were increasingly black. Cities which were still predominantly white had a school population which was predominantly black. The racial problems which had, in the 1930's, seemed to be southern were now northern ones and the *de facto* segregation of the North appeared at least as rigid as the *de jure* segregation of the South. Blacks had once again become the center of national instead of regional attention.

The urbanization of Blacks intensified other anxieties. Concerned over the impact of poverty and the depersonalization of urban life, social scientists continued to view pessimistically the disorganization of the black family in the city. Prominent among these Jeremiahs was Daniel P. Moynihan whose report, *The Negro Family* (1965), done for the Office of Policy Planning and Research of the Department of Labor, pointed to the increasing number of broken homes in the black ghetto and found the black family to be in deep trouble. Moynihan indicated that the connection between the incidence of poverty and the number of families headed by black women made optimism difficult. (In 1968, 56 percent of all black families in the North whose annual income was less than $3,000 were headed by women.) The continued high proportion of young black persons who were unemployed also presented a seemingly insoluble problem for an economic system that was less and less geared to providing jobs for all.

Interracial violence seemed to prove pessimists right as Whites responded savagely to the pressure of civil rights. The Montgomery bus boycott of 1955 to 1956 led to beatings and bombings. The era of the 1960's witnessed the assassination of two major civil rights leaders, Malcolm X and Martin Luther King. In addition, there was a return to large scale urban disturbances such as had not been seen since the tension-filled years just before and after World War I and during World War II. The first major urban riot was in the Watts section of Los Angeles in 1965, where 34 people died and rioters looted and burned many stores. In the summer of 1967, two other large disturbances troubled American cities. The first was in Newark, New Jersey, a city that was populated by a majority of black citizens. The police and National Guard killed twenty-five people in their attempts to prevent looting and to cordon off the city. The second riot was in Detroit, Michigan, where 43 persons were killed and a quarter of a billion dollars's worth of property damage was done in a six-day outburst. These riots, like earlier ones, took place in black sections, but unlike the earlier ones, much of the significant property damage was done by Blacks rather than Whites. Another new element was increased militancy of black resistance as shown by reports of black snipers shooting at police and firemen. The initiative for the disturbances had passed to Blacks, who reacted to incidents of real or assumed brutalities. The violence also differed in that it became standard television fare. Viewers could watch the burning buildings in Watts or the attack dogs of Bull Connor in living color; the visual involvement made a vicarious experience appear a near physical one, confirming the violent and brutal images that both Whites and Blacks had of each other. Arming of Blacks and Whites increased at a steady pace against the day when the members of the other race might attack a nearby neighborhood; civil war seemed imminent to many people. Fortunately, by the end of the 1960's, the number and extent of urban disturbances lessened.

The drive for civil rights accelerated in the 1950's and early 1960's. A successful bus boycott in Montgomery, Alabama, catapulted Martin Luther King, Jr., into national prominence in 1955. King, a Baptist minister, espoused nonviolence and practiced sit-ins and marches to draw white attention to black demands and to dramatize the brutality of those who opposed lowering the bars of segregation. He, along with others of the same persuasion, founded the SCLC, the Southern Christian Leadership Conference, to spearhead civil rights programs. In 1960, a new wave of sit-ins began in Greensboro, North Carolina, and another civil rights group, SNCC, was born. SNCC, the Student Nonviolent Coordinating Committee, began as a body designed to obtain maximum efficiency from already existent protesting groups but eventually came to advocate programs of its own. Freedom rides, travelling south to test the segregation of public facilities, proliferated in 1961 and resulted in the ICC banning segregation on all interstate buses and trains, as well as in terminals. The high point of the movement for civil rights was the March on Washington for Jobs and Freedom on August 28, 1963. The original March on Washington movement, which had faded after Roosevelt had created the FEPC, seemed fulfilled in this actual march which culminated in King's "I have a dream" speech. In this speech, he articulated his hopes for a truly multiracial society in America.

At the same time, the SNCC had been organizing Negro voters in Mississippi and Alabama. The national election of 1964 attracted attention to black demands. In that year, the Mississippi Summer Project was the significant civil rights event. This action, led by SNCC and sponsored by the Council of Federated Organizations and the National Council of Churches, registered 40,000 black voters in Mississippi. The cost of the action was high; 15 people, including James Chaney, Andrew Goodman, and Michael Schwerner, were murdered. In 1965, the Selma March to protest the difficulty of voter registration in Alabama, and attacks on the protesters by the police attracted widespread support, but the success of the Selma march concealed the problems within the civil rights movement. The SNCC had begun to limit white membership in 1963. In 1966, the head of the organization, Stokely Carmichael, uttered the famous words "Black Power" and signaled the new direction of civil rights toward black control. The great moderate, Martin Luther King, Jr., died from an assassin's bullet on April 4, 1968; his successor as the head of SCLC, Ralph Abernathy, proved unable to duplicate the success of the March on Washington for Jobs and Freedom in his Poor People's Campaign that summer. More radical black groups emerged, including the Black Panthers and the Republic of New Africa. By this time, the civil rights movements seemed fragmented and the new organizations denied the validity of older civil rights goals.

As far as legal developments were concerned, the decades of the 1950's and the 1960's were ones of considerable accomplishment. The Korean War speeded up the lagging process of integration in the Armed Services, and in 1954, the monumental Supreme Court decision of *Brown* v. *the Board of Education* culminated the long series of decisions leading to a declaration that racial segregation of schools was unconstitutional. The Brown decision held that schools should be open to all regardless of race. However, enforcement of this decision was left up to Federal district judges, and the Court asked for compliance with "all deliberate speed." Because of the ambiguity of the latter phrase, the reluctance of some unsympathetic judges to push integration, and continued determined white resistance to integration, the ending of segregation became a long and difficult process. In 1957, 1960, 1964, and 1965, the first four civil rights acts of the twentieth century were passed. The Civil Rights Act of 1964 forbade discrimination—racial, religious, and sexual—in housing, employment, and accommodations, while the Voting Rights Act of 1965 outlawed the use of literacy tests and poll taxes in federal elections. The Act of 1964 removed the last vestiges of legal discrimination while the Act of 1965 made possible growing political participation in the formerly restricted South.

However, because of continued migration to cities and because of residential patterns in the cities, schools were more segregated at the end of the 1960's in the North than at the beginning. While individual economic improvement was noticeable among middle-class Blacks, the displacement of unskilled labor and persistent high unemployment still kept Blacks at an inferior income level and seemed to prove the more optimistic assumptions of earlier decades about the ability of American society to overcome years of economic deprivation wrong.

I

The movie treatment of the Negro also changed in the recent past. The 1950's and 1960's saw a large increase in the production of all-black movies; these were of a different kind from those of the

1930's. In addition, movies showed more and more social integration; they even portrayed intentional black and white marriages as desirable. The general trend can be traced in the movie career of Sidney Poitier, who went from an asexual helper of a group of isolated nuns in the Southwest, in *Lilies of the Field* (1963), to an educated suitor of a white girl, in *Guess Who's Coming to Dinner* (1967). In the latter movie, Poitier played the part of a black man whose high qualities were so obvious that at least one critic claimed that the major question raised by the movie was why the black man wished to marry beneath himself. The image Poitier conveyed was of a black man who had proved himself superior by mastering all of the values of middle-class white society. This image reached its zenith in *Heat of the Night* (1967), in which Poitier assumed the role of a Philadelphia detective, Virgil Tibbs. Forced to remain in a small town, Sparta, Mississippi, Tibbs helped a white police chief solve a murder. Neither the white police chief nor the black detective liked the other nor the job they had to do, but the white power elite of the town insisted that the case be resolved. The black detective caught the murderer and amazed the ignorant, ill-trained chief. Poitier's movies accepted the vision of the social scientists in the 1930's and showed how a black man who was intelligent, educated, and middle-class could achieve wealth and even a white girl. This was the movie-studio solution of the American dilemma.

Not all the movies involving Blacks tried to present them as plaster saints. There were also attempts to make Blacks seem human and real. Poitier also portrayed this kind of role. In *A Raisin in the Sun* (1961), a movie adaptation of a black playwright's (Lorraine Hansberry) play, Poitier played the part of the married son whose mother had just received a $10,000 insurance settlement. Because the family lived in a Chicago ghetto, the mother wished to use her windfall to buy a better house, one located in a white neighborhood. The daughter wanted to spend the money on a medical education while the son's desire was to buy a liquor store and achieve financial security. He won the discussion but lost the money in an unsuccessful venture. While the movie's attempt at a realistic portrayal, according to film critic Stanley Kauffmann, was unsuccessful (Kauffman says in *A World of Film* [1966] that "*A Raisin in the Sun* is to Negroes what the *Rise of the Goldbergs* was to the Jews: a facile vaudeville of 'true characteristics' intended to prove that 'they' are just like us"), black audiences found it compelling.

Other movies that focused on the problem of being black in white America were *Take a Giant Step* (1961) and *Nothing But a Man* (1964). The former concerned a black adolescent who was abandoned by his white friends at the onset of puberty and who went through an identity crisis with a prostitute. The second involved a black man in a southern town who was caught in a moral struggle between his minister father-in-law, who was an Uncle Tom, and his own civil rights leanings. Neither film was an artistic nor a popular success, but each tried to show the Black as a middle-class person, striving for recognition in a white-dominated society.

In the early 1970's, another kind of black movie evolved. This was the fantasy of a super "nigger." In films such as *Shaft* (1971) and *Super Fly* (1972), the black hero was marginally engaged in the world of the private detective or in the illegal activity of dope peddling. He lived well, wearing expensive clothes and driving big cars; he had no white wife, but he had white women. Violence was commonplace and the amorality of the hero's actions often resulted in injury to others. In *Super Fly* the "bad nigger" was brought to the screen with a vengeance, fulfilling the fantasies of both Blacks and Whites and bringing into the open the underground stereotype of the black man as physically aggressive, violent, and overtly sexual. Because of this image, *Super Fly* provoked much negative comment from white and black critics alike, but its financial success ensured imitation. Regardless of critical reaction, the "bad" Black was once again on the silver screen.

A trend moving from an image of middle-class respectability to lower-class earthiness can be found in television. Black pressure helped terminate *Amos 'n Andy* in the early 1960's, even though the actors in the series were black and the portrayal was purported to be of lower-class ghetto life. The urge for black respectability was such that the roles written into television programs were, like those for Sidney Poitier, eminently middle-class. In 1963, the first black actors appeared in a television commercial on Art Linkletter's *House Party,* but the persons involved could easily have been white. The first black male in a leading role in a significant network series was Bill Cosby in *I Spy* (1963). Cosby played the part of a tennis trainer cum secret agent who, with his white partner, traveled the world hobnobbing with the rich and beautiful. The role was more than middle-class; it was upper-class. Both protagonists were cool and obviously in control no matter what the circumstances. The first successful series featuring a black female was

Julia, also in the mid-1960's. The heroine was supremely middle-class, being light-skinned, living in an expensive apartment, working in an antiseptic atmosphere, wearing fine clothes, and possessing a precocious son. Neither *I Spy* nor *Julia* showed Blacks as being in any way different than Whites; white actors could have been substituted without there being any necessity to rewrite scripts.

In the 1970's, T.V. Blacks took on more conspicuously ethnic roles. These roles were often either attempts to parody or genuine attempts to depict lower-class black life styles. Flip Wilson, in his show, satirized the conniving minister in "The Church of What's Happening Now" and the aggressive black woman in "Geraldine," which he played in drag. Both skits reflected black experiences and showed traditional black humor in an undisguised form. Redd Foxx in the *Sanford and Son* series acted out the comic adventures of a junkman in Watts. Like the British version, *Steptoe and Son,* on which it was based, *Sanford and Son* presented a generational struggle between a father and son, between the lower–middle-class values of the former and the upwardly mobile aspirations of the latter. Ironically, much of the humor of both programs resembled that of *Amos 'n Andy;* the major difference was that it was now respectable and the black characters were in control of the situations rather than being the victims of them.

Black faces had become common on the television screen, and viewers could choose between the gyrations of Tina Turner, the cartoon adventures of *The Harlem Globetrotters* and *Fat Albert and the Cosby Kids,* and the series *Good Times.* No longer were these faces necessarily light and handsome by white standards; some were dark and even ugly by any standards. No longer did the audience only hear standard English spoken in modulated tones; the dialect and structure of ghetto language began to be as familiar. Television, like the movies, was much blacker.

Blacks continued to appear in white literature in the traditional roles. Southern writers continued to view the Black as possessed of special racial qualities, which were sometimes bizarre and occasionally superior, and to use the mulatto either as a tragic figure or as a reminder of past white sins.

Robert Penn Warren had a mulatto heroine in the latter tradition in his *Band of Angels* (1955), a novel that centered on the life of a New England abolitionist, Tobias Sears, who tried unsuccessfully to create a relationship with Blacks that would be tempered with justice and result in freedom. The failure of Sears' attempt to establish a community thrust a young mulatto girl into the world, and the rest of the novel recounted her dilemmas.

Eudora Welty used the Black as a bizarre figure in her short story, "Kella, The Outcast Indian Maiden." The heroine was, in reality, Little Lee Roy, a black dwarf masquerading as an Indian princess. Although his life was horrible—he ate live chickens in a carnival act—Little Lee Roy triumphed over his degradation and, in the process, reflected genuine humanity. The stereotype of the grotesque Black was also prominent, though combined with an intense religiosity, in the fiction of Flannery O'Connor. The Black to O'Connor represented the unfathomable divinity that God sees in even the most downcast persons. In her first collection of short stories, *A Good Man Is Hard to Find* (1955), O'Connor used a black lawn figure to symbolize the mysterious ways of God. In "The Artificial Nigger," the sight of a cast-iron statue of a Black on a suburban lawn gave a white man an insight into the ultimate reality of life and made possible a reconciliation with his grandson, whom he had betrayed in a moment of weakness. In her second collection of short stories, *Everything That Rises Must Converge* (1965), O'Connor used the century-old stereotype of the Black as being Christlike. In "Revelation," Mrs. Turpen, a good middle-class white woman, had a vision of people going to heaven.

There were whole companies of white-trash, clean for the first time in their lives, and bands of black niggers in white robes, and battalions of freaks and lunatics shouting and clapping and hopping like frogs.

She saw her own white sort last in line with their supposed virtues burned away. Taking the biblical injunction "The last shall be the first" literally, O'Connor conceived of Blacks as they had been conceived of by some abolitionists, as possessing greater qualities of spirituality because of their terrible life on this earth.

William Styron, another Southerner, also utilized Blacks in conventional roles in his novels. In *Lie Down in Darkness* (1951), Styron included an eccentric black evangelist named Daddy Faith who traveled in a maroon Packard and baptized members of his congregation from the sanctuary of a device-covered raft in the middle of the river. Although white characters in the novel ridiculed Daddy Faith's actions, Styron indicated that both the black minister and his congregation received and gave love. In a later novel Styron made a black man the protagonist. This novel, *The Confessions of Nat Turner* (1968), won Styron a Pulitzer Prize and became a best-seller. Styron tried to get inside the character of the most famous rebel in the annals of American slavery. Using Turner's own confessions, as told to a white man named Gray, Styron reconstructed a fictional account of the psychological motives of the black revolutionary. Styron emphasized the sexual drives of Turner, suggesting that he had lusted after a white girl whom he later killed during his revolt. While Styron made Nat Turner seem quite human, he aroused antagonism in the black intellectual community. John Hendric Clarke edited a book in reply, *William Styron's Nat Turner: Ten Black Authors Reply* (1968), which accused Styron of ignoring Turner's political motivations and substituting instead the white view of the sexually-motivated black man. The contributors also claimed that Styron had made Turner too white. While a number of Whites continued to admire *The Confessions of Nat Turner*, the heated reaction among black critics cast doubt on the legitimacy of the effort.

A new view of the Black, however, emerged in the literature of the 1950's. The Beat generation came to see the Black as possessed of a way of life that might be worth imitating. In Jack Kerouac's *The Subterraneans* (1958), the white hero, Leo, was paranoid and impossible to live with and had a black mistress who also needed psychiatric care. The two lived together in jarring disharmony until Leo's black mistress moved on to another man. Neither white man nor black woman were particularly strong characters, and both had a life-style diametrically opposed to that of straight America. However, the black woman showed superior insight, even if it was a disturbed insight, compared to that of the white man.

It was Norman Mailer who drew attention to the supposed sensual superiority of the Black in an essay entitled "The White Negro," which was published in *Advertisements for Myself* (1959). Mailer argued that the white hipster had taken his lifestyle from the Black. Combining the beliefs of Wilhelm Reich, who developed a theory that psychic disorders were a result of sexual repressions and that orgone (orgasmic) energy could heal these disorders, with an existential view derived from Sartre, who said humans had to give meaning to themselves, their lives, and their experiences, Mailer claimed that the Black was the only fully human animal. Because of black experiences, which had somehow entered into the black genetic heritage, Blacks supposedly provided a model for the urban adventurer, the bohemian, and the juvenile delinquent. Most Whites, according to Mailer, had to make do with a nervous system that contained all the problems generated by their own and their parents' experiences. Therefore, rebels, the new psychopaths, supposedly strove to acquire a new nervous system, that of the Black. For Mailer, Blacks were superior because of their lack of sexual inhibition, which, in turn, contributed toward their memorable music. By the 1960's, Mailer's views had become commonplace. As the literary critic Ronald Berman said in his *America in the Sixties*, "it is one of the literary myths of this decade that the higher life of the unconscious is incarnated by sex and explained by music."

Mailer said nothing that had not been said earlier, but the increasing frankness and larger audiences of the era permitted wider circulation of his views. In an ironic way, Mailer had accepted the description of Blacks offered by nineteenth-century southern apologists; Blacks lacked civilized restraint and possessed greater sexual vitality than Whites. Mailer, however, considered this characterization a sign of superiority and not inferiority. The "bad nigger" had become the funky Black, the hope of the future. However, the concept of negritude could not include both a Reichian sexuality and Christian spirituality at the same time. The romantic racialism of the preacher was at odds with the sensualism of the hipster.

The White view of the Black as a more sexually liberated person continued into the 1960's. Susan Sontag, in a review of *Blues for Mister Charlie,* said that, compared to Blacks, Whites were pasty-faced, graceless, lying, sexually dull, and murderous. Leslie Fiedler suggested that Blacks be used to return sexuality to the Western. Precedent for this use had been established by the black characters in Berger's *Little Big Man* and in Fiedler's own short story, "The First Spade in the West" in *The Last Jew in America*. These black characters supposedly represented the dual hope and fear of white Americans, the hope of sexual union with and the fear of physical violence from another race.

Fiedler retained the hope that Black, White and Red would emerge into one race, creating a new American in the West. In his *The Last Jew in America* (1966), Fiedler discussed the Americanization of peoples of divergent origins into a new homogenous society. "The First Spade in the West," Ned York, the great-great-grandson of a black slave, worked as a tavern owner in the West. Taking advantage of a drunken white patron, whom he has had to drive home, York slept with the patron's rich old wife, which contributed to her death. York's deed escaped detection, however, and the story ended with everyone reconciled at the graveside of the white woman. In "The First Spade in the West," the connection holding the races together was a sexual one. Like Mailer, Fiedler saw the Black as representing sexuality, and like Jack Kerouac, a "beat" writer of the 1950's, he saw the possibility of racial reconciliation through this sexuality.

II

The revival of romantic racialism in literature paralleled a revival of racial explanations in other areas. Despite the work of Klineberg and Montagu, race did not disappear from popular vocabularies, and the use of I.Q. tests to show racial differences persisted. In 1955, Audrey M. Shuey published a controversial volume called *The Testing of Negro Intelligence.* Her book attacked the new social science orthodoxy, represented by the ideas of Boas and Klineberg. She utilized the data collected from tests made in two periods, from 1920 to 1940 and from 1940 to 1955. From these, she concluded that there had been little change in the discrepancy between black and white scores from 1920 to 1950, and that this reflected differences in racial intelligence because the tests were valid and reliable.

Shuey began her book by reviewing textbooks in general psychology. As might be expected, she found that the term racial intelligence rarely occurred; only about half of the books reviewed discussed race in connection with intelligence. (Montagu's work had been well done.) The half that did discuss race accounted for differences in test results by indicating the importance of such environmental factors as the lack of common cultural backgrounds, cultural bias in the tests, and by social-economic differences. Moreover, the discussions of test results invariably ended with the hope that an improved environment would eventually end the discrepancy. Shuey's research confirmed that Klineberg's work had become the conventional wisdom.

Shuey then set about disproving this conventional wisdom. She quoted nine studies of preschoolers showing an average I.Q. difference between Blacks and Whites of 9 to 10 points. She turned to individual verbal tests taken by elementary school children (she recognized the questionable validity of group tests) and discovered that in 9 of 12 studies, Blacks scored lower than Whites. Shuey claimed that out of the three tests where Blacks scored higher than Whites, two used a selected rather than random sample. She concluded that only one test validly showed equal ability. On nonverbal tests, she found results that were not too different. Shuey claimed that scores of 297 nonverbal studies showed white superiority while only 13 showed black superiority, and she disqualified all of the latter studies for containing some kind of testing error. She also maintained that results had not been changed by the attempts, made since 1940, to remedy test bias. Some of the tests had even been given by Blacks, thus removing Klineberg's objection that the race of the tester affected results. Other tests involved white subjects of inferior socioeconomic status to that of Blacks, thus removing another objection of Klineberg, that lower-class Blacks should not be compared to upper-class Whites. The black children continued to test lower than the white ones.

In a chapter on I.Q. tests in high schools and colleges, Shuey maintained that similar results were again obtained in spite of the use of Blacks as test supervisors and in spite of the more highly selected subjects (a smaller percentage of the total black population than white went to high school and college). A significant portion of her attack on Klineberg centered on two ideas that she claimed as facts: that Blacks scored higher on verbal versions of I.Q. tests than on non-verbal ones, and that I.Q.'s decreased as subjects tested became older. If the poorer results of Blacks had been a function of language, the verbal scores should have been lower than the non-verbal; if education had been the key, verbal scores should have improved as individuals advanced in school.

Shuey attacked the analyses by Klineberg and Montagu of the I.Q. tests given in World War I; both Klineberg and Montagu said that the differences between black and white test scores was less than between scores of individuals from North and South and that northern Blacks performed better than southern Whites. Shuey, however, saw the results of tests differently. She found particular support for her thesis of black inferiority in the World War II tests, which, unlike those of World War I, excluded officers. This, according to Shuey, meant that brighter Whites were not tested while brighter Blacks were. Other selective factors that ought to have improved black scores were the high deferment rate for superior Whites and the rejection of many Blacks for educational reasons. However, the differences between scores remained the same. Shuey also revived the question of a connection between race and social deviation, delinquency, and crime. She blamed the higher rate of crime, delinquency, and deviation in the black population on inferior mental ability. Attacking Klineberg's denial that selective migration had any influence on test scores, Shuey claimed that the higher scores of black city children were only partly the result of better schools but partly the result of social selection, which she thought operated as Blacks migrated to urban areas. She concluded her book with four propositions: that I.Q. tests showed consistent racial differences, that these differences were not the result of language factors, that they were not the result of cultural deprivation, and that the I.Q. tests had measured the most competent Blacks. All of these confirmed her in her belief in innate racial differences in intellectual capacity.

The broader intellectual community severely attacked Shuey for her Southern sympathies and for her use of an antiquated and outmoded thesis. She was criticized for not recognizing the questionableness of I.Q. tests in general, the cultural assumptions inherent in the tests, and the effect of the separate black subculture on testing. Psychologists and anthropologists used her book as an example of perverse scholarship. Although Shuey had done nothing that psychologists of the 1920's had not done, what she did was no longer respectable. She had ignored the new paradigm of cultural determinism in an attempt to return to the older one of racial determinism.

There were others who also held to the older paradigm. Prominent among these was Carleton Putnam, a lawyer who had been president of the Chicago and Southern Air Lines and chairman of the board of Delta Air Lines. In *Race and Reason: A Yankee View* (1961), Putnam articulated a gut response to the *Brown v. Board of Education* decision (which said that conscious racial segregation was unconstitutional). This response was as much a reaction to what happened in America in the 1950's as to the Supreme Court decision and reflected Putnam's gross misunderstanding of the academic discipline of sociology. Putnam wrote a letter that denounced the Supreme Court's decision. This letter appeared in several newspapers and provoked a number of replies, many of which criticized Putnam's knowledge and scholarship. Stung by criticism that said that he did not know the new anthropology, Putnam read Boas and became more disquieted. Putnam was suspicious of Boas and many of his students because they had foreign names; he felt that Boas had possibly been influenced by one of his students, Gene Weltfish, whom Putnam believed to be a Communist. In addition to the questionable Americanism of Boas, Putnam saw a lack of intellectual respectability. As proof of the latter, Putnam indicated that Ralph Linton, chairman of the Columbia anthropology department, had fired all of Boas's students except for those who had tenure (thus did Putnam confuse academic politics with intellectual orthodoxy). So concerned was Putnam that he wrote the Attorney General of the United States in 1959 complaining of the nationality and the ideas of Boas and his students.

In his *Race and Reason,* Putnam relied heavily on evidence from I.Q. tests. Quoting Shuey, Putnam said that the Black was inferior; refuting Montagu, Putnam ridiculed the idea that race did not exist; and, discounting Clyde Kluckhohn, Putnam denied that any African state had ever reached a high level of civilization or achieved political stability without outside aid. Blacks, said Putnam, dragged down white civilization by intermarrying with Whites—Putnam referred to Adam Clayton Powell, Jr., and Sammy Davis, Jr., as examples, of persons introducing inferior black genes into the genetic pool of the White American population.

Putnam's explanation for why his so-called facts no longer appeared in American anthropology was based on his view of the history of America. Immigrants who wanted to prove their racial equality won places in American universities and supposedly subverted social anthropology. Gaining control of anthropology departments, these persons, according to Putnam, prevented open discussion of race traits and ignored the problems of miscegenation and the dangers of the mulatto. (Putnam maintained that all famous Blacks—Harry Belafonte, Ralph Bunche, Booker T. Washington, and George Washington Carver—were part white.) For Putnam, the villains were foreign intellectuals who subverted American ideas of racial inequality.

If Putnam had written these ideas in 1890, they would probably have been accepted. He was not accepted in the 1960's, although white racists quoted him widely in the South. He did, however, illustrate the problems implicit in the anthropological attack on race. The word race, with all of its implicit value assumptions, had become so firmly fixed in the common usage that the attempt to discard it met with considerable resistance and outrage.

The use of the I.Q. tests as evidence for black racial inequality had declined despite the efforts of the psychologist Shuey and the lawyer-businessman Putnam. In the late 1960's, however, I.Q. evidence was revived. This, together with three social documents, the Moynihan Report, the Coleman Report, and Arthur Jensen's article in the *Harvard Educational Review,* led to pessimism about elevating black prospects.

The Moynihan Report appeared under embarrassing circumstances in 1965. The document originated from an Irish urban sociologist, Daniel Moynihan, who was an Assistant Secretary of Labor (the youngest Assistant Secretary in President Johnson's administration). Moynihan's study had begun as one that was to have limited circulation; however, President Johnson promised major attention to the goal of racial equality at Howard University on June 4, 1965, and White House aides subsequently released portions of the report. Public clamor forced the issuance of the entire report, which resulted in a political fiasco since it elicited a negative reaction from the black community, erasing the favorable impact of Johnson's speech.

Moynihan's study was an analysis of the black family. Its attitude was pessimistic and its intent was to stir governmental bureaucracy into action. The study portrayed the black family as unstable, the black community as pathological, the black female as the dominant figure in the family, and the black male as both psychologically insecure and economically deprived. The report did not blame Blacks; slavery, discrimination in the South, urban decay, and restrictive and unthinking welfare laws were the ascribed causes of deprivation. Moynihan's ideas were not new; the black sociologists, Johnson and Frazier, had advanced similar arguments in the 1930's. What was different was the tone. Moynihan said that the increase in black illegitimacy was "drastic" and that the black family was "approaching complete breakdown." He claimed that the situation had grown worse, that the black family had regressed, and that the trend might not be reversible.

The Coleman Report, also bearing the title of *Equality of Educational Opportunity,* appeared the following year, 1966, and reflected much the same pessimism about the possibility of black student achievement as the Moynihan Report had about the stability of the black family. James S. Coleman, a Johns Hopkins sociologist, undertook a massive study of American schools under the sponsorship of the United States Department of Health, Education, and Welfare. The results seemed to undermine the premise that education could overcome the educational disabilities of the black child that were generated by prejudice and inferior social environment. Coleman's analysis discounted the effect of a school's physical facilities or teachers on pupil achievement, emphasizing the influence on students of peers and the socioeconomic class of their parents, neither of which the school could control. This conclusion made the task of upgrading the black child scholastically more formidable. Since it was obvious by 1966 that the schools in the large cities were becoming more rather than less segregated, the Coleman report offered little hope for Blacks breaking out of the circle of poverty and ignorance. The environmentalists of the 1930's and 1940's had put their faith in the ability of the schools to remedy the racial problems of the larger society; now the Coleman Report challenged this faith. Other evidence seemed to support Coleman's findings. The Office of Economic Opportunity, Johnson's chief weapon in the War on Poverty, had relied heavily upon Head Start to prepare deprived preschoolers for school by overcoming early environmental disabilities. But Head Start, like other agencies of the War on Poverty, lacked adequate funds, and its efforts proved less successful than had been hoped.

Out of this disillusion with the results of educational input came Arthur R. Jensen's "How Much Can We Boost I.Q. and Scholastic Achievement?," an article which appeared in the *Harvard Educational Review* in 1969. Jensen, a University of California psychologist, began with the thesis that the apparent failure of compensatory education for the disadvantaged child resulted from the doubtful principle on which it rested—the essential plasticity of the human intellect. Jensen denied the validity of that principle and insisted instead that social class and racial difference were, in part, a product of genetic inheritance.

Jensen also asserted his faith in I.Q. tests. "No doubt intelligence testing is imperfect, and may even be in some sense imperfectible, but there has already been too much success for it to be repudiated on technical grounds alone." He, like Shuey, reviewed the research on the factors affecting these tests—genetic, environmental, and cultural—and concluded that the correlations between high I.Q.'s, success in education, and social origin were primarily genetic. Jensen did not deny the influence of experience and environment on I.Q., but he claimed heredity to be most significant. He derived his evidence from studies of North American and western European Whites who showed an intelligence heritability factor ranging between .80 and .85, indicating that 80 to 85 percent of intelligence was genetic. Jensen also quoted his own study of identical twins, which revealed that the variation in I.Q. scores was very small, only seven points, for individual twins in completely different environments. In an ordinary, random population, the variation between individual scores was 17 points. Jensen attacked environmental explanations of intellectual variation and argued for heredity determinism. Jensen was not dogmatic; he acknowledged that his own arguments were deficient because of insufficient studies on the heritability of intelligence in black populations. But he clung to his major point, that intelligence was primarily innate and that environmental manipulation had no great effect upon it.

Jensen inspired further research of identical twins. One such study was that of Dr. R. S. Wilson, reported in *Science* (February 1972). Wilson studied 261 pairs of twins in Louisville, Kentucky, and administered sequential tests at 3, 9, 12, 18, and 24 months of age. From these, he concluded that mental development depended mainly upon genetic factors and little upon environmental ones, except in extreme instances of malnutrition and emotional deprivation. Identical twins, for example, showed the same pattern of mental development with spurts and lags occurring at the same time. Nonidentical twins did not. From this, Wilson concluded that cultural environment had little effect upon the development of the child's I.Q. prior to the age of two. This conclusion supported Jensen's thesis.

The consequences of Jensenism were obvious. Richard Herrnstein outlined them in a syllogism in "I.Q.," *Atlantic* (September, 1971). "If differences in mental ability are inherited, and if success requires those abilities, and if earnings and prestige depend on success, then social standing (which reflects earnings and prestige) will be based to some extent on inherited differences among people." Herrnstein predicted that American society will become more structured and that Americans will become less mobile, that society will be less equalitarian and will have a permanent underclass, and that there will evolve a society where equality is no longer a goal.

The reaction to Jensen's study was lively and immediate. The American Anthropological Association passed a resolution rejecting the findings of Jensen; critics claimed Jensen was irresponsible to advance arguments that would increase racial tensions and support racists' arguments. Both responses showed the strength of the paradigm of cultural determinism and the outrage over the revival of another paradigm that had supposedly been demolished. More thoughtful critics maintained that the questions Jensen posed in his studies were superficially straightforward but could not be properly answered or, if answered, merely compounded confusion. The questions framed by Jensen had no scientific meaning, only a political one. For while mental tests dated from at least the beginning of the twentieth century and were standardized instruments based upon empirical data, the construction of such tests had not and did not spring from any well-established theory about the nature of intellectual performance and, according to these critics, lacked scientific validity. The tests had a circular logic; they predicted success in school based upon the characteristics of those who succeeded. Their continued use reflected the needs of a society to rationalize the social and economic positions of its members but did not reflect the needs of research scientists.

Professor Steven Rose, a biologist, has argued that Jensenism is a pseudo-science, that intelligence, like human behavior, is an extremely complex process involving the interaction of a physical system with an environment. He felt that certain physical conditions, such as malnutrition and ill-health as caused by poverty or a disease-encouraging environment, can influence both the observed behavior and the internal biochemistry of later generations without being transmitted genetically. Yet, this effect cannot be distinguished from such genetic inheritance. Other critics of Jensen maintained that experiential influences significantly affect test results and are distinguishable from genetic ones. Housing, educational and occupational opportunities, child-rearing practices, and language patterns, all combined, result in repressed scores for poor black and white children, according to these critics. Lists of environmental influences can be expanded indefinitely as Bryan Bett has shown in "Jensen, Race, and Genes," *Times Higher Education Supplement* (March 3, 1972).

At an empirical level, we must consider the possibility that social depression, held by many to be the effective cause of intellectual stunting, may itself be a partial consequence of genetic constitution. At an epistomological level, since we have very little idea of what constitutes a benign or a malign environment, the set of possible experiential explanations is virtually unbounded. Thus the dedicated environmentalist who finds that one line of inquiry is abortive can fairly easily generate another—a kind of scholarly filibuster.

Since neither intelligence nor environment have been adequately defined, one might feel that the use of I.Q. tests was a mistake from the start. (That is my position.) Civil rights leaders, sharing this premise, have successfully barred the giving and use of tests in some urban schools. However, like the concept of race, the concept of I.Q. has become part of the common language of American society and would probably be as difficult to erase. Seventy-five years of test usage have hallowed the concept of I.Q., and the explanation of the meaning of I.Q., while a circular explanation, continues to have social utility. If the black population continues to remain in poverty and continues to be regarded as a problem by the white majority as a result, explanations like Jensen's can be expected to proliferate.

One difficulty in the genetic concept of race, which the psychologists and anthropologists had exploited to bolster their arguments against the use of the concept, proved to be surmountable. This difficulty, which originated in the 1930's, was that the complexity of the genetic structure made the tracing any kind of inheritable traits except for the most simple ones impossible. Since the simple, traceable traits were usually pathological and were abnormal instead of normal occurrences, their use to describe large population groups was inappropriate. The argument was essentially a know-nothing one. Scientists could not determine what various individuals had inherited; they could determine statistically the existent gene pool of a population, but they could not reconstruct its past. Several developments, however, greatly increased the possibility of determining genetic traits previously thought indeterminable. One was the increased use of electron microscopes, which enabled researchers to see chromosomes in 1959. As a result, chromosome tests became common; by 1964, such tests were used to determine the sex of athletes who participated in the Olympic Games. Another instrument also aided genetic researchers. This was the computer, which came into widespread use after World War II. Both the improved microscope and the computer made possible the uncovering and exploitation of data formerly unobtainable. A third discovery, that of the structure of the DNA molecule, added to the theoretical knowledge of hereditary transmission.

The technological advances that aided genetic research coincided with a renewed interest in a Darwinian neo-naturalism. In 1959, the centennial anniversary of *Origin of Species*, there was an atmosphere that was congenial to the discussion of evolution and that stimulated the application of biological naturalism to social theory. Like the earlier Darwinism, the new naturalism emphasized the influence of man's genetic inheritance and explained his behavior, not by cultural conditioning, but by the past history of the species. Two books to which scholars returned were Darwin's *The Expression of the Emotions in Man and Animals* (1872) and Galton's *Inquiries into Human Faculties* (1883). The scholars who promoted the ideas of Darwin and Galton did so in two areas, ethology and behavior genetics.

Ethology had originated in Germany in the 1930's and involved the study of instinctive behavior of animals in a natural rather than artificial environment. Peter Knapp, in *Expressions of the Emotions in Man* (published papers of a symposium held by the American Association for the Advancement of Science, 1963), defined instinctive behavior as "groups of patterns of neural and behavioral organizations, unfolding at or after birth in constant interaction with experience." The ethologists claimed that animals had releaser mechanisms within their nervous systems; these triggered complex behavior patterns that previous observers had called mind-guided learned behavior but that were actually instinctive. For example, the chick of the herring gull begins to beg for food when it sees a particular patch of color on the mandible of the adult herring gull. The color appeared to be the key; the same behavior in the chick could be produced by a cardboard dummy with an equivalent patch. Ethologists believed that instinctive behavioral patterns had evolved through natural selection. At some time in the past, a certain kind of behavior had proved adaptive for a species; individuals who behaved in this fashion had had selective advantage, had survived, and had passed the behavior pattern on to their descendants. Konrad Lorenz, director of the Max-Plank-Institute for behavioral physiology in Bavaria and author of a number of books, including *King Solomon's Ring* (1952), *Man Meets Dog* (1954), and *On Aggression* (1966), was one of the pioneers in the discipline of ethology and illustrated the usefulness of certain behavioral patterns with an example from wolves. When wolves fight, the loser signals his defeat by turning his head and thus exposing his throat to the teeth of the victor; the victor recognizes the signal and never severs the jugular vein. This behavior assures that the species will be continued, that individual wolves will not kill each other to the detriment of the group.

When closely examined, ethological explanations proved to be neo-Lamarckian. Somehow, individual behavior that was adaptive became part of a neural network and entered into the genetic pool. Just how this process operates is unclear; ethologists assume that the experiences of the wolf become its future, just as Mailer assumed that the experiences of the black man became his future. Ethological explanations have a built-in problem of origins. The behavior that Lorenz described has to occur in two separate individuals with the same neural network. In other words, the wolf that exposes his jugular and the one who refuses to bite it must have similar behavior patterns or the first wolf is dead. What is to ensure that two individuals of like behavior meet?

Nonetheless, the ethological ideas of thinkers such as Konrad Lorenz became popular in the 1960's. Ethological concepts provided the framework of such bestsellers as Robert Ardrey's *African Genesis* (1961) and *Territorial Imperative* (1966), and Desmond Morris's *The Naked Ape* (1967). Lorenz also resurrected the beliefs of the instinct psychologist McDougall, who had maintained that animals and humans had similar emotions, a belief he supported with the use of photographs of the expressions on dogs' faces. Lorenz used the same technique, claiming that much animal behavior appeared to correspond to human behavior. Although many psychologists still believed that the largest part of human behavior was mind-controlled, Lorenz did not. He believed that much of man's behavior was neither rational nor the product of thought but was, instead, the result of adaptive responses of ancestors to an earlier environment.

The behavior that most interested Lorenz was aggression, which he saw as being an obsolete instinctive reaction in man, the product of a territoriality that had originally made possible the rapid development of the species. The idea of territoriality was not new; it had originated in the 1930's as an explanation of animal behavior. E. A. Hooton said in his *Man's Poor Relations* (1942) that "territoriality, or the residence of a primate group within well-defined territorial limits, has been established for howler monkeys, red spider monkeys, various baboons, gibbons, and, in all probability, orang-utans." Lorenz applied the concept to man and indicated that human wars were a result of leftover intra-species aggression.

For the ethologists, instinct prompted almost all of man's behavior. Humans were still animals; indeed, they were the only animals who had failed to develop an inhibiting mechanism to prevent aggression. Supposedly, only humans were cannibals; other primates did not eat each other (this fact was proved erroneous through further observation of chimpanzees by Jane Goodall). The usual conception of humans as rational beings did not match reality as seen by ethologists, who described humans as inferior primates, lacking in instinctual restraints.

Ethological ideas were not confined to popular nonfiction. In 1955, the American Psychological Association had its first session on behavior and evolution; in 1958, G. G. Simpson and A. Roe edited *Behavior and Evolution,* a book that maintained that emotional phenomena was adaptive. In 1960, the American Association for the Advancement of Science held a symposium, the papers of which were later published as *Expression of the Emotions in Man,* on the topic of man's emotional behavior. The contributors agreed that not enough had been made of Darwin's ideas on emotions. Peter Knapp, the editor of the book, advanced the thesis that emotions were physical phenomena of a natural origin and scoffed at the idea that the soul existed outside nature. Knapp also critically reviewed Darwin's work. Darwin had assumed three principles of emotions—that emotions were associated with habits (a dog bares teeth prior to biting), that there were antithetical behaviors (a dog fawns while preparing to bite), and that these behaviors resulted from the direct action of an outside stimulus to the nervous system. Knapp claimed that while the last principle had been proven wrong, the first two were still usable. He called for the expansion of Darwin's work to further the instinctive and natural explanation for human emotion.

Other contributors to the book explored phylogenesis, the race history of man. The participants agreed that, phylogenetically considered, humans had had three brains—the first was reptilian, the second was lower mammalian, and the third was higher mammalian. Human brains resembled those of other primates and their structures had supposedly developed for the preservation of the species. The contributors described the existence of a "neural ladder" in humans and in other primates; it included the most primitive sexual feelings and the highest levels of altruistic sentiments, all of which were reflected in the bodily movement and facial expressions of humans and animals.

The conclusion of the book was written by Margaret Mead. As usual, Mead reflected the changing times. She had been first introduced to Darwin's book on the expression of emotions in 1954 when she was asked to write an introduction to a new edition of it. After reading the book, Mead recalled, she contacted the paleontologist G. G. Simpson to solicit his opinion of it. He denigrated it, Mead says in her conclusion, saying "it was right off the main line." Later, however, Simpson changed his mind and found merit in it as did Mead, within limits. She questioned whether all of the behavior that Darwin described as instinctive really was so, and she still retained a belief in the possibility of there being human behavior distinct from that of animals. But she agreed that the case for the natural origin of human behavior was stronger than she had originally thought.

The movement to revive Darwin's *The Expressions of the Emotions in Man and Animals* was not specifically racist, although it had the potential of being so. The ethologists and their popularizers assumed that humans were of one species and that the behavior they described as natural was possessed by all humans. But ethological theory could also accommodate a polygenetic theory of origins. If human races were subspecies, the adaptive histories of these subspecies might have been different enough so that they would have evolved different neural ladders (thus different emotional responses and patterns of behavior). Even if the question of human origin ceased to be of interest, the natural explanation of emotions in men and animals, depending as it did upon the determining feature of experience, still led to the hypothesis that varying human populations might have different emotional responses because of differing experiences.

A second discipline that revived racial explanations for group differences was behavior genetics. Behavior genetics derived from Galton's *Inquiries into Human Faculties* (1883), and was further stimulated by the results of three kinds of research: unsatisfactory conditioning attempts in psychological research after World War II, ethological research that showed species-specific innate behavior, and neuroendrocrinological research that showed the influence on behavior of such glands as the hypothalamus, pituitary, thyroid, adrenal, and gonads.

The behavior geneticists started with two premises: first, natural selection did occur in man, and second, it could be measured thanks to Galton, who originated biometry—the science of quantitative biology. According to these scientists, the basis for natural selection was diversity; since man was the most genetically diverse of any species, he was highly subject to selection, having the most traits to be selected from. The behavior geneticists carefully limited natural reasons for human behavior; they claimed that while evolution was "rooted in" biology, the main agent of evolution was education. Human variation supposedly took two forms, a discontinuous form (with a clear contrast between varieties and no intervening types in between) or a continuous form (with change from one variety to another occurring in essentially small quantitative steps). Continuous variation could be measured and used to determine the racial history of a group. An example was provided by Kenneth Mather and concerned the inheritance of the tendency to sickle-cell anemia, a trait that was adaptive in areas subject to malarial disease. The incidence of the trait in West African tribes prior to enslavement was estimated to have been 22 percent; given the infusion of white and Indian genes in the black population of the United States, the incidence of sickle-cell anemia in American Blacks should have fallen to no lower than 15 percent. Instead, it was discovered to be 9 percent. It was believed that twelve generations of natural selection had contributed to the lowered figure.

Behavior geneticists believed that intelligence could be measured because it also was supposed to be the result of continuous variation. The study of intelligence was difficult because intelligence depended upon a combination of genes, but it was not considered impossible. Although I.Q. tests were believed to measure intelligence inaccurately and although scholars, as a result, were unable to determine the exact influence of heredity, variations in intelligence they believed to be at least 50 percent genetically determined. (Some behavior geneticists said that intelligence was over 80 percent genetically determined.) While behavior genetics was primarily involved in the study of individual variations of intelligence, the discipline does not dismiss the possibility of comparing groups and of looking for genetic reasons for group differences.

The state of the discipline in the late 1960's was revealed in a symposium sponsored by the Wenner-Gren Foundation for Anthropological Research in The Burg in Austria. The papers, published as *Genetic Diversity and Human Behavior* (1967), revealed a deep underlying faith in a physical basis for behavior. The participants attacked the assumptions of many psychologists for excessive reliance upon the concept of conditioning and projected a future where individual variations, whether physical or mental, would be explained on a genetic basis. Two statisticians, Ruth and Louis Guttmann, maintained that intelligence could be measured through use of culture-free I.Q. tests and that variations in intelligence showed genetic determination. Gardner Lindzey, another participant and a psychologist, returned to the nineteenth-century claim of a connection between human behavior and morphological (body shape) variations.

Behavior geneticists have revived the hereditarian arguments of the early twentieth century without, however, including the explicit racial assumptions that were connected with them. Again, like the ethological explanation of natural emotions, the genetic explanation for behavior does have racist possibilities. The geneticists, using the idea of population groups, do believe that behavior is connected with gene pools; they believe in the possibility of establishing an empirical connection between individual intelligence and genetic inheritance; and they believe that the question of group comparison is not fully answered and could be explored.

Carl Larson, a leading Swedish geneticist, has pioneered the exploration of military exploitation of genetic variations between population groups. Larson, writing in the *U.S. Army Military Review,* has concluded that "ethnic weapons would employ differences in human genetic configuration to make genocide a particularly attractive form of war." The base for ethnic weapons is the known differences in enzyme levels between racial groups. Since enzymes are catalysts which trigger important biochemical reactions, they can be utilized to kill in a naturally selective manner (a theme in the movie *Three the Hard Way* [1974]). For example, an enzyme deficiency that causes cow milk to be poisonous to Southeast Asians and that causes Africans to vomit and have diarrhea after drinking it is not often present in Europeans. This deficiency could be deepened with chemical inhibitors, making racial genetic war not only possible but, because of its selectivity, more effective than ordinary weapon warfare. Although the Pentagon has supposedly dismantled its biological warfare apparatus, one wonders whether some scientists are not exploring Larson's idea in some remote laboratory and whether the idea of race is not sometimes mentioned in the Defense Department.

III

One explanation both for the existence of prejudice and for the failure of assimilation in American society referred to the severity of the institution of slavery. This was not a new argument, but it received new life in 1950 when Oscar and Mary Handlin argued that Blacks had become slaves in the American colonies only after 1660. Prior to that time they had supposedly been indentured servants and equal in status with white servants. A connected proposition advanced by the Handlins was that prejudice was a product of slavery and was not based on a natural antipathy to the Black by the white population as many earlier historians had claimed.

Oscar Handlin expanded the thesis that slavery caused prejudice in a later book, *Race and Nationality in American Life* (1957). In this work, Handlin maintained that the majority of the population of Virginia, White and Black, had had service obligations during the first two decades of colonial existence and that the word slave had had no legal meaning at that time but had rather been a derogatory term applied indiscriminately to persons of varying statuses. There had been no clear-cut distinction between the lengths of servitude of a slave and a servant. In the early seventeenth century, the duration of an indenture meant little to the master; when a servant's time was up, the master frequently indentured him again. So, the difference between servant and slave was insignificant. It was not until the end of the seventeenth century that the black slave and the indentured servant could be distinguished, according to Handlin. He concluded from this that slavery and prejudice both developed as mature social phenomena only in the eighteenth century.

The Handlins' explanation for the origin of slavery and prejudice became quite popular in the 1950's. Kenneth M. Stampp's definitive work, *The Peculiar Institution: Slavery in the Ante-Bellum South* (1956) extended the argument even further; in the book, Stampp made his famous statement "that innately Negroes *are*, after all, only white men with black skins, nothing more, nothing less." Arnold Rose, a sociologist who had done research for Myrdal's *An American Dilemma*, took the same position in a chapter, "The Roots of Prejudice," of a UNESCO publication entitled *The Race Question in Modern Science*, claiming that racial prejudice had begun only with the invention of the cotton gin, thus stretching the Handlins' period of tolerance from 40 years to 170. The ultimate, and the most controversial, expression of the link between slavery and prejudice, however, appeared in 1959 with the publication of Stanley Elkins's book *Slavery*. Elkins claimed that slavery in North America was the product of several intersecting historical trends: a general decline in tobacco prices in Virginia and Maryland in the latter part of the seventeenth century; a lack of experience with slavery in English history and law; and the absence of constraints, either religious or secular, on the slaveowners who defined the institution. These all contributed to making American slavery the most severe of any of the known forms of slavery, from classical times in Europe and Africa to contemporary Latin America. Elkins argued that American slavery had destroyed black families, supplanting the natural father as an authority figure with the slaveowner and making the slave family mother-dominated. Using a concentration camp analogy, Elkins portrayed American slavery as a vast enterprise devoted to brainwashing Blacks and to converting them from autonomous persons into servile, dependent "Sambos." Once this was accomplished, slave became synonymous with "Sambo" and black with slave. Elkins had contributed a mechanism, psychological change, to a theorem that was already accepted, but he had not suggested how to reverse this psychological process. Still, his thesis was implicitly optimistic because it based the origin of prejudice on an institution that had been destroyed.

Even as Elkins's book was published, the explanation of slavery as the cause of prejudice was itself under attack. Carl Degler's article, "Slavery and the Genesis of American Race Prejudice," which appeared in *Comparative Studies in Society and History,* cast doubt on the supposed tolerance of white settlers and denied that slavery had developed only after 1660. Degler maintained instead that prejudice and enslavement had existed from the beginning of Black-White contact in America. His position was reinforced by Winthrop Jordan who wrote an article with a similar title, "Modern Tensions and the Origins of American Slavery," in the *William and Mary Quarterly* in 1962. Jordan proposed that there had been a dialectic relationship between slavery and prejudice with each influencing the other and both existing from the very start. According to this argument, slavery and prejudice had been mutually causes and effects; both had been part of a general debasement of black persons. Jordan's preliminary article was followed by the National Book Award–winning *White Over Black* (1968), which, though retreating somewhat from Jordan's earlier position that there was considerable prejudice at the time of colonization, still held that earlier attitudes combined with slavery accounted for contemporary white views of Blacks.

A second attack on Elkins's evaluation of American slavery came from comparative studies of slave systems. The best of these was David Brion Davis's *The Problem of Slavery in Western Cul-*

ture (1966), which analyzed slavery as it had existed in classical and medieval European, Asiatic, and African societies. Davis concluded that the features supposedly unique to modern American slavery could be found in all slave systems. He denied that slavery in the United States was different or worse than slavery anywhere else in the world and, by inference, severed the causal link between slavery and prejudice. If classical slavery was as cruel as modern slavery, why did it not also create prejudice against the slave?

Two vastly different works in the early 1970's also had the effect of denying that the black plight in America resulted from the slave experience. Both works claimed to answer questions and refute positions of earlier historians. The first was a study by John W. Blassingame, a black scholar, which was entitled *The Slave Community* (1972) and specifically rejected Elkins's work. Blassingame insisted that slaves had retained elements of African culture, created new cultural forms, used the family as a defense against slavery, and evolved several meaningful roles in the black community. While Blassingame did not deny the rigors of slavery, he regarded it as a far less total institution than Elkins had.

The second book was *Time on the Cross* (1974), a two-volume work by Robert William Fogel and Stanley L. Engerman that relied upon statistical data for an economic consideration of slavery. While the authors insisted that they had no intention of minimizing the horrors of slavery, their conclusions did have that effect. Slavery, as they pictured it, relied upon stable families and did not separate families; it did not rely on much coercion nor did it exploit the slave terribly. The slave learned skills, so that by 1870 there were more slave artisans in proportion to the general population than there had been in 1850. The slaves had received 90 percent of what they earned in supplies and services—an amount that was 15 percent more than that received by the free white agricultural worker, according to these authors.

The net effect of the latest look at the slave system was to minimize the impact of the institution on Blacks and to deny that their experience in America was much different than that of other immigrant groups. Indeed, the Fogel and Engerman study seemed to say that slaves benefited from slavery more than immigrants did from early industrial experience. It also meant that the belief that slavery had caused prejudice was almost abandoned among historians. America had not begun as a racial utopia, historians now said, but had had a flawed vision of racial potential from the start. This, combined with the earlier denial of ethnic assimilation in the present, altered the model of American history that claimed that race relations had degenerated from an earlier, more equalitarian model to a prejudiced one that, after emancipation, began to change for the better. The newer view projected the problem of racial prejudice back to events and attitudes existent before colonization and had the same effect as the sociological view that said that the problem of racial prejudice was more deep-seated and more intertwined with the whole of American history and society than was commonly thought.

IV

There were other approaches to the idea of group identity in America. One such approach was through ethnomusicology; another was through folklore. The first approach appeared in Charles Keil's *Urban Blues* (1966), and the second in Roger D. Abrahams's *Positively Black* (1970). Both authors arrived at the same conclusions: black culture was not solely a product of universal lower-class experiences, and black Americans did have significant ethnic traditions to value and defend. Both authors were white but both looked at black lower-class society with sympathy and with appreciation. Both aimed at understanding black culture, and both believed that this understanding had been lacking in the work of other social scientists. The Moynihan report, for example, had failed to show the bonds holding the black family together; it had seen black communities only as "suffused" with dysfunction and had ignored or skipped over the meaningful social organizations and communications systems that did exist.

In *Urban Blues*, Keil argued that those who regarded the black male as weak and insecure because of his supposed numerous sexual affairs and because of his desertions of his family were wrong; these observers never asked the opinions of the persons who were involved with the black man. A black man's mother, his wife, and his girl friend often viewed him as strong and adequate rather than weak and insecure. In *Positively Black*, Abrahams attacked racial stereotypes that reflected cultural differences. He identified three common educational stereotypes of Blacks: Blacks supposedly had language disabilities, lacked cultural background, and were unable to communicate well. Abrahams denied the truth of all three. He said that what were called language disabilities were merely the results of different speech patterns and different black attitudes.

Most Blacks, according to Abrahams, derived most language education from peers rather than from adults. Within their own speech patterns and on their own terms, they could communicate perfectly well.

Abrahams claimed that lower-class Blacks did not conceive of the existing social system in terms of equilibrium, as most Whites did, but rather thought of it in terms of a conflict model. This meant that Blacks could justify the use of personal and collective violence to achieve social status and material goods. Aggression was also expressed in other ways. Abrahams found much aggression expressed in folklore as told by "men-of-words," who vented their aggression by playing the dirty dozens (the exchanging of insults) and who were admired for their verbal skill. Aggression was also displayed by the physical exploits of the legendary black hero Stackalee. Abrahams claimed that even accommodationist behavior could be aggressive (contrary to the views of Dollard and Elkins) in that stupidity, literal mindedness, servile fawning, and irresponsibility, if successful in attaining desired goals, both reflected contempt on the person deceived and provided status for those using it. The verbal aggression of Whites on Blacks, such as references to black sexuality, also could be turned to black advantage and could encourage black pride. Thus, weakness could become strength. Abrahams also discovered that Blacks' perception of role images differed from Whites' perception. Blacks viewed men as either cats or gorillas, gaining power through words or muscles; they were also seen as either country-boys or preachers, being either naive or hypocritical. Women were to be exploited through openly sexual approaches. But, paradoxically, black men also recognized the importance of women.

Abrahams questioned whether Blacks constituted a minority group in the same sense that Jews, Italians, or Mexicans did. Blacks lacked a sense of cultural identity distinct from that of the dominant culture, he said, defining themselves in terms of the mainstream white culture and seeing themselves as the antithesis of this culture. According to Abrahams, other true minorities defined themselves as intrinsically different from the dominant culture, which they did not attempt to change. Blacks supposedly tried to change the dominant white culture by emphasizing those values that were in opposition to it. A good example of this process, according to Abrahams, was the use of the concept of soul, which he defined as the ability to share communal emotions and to have interpersonal contact. Abrahams felt that Blacks spoke of having soul in order to convince themselves and their audiences of their own worth and to bridge the gap between themselves and the white culture. The concept of soul contributed to a revitalization movement among Blacks, which eventually converted middle-class Blacks to the acceptance of soul. Finally, soul became sass, which made it socially acceptable to attack others verbally. While not resolving conflicts, sass provided Blacks with a role possessed of some power, the power of the tongue and the pen.

The idea of a separate black society that reversed the values of the dominant white one elicited much adverse reaction from the sociological community. Bennett M. Berger denounced Keil as a romantic, arguing that black culture was merely a version of lower-class culture. Since lower-class culture had no future, Berger felt, the sympathetic appreciation of it weakened the drive toward integration and equality. The fears Berger expressed were not uncommon; if a black lower-class culture existed and possessed stability, it would be difficult to change. Further, if the values of Blacks and Whites were in opposition, this could lead to perpetual conflict.

Robert Blauner took a less extreme position on black culture. He felt that the classic definition of a separate culture, which was used to describe immigrant Europeans, probably did not apply to Blacks. According to Blauner, black culture was moving toward both a specifically ethnic and a generally American society, moving either alternately or simultaneously, depending upon the nature of black leadership. The ghetto subculture, as Blauner saw it, was a mixture of both lower-class American and black ethnic characteristics. Thus, while black culture encompassed shared memories and frames of reference from black historical experience, it also contained white shared memories and frames of reference. Blauner felt that white racism had cut the African roots of the black slave population and that it had also prevented black participation in the larger white society, encouraging a separate cultural definition. Neither Berger nor Blauner settled the question of the meaning of the black ghetto experience, which question persisted into the late 1960's in such books as Elliot Liebow's *Tally Corner* (1967), Charles Valentine's *Culture and Poverty* (1968), and J. Alan Winter's *The Poor: A Culture of Poverty or a Poverty of Culture?* (1971).

The problem of a flawed black identity concerned white and black scholars alike. Thomas I. Pettigrew, a Harvard social psychologist, reviewed the relevant research on this question in his *A Profile of the Negro American* (1964). Having analyzed the studies on the black child made by Kenneth Clark, a black psychologist, Pettigrew outlined three major crises in black personality development. The first crisis was believed to occur at about the age of 3 years, when the child discovered race and rejected blackness in favor of whiteness. The second occurred during adolescence; black children lost their white friends when they began to mature sexually. The last crisis occurred when the young black attempted to get a job and failed because of his race. The black experience took a psychic toll, according to Pettigrew, as shown by the numerous incidence of mental illnesses among Blacks. Although admitting that records of mental illness were unreliable and that the lack of money for private psychiatric treatment among Blacks resulted in a higher rate of public institutionalization, Pettigrew showed that the psychosis rate for Blacks was twice as high as that for Whites. Neuroses, however, appeared to occur less often among Blacks than Whites as did suicide. Pettigrew pointed to social class as a significant variable, but he also blamed prejudice for black mental imbalance.

Some scholars attributed black psychological problems to their past immigrant experiences and compared the black experience with that of other immigrants. Oscar Handlin was in the forefront of historians analyzing the immigrants' experiences. In his prize-winning book, *The Uprooted* (1951), Handlin described the many problems that the immigrant encountered in America, as well as detailing the great psychic price that the immigrant was forced to pay. Unlike earlier historians who had emphasized the ultimate triumph of the immigrants, Handlin focused upon their traumas. In *The Newcomers: Negroes and Puerto Ricans in a Changing Metropolis* (1959), Handlin evaluated the historic migration of southern Blacks and Puerto Ricans to New York City, Handlin described demographic and social changes in the black community as well as in the Puerto Rican ones and concluded that the newer immigrants had problems similar to earlier immigrants, with two significant exceptions. The first exception was related to color and the second was related to a change in the character of the metropolitan community beginning in 1920. At this time, rapid flight to the suburbs by upwardly mobile city families was not accompanied by extension of adequate public transport, as earlier movements had been. This made it difficult for newcomers to move out and magnified income differences between city and suburb, which were further accentuated by the severe impact of the depression of the 1930's. While economic conditions forced black and Puerto

Rican males to take low paying jobs and pressured their wives to work, this had also been the experience of earlier immigrants. What was different was that the new immigrants were oppressed by institutional racism that froze them into housing patterns and, in turn, resulted in de facto segregation in other facilities.

Handlin found fault with some of the characteristics of the newer immigrants. They lacked the will to save, probably because of feelings of uncertainty about their future and because of the nonexistence of attainable goals. They had no voluntary organizations for mutual aid which, like individual personal thrift, characterized earlier immigrant groups. They failed to develop serious communications media, a marked contrast to the development of fine newspapers by the Irish and Germans. Handlin believed these differences arose because the migration of the Blacks and Puerto Ricans did not constitute the sharp break with place of origin that European migrations did (the newcomers could easily return), the new immigrants used already existing communications media in English and Spanish, they lacked creative leadership, and the welfare state had effectively ended collective self-help. Handlin concluded, however, that the social disorder blamed on the newcomers, while real and, in part, a function of a lack of leadership and a lack of social cohesion, had been an inescapable accompaniment of American urban growth. The new immigrants were like the old immigrants but had more difficult problems and less social resources with which to solve them.

The most famous attempt to show the psychic cost of segregation for Blacks was Kenneth Clark's *Dark Ghetto* (1965). Clark viewed the black ghetto as pathological, unlike Keil and Abrahams, and indicated that the ghetto environment was complicated by a white belief in black racial inferiority. This feeling of white superiority was shared by social scientists (who questioned the validity of sociological and psychological data used in the *Brown* v. *Board of Education* decision), social workers, clinical psychologists, and psychiatrists, all of whom treated Blacks but who were isolated from the black communty. Clark stressed that the necessary psychological defenses of the Black resulted in attempts to appear either whiter or blacker, to conform to white images or react against them. Clark described the fantasy world of black youths, who pretended that they were lighter-colored, that they had sexual urbanity, and that they were succeeding in college or in a high-status occupation. The reality was different; according to Clark, the black male in the ghetto was (of course) black, poor, and barely adequate sexually. The last was attributed to the fact that the black male child lacked a strong father figure in a female-dominated family, and that black girls used sex as a device for personal affirmation of worth. The ghetto, as described by Clark, contained a population of psychologically scarred and handicapped persons.

The image of the Black as a psychologically scarred individual became a common one for black writers in the late 1960's. Alvin E. Poussaint, in "The Negro American: His Self-Image and Integration," *Journal of the National Medical Association* (1966), said that Blacks tended to distrust and hate themselves and other Blacks because of their color, that black children preferred to play with white rather than black dolls, and that their spontaneous drawings denigrated black persons as small and incomplete figures. He also maintained that some black persons feared success even more than failure and that while the civil rights movement brought a sense of dignity and respect to deprived Blacks, the failure to assimilate into white society and the lack of political power depressed any sense of black worth and pride. The ultimate expression of the thesis that psychological damage to the Black resulted from a white racist society appeared in William H. Grier's and Price M. Cobb's *Black Rage*. Grier and Cobb, black psychiatrists at the University of California Medical Center in San Francisco, deduced several theorems from their treatment of black patients. They claimed that the survival of Blacks in America necessitated the formation of what the authors called a "healthy" cultural paranoia. The black man "must maintain a high degree of suspicion toward the motives of every white man and at the same time never allow this suspicion to impair his grasp of reality." Grier and Cobb postulated that cultural depression and cultural masochism, which were considered pathological mental states in Whites, were culturally inspired in Blacks, were functional derivatives of the black experience in America. They concluded that the black experience prevented the development of the psychological reactions that were considered normal in Whites.

The thesis that the black experience had deep psychological consequences explained why Blacks had not achieved full equality in America and showed the perniciousness of white racism. It explained the low black test scores and the high amount of black violence, but it also impeded the achievement of an equalitarian society (in the same way that knowledge of the effect of the experience of slavery had complicated nineteenth-century American society). If black experience was so scarring (whether this experience was of the urban ghetto or of plantation slavery), did not these scars hinder white acceptance of Blacks as equals? As one critic of Clark asked, would a white parent reading Clark's *Dark Ghetto* be persuaded to send his child to an integrated school with black students from the inner city? The argument that the black experience was a very bad and harmful one evoked feelings of guilt but also feelings of aversion.

The psychological repression of Blacks was attributed by some to the failings of a white colonial society. Frantz Fanon, a black psychologist from the French Carribean who became the prophet of the black revolutionary movement, provided the rationale for this argument. His ideas permeated black urban society. Don Watts, a black reporter, told Jimmy Breslin of the Chicago *Sun-Times,* after the riots in Newark and Detroit, that "every brother on a rooftop can quote Fanon." Although he died at an early age, Fanon achieved considerable fame.

Fanon's first book, *Black Skins, White Masks* (1952) discussed racism as a Western phenomenon. Fanon believed that Blacks in a white society had to assume an identity not their own; they had to hide their black faces behind white masks in order to disguise their true feelings. Despite this attempt to become Whites, Blacks failed to gain acceptance because of the racism of Western society, which was based upon sexual repression, high individual achievement, and an authoritarian family. According to Fanon, two groups threatened the basis of Western society. They were the Jews, who achieved more than other Whites, and Blacks, who lacked sexual repression and were supposedly more sexually powerful than Whites. Because of these threats, both Jews and Blacks became outcasts. Fanon believed that the effort to overcome white racism could not succeed unless the Blacks achieved a sense of pride in their blackness. Fanon agreed that this was a kind of antiracist racism but argued that it was necessary. In *The Wretched of the Earth* (1963), his most famous book, Fanon described the world as a colonial world, which consisted of two societies—white and colored—and which offered colored natives—yellow or black or brown—two choices: either to become "Ariels," good persons as defined by whites, or raging "Calibans," violent revolutionaries. Fanon believed that the act of becoming a "Caliban" served as a psychological release, making the colonized person whole and ending his spiritual bondage. By an act of violence, he both healed his own inner wounds and secured his outward freedom. Fanon argued that the salvation of the colonial world lay in violence directed against white oppressors.

Fanon's ideas were a component of the "Black Power" movement in America, although in a somewhat changed form. The concept of black power first appeared during James Meredith's march in Mississippi in 1966 and was articulated by Stokely Carmichael and Willie Ricks. The concept had many facets, but usually started with a condemnation of white America. Stokely Carmichael put it this way in "What We Want," *The New York Review of Books* (Sept. 22, 1966):

The reality is that this nation, from top to bottom, is racist; that racism is not primarily a problem of "human relations" but of an exploitation maintained—either actively or through silence—by the society as a whole. Camus and Sartre have asked, can a man condemn himself? Can whites, particularly liberal whites, blame their own system?

The extent of white racism in American society, according to the black scholar W. Aggrey Brown, could hardly be overestimated. It was believed to be instinctive rather than learned behavior; thus it could not be eliminated but only controlled.

While they condemned white racism, black proponents of black power advocated a raising of black consciousness. However, although they agreed on the necessity of black consciousness, the proponents of black power were divided on what black power meant. In Mississippi it meant voter registration of Blacks with subsequent black political control of local black communities. To Blacks in a Northern urban area it might mean black separatism. One view of black power was revealed at the National Black Government Conference, which met in Detroit in April, 1968. This group elected Robert F. Williams president of the Republic of New Africa and asked for five Southern states—Louisiana, Mississippi, Alabama, Georgia, and South Carolina—for black colonization. The Black Panthers' version of black power included black control of the ghetto and the creation of a separate black state; this version shifted to include general political participation of Blacks when Bobby Seale ran for office in Oakland, California. Whatever black power meant to Blacks, it did not mean integration. John H.

Bracey, Jr., a black historian, attacked integration as a product of the mistaken views of middle-class white and black liberals and of Gunnar Myrdal in *An American Dilemma,* that black communities and institutions were pathological while integrated communities were normal.

The colonial model also appealed to some Whites. W. H. Perry of the Center for the Study of Democratic Institutions, a West Coast think-tank, suggested that the racial problem in America has resulted from implicit colonialism and that it could be solved by making the implicit colonialism explicit. Perry advocated the creation of a Department of Colonial Affairs in Washington. This Department would operate under the authority of a statute legalizing the establishment of colonies with a minimum size of one square mile and a minimum population of 25,000, 75 percent of which must be black. The citizens of these colonies would be allowed to travel outside their areas only on condition that they be prepared to suffer discrimination without complaint. Perry offered his suggestion seriously as an answer to a problem he saw as otherwise incapable of resolution; he predicted that major American cities would be black in less than a generation and racial integration would prove impossible because of white opposition. Therefore, only a few years of grace remained to develop a political theory that would sustain a democratic society and yet recognize separate minority enclaves. Perry only tried to legitimize the reality he thought already existed.

The concept of black power had many critics, white and black. Perhaps the most trenchant of these critics was Harold Cruse, who, in his *The Crisis of the Negro Intellectual* (1967), argued that advocacy of black power was a strategic retreat from earlier civil rights movements of the 1920's. Cruse felt that the advocates of black power and black nationalism were often romantic and escapist in both their rhetoric and their solutions, failing to see that black intellectuals depended upon white intellectuals and vice-versa. Cruse also denounced those who equated pro-blackness with the ability and design to change white society. Cruse, himself black, denied that the black power advocates had devised a revolutionary program; he said that more revolutionary ideas had been promulgated by black leaders in the 1920's. He castigated black intellectuals for their facile and surface slogans and their lack of well thought-out programs of action.

White observers added their own evaluations. Two of the most astute of these observers were Lewis M. Killian and Christopher Lasch. Killian maintained that the black power movement had developed from the civil rights movement because of black despair over the slow rate of social change and because of CORE and SNCC's experiences of southern white intransigence. Killian believed that the white reaction to black power, which was labeled revolutionary despite its record, negated any progress made in furthering black pride. Christopher Lasch agreed and claimed that riots, armed self-defense, and conflicts over community control did not signal the opening of a new era of race relations but rather the final disenchantment with integration. Lasch believed that the old civil rights movement had been based upon a black subculture in the South and that this subculture had been transferred to the urban ghetto without the means or morals to support itself. As he said in "The Trouble with Black Power," *The New York Review of Books* (Feb. 29, 1968):

In the South, the Negro church implanted an ethic of patience, suffering, and endurance. As in many peasant or precapitalistic societies, this kind of religion proved surprisingly conducive—once endurance was divorced from passive resignation—to effective political action. But the ethic of endurance, which is generally found among oppressed people in backward societies, cannot survive exposure to modern materialism. It gives way to an ethic of accumulation. Or, if real opportunities for accumulation do not exist, it gives way to hedonism, opportunism, cynicism, violence, and self-hatred—the characteristics of what Oscar Lewis calls the culture of poverty.

The prospect of black revolution was slim, according to Lasch. Blacks lacked a terrain suitable to guerrilla action; there was small prospect of becoming a majority or of expelling white colonial power and gaining control of the economy. Lasch felt that even the idea of nationalism was unsuitable to the black situation in America. Ethnic nationalism, as shown by the Irish-Americans, was inherently romantic and oriented to an overseas homeland rather than to internal domestic divisions. Unlike Cruse, who believed that black nationalists were sometimes romantic and escapist, Lasch held that they were always romantic and escapist.

The image of Blacks as Christ-like figures was absent in the concept of black power, although the idea of a community based on persons with soul was present. Martin Luther King, Jr. in sermons and books like *Stride Toward Freedom* (1958), still proclaimed the hope that the black man might save America, that his qualities of patience, endurance, and love would make America at last the nation where high ideals and practical reality merged. His views, echoing a kind of nineteenth-century romantic racialism, stirred the religious sentiments of white and black Americans alike and contributed to the spiritual aura that surrounded the civil rights movement in the early 1960's.

The two most widely read books written by black authors in the 1960's were *The Autobiography of Malcolm X* (1964) and *Soul On Ice* (1968) by Eldridge Cleaver. Both books were descriptions of prison experiences; both related the lives of black rebels against white society. Both authors had been influenced by an older American tradition of self-education and religious conversion. Malcolm X was converted to a belief in a human brotherhood after his pilgrimage to Mecca, and Eldridge Cleaver was persuaded that all Whites were not devils after an encounter with his white lawyer. Both authors also denounced the great waste of artistic talent in black America; the subsequent fate of each man—Malcolm X was assassinated and Cleaver went into exile—showed that the waste had not yet been ended.

Both Malcolm X and Cleaver believed American society to be sick. Cleaver said, "I think America has already committed suicide and we who now thrash within its dead body are also dead in part and parcel of the corpse." Both believed in the need for black consciousness; Malcolm X deliberately rejected his white ancestors and denounced white rapists of black women. Cleaver believed that Blacks had a land hunger and that this hunger could only be satisfied by a black homeland; he said that the situation of the Blacks paralleled that of the Jews at the height of the Zionism movement. Both men preached that an end to a slave psychology could be achieved through a conscious effort, but they differed on what that effort should be. Malcolm X became an ascetic, preaching a religious commitment to chastity and clean living. Cleaver, influenced by Reich, argued that white Americans needed the sexuality of the Blacks to improve the white physique as Blacks needed the rationality of the Whites to improve the black intellect. Both, however, deliberately cultivated the image of the bad Negro, the rebel, the one who resisted white prejudice and the strictures of a racist society. They saw themselves as Cleaver described a fellow Black Panther in *Post Prison Writings and Speeches* (1968), "the baddest motherfucker ever to set foot inside history."

However, this image was not at first evident in the 1950's. The best novel written by a black man in the 1950's was Ralph Ellison's *Invisible Man,* which won a National Book Award in 1952. Ellison was born in Oklahoma and was a friend of Richard Wright; he had lived in urban ghettos and had seen and heard many would-be Messiahs, black and white. These experiences were reflected in *Invisible Man,* a book that explored what it was like to be a Black in America. The first half of the book expressed disillusion with American society; the second half expressed disillusion with the Communist Party (the Brotherhood). American society, as portrayed in *Invisible Man,* represented the superego—morality imposed by the power structure; the Communist Party represented the ego—reason applied through the normal perception of reality. Blacks stood for the id, which combined emotion and chaos. All three—American society, Communism, and Blacks—existed by manipulating and deceiving the others. The only persons who did not compromise were black jazz musicians, who played what they wanted to play and thus retained their integrity.

The book began by describing an enlightening but terrible experience. The hero participated in a boxing match at a smoker for the amusement of a white audience. The promoters of the event confronted him with a naked blonde woman and rewarded him with coins lying on an electrified rug. The hero went to a Negro college, which expelled him after he took a white trustee into a roadhouse to introduce him to the true reality of black life. Going to New York City, the hero obtained a job, putting 10 drops of black pigment in "Optic White" paint; the injected black element became invisible in the white paint, symbolizing the state of Blacks in white America. Later, the paint factory exploded, and the authorities, judging him insane for his social views, committed the hero to a hospital where he endured shock treatments. Released from the hospital, he encountered the Brotherhood (Communist Party) before becoming a con-man who survived by putting-on those around him. The book ended with a symbolic representation of the Harlem riot of 1943 as the hero, after escaping being speared by Ras the Destroyer, a Garvey-like figure, fell into a coal cellar. There he remained as an invisible man concealed by physical as well as social circumstances.

While Ellison utilized the rhetoric of black America, he also borrowed from such writers as Joyce, Kafka, and Faulkner. Critics saw his book as having been written not only in the black tradition but in the Western tradition; both the critics and Ellison agreed that Ellison went beyond the black experience to a broader human one, that he was a writer first and a Black second.

The problem of black identity was the major issue in the novels of black authors in the 1950's. James Baldwin, who with Ralph Ellison, achieved fame as the leading black writer of the decade, discussed this problem in his first novel, *Go Tell It on the Mountain* (1952). The story reflected Baldwin's life experiences through the conflicts and struggles of Gabriel Grimes, a proud, lust-driven minister, and Johnny, his illegitimate stepson. Grimes was at first successful in an attempt to convert his stepson to his church, The Temple of the Fire Baptized. Johnny, however, renounced his conversion in a state of adolescent rebellion, damning his race, cursing his stepfather, and abandoning Grimes in a search for human status and love. His search ended in self-realization when he discovered that happiness entailed the acceptance of responsibility for his own imperfections and when he saw his stepfather as a victim as well as an oppressor.

Baldwin continued to write about the search for black identity in the essays in *Notes of a Native Son* (1959), but he broadened his discussion to one on the problems of white identity as well. As Baldwin said in *Notes*, "at the roots of the American Negro problem is the necessity of the American white man to find a way of living with the Negro in order to live with himself." In *Another Country* (1962), Baldwin developed an explanation for racial prejudice. The white American had supposedly escaped his own humanity by shifting his feelings of guilt from himself to Blacks, whom he had brought to the New World, enslaved, exploited, and made into Bigger Thomases. Baldwin, unlike Martin Luther King, did not believe that the burden of white guilt made the Black Christ-like, although Baldwin believed that Blacks might, by confronting Whites, help humanize them. In *Another Country* Baldwin identified himself with the underclass of black society—the pimps, whores, and racketeers—whom he had seen as villains when he was a boy preacher. He now saw them as free and authentic people who knew how to live and feel.

With *The Fire Next Time* (1963), a reprint of articles earlier published in the *New Yorker* on a variety of topics including the Black Muslims and racial difficulties in America, Baldwin had come to believe that white civilization was unfit to survive; like Mailer and Cleaver, he suggested a Reichian reason for this unfitness.

Baldwin said that white Americans were terrified of sensuality and, hence, of the black man, who symbolized this personally and in his music, which had deep roots in sexual feeling. Because of this antipathy, Baldwin was pessimistic about the chance for the survival of American society. If white Americans did not overcome their own fears, God's promise to Noah would be kept, the fire would consume us.

The following year, 1964, Baldwin's play *Blues for Mister Charlie* elaborated the theme implicit in *The Fire Next Time*. The plot of the play, which concerned the lynching death of Emmet Till, was a vehicle for Baldwin's opinions. The Whites in the play were either sexual sadists who wanted to castrate Blacks physically or symbolically or they were vacillating liberals who befriended Blacks only to betray them. Regardless of the kind of Whites they were, they were all sexually inferior to the Blacks. The play ended on a tragic note as the black hero goaded a lower-class White into shooting him; thus, violence was shown to be the fate of the Black in America.

Robert Brustein, a noted white critic who reviewed the play, was quite caustic toward it. Reflecting on Baldwin's essay entitled "Everybody's Protest Novel" (1949), Brustein called *Blues for Mister Charlie* "Everybody's Protest Play." Baldwin had protested didactic literature in his 1949 essay, but in 1964, according to Brustein, Baldwin wrote that kind of literature. While Baldwin had once tried to explode the myth of black sexuality, now he defended it. In so doing, Brustein felt that Baldwin's work had degenerated. *Blues for Mister Charlie,* Brustein concluded, was an "inflammatory broadside of race hatred which will profit nobody but the author."

Nowhere was the image of the black rebel reveling in his badness and sexuality more evident than in the black literature of the 1960's. By the middle 1960's, Blacks had become the center of intellectual attention on Broadway. Plays like *The Sign in Sidney Brustein's Window* (1964), *The Owl and the Pussycat* (1964), and *Slow Dance on the Killing Ground* (1964), all involved Blacks. Three plays of Le Roi Jones showed the greatest White-Black tension; these plays were *Dutchman* (1964), *The Toilet* (1964), and *The Slave* (1964). In the first, a white woman who understood neither jazz nor sex, let alone the Black who represented both, killed a black man. Before his death, however, the black man provided a sexual education for the white woman, although he conceived of this lesson as an act of revenge. *The Toilet* portrayed life in the men's room of a predominantly black high school. The black students in the toilet insulted each other and attacked other students, most particularly a Puerto Rican homosexual who had written a love letter to one of them. Although violent in tone and language, the play seemed to end on a note of reconciliation as the black student cradled the beaten Puerto Rican in his arms. The third play, *The Slave,* showed a Genet-like war between Black and White. The play began with a black military leader, who was also a poet and intellectual, returning to the home of his white ex-wife, who was married to a white university professor. The Black attacked the liberalism of the Whites; he insulted the professor by calling him "Professor No Dick," then attacked and finally killed him and the white ex-wife. Like Baldwin's efforts, all three plays by Jones proclaimed black sexual superiority and white weakness.

Jones, according to Brustein, was inspired by race hate. His plays, which were tied to the black revolution, marked the end of the theater of realism of the 1930's. The tradition of the political drama of Clifford Odets, Lillian Hellman, and Arthur Miller had been distorted by Jones; he had turned the bohemianism of O'Neill and Tennessee Williams into a homosexual camp. Jones' drama, as Brustein saw it, was self-righteous, dramatic, and lacking in art. Brustein said that *The Toilet* was little more than a "psychodrama for acting out sado-masochistic racial fantasies" and that, in *The Slave,* Jones had "shown little theatrical purpose beyond expression of raging chauvinism, and few theatrical gifts beyond a capacity to record the graffiti scrawled on men's rooms walls."

Jones continued his portrayal of the bad black man and his implicit Fanonism in *Home: Social Essays* (1966) and in *Raise Race Rays Rage: Essays Since 1965* (1971). The last book contained an account of the Newark riot as well as a dialectic on the liberation of black colonized people. According to Jones, Blacks first imitate Whites, then exorcise the racism that has been internalized, and end by becoming liberated. By this time, Jones had changed his name to Imamu Amiri Baraka and had relegated his writing efforts to a position subordinate to his major concern, black economic development in Newark. In 1972, he acted as chairman of the National Black Political Convention at Gary, which called for an "independent black political movement."

By the 1970s, the image of the bad black man had seemed to overcome the image of the Christ-like Negro in the literature. Blacks posed a black hero who was spontaneous, funky, and sexual, in contrast to Whites who were sexually weak and jealous. The black mission consisted of the creation of a true community of brothers and sisters, but this community would not include Whites. The dream of integration seemed over, buried with the body of Martin Luther King. The victory of the body over the spirit seemed complete.

Whether this victory was real or apparent, the belief in black racial characteristics still lingered. By some great irony, the racial attributes of Negroes that were considered by Whites as bestial in 1900, had come to be the very ones upon which Blacks based their superiority in 1970. This crowning irony can be seen in a dialogue between the white anthropologist Margaret Mead and the black author James Baldwin that was published as *A Rap on Race* (1971). The book was not a good one; one reviewer called it a lot of bilge, instant wisdom unsullied by reflection. Despite its low quality, however, it reflects the nature and the attitude of the times. It is doubly ironic in that Margaret Mead, one of the original anthropological crusaders against the use of the idea of race, seemed to have capitulated to it.

Mead admitted that 25 years earlier she had advocated ignoring race but that now she realized she was wrong. Race—which she equated with skin color—could not be erased from consciousness. Instead, she said, we must simply learn to forget it. Baldwin agreed and maintained, in turn, that the Blacks who attempted to become like Whites but who knew that Whites really hated them were candidates for a mental institution. Mead agreed. Thus, the bubble of integration was burst. Mead said that Black was beautiful and that Whites looked sick in the tropics because they were not physically suited for that climate. Baldwin agreed. Thus, Jefferson's argument that humans could adjust to any climate was rejected and Agassiz's natural provinces returned. Finally, Mead claimed that she lacked a sense of rhythm because of her biological inheritance. She further maintained that half-Blacks in Liverpool had lost their sense of rhythm because they had white mothers. Baldwin agreed. Thus, Mead accepted the idea of the biological transmission of cultural traits. *A Rap on Race* seemed oddly antiquated as if the discussions on race from the 1930's to the 1950's had never really happened.

Mead and Baldwin illustrate the dilemma of Americans. For, as George Frederickson has said in *The Black Image in the White Mind* (1971):

Although inherent racial differences of a socially significant kind cannot be demonstrated and probably do not exist, the consciousness of race as a basis of personal identity seems much more difficult to eliminate than the more optimistic liberal environmentalists have led us to believe.

The concept of race has survived despite its imprecision and its implicit assumptions of superiority and inferiority. Whether it can be eliminated from the language is questionable; perhaps the most that can be hoped is that it will lose its pernicious meaning. Since the task of building American society goes on, each generation must answer anew for itself how it will categorize persons in that society. If race continues to be used to indicate inferiority, the cost may, as Lincoln said of the cost of slavery, have to be paid in blood. As he also said, God's will be done. And having said this, one could also hope that the religious faith that caused early Americans to believe that all humans were equally children of Adam and Eve might still lurk in the inner recesses of this generation of Americans' hearts.

Bibliography

There are a number of indispensable works in the area of race. The standard book in the field is Thomas Gossett's *Race: The History of an Idea* (Dallas, Tex., 1963). This book concentrates mainly on the nineteenth century and contains little on ideas after 1930. It has, in addition, a strong emphasis upon literary images of race. Winthrop Jordan's *White Over Black* (Chapel Hill, N.C., 1968) is the best account of English and American racial attitudes toward Blacks and Indians from 1550 to 1812. The book is encyclopedic in treatment and has a particularly detailed analysis of eighteenth-century thought on race. Jordan has recently published a shorter version called *The White Man's Burden* (New York, 1974). David Brion Davis's *The Problem of Slavery in Western Culture* (Ithaca, N.Y., 1966), which is both richer and more comprehensive than one might suspect from the title, covers much the same time period as Jordan's book, ending, however, at 1775. Davis traces slavery back to classical times, emphasizing the similarities between classical and modern slavery. He thus de-emphasizes slavery as the cause of prejudice. George M. Fredrickson's *The Black Image in the White Mind* (New York, 1971) is the best study available on racial ideas in the nineteenth century and should be used after *White Over Black*. Fredrickson, like Gossett, covers material up to the twentieth century. There is no adequate study of racial ideas in the twentieth century, a lack that needs to be remedied.

Chapter One

Philip Curtin is the leading authority on the demography of the slave trade. In his book, *The Atlantic Slave Trade: A Census* (Madison, Wisc., 1969), he separates fact from fiction and has the best estimate of the number of Blacks brought to the New World and where they settled. His article, "Epidemiology and the Slave Trade," *Political Science Quarterly* 83 (1968): 190–216, contains his theory on why Blacks replaced Indians as the source of labor in the Americas. He also discusses the slave trade as it operated in Europe prior to the starting of the trans-Atlantic trade in his chapter, "The Slave Trade and the Atlantic Basin: Intercontinental Perspective," in Nathan I. Huggins, Martin Kilson, and Daniel M. Fox, eds., *Key Issues in the Afro-American Experience*, Vol. I (New York, 1971). There are several good books describing the slave trade; one is James Pope-Hennesey's *Sins of the Fathers: A Study of the Atlantic Slave Traders, 1441–1807* (New York, 1968), which has a popular appeal.

The legends concerning wild men and apes can be found in Richard Bernheimer's *Wild Men in the Middle Ages: A Study in Art, Sentiment, and Demonology* (Cambridge, Mass., 1952) and in H. W. Janson's *Apes and Ape Lore in the Middle Ages and the Renaissance* (London, 1952). The latest anthology on the topic, edited by Edward Dudley and Maximillian Novak, is *The Wild Man Within: An Image in Western Thought from the Renaissance to Romanticism* (Pittsburgh, Penn., 1972). Rudolph Altrocchi in *Sleuthing in the Stacks* (Cambridge, Mass., 1944) discusses European attitudes toward ape legends.

John H. Rowe's "The Renaissance Foundations of Anthropology," *American Anthropologist* 67 (1965): 1–20, is a controversial historical article. A discussion of the legend of Noah appears in Don Cameron Allen's *The Legend of Noah: Renaissance Rationalism in Arts, Science, and Letters* (Urbana, Ill., 1949). This is the most comprehensive treatment of the early modern account of human origins. An account of human origins can also be found in Margaret T. Hodgen's *Early Anthropology in the 16th and 17th Centuries* (Philadelphia, Penn., 1964), an indispensable book for anyone interested in European views of American Indians and one that points out the rigorousness of early thinkers on this subject. John H. Rowe's "Ethnography and Ethnology in the 16th Century," *Kroeber's Anthropological Society Papers* No. 30 (1964): 1–19, is an important summary of the ideas of the sixteenth century. Robert Wauchope, in his popularly written *Lost Tribes and Sunken Continents* (Chicago, 1962), concentrates on the theories of Indian origins; he takes these theories less seriously than Hodgen and tends to ridicule them.

The most recent book on Blacks in England is James Walvin's *Black and White: The Negro and English Society* (London, 1973). The images of Blacks in English drama are best described by Eldred Jones in his *Othello's Countrymen: The African in English Renaissance Drama* (New York, 1965) and are also discussed in Robert R. Cowley's *The Voyagers and Elizabethan Drama* (Boston, 1938). Cowley's book also treats the images in English drama of the natives of the New World. Henri Baudet's *Paradise on Earth: Some Thoughts on European Images of Non-European Man* (New Haven, Conn., 1965) is a brief but significant book.

Carolyn Thomas Foreman discusses the Indians who returned with explorers to Europe in *Indians Abroad, 1493–1938* (Norman, Okla., 1943), while Lee Eldridge Huddleston's *Origins of the American Indians: European Concepts, 1492–1729* (Austin, Tex., 1967) analyzes the theories about how Indians got to the New World. Lewis Hanke's *Aristotle and the American Indians: A Study in Race Prejudice in the Modern World* (London, 1959) is a microcosmic study of the Spanish debate over whether the Indian was a "natural slave." Gary B. Nash, in "The Image of the Indian in the Southern Colonial Mind," *William and Mary Quarterly*, 3rd Series 29, No. 2 (1972): 197–230, describes the early views of English settlers on the Indians as does Leslie A. Fiedler in *The Return of the Vanishing American* (London, 1968). The latter work, however, deals more exclusively with these views as they appear in literary images. T. D. Stewart and Marshall Newman's "An Historical Resumé of the Concept of Differences in Indian Types," *American Anthropologist* 53 (1951): 19–36, is an important article discussing the constancy of the Indian stereotype. For the image of the Indian in America, see also the first two chapters of Howard Mumford Jones's *O Strange New World: American Culture in the Formative Years* (New York, 1964).

Chapter Two

An Indian view of white settlers is reconstructed by Nancy Oestreich Lurie in "Indian Cultural Adjustment to European Civilization," in James M. Smith, ed., *Seventeenth-Century America* (Chapel Hill, N.C., 1959). The early attitudes of the English toward America, and the relations between the English and colonial society are described in A. L. Rowse's *The Elizabethans and America* (London, 1959). Gary B. Nash's "Red, White and Black: The Origins of Racism in Colonial America," a chapter in Gary B. Nash and Richard Weiss, eds., *The Great Fear: Race in the Mind of America* (New York, 1970), touches on the general attitude of the English colonists toward alien racial groups. Nash's book, *Red, White and Black* (Englewood Cliffs, N.J., 1974) traces attitudes toward Blacks and Indians from 1550 to 1776 and is an excellent book. Howard Peckham and Charles Gibson have edited *Attitudes of the Colonial Powers Towards the American Indians* (Salt Lake City, Utah, 1969); the book is short and easy to read. This may be supplemented by James Axtell's "The Scholastic Philosophy of the Wilderness," *William and Mary Quarterly*, 3rd Series 29, No. 3 (1972): 335–66, which article gives an account of the attitude held by Europeans toward the natural setting where Indians were found.

Wesley Craven's "Indian Policy in Early Virginia," *William and Mary Quarterly* 1 (1944): 65–82, and W. Stitt Robinson, Jr.'s "The Legal Status of the Indian in Colonial Virginia," *Virginia Magazine of History and Biography* 61 (1953): 247–59, are the standard articles on the relations between early colonists and Indians in Virginia. Douglas Edward Leach writes of the Indian wars in New England in *The Northern Colonial Frontier, 1607–1763* (New York, 1966), and in *Flintlock and Tomahawk: New England in King Philip's War* (New York, 1958). Yasu Kawashima has two helpful articles on the legal position of Indians in colonial Massachusetts. These articles are: "Jurisdiction of the Colonial Court over the Indians in Massachusetts, 1689–1763," *New England*

Quarterly 42 (Dec., 1969): 532–50; and "Legal Origins of the Indian Reservation in Colonial Massachusetts," *The American Journal of Legal History* 13 (1969): 42–56. A view sympathetic to the plight of the Christian Indian is contained in Alden T. Vaughan's *New England Frontier: Puritans and Indians, 1620–1675* (Boston, 1965). For an opposite view, see Francis Jennings's "Virgin Land and Savage People," *American Quarterly* 23 (1971): 519–41.

Frank Craven, in *White, Red and Black: The Seventeenth Century Virginian* (Charlottesville, Va., 1971), tries to understand the race relations in that colony in terms of the size and character of the population. The controversy over whether the first Blacks were slaves is summed up best by Winthrop D. Jordan in "Modern Tensions and the Origins of American Slavery," *Journal of Southern History* 28, No. 1 (1962): 18–32, and in the most recent study of the status of Blacks in Virginia is Alden T. Vaughan's "Blacks in Virginia: A Note on the First Decade," *William and Mary Quarterly*, 3rd Series, 29, No. 3 (1972): 469–78.

Edmund S. Morgan suggests that the price of social mobility in colonial America was slavery in his "Slavery and Freedom: The American Paradox," *American Historical Review* 59 (1972): 5–29. T. H. Breen's "A Changing Labor Force and Race Relations in Virginia, 1660–1710," *Journal of Social History*, Fall, 1972: 3–18, admits that there were many problems concerning both white indentured servants and black slaves until 1684 when tobacco prices rose and the number of indentured servants fell. George M. Fredrickson says much the same thing in a more general presentation in "Toward a Social Interpretation of American Racism," in Nathan I. Huggins, Martin Kilson, and Daniel M. Fox, eds., *Key Issues in the Afro-American Experience*, Vol. I (New York, 1971).

The social backgrounds of English settlers are described in Mildred Campbell's "Social Origins of Some Early Americans," in James M. Smith, ed., *Seventeenth-Century America* (Chapel Hill, N.C., 1959). Christopher Hill describes Puritan social attitudes in *Society and Puritanism in Pre-Revolutionary England* (London, 1964) and particularly emphasizes their attitudes toward work. John Demos, in *A Little Commonwealth: Family Life in Plymouth Colony* (New York, 1970), shows the significance of family discipline for the separatists as Edmund S. Morgan does for the Puritans in *The Puritan Family* (Boston, 1944). Philip J. Greven in "Family Structure in Seventeenth-Century Andover, Massachusetts," *William and Mary Quarterly*, 3rd Series, Vol. 24, No. 3 (1967): 224–42, and Kai Erickson in his *Wayward Puritans* (New York, 1966) report an absence of racially defined social deviance.

Louis Ruchames has edited *Racial Thought in America: From Puritans to Lincoln* (Amherst, Mass., 1968), which is a useful survey. Sympathetic to the Puritans' attitudes is Alden T. Vaughan in his *New England Frontier: Puritan and Indians, 1620–1675* (Boston, 1965); Vaughan believes that the Puritans made a genuine attempt to convert the Indians. See also Peter Carroll's *Puritanism and the Wilderness:*

The Intellectual Significance of the New England Frontier, 1620–1700 (New York, 1969). The effort to convert the Indians is recounted in John Eliot's *A Brief Narrative of the Progress of the Gospel Among the Indians of New England in the Year 1670* (London, 1671). William Kellaway's *The New England Company, 1649–1776* (New York, 1961) is the authoritative work on the organization which financed much of the Indian missionary effort. Samuel Eliot Morison lists the attempts made by the Puritans for the education of Indians in *The Founding of Harvard College* (Cambridge, Mass., 1935). The Puritan sense of failure after King Philip's War is expressed in Peter Gay's study of Puritan historiography, *A Loss of Mastery* (New York, 1966), and in Perry Miller's *The New England Mind: The Seventeenth Century* (New York, 1939).

Thomas Thorowgood's *Jewes in America* (London, 1650), reopened the question of Indian origins in English minds; it is short and readable. Harmon L'Estrange's answer, *Americans no Jewes* (London, 1651) is likewise. Roy Harvey Pearce's "The 'Ruines of Mankind', the Indian and the Puritan Mind," *Journal of the History of Ideas* 13 (1952): 200–17, advances the argument that the Indian represented the degeneracy of natural man, an argument he later elaborated in *The Savages of America* (Baltimore, Md., 1953). Richard Slotkin's *Regeneration Through Violence* (Middletown, Conn., 1973) touches on the mythology of the frontier from 1600 to 1860. In addition, Roger Williams's *A Key into the Languages of America* (London, 1943), William Wood's *New England's Prospect* (London, 1634), Thomas Lechford's *Plain Dealing* (London, 1642), and Thomas Morton's *New English Canaan* (New York, 1967) contain worthwhile material about the Indians.

Finally, the Indian captivity stories appear in Arthur Ray Buntin's "The Indian in American Literature, 1680–1760," (unpublished Ph.D. Dissertation, University of Washington, Seattle, 1961) and in Leslie Fiedler's *The Return of the Vanishing American* (London, 1968). The standard article is Roy Harvey Pearce's "The Significance of the Captivity Narrative," *American Literature* 19 (1947): 1–20. An anthology on the topic is Richard Van Der Beets's *Held Captive by the Indians: Selected Narratives, 1642–1836* (Knoxville, Tenn., 1973). Joseph Norman Heard's *White into Red: A Study of the Assimilation of White Persons Captured by Indians* (Metuchen, N.J., 1973) is not particularly enlightening but does make the point that captives under 12 years of age were least likely to return.

Chapter Three

J. Potter's population estimates in "The Growth of Population in America, 1700–1860," in D. V. Glass and D. E. C. Eversley, eds., *Population in History* (Chicago, 1965), reflect the growing interest in demography and the increasing accuracy of such studies. Philip D. Curtin's *The Atlantic Slave Trade: A Census* (Madison, Wisc., 1969) confirms Potter's estimates and shows that the eighteenth century was the one in which most slaves came to North America. His *The Image of Africa: British Ideas and Actions* (Madison, Wisc., 1964) is good on English images of Blacks between 1780 and 1850. The organization of American society into which the black and white immigrants fit is described by Richard Hofstadter in *America at 1750: A Social Portrait* (New York, 1971), a volume of the high quality to be expected from Hofstadter despite his death before its completion. Jackson Turner Main's *The Social Structure of Revolutionary America* (Princeton, N.J., 1965) is more pedestrian but is equally informative on the subject. For specific material on how Blacks fit into the colonial social system, the best book is Thad W. Tate, Jr.'s *The Negro in Eighteenth-Century Williamsburg* (Williamsburg, Va., 1965). William S. Willis shows the deliberate policy of the lower southern colonies to set one race against the other in "Divide and Rule: Red, White, and Black in the Southeast," *The Journal of Negro History* 48 (1963): 157–76.

The successful emancipation efforts in the North at the time of the Revolution are discussed in David Brion Davis's *The Problem of Slavery in Western Culture* (Ithaca, N.Y., 1966) and in his "New Sidelights on Early Antislavery Radicalism," *William and Mary Quarterly*, 3rd Series 28, No. 4 (1971): 585–94. Davis describes the ambivalence that afflicted eighteenth-century thinkers as does Leon F. Litwack in *North of Slavery* (Chicago, 1961). Both William W. Freehling in "The Founding Fathers and Slavery," *American Historical Review* 77, No. 1 (1972): 81–93, and Howard A. Ohline in "Republicanism and Slavery: Origins of the Three-Fifths Clause in the United States Constitution," *William and Mary Quarterly*, 3rd Series, 28, No. 4 (1971): 563–84, portray the founders of the Republic as unsympathetic to slavery and desirous of eventually ending it. These are obvious reactions to the New Left historians, such as Staughton Lynd, who emphasize the key role of slavery in American history.

Douglas Edward Leach's *The Northern Colonial Frontier, 1600–1763* (New York, 1966) details the problems with Indians on the frontier. J. Ralph Randolph's *British Travelers Among the Southern Indians, 1660–1773* (Norman, Okla., 1973) consists of reports from the Southern colonial area. Milo Milton Quaife edited *Alexander Henry's Travels and Adventures in the Years 1760–1776* (Chicago, 1921); his book is a classic account of Indian life. Roy Harvey Pearce's *The Savages of America* (Baltimore, Md., 1953) is justly famous. A simple version of the idea of the noble savage is in A. L. Dicket's "The Noble Savage Convention Epitomized in John Lawson's 'A New Voyage to Carolina,'" *North Carolina History Review* 63 (October, 1966): 413–29. An older view, but still a good one, is Hoxie Fairchild's *The Noble Savage: A Study in Romantic Naturalism* (New York, 1928). This book relies heavily upon literary sources and reveals the persistent use of the image of the noble savage. Jonathan Edwards's ideas are expressed in his *History of the Work of Redemption,* Volume 3 in his *Works* (New York, 1830). The Indian policy of the Revolutionary and early National period is discussed in Wilbur R. Jacob's *Dispossessing the American Indian* (New York, 1973), which has been criticized as being unsympathetic to the Indian; and in Reginald Horsman's *Expansion and American Indian Policy, 1783–1812* (East Lansing, Mich., 1967), which is a useful description of the attempts of early Americans to come to terms with the Indians. The most recent book concerning the Iroquois and the Revolution is Barbara Graymont's *The Iroquois in the American Revolution* (Syracuse, 1972). Bernard W. Sheehan's *Seeds of Extinction: Jeffersonian Philanthropy and the American Indian* (Chapel Hill, N.C., 1973) combines a history of Indian policy and ideas.

The idea of millenialism and its connection to the American past is the theme of Ernest Lee Tuveson's *Redeemer Nation: The Idea of America's Millenial Role* (Chicago, 1968). The book is especially useful on the Revolutionary and early National periods. A good survey of the eighteenth-century idea of degeneracy is in Stow Persons's article, "The Cyclical Theory of History in Eighteenth Century America," which originally appeared in the *American Quarterly* 2, No. 2 (Summer, 1954): 147–63, and is reprinted in Hennig Cohen, ed., *The American Culture* (Boston, 1968). Antonello Gerbi's *The Dispute of the New World: The History of a Polemic* (Pittsburgh, Pa., 1973) is the most complete work on the topic of degeneracy. Charles Brewster Tinker's *Nature's Simple Plan* (Princeton, N.J., 1922) and John C. Greene's *The Death of Adam* (Ames, Ia., 1959) concentrate on biological thought. The beginnings of developmental biology are discussed by Maurice Mandelbaum in "The Scientific Background of Evolutionary Theory in Biology," *Journal of the History of Ideas* 18 (1957): 344–46.

The controversy over who built the Indian mounds can be found in Henry C. Shitrone, *The Mound Builders* (New York, 1930). Three contemporary accounts of Indian customs that are indicative of the view of the eighteenth century are Robert Beverley's *The History and Present State of Virginia,* Louis B. Wright ed., (Chapel Hill, N.C., 1947); Cadwallader Colden's *The History of the Five Indian Nations Depending on the Province of New York in America* (Ithaca, N.Y., 1958); and James Adair's *The History of the American Indians* (London, 1775). Albert Keiser's *The Indian in American Literature* (New York, 1933) is old but comprehensive. Margaret T. Hodgen, in *The Doctrine of Survivals* (London, 1936), discusses the anthropological conception of survivals, as used by Tylor, and shows how this conception was central to the anthropology of the eighteenth century. Marvin Harris's *The Rise of Anthropological Theory: A History of Theories of Culture* (New York, 1968) is strongest on recent anthropology, but he, like Hodgen, points out the consistent use of anthropological theory by early thinkers. Two collections are helpful for a study of anthropological theory; these are Frederick de Laguna, ed., *Selected Papers from the American Anthropologist, 1880–1920* (Evanston, Ill., 1960) and Fred Eggan, ed., *Social Anthropology of North American Indians* (Chicago, 1955). In the latter collection, Sol Tax's "From Lafitau to Radcliffe-Brown, A Short History of the Study of Social Organization," offers particularly good insights.

Clarence J. Glackens's *Traces on the Rhodian Shore: Nature and Culture in Western Thought from Ancient Times to the End of the 18th Century* (Berkeley, Calif., 1967) is a monumental survey of environmental theory and geography. The enlightened concept of man is expressed in Gladys Bryson, *Man and Society: The Scottish Inquiry of the Eighteenth Century* (Princeton, N.J., 1945) and in E. A. Hoebel, "William Robertson: An 18th-Century Anthropologist-Historian," *American Anthropologist* 62 (1960): 648–55. Reverend John Adams's *Curious Thoughts on the History of Man* (London, 1789) contains an abridgement of works on man of Lord Kaimes, Lord Monboddo, Dr. Dunbar, and Montesquieu. Margaret T. Hodgen's "The Negro in the Anthropology of John Wesley," *Journal of Negro History* 19 (1934): 308–23, is an interesting sidelight on the racial views of the eighteenth-century enthusiast. American concepts of the past histories and future destinies of the Indians and Blacks are clearly presented in Daniel J. Boorstin's *The Lost World of Thomas Jefferson* (Boston, 1948) and in Francis W. Pennell's "Benjamin Smith Barton as Naturalist," *Proceedings of the American Philosophical Society* 86 (1943): 108–22. Finally, Samuel Stanhope Smith's *An Essay on the Causes of the Variety of Complexion and Figure in the Human Species...* (New Brunswick, N.J., 1810) recapitulates as well as any other work the religious paradigm of the eighteenth century.

Chapter Four

Wilcolm E. Washburn's "The Moral and Legal Justifications for Dispossessing the Indian," in James M. Smith, ed., *Seventeenth Century America* (Chapel Hill, N.C., 1939) is a helpful survey of the arguments for taking Indian land. Mary E. Young's "Indian Removal and Land Allotment: The Civilized Tribes and Jacksonian Justice," *American Historical Review* 64 (1958): 31–45, treats the process of Indian removal in the South in the 1820's and 1830's and is a standard work. Robert H. Berkhofer, Jr. offers anthropological insights in his book *Salvation and the Savage: An Analysis of Protestant Missions and American Indian Response, 1787–1862* (Lexington, Mass., 1965) and relates what happened to those Indians who were Christianized and supposedly civilized. R. W. B. Lewis's classic study of nineteenth-century thought, *The Amer-*

ican Adam (Chicago, 1955) contains some material on the assigned place of the Indians in the American Garden of Eden in which Europeans supposedly returned to a pre-fall Adamic state. John Heckewelder's *Account of the History, Manners, and Customs of the Indian Nations, Who Once Inhabited Pennsylvania and the Neighboring States* (Philadelphia, Pa., 1818) is a classic account of Indian life. The different images that early fur traders had of Indians are well described in Lewis O. Saum's *The Fur Trader and the Indian* (Seattle, Wash., 1965).

Nineteenth-century speculation on the origin of the Indians was rich and varied. DeWitt Clinton's *A Memoir on the Antiquities of the Western Parts of the State of New York* (Albany, N.Y., 1818) recounts that prominent New Yorker's view of the creators of the Indian Mounds in his state. John Ranking's *Historical Researches on the Conquest of Peru, Mexico, Bogata, Natchez, and Talomeco, In the Thirteenth Century, by the Mongols, accompanied with Elephants* (London, 1827) is an interesting curiosity founded on presumed natural and historical evidence of the time.

Material is also plentiful on Henry Rowe Schoolcraft. The relationship between Schoolcraft and Lewis Cass, governor of the Michigan Territory, is shown in Frank B. Woodford's *Lewis Cass, The Last Jeffersonian* (New Brunswick, N.J., 1950); and an evaluation of Schoolcraft's contribution to anthropology may be found in H. R. Hays's popularly written *From Ape to Angel, An Informal History of Social Anthropology* (New York, 1958). A. Irving Hallowell's article "The Beginning of Anthropology in America," in *Selected Papers from the American Anthropologist, 1880–1920* (Evanston, Ill., 1960) is an encyclopedic treatment of early American anthropologists. Of the books by Schoolcraft, *Algic Researches* (New York, 1839), *The Indian in His Wigwam* (New York, 1848), and *Notes on the Iroquois* (Albany, N.Y., 1847) most comprehensively include his ideas concerning the Indians. On Schoolcraft's fellow scholar, Lewis Henry Morgan, Bernard J. Stern's *Lewis Henry Morgan: American Scholar* (Chicago, 1960) is the most recent book. Morgan's own book *League of the Ho-De-Na-Law-Nee or Iroquois* (Rochester, N.Y., 1966), is easy to read and catches the flavor of Morgan's early thinking.

The image of the Indian in the literature of the nineteenth century is described by Albert Keiser in *The Indian in American Literature* (New York, 1933). Leslie A. Fiedler, in his *Love and Death in the American Novel* (New York, 1966), also discusses Indians in the literature of the time and describes how Henry David Thoreau reacted to Alexander Henry and how James Fenimore Cooper borrowed from John Heckewelder. Daniel G. Hoffman says only a little on the Indian and the Black in *Form and Fable in American Fiction* (New York, 1961), but what he does say is significant. The Indian hater can be found in Herman Melville's *The Confidence Man: His Masquerade* (London, 1857) and is discussed in Roy Harvey Pearce's article, "Melville's Indian Hater: A Note on the Meaning of *The Confidence Man*," *PMLA* 67 (1952): 942–48. Ruth Elson's *Guardians of Tradition: American Schoolbooks of the 19th Century* (Lincoln, Nebr., 1964) has one chapter on race in the textbooks of the time. David Levin analyzes the view of the Indian held by America's first great generation of historians in his *History as Romantic Art* (New York, 1963).

Chapter Five

The population figures for Blacks during the pre-Civil War period come from Philip D. Curtin's *The Atlantic Slave Trade: A Census;* Frank Pollara's "Trends in U.S. Population," in Daniel Callahan, ed., *The American Population Debate* (Garden City, N.Y., 1971); and J. Potter's "The Growth of Population in America, 1700–1860," in D. V. Glass and D. E. C. Eversley, eds., *Population in History* (Chicago, 1965). Eugene O. Genovese's *The Political Economy of Slavery* (New York, 1965) contains economic data on the development of slavery in the nineteenth-century South.

The treatment of the free Black in the North is summarized best in Leon F. Litwack's *North of Slavery* (Chicago, 1961), which is a very valuable book. Litwack insists that there was as pervasive a prejudice against Blacks in the North as in the South. A similar view appears in George M. Fredrickson's *The Black Image in the White Mind* (New York, 1971) and in John L. Stanley's "Majority Tyranny in Tocqueville's America: The Failure of Negro Suffrage in 1846," *Political Science Quarterly* 34 (1967): 412–35. See also C. Vann Woodword's *American Counterpoint: Slavery and Racism in the North-South Dialogue* (Boston, 1971). Linda K. Kerber's "Abolitionists and Amalgamators; The New York City Race Riots of 1834," *New York History* 48 (1967): 28–39, shows how sensitive nineteenth-century Americans were to any hints of racial mixing. The racial views of three early American presidents can be found in Frederick M. Binder's *The Color Problem in Early National America as Viewed by John Adams, Jefferson and Jackson* (Amsterdam, 1968).

Frederick Merk's "A Safety Valve Thesis and Texas Annexation," *Mississippi Valley Historical Review* 49 (1962): 413–36, tells the story of those who believed that Texas could be a staging area for black slaves who would eventually be freed because of the prohibition of slavery in Mexico. Theodore Draper surveys black attitudes toward colonization in *The Rediscovery of Black Nationalism* (New York, 1970); the positions of black leaders on the subject can be found in Benjamin Quarles's *Black Abolitionists* (New York, 1969), and in Hollis R. Lynch's "Pan-Negro Nationalism in the New World, Before 1862," in Jeffrey Butler, ed.,

African History, Vol. II in the *Boston University Papers on Africa* (Boston, 1966). White attitudes on the topic appear in *An Address to the Public on the Subject of the African School*, published by the Synod of New York and New Jersey (New York, 1816).

There is a voluminous literature on all aspects of slavery. The Northern view is best shown in an article by Martin Duberman entitled "The Northern Response to Slavery," in Martin Duberman, ed., *The Antislavery Vanguard: New Essays on the Abolitionists* (Princeton, N.J., 1965). Eugene H. Berwanger details the racial attitude in the old Northwest in *The Frontier Against Slavery: Western Anti-Negro Prejudice and the Slavery Extension Controversy* (Urbana, Ill., 1967). The Brazilian slave experience and its impact on race relations has most recently been brilliantly discussed in Carl N. Degler's *Neither Black nor White* (New York, 1971). Degler's book is a comprehensive survey of race relations in Brazil and the United States from colonial times to the present. It can be supplemented by Herbert Klein's *Slavery in the Americas* (Chicago, 1967), which is a more comprehensive and general study of slavery. Two other works are classics on the area of race relations in Brazil: Donald Pierson, *Negroes in Brazil: A Study of Race Contact*, rev. ed., (Carbondale, Ill., 1967) and Charles Wagley, ed., *Race and Class in Rural Brazil*, 2nd ed., (New York, 1963). The later book contains a justly praised chapter by Marvin Harris entitled "Race Relations in Minas Vilhos, A Community in the Mountain Region of Central Brazil." Two new books on American slavery have been influential: John W. Blassingame, in *The Slave Community* (New York, 1972), attempts to capture the black social relations within slavery, while Robert William Fogel and Stanley L. Engerman's *Time on the Cross* (Boston, 1974) is a controversial study of the economics of slavery.

For those interested in the development of nineteenth-century anthropology, there is no better place to begin than George W. Stocking, Jr.'s *Race, Culture, and Evolution: Essays in the History of Anthropology* (New York, 1968). This book is a collection of disparate articles that hold together quite well. James Cowles Prichard wrote a number of books; *The Natural History of Man* (London, 1843) is as representative of his anthropological ideas as any. A useful article on pre-Darwinian racial ideas is John C. Greene's "Some Early Speculation on the Explanation of Race," *American Anthropologist* new series 56, (1954): 31–41. The standard work on the American school of anthropology is W. R. Stanton's *The Leopard's Spots* (Chicago, 1960). On phrenology, the best-known work is John D. Davies's *Phrenology: Fad and Science* (New Haven, Conn., 1955). Samuel George Morton's *Crania Americana* (Philadelphia, 1893) and *An Inquiry into the Distinctive Characteristics of the Aboriginal Race of America* (Philadelphia, 1844), 2nd ed., are both based upon considerable investigation of Indian skulls and show the diligence of the dedicated amateur physical anthropologist. The problem of how to account for the expanding number of years in human history appears in Stephen Toulmin and Jane Goodfield's, *The Discovery of Time* (London, 1965).

Charles Caldwell, M.D., in *Thoughts on the Original Unity of the Human Race* (New York, 1830), shows how the biblical explanation of human unity had lost support by 1830. Samuel Morton's ideas about monogenesis appear in "Hybridity in Animals, Considered in References to the Question of the Unity of the Human Species," *American Journal of Science and Art*, 2nd Series, 3 (1847): 39–50, 203–11. A synthesis of racial ideas can be found in *Types of Mankind* (Philadelphia, 1854) by J. C. Nott and George R. Gliddon, two disciples of Morton, and in Alfred Maury, Francis Pulszky, J. Aitken Meigs, J. C. Nott, and George R. Gliddon, *Indigenous Races of the Earth* (Philadelphia, 1857). Edward Lurie is the recognized expert of the life and thought of Louis Agassiz. His biography *Louis Agassiz: A Life in Science* (Chicago, 1960) describes the prestige and accomplishments of the Swiss-born scientist and his reputation in America. Lurie's "Louis Agassiz and the Races of Man," *Isis* 45 (1954): 227–42, is a good, short summary of Agassiz's position on the issue of race. For Agassiz's own summation of polygenesis, the reader is advised to turn to Louis Agassiz, "The Diversity of Origin of the Human Race," *Christian Examiner*, July, 1850, 110–45. The first American scientific effort on the gorilla was Thomas S. Savage, M.D., and Jeffries Wyman, M.D., *A Description of the Characters and Habits of Troglodytes Gorilla* (Boston, 1847). The rear-guard defense of monogenesis by an informed theologian is best seen in John Bachman's *An Examination of the Characteristics of Genera and Species as Applicable to the Doctrine of the Unity of the Human Race* (Charleston, Va., 1850).

The apocalyptic nature of the Civil War and the millenial expectation it inspired has not been explored as much as it might. George M. Fredrickson shows how even Northerners who were conservatives on the race question supported the War as a presumed chastening of American society in *The Inner Civil War: Northern Intellectuals and the Crisis of the Union* (New York, 1965). Ernest Lee Tuveson in *Redeemer Nation: The Idea of America's Millenial Role* (Chicago, 1968) describes the function of the idea of the millenium in early nineteenth-century America and convincingly demonstrates its significant impact on behavior.

Some of the impatience of the abolitionists, because of their hopes for a transformed society, is caught by William H. Pease and Jane H. Pease in "Antislavery Ambivalence: Immediatism, Expediency, Race." *American Quarterly* 17 (1965): 687–95. Stanley Elkins is unsympathetic to this vision of society in *Slavery* (Chicago, 1959). One good place to start reading on abolitionism is Theodore Parker's *Centenary Edition* (Boston, 1907). Earl E. Thorpe's *Black Historians: A Critique* (New York, 1971) is poorly written but has useful data on this issue. Two re-issues of nineteenth-century black narratives outline the theories of Blacks about themselves. These are *An Autobiography of Reverend Josiah Henson,* with an introduction by Robin W. Winks (Reading, Mass., 1969), and *The Narrative of William Wells Brown, A Fugitive Slave,* with an introduction by Larry Gara (Reading, Mass., 1969). The definitive biography of William Wells Brown is William Edward Farrison's *William Wells Brown: Author and Reformer* (Chicago, 1969).

Scholars have recently turned to a study of popular culture and folklore to ascertain the feelings and opinions of large groups of the population. One such analysis, which looks at white views of blacks, is Joseph Boskin's "Sambo: The National Jester in the Popular Culture," in Gary B. Nash and Richard Weiss, eds., *The Great Fear* (New York, 1970). Joel R. Williamson, "Black Self-Assertion Before and After Emancipation," in Nathan I. Huggins, Martin Kilson, and Daniel M. Fox, eds., *Key Issues in the Afro-American Experience,* Vol. I (New York, 1971) and Sterling Stuckey, "Through the Prism of Folklore: The Black Ethos in Slavery," *The Massachusetts Review* 9 (1968): 417–37, both rely heavily on slave songs and other folk material to build a case for black resistance to the slave system. The pioneer collection of folklore is B. A. Botkin's *A Treasury of American Folklore* (New York, 1944); another useful collection is Bruce Jackson's *The Negro and His Folklore in Nineteenth-Century Periodicals* (Austin, Texas, 1967). David Brion Davis's "Some Ideological Functions of Prejudice in Anti-Bellum America," *American Quarterly* 15 No. 2, Pt. 1 (1963): 115–25, suggests that prejudice was intrinsic to the nature of a free society.

Chapter Six

Philip Borden's "Found Cumbering the Soil: Manifest Destiny and the Indian in the Nineteenth Century," in Gary B. Nash and Richard Weiss, eds., *The Great Fear* (New York, 1970), is a general statement on post-Civil War American attitudes toward the Indians. Peter Farb, although overly influenced by evolutionism, reviews post-war Indian policy in his *Man's Rise to Civilization as Shown by the Indians of North America from Primeval Times to the Coming of the Industrial State* (New York, 1968). More specific details of the policies and the motives behind them are found in Henry E. Fritz, *The Movement for Indian Assimilation, 1860–1890* (Philadelphia, 1963) and in Robert Winston Mardock, *The Reformers and the American Indian* (Columbia, Mo., 1971). Helen Hunt Jackson's *A Century of Dishonor* (New York, 1960) has been reissued with an introduction by Andrew F. Rolle and shows the passion of the Indian reformers. Paul Prucha has put together original sources from the post-Civil War period in his *Americanizing the American Indian: Writings by the "Friends of the Indians," 1880–1900* (Cambridge, Mass., 1973).

The impact of Darwinism is the theme of John C. Greene's *Darwin and the Modern World View* (Baton Rouge, La., 1961). This book, used in conjunction with George Stocking, Jr.'s *Race, Culture, and Evolution: Essays in the History of Anthropology* (New York, 1968), provides an overview of the influence of the theory of natural selection on anthropological thought. Two other books which are helpful on biological thinking are William Coleman's *Biology in the Nineteenth Century: Problems of Form, Function, and Transformation* (New York, 1971) and Michael Gheselin's *The Triumph of the Darwinian Method* (Berkeley, Calif., 1969). The most recent book on evolution and racial thought is John S. Haller, Jr., *Outcasts from Evolution: Scientific Attitudes of Racial Inferiority, 1859–1900* (Champaign, Ill., 1971). Margaret T. Hodgen's book, *The Doctrine of Survivals* (London, 1936) is old but is still significant; she showed that the idea of survivals, as used by Edward B. Tylor, neither originated with Tylor nor ended with him. A more recent article on nineteenth-century anthropology is Idus Murphree's "The Evolutionary Anthropologists: The Progress of Mankind, The Concepts of Progress in the Thought of John Lubbock, Edward B. Tylor, and Lewis H. Morgan," *Proceedings of the American Philosophical Society* 105 (1961): 265–300.

Marshall T. Newman describes the measurements of Senecas in "The Physique of the Seneca Indians of Western New York State," *Journal of the Washington Academy of Sciences* 47 (1957): 357–62. A. Hunter Dupree analyzes the naturalistic ideas of a prominent American scientist in "Jeffries Wyman's Views on Evolution," *Isis* 44 (1953): 243–46. The ideas of the three dominant American anthropologists—Morgan, Powell, and Brinton—of the post-Civil War decades can be found in Carl Resek's biography, *Lewis Henry Morgan: American Scholar* (Chicago, 1960); in Wallace Stegner's *Beyond the Hundredth Meridian, John Wesley Powell and the Second Opening of the West* (Boston, 1954), which, as the title suggests, concentrates mostly on Powell's career as explorer; and in works of Daniel G. Brinton such as *The Myths of the New World* (New York, 1968) and *Aboriginal American Authors and Their Productions* (Philadelphia, 1883). Two juvenile potboilers, by Edward Eggleston and Lillie Eggleston Seelye, are *The Shawnee Prophet; or the Story of Tecumseh* (London, 1880) and *The Indian Princess; or the Story of Pocahontas* (London, 1881).

Chapter Seven

The attitude of the North toward the Blacks prior to the Civil War was often like that of the South, or so claims V. Jacque Voegeli in "The Northwest and the Race Issue, 1861–1862," *Mississippi Valley Historical Review* 50 (1963): 235–51. Leslie H. Fishel, Jr., makes the same point in his "The North and the Negro, 1865–1900: A Study in Race Discrimination" (unpublished Ph.D. dissertation, Harvard University, Cambridge, Mass., 1953). A case study of the difficulty in obtaining black suffrage in a Western state after the Civil War is Robert P. Dykstra and Harlan Hahn, "Northern Voters and Negro Suffrage: The Case of Iowa, 1869," *Public Opinion Quarterly* 32 (1968): 202–15. William Leckie's *The Buffalo Soldiers: A Narrative of the Negro Calvary in the West* (Norman, Okla., 1967) is an excellent history of the black man's role in the conquest of the West. This should be supplemented by Arlen L. Fowler's *The Black Infantry in the West* (Westport, Conn., 1971).

James M. McPherson claims that the abolitionists persisted in striving for racial equality in his essay, "A Brief for Equality: The Abolitionist Reply to the Racist Myth, 1860–1865," in Martin Duberman, ed., *The Antislavery Vanguard: New Essays on the Abolitionists* (Princeton, N.J., 1965), but he admits the split caused by the issue of women's suffrage in "Abolitionists, Woman Suffrage and the Negro, 1865–1869," *Mid-America* 47 (1965): 40–47.

Allan Spear's "The Origins of the Urban Ghetto, 1870–1915," in Nathan I. Huggins, Martin Kilson, and Daniel M. Fox, eds., *Key Issues in the Afro-American Experience*, Vol. II (New York, 1971), is an excellent description of early black migration to the city. For specific cities, the reader may turn to Spear's *Black Chicago* (Chicago, 1969) or Gilbert Osofsky's *Harlem: The Making of a Ghetto* (New York, 1963). Two general works about the nature of American society are particularly helpful. One is Robert H. Wiebe's *The Search for Order, 1877–1920* (New York, 1967) which sets out a hypothesis that Americans were trying to bring their society under control. The other is an anthology put together by Richard Hofstadter and Michael Wallace called *American Violence: A Documentary History* (New York, 1970), which shows the extent to which white violence was used to intimidate Blacks. George Sinkler's *The Racial Attitudes of American Presidents from Abraham Lincoln to Theodore Roosevelt* (Long Island, N.Y., 1971) is a summary of some value. The two comprehensive works on southern racial thought after the Civil War are Claude H. Nolen's *The Negro's Image in the South* (Lexington, Ky., 1967) and Lawrence J. Friedman, *The White Savage: Racial Fantasies in the Post-bellum South* (Englewood Cliffs, N.J., 1970). Martin Gardner's popular book, *In the Name of Science* (New York, 1952), has one chapter on racist thought which is perceptive but superficial.

Charles Carroll's attempts to rationalize the biblical account of creation by combining it with recent biological developments appear in *The Negro Not the Son of Ham; or, Man Not a Species Divisible* (Chattanooga, Tenn., 1898), and in *The Tempter of Eve or the Criminality of Man's Social, Political, and Religious Equality, with the Negro, and the Amalgamation to Which These Crimes Inevitably Lead* (St.

Louis, Mo., 1902). William G. Schell's answer to Carroll, *Is the Negro a Beast?* (Moundsville, West Va., 1901), rejects the idea that the Negro was created as an animal prior to Adam and tries to defend monogenesis and racial equality.

The two significant post-Civil War books of Hinton Rowan Helper are *Nojoque: A Question for a Continent* (New York, 1867) and *The Negroes in Negroland; The Negroes in America; and Negroes Generally* (New York, 1868). Francis Brownell in "The Role of Jim in *Huckleberry Finn*," *Boston University Studies in English I* (Boston, 1955) traces the development of Mark Twain's character in that novel.

Both Charles H. Pearson's *National Life and Character* (New York, 1893) and Benjamin Kidd's *The Control of the Tropics* (New York, 1898) typify the growing belief that climate prevented white expansion in the tropics and modified the early social Darwinism that postulated a white-controlled world. John Beddoe talks of the index of nigrescence in *The Races of Britain* (Bristol and London, Eng., 1885), while L. P. Curtis, Jr., has analyzed the idea in "Of Images and Imagination in History," in L. P. Curtis, Jr., ed., *The Historians' Workshops* (New York, 1970), and in his *Apes, Angels, and Irishmen, A Study in Victorian Physiognomy and Caricature* (Washington, D.C., 1970). Daniel G. Brinton wrote several books on race and human origin in the 1890's. Three of the most significant are *Races and People* (New York, '890), *An Ethnologist's View of History* (Philadelphia, 1896), and *The Factors of Heredity and Environment in Man* (Washington, 1898).

The expert on Bishop Turner is Edwin S. Redkey. Three of his efforts are worth reading: they are "Bishop Turner's African Dream," *Journal of American History* 54 (1967): 271–90; "The Flowering of Black Nationalism; Henry McNeal Turner and Marcus Garvey," in Nathan I. Huggins, Martin Kilson, and Daniel M. Fox, eds., *Key Issues in the Afro-American Experience*, Vol. II (New York, 1971); and *Black Exodus: Black Nationalist and Back-to-Africa Movements 1890–1910* (New Haven, Conn., 1969). The racial views of Booker T. Washington appear in *Up From Slavery* (New York, 1965) and his ideas on Africa in Louis R. Harlan's "Booker T. Washington and the White Man's Burden," *American Historical Review* 71, No. 2 (1966): 441–67. The definitive biography of Booker T. Washington is being written by Louis R. Harlan. His first volume, *Booker T. Washington, The Making of a Black Leader 1865–1901* (New York, 1972), tells much of the background of Washington's ideas. Frederick Douglass remained remarkably constant in his commitment to full equality in America as shown in his autobiography, *Life and Times of Frederick Douglass* (New York, 1892) and in August Meier's "Frederick Douglass' Vision for America: A Case Study in Nineteenth-Century Negro Protest," in Harold M. Hyman and Leonard W. Levy, eds., *Freedom and Reform, Essays in Honor of Henry Steele Commager* (New York, 1967). Meier's book, *Negro Thought in*

America 1880–1915 (Ann Arbor, Mich., 1963) is the standard general survey of Negro thought of the time.

Emma Lou Thornbrough's *T. Thomas Fortune: Militant Journalist* (Chicago, 1972) is an up-to-date and judicious treatment of this outspoken black journalist. Frederick W. Bond's *The Negro and the Drama* (Washington, D.C., 1940) is not particularly insightful, but Robert A. Bone's *The Negro Novel in America* (New Haven, Conn., 1958) is. Another helpful book on black literature is David Littlejohn's *Black on White: A Critical Study of Writing by American Negroes* (New York, 1966). Helen M. Chesnutt's *Charles Waddell Chesnutt: Pioneer of the Color Line* (Chapel Hill, N.C., 1952) is, as might be expected, sympathetic to Chesnutt and his works. Bernard Wolfe's "Uncle Remus and the Malevolent Rabbit," *Commentary* (July, 1949): 31–41, shows how aggression lurks beneath the surface of seemingly innocent stories.

Chapter Eight

Randolph C. Downes traces the steps leading to the Indian Reorganization Act of 1934 in his "A Crusade for Indian Reform, 1922–34," *Mississippi Valley Historical Review* 32 (1945): 331–54. Paul Radin transcribed the words of Crashing Thunder in a book, *Crashing Thunder: The Autobiography of an American Indian* (New York, 1926). How much Radin's own values intruded is difficult to determine. For a view from the distaff side, see Mountain Wolf Woman, *Mountain Wolf Woman, Sister of Crashing Thunder: The Autobiography of a Winnebago Indian,* edited by Nancy O. Lurie and with a forward by Ruth Underhill (Ann Arbor, Mich., 1961).

Lewis M. Terman's early views on mental tests can be found in his *The Intelligence of School Children* (London, 1921). A recent history of early sociology, Herman and Julia R. Schwendinger's *The Sociologists of the Chair: A Radical Analysis of the Formative Years of North American Sociology, 1883–1922* (New York, 1974), is a useful synthesis, although the authors are unsympathetic to the pioneers. Two general surveys of anthropological theory are invaluable. The first is David Bidney's *Theoretical Anthropology* (New York, 1953), which appeared at the peak of the prestige of the culture concept, and the second is Marvin Harris's *The Rise of Anthropological Theory* (New York, 1968). Robert H. Lowie's *The History of Ethnological Theory* (New York, 1937) is mainly helpful in discussing the currents of controversy in the decade when the book was written.

There is a wealth of information on Franz Boas. Two issues of the *American Anthropologist* were devoted to him. The first was "Franz Boas," *American Anthropologist* 45, No. 3, Part 2 (1943) and the second was Walter Goldschmidt, ed., "The Anthropology of Franz Boas,"

American Anthropologist 61, No. 5, Part 2 (1959). Melville J. Herskovits's *Franz Boas: The Science of Man in the Making* (New York, 1953) is the standard biography. Boas was a prolific writer but his books are collections of articles that lack unity or a central theme. His *The Mind of Primitive Man* (New York, 1911) should be consulted for his early ideas and *Race, Language, and Culture* (New York, 1940) for his later ones.

The branching of physical anthropology away from cultural anthropology is detailed in Harry L. Shapiro's "The History and Development of Physical Anthropology," *American Anthropologist* 61, No. 3 (1959): 371–78.

Chapter Nine

The population figures cited in the chapter are from Frank Pollara's "Trends in U.S. Population," in Daniel Callahan, ed., *The American Population Debate* (Garden City, N.Y., 1971). August Meier and Elliott Rudwich have a series of articles on unsuccessful boycotts mounted by Negroes in the Progressive Era. These include "The Boycott Movement Against Jim Crow Streetcars in the South, 1900–1906," *Journal of American History* 55 (1970): 765–75; "Negro Boycotts of Jim Crow Schools in the North, 1897–1925," *Integrated Education* 5 (1967): 1–12; and "Negro Boycotts of Jim Crow Streetcars in Tennessee," *American Quarterly* 21 (1969): 755–63. Two race riots are analyzed in Elliott Rudwick's *Race Riot in East St. Louis* (Carbondale, Ill., 1964) and William M. Tuttle, Jr.'s, *Race Riot: Chicago in the Red Summer of 1919* (New York, 1970). Two contemporary views of the Atlanta riots, one white and the other black, are A. J. McKelway, "The Atlanta Riots, I—A Southern White Point of View," *Outlook* 84 (November 3, 1906): 557–66; and Carrie W. Clifford, "The Atlanta Riots, I—A Northern Black Point of View," *Outlook* 84 (November 3, 1906): 557–66.

Robert Moats Miller has written extensively on the views of American Protestants on racial problems; two of his articles that reflect these views are "The Attitudes of American Protestantism Towards the Negro, 1919–1939," *Journal of Negro History* 41 (1956): 215–40, and "The Protestant Churches and Lynching," *Journal of Negro History* 42 (1957): 118–31. David Reimers's *White Protestantism and the Negro* (New York, 1965) provides a more detailed analysis of the prejudice existing in American churches.

The classic study of the problem of the Negro is still Ray Stannard Baker's *Following The Color Line: American Negro Citizenship in the Progressive Era* (New York, 1964). The program of the reactivated Klan in the twentieth century is the topic of Kenneth T. Jackson's *The Ku Klux Klan in the Cities* (New York, 1967). For a first-hand account of the rhetoric and thought of the Klan, the reader should turn to Hiram Wesley Evan's, "The Klan's Fight for Americanism," *The North American Review* 223 (1926): 33–61.

William McDougall's, *The Indestructible Union: Rudiments of Political Science for the American Citizen* (Boston, 1925), is the work of a transplanted English psychologist that still reflects a strong belief in black inferiority. The results of army intelligence testing appear in Robert M. Yerkes and Clarence S. Yoakum, eds., *Mental Tests in the American Army* (New York, 1920) and Robert M. Yerkes, ed., *Psychological Examining in the United States Army, Memoirs of the National Academy of Sciences* 15 (Washington, D.C., 1921). Yerkes's popularity written book on his experiments on primates is *Almost Human* (New York, 1925). Howard W. Odum's *Social and Mental Traits of the Negro* (New York, 1910) does not show his latest view of the Negro but argues black inferiority. Edward Byron Reuter's *The Mulatto in the United States* (Boston, 1918) reveals his own interest in the results of miscegenation, a common preoccupation at that time. Aleš Hrdlička, *The Old Americans* (Baltimore, Md., 1925) is an ambitious attempt to categorize native Americans by anthropometric techniques. Melville J. Herskovits applied the same methods to the Negro and published his findings as *The American Negro: A Study in Racial Crossing* (New York, 1928) and as *The Anthropometry of the American Negro* (New York, 1930).

Representative racist views of the Negro based on older theories are shown in W. B. Parks, *The Possibilities of the Negro in Symposium: A Solution of the Negro Problem Psychologically Considered, The Negro Not "A Beast"* (Atlanta, Ga., 1904), H. A. Eastman, *The Negro* (Boston, 1905), Alfred Hall Stone, *Studies in the American Race Problem* (New York, 1908), and Edward Eggleston, *The Ultimate Solution of the American Negro Problem* (Boston, 1930). I. A. Newby's *Jim Crow's Defense: Anti-Negro Thought in America 1900–1930* (Baton Rouge, La., 1965) outlines the continuing racial views in America during this period.

The three best books on the newly developing discipline of genetics and its impact on racial theory are Donald K. Pickens, *Eugenics and the Progressives* (Nashville, Tenn., 1968), Mark H. Haller, *Eugenics: Hereditarian Attitudes in American Thought* (New Brunswick, N.J., 1963), and Kenneth M. Ludmerer, *Genetics and American Society* (Baltimore, Md., 1972). William C. Boyd, a contemporary physical anthropologist, shows a little of the controversy over genetics and race in his *Genetics and the Races of Man* (Boston, 1950). Two recent works on genetics are useful for the general reader. They are L. C. Dunn's *A Short History of Genetics* (New York, 1965) and Elof A. Carlson's *The Gene: A Critical History* (Philadelphia, Pa., 1966). The most famous popularizers of a racism based on a genetic model were Madison Grant and Lothrop Stoddard. Madison Grant wrote his *The Passing of the Great Race or the Racial Basis of European History* (New York, 1916) first; Lothrop Stoddard followed with two significant works, *The Rising Tide of Color Against White World-Supremacy* (New York, 1920) and *The Revolt Against Civilization: The Menace of the Underman* (London, 1922). Another hereditarian work that concentrated more upon the American Negro is Samuel J. Holmes' *The Trend of the Race* (New York, 1921).

S. P. Fullenwider's *The Mind and Mood of Black America* (Homewood, Illinois, 1969) is, in my opinion, the best treatment of twentieth century black thinking. June Sochen's *The Unbridgeable Gap: Blacks and Their Quest for the American Dream, 1900–1930* (Chicago, 1972) is short and relies most heavily on newspaper sources. W. E. B. DuBois' *Souls of Black Folks* (New York, 1903) is a classic that still reveals much about the emotions and the thoughts of that black leader. U. B. Thompson, *Africa and Unity: The Evolution of Pan-Africanism* (London, 1969), touches on the growth of the belief in the necessity of a free Africa and unified Africans, wherever they lived. E. David Cronon's *Black Moses: The Study of Marcus Garvey and the Universal Negro Improvement Association* (Madison, Wisc., 1955) gives a good account of the life and ideas of Garvey. Amy Jacques-Garvey has edited Marcus Garvey's *Philosophy and Opinions* (New York, 1970) in two volumes; these show how much Garvey owed to other thinkers.

Everett Carter has the best discussion of the black image in the early movies in "Cultural History Written with Lightning: The Significance of *The Birth of a Nation*," *American Quarterly* 12, No. 3 (1960): 347–57. Donald Bogle's *Toms, Coons, Mulattoes, Mammies, and Bucks* (New York, 1974) is the latest history of the stereotypes of Blacks in the movies and is popularly written. Two older books on the Negro in fiction are somewhat useful, although their basic frameworks now seem antiquated. The first is Elizabeth Loy Green's *The Negro in Contemporary American Literature* (Chapel Hill, N.C., 1928) and the second is Sterling Brown's *The Negro in American Fiction* (Washington, D.C., 1937). Leonard C. Archer's *Black Images in the American Theatre* (New York, 1973), an updated version of a 1956 Ph.D. dissertation, is not particularly illuminating. Seth M. Scheimer sets the stage for the Harlem Renaissance in his study of Harlem, *Negro Mecca* (New York, 1965). The most recent discussion of that renaissance is in Nathan Huggins, *Harlem Renaissance* (New York, 1971). James Weldon Johnson has three books well worth reading, his novel, *The Autobiography of an Ex-Colored Man* (New York, 1912), his history of Harlem, *Black Manhattan* (New York, 1930), and his own autobiography, *Along This Way* (New York, 1933). The problems encountered by the Negro writer are described in Langston Hughes's "The Negro Artist and the Racial Mountain," *The Nation*

June 23, 1926: 692–94, and the concept of the New Negro is described in Alain Locke, ed., *The New Negro: An Interpretation* (New York, 1925).

Chapter Ten

Ruth Benedict's *Patterns of Culture* (Boston, 1934) contains her thoughts on Indian societies, and her *Race, Science and Politics* (New York, 1940) contains her thoughts on race. The latter book is superficial but shows what the prevailing orthodoxy on race was. *Ruth Fulton Benedict: A Memorial* (New York, 1949) is a tribute given her by friends and associates and tells much about her personal and intellectual life. Victor Barnouw is very critical of her ideas in "Ruth Benedict: Apollonian and Dionysian," *University of Toronto Quarterly* 18, No. 3 (1949): 241–53.

The two novels mentioned in chapter ten as typical of the times are Edwin Carle's *Fig Tree John* (New York, 1935) and Oliver La Farge's *Laughing Boy* (Cambridge, Mass., 1929). John G. Neihardt's *Black Elk Speaks: Being the Life Story of a Holy Man of the Oglala Sioux* (Lincoln, Nebr., 1961) is a reissue of the 1930 edition. Another related book is Joseph Epes Brown, *The Sacred Pipe: Black Elk's Account of the Seven Rites of the Oglala Sioux* (Norman, Okla., 1953). Two articles on Indians and the media are useful. The first, Peter Dillingham's "The Literature of the American Indian," *English Journal* 62 (1973): 37–41, discusses the writings done by Indians, while the second, Don Geargakas's "They Have Not Spoken: American Indians in Films," *Film Quarterly* 25 (1972): 26–32, concerns the representation of Indians in Hollywood movies.

A. L. Kroeber, ed., *Anthropology Today* (Chicago, 1953) contains the developments of physical anthropology during the decades of the 1930's and 1940's. Theodosius Dobzhansky's *Mankind Evolving* (New Haven, 1962) and William C. Boyd's *Genetics and the Races of Man* (Boston, 1950) both discuss the interest in blood groups that grew during the same two decades. Sir R. A. Fischer's *The Genetical Theory of Natural Selection* (Oxford, England, 1930) and William B. Provine's *The Origins of Population Genetics* (Chicago, 1970) provide insight into the changing position of geneticists toward their discipline. E. A. Hooton's two books, *Up From the Ape* (New York, 1931) and *Apes, Men and Morons* (New York, 1938), are aimed at a popular audience.

The about-face of psychologists in the 1930's is signaled by Thomas Russell Garth's *Race Psychology: A Study of Racial Mental Differences* (New York, 1931) and by "A Review of Racial Psychology," *Psychological Bulletin* 27 (1930): 331–48. M. F. Ashley Montagu's "Intelligence of Northern Negroes and Southern Whites in the First World War," *American Journal of Psychology* 68 (1945): 161–88, criticizes intelligence testing procedures and the conclusions drawn from the mental tests. He points out that Northern Negroes did better than southern Whites. Anne Anastasi uses the new psychological orthodoxy in her *Differential Psychology: Individual and Group Differences in Behavior* (New York, 1937). Otto Klineberg's *Race Differences* (New York, 1935) and *Negro Intelligence and Selective Migration* (New York, 1935) both emphasize environmental influences on lower Negro test scores.

Robert H. Lowie tells his story candidly in *Robert H. Lowie, Ethnologist: A Personal Record* (Berkeley, Calif., 1959). The rejection of race as an explanation of group difference in the early 1940's can be seen in Ruth Benedict and Gene Weltfish, *The Races of Mankind* (New York, 1943); Gunnar Myrdal, *An American Dilemma: The Negro Problem and Modern Democracy* (New York, 1942); Otto Klineberg, ed., *Characteristics of the American Negro* (New York, 1944); and, especially, M. F. Ashley Montagu, *Man's Most Dangerous Myth: The Fallacy of Race*, 2nd ed. (New York, 1945). See also Earl W. Count, ed., *This Is Race: An Anthology* (New York, 1950).

Chapter Eleven

Reynolds Farley discusses demographic trends in the black population in the 1930's and 1940's in his "The Urbanization of Negroes in the United States," *Journal of Social History*, 1 (1968): 24–58. There has been recent interest in the effect of the years of depression and war on Blacks. Leslie H. Fishel, Jr., in "The Negro in the New Deal Era," *Wisconsin Magazine of History* 48 (1969): 111–26, provides a good, brief overview of what happened during this period. Frank Freidel's *F.D.R. and the South* (Baton Rouge, La., 1965) analyzes Roosevelt's slow movement in the direction of civil rights. The operation of the federal government in areas affecting Negro workers and farmers is described in Donald Eugene Conrad's *The Forgotten Farmers: The Story of Sharecroppers in the New Deal* (Urbana, Ill., 1965) and in John A. Salmond's *The Civilian Conservation Corps, 1933–1942: A New Deal Case Study* (Durham, N.C., 1967).

Richard M. Dalfuime in "The Forgotten Years of the Negro Revolution," *Journal of American History* 55 (1968): 90–106, recounts the gains obtained by the Negro in World War II while Howard Sitkoff's "Racial Militancy and Interracial Violence in the Second World War," *Journal of American History* 58 (1971): 661–81, records the cost of the efforts to achieve civil rights during that era. The success of the NAACP in legal battles appears in Loren Miller's *The Petitioners: The Story of the Supreme Court of the United States and the Negro* (New York, 1966); the NAACP's success in resisting blandishments from the Left is described in Wilson Record's *Race and Radicalism: The NAACP and the*

Communist Party in Conflict (Ithaca, N.Y., 1964). Inge Powell Bell traces the founding and operation of the Congress of Racial Equality in *CORE and the Strategy of Non-Violence* (New York, 1968), as do August Meier and Elliott Rudwick in *CORE: A Study in the Civil Rights Movement, 1942–1968* (New York, 1973). Herbert Garfinkel does the same for the MOWM in an excellent book, *When Negroes March: The March on Washington Movement in the Organizational Politics for FEPC* (Glencoe, Ill., 1959). The Truman turn-around on civil rights plays a prominent part in Barton J. Bernstein, ed., *Politics and Policies of the Truman Administration* (Chicago, 1970). The struggle to desegregate the Armed Forces is the topic of Richard M. Dalfuime's *Fighting on Two Fronts: Desegregation of the Armed Forces* (New York, 1968).

General background on the film industry appears in Paul Rotha, *The Film Till Now* (London, 1967) and Richard Griffith and Arthur Mayer, *The Movies* (New York, 1957). Two perceptive critics of the films of the 1940's were James Agee and Parker Tyler. Agee's ideas emerge from his collected reviews, *Agee on Film* (London, 1963), and Parker Tyler's emerge from his article, "Hollywood as a Universal Church," *American Quarterly* 2, No. 2 (1950): 165–76, and his book, *The Three Faces of the Film* (New York, 1960). Two books of literary criticism, which touch on violence in literature, also give considerable insight into racial attitudes; they are Louise Y. Gossett's *Violence in Recent Southern Fiction* (Durham, N.C., 1965) and W. M. Frohock's *The Novel of Violence in America* (Dallas, Tx., 1958). Philip Rahv's criticism in *Image and Idea* (London, 1949) is provocative and insightful.

The retreat of Grant and Stoddard into a fortress America can be traced in their later works: Madison Grant, *The Conquest of a Continent, or the Expansion of Races in America* (New York, 1933), and Lothrop Stoddard, *Lonely America* (Garden City, N.Y., 1932), *Clashing Tides of Color* (New York, 1935), and *Into the Darkness* (New York, 1940). S. J. Holmes continued his hereditarian pessimism in *The Negro's Struggle for Survival: A Study in Human Ecology* (Berkeley, Calif., 1937). Holmes's use of the term ecology predated its fashionable use in the 1950's.

The new sociology of the 1930's is somewhat evident in E. B. Reuter's *Race Mixture* (New York, 1931); the author had considerably modified his earlier thoughts on race. Peter I. Rose's *The Subject is Race: Traditional Ideologies and the Teaching of Race Relations* (New York, 1968) is a history of the racial ideas of sociologists. Robert E. Park's *Race and Culture* (New York, 1949) represents the culmination of the assimilationist tradition. Stanford M. Lyman, *The Black American in Sociological Thought* (New York, 1973), discusses the ideas of Park and Dollard. John Madge's *The Origins of Scientific Sociology* (New York, 1962) touches on the generation of sociologists who were prominent in the 1930's including Myrdal. Ralph Ellison, a black writer, criticizes

Park's characterization of the black race as feminine in *Shadow and Act* (New York, 1964).

There are a number of studies of the South of just prior to the Second World War that use anthropological methods; these describe the Southern social system basically as one of caste. Three representative books are John Dollard, *Caste and Class in a Southern Town* (New Haven, Conn., 1937); Allison Davis and John Dollard, *Citizens of Bondage* (New York, 1940); and Allison Davis, Burleigh B. Gardner, and Mary R. Gardner, *Deep South* (Chicago, 1941). Melville J. Herskovits makes the case for the persistence of African culture in his *The Myth of the Negro Past* (New York, 1941).

Robert Russa Moton analyzes the mood of Negroes in the South in *What the Negro Thinks* (New York, 1929). While Charles S. Johnson's *Growing Up in the Black Belt* (Washington, D.C., 1941) could as easily have been written by a white scholar as by the black one who did it, it does reveal black thought. August Meier and Elliott Rudwick describe the reaction of Blacks to the Depression and the Second World War in their chapter "Black Protest in Twentieth-Century America," in Peter I. Rose, ed., *Old Memories, New Moods* (New York, 1970) as does St. Clair Drake in "Hide My Face," in Herbert Hill, ed., *Soon One Morning* (New York, 1963). Samuel W. Allen discussed black writers of the 1930's and 1940's in *The American Negro Writer and His Roots* (New York, 1960). Arthur Huff Fausett's *Black Gods of the Metropolis: Negro Religious Cults of the Urban North* (Philadelphia, Penn., 1949) is a good review of the attempts to soften the problems of ghetto life by religious means while Robert A. Parker's *The Incredible Messiah: The Deification of Father Divine* (Boston, 1937) describes the rise of one of the more successful religious leaders of the period. Finally, C. Eric Lincoln's *The Black Muslims in America* (Boston, 1961) details the rise of that sect in American society. Susan Frutkin, *Aimé Césaire: Black Between Worlds* (Washington, D.C., 1973) is the most recent study of the paradoxical views of the Martinique-born proponent of negritude.

Chapter Twelve

Stan Steiner discusses the arousal of the Indians in the recent past in his *The New Indians* (New York, 1968), as does Hazel W. Hertzberg in *The Search for American Indian Identity* (Syracuse, N.Y., 1971). Vine Deloria, Jr.'s first book, *Custer Died for Your Sins* (New York, 1969), is an impassioned plea for Indian self-determination and is superior to his second one, *We Talk, You Listen* (New York, 1970). Murray Wax has written an important article and a book on Indians. His "The White Man's Burdensome 'Business': A Review Essay on the Change and Constancy of Literature on the American Indians," *Social Problems* 16

(1968): 106–13, contains material on Indian stereotypes in textbooks. His *Indian Americans: Unity and Diversity* (Englewood Cliffs, N.J., 1971) has a useful chapter on Indian nomenclature. See also Robert Berkhofer, Jr.'s "Political Context of the New Indian History," *Pacific Historical Review* 40 (1971): 357–64. Edmund Wilson's *Apologies to the Iroquois* (London, 1960) is up to his usual standards, although his discovery of the Indians seems to have come rather late. Theodore Roszak's *Where the Wasteland Ends* (New York, 1972) and William Irwin Thompson's *At the Edge of History* (New York, 1971) are perhaps the best known of the counterculture histories. Thompson's book, in particular, argues the validity of old myths about Indian origins.

Ken Kesey's *One Flew Over the Cuckoo's Nest* (New York, 1962) is one of that author's better novels and uses the Indian as a sympathetic character. Two collections on film are useful sources of information on the movies of the period; they are Stanley Kauffmann, *A World on Film; Criticism and Comment* (New York, 1966) and Richard Schickel, *Second Sight* (New York, 1972). Ralph E. Friar and Nataska Friar's *The Only Good Indian* (New York, 1972) touches on Hollywood images of the Indian.

The work of Leslie Fiedler is always provocative and his *Waitng for the End* (New York, 1964), *The Last Jew in America* (New York, 1966), and *The Return of the Vanishing American* (London, 1968) contain essays and creative pieces on both Indians and Blacks as well as reflections on the state and future of American society. The material on sociological investigation of race relations is voluminous. Talcott Parsons' *Essays in Sociological Theory* (New York, 1964) contains his views on the frustration that the American social system engenders. Like other works by Parsons, it is not easy reading. Two books that are important for the purposes of sociological theory are Rolf Dahrendorf's *Class and Class Conflict in Industrial Society* (Stanford, Calif., 1959) and Gerhard E. Lenski's *Power and Privilege: A Theory of Social Stratification* (New York, 1966). Typical articles on race relations are Stanley L. Singer and Buford Steffler, "A Note on Racial Differences in Job Values and Job Desires," *Journal of Social Psychology* 43 (1956); 333–37; J. Milton Yinger, "Recent Developments in Minority and Race Relations," *The Annals* 378 (1968): 130–45; and Milton M. Gordon, "Recent Trends in the Study of Minority and Race Relations," *The Annals* 350 (1963), 148–56. The two standard books in the area are George E. Simpson and J. Milton Yinger, *Racial and Cultural Minorities* (New York, 1965), 3rd ed., and Hubert M. Blalock, Jr., *Toward a Theory of Minority-Group Relations* (New York, 1967). Francis L. K. Hsu's comments on the American character appear in his "American Core Values and National Character," in Francis L. K. Hsu, ed., *Psychological Anthropology* (Homewood, Ill., 1961). Racism in a cross-cultural perspective is the topic of Pierre L. Van den Berghe, *Race and Racism: A Comparative*

Perspective (New York, 1967) and H. Hoetink, *The Two Variants in Caribbean Race Relations* (New York, 1967). The former is one of the most significant books on the topic. The latter compares racism in Curacao and Surinam.

The problem of what happened to the immigrant in America occupies a number of people, including Daniel Bell in his essay on Italian-Americans, "Crime as an American Way of Life," in Daniel Bell, ed., *The End of Ideology* (Glencoe, Ill., 1959); Nathan Glazer and Daniel Moynihan in their analysis of ethnic groups in New York City in *Beyond the Melting Pot* (Cambridge, Mass., 1963); Nathan Glazer in "America's Race Paradox," *Encounter* 31 (October, 1968): 63–68; and Glazer's "Blacks and Ethnic Groups: The Difference, and the Political Difference It Makes," in Nathan I. Huggins, Martin Kilson, and Daniel M. Fox, eds., *Key Issues in the Afro-American Experience*, Vol. II (New York, 1971). The best general treatment of the topic of assimilation and a theoretical statement of the operation of the triple melting pot is Milton M. Gordon's *Assimilation in American Life* (New York, 1964).

Oscar Handlin, in *Race and Nationality in American Life* (New York, 1957), echoed his early position on the impact of the American experience upon attitudes. The culmination of the culture concept appears in A. L. Kroeber's *The Nature of Culture* (Chicago, 1952), but David Bidney had already begun to question the objectivity of those who used the concept in "The Concept of Value in Modern Anthropology," in A. L. Kroeber, ed., *Anthropology Today* (Chicago, 1953) and in his own *Theoretical Anthropology* (New York, 1953). Two recent books on the concept of culture that are essential are Ervin Hatch's *Theories of Man and Culture* (New York, 1973), which is an historical treatment of the idea of culture, and Louis Schneider and Charles M. Bonjean's *The Idea of Culture in the Social Sciences* (Cambridge, England, 1973), which is a theoretical overview. Marvin Harris points to weaknesses in the concept in his massive *The Rise of Anthropological Theory: A History of Theories of Culture* (New York, 1968). Two of the more significant articles on the idea of culture are James Boon, "Further Operations of 'Culture' in Anthropology: A Synthesis of and for Debate," *Social Science Quarterly* 53, No. 2 (1972): 221–52, and Robert F. Berkhofer, Jr., "Clio and the Culture Concept: Some Impressions of a Changing Relationship in American Historiography," *Social Science Quarterly* 53, No. 2 (1972): 297–320.

The growing respectability of evolutionism is reflected in John P. Greene's *Darwin and the Modern World View* (Baton Rouge, La., 1961) and Julian S. Huxley's "Evolution, Cultural and Biological," in William L. Thomas, Jr., ed., *Current Anthropology* (Chicago, 1956). Leslie A. White's ideas appear in his *The Evolution of Culture: The Development of Civilization to the Fall of Rome* (New York, 1959), and an evaluation of his ideas appears in Gertrude E. Dole and Robert L. Carneiro, eds., *Essays in the Science of Culture in Honor of Leslie A. White* (New York, 1960). William C. Boyd and Theodosius Dobzhansky have thought much about the impact of human genetics on anthropology; their ideas can be found in William C. Boyd, "The Contributions of Genetics to Anthropology," in A. L. Kroeber, ed., *Anthropology Today* (Chicago, 1953); in William C. Boyd and Isaac Asimov, *Races and People* (New York, 1958); and in Theodosius Dobzhansky, *Mankind Evolving* (New Haven, Conn., 1962). Margaret Mead indicates her partial conversion to evolutionism in *Continuities in Cultural Evolution* (New Haven, Conn., 1964) and in Margaret Mead, Theodosius Dobzhansky, Ethel Tobach, and Robert Light, ed., *Science and the Concept of Race* (New York, 1968).

Chapter Thirteen

The standard work on urbanization of Blacks is Karl E. and Alma F. Taeuber's *Negroes in Cities* (Chicago, 1965). Daniel P. Moynihan's *The Negro Family: The Case for National Action* (Washington, D.C., 1965) is remarkable less for its content than its timing. It sums up the concerns of white sociologists about black family structure. Herbert G. Gutman, a historian, claims that these concerns were misplaced and that the black lower-class family was more, rather than less, patriarchal than its white equivalent, based on his research on northern cities in the latter part of the nineteenth century. Gutman's findings appear in "Persistent Myths About the American Negro Family" (Paper read at the 54th Annual Meeting of the Association for the Study of Negro Life and History, Birmingham, Ala., October 10, 1969).

Tom Hayden analyzes one of the significant urban riots of the 1960's in *Rebellion in Newark: Official Violence and Ghetto Response* (New York, 1967). Robert Conot, *Rivers of Blood, Years of Darkness* (New York, 1967), discusses the events in Watts. Howard Zinn's *SNCC: The New Abolitionists* (Boston, 1964) is a standard work on the formation of the Student Nonviolent Coordinating Committee.

Ihab Hassan, *Radical Innocence: Studies in the Contemporary American Novel* (Princeton, N.J., 1961) is a balanced overview of the novels of the 1960's and 1970's. Robert Drake emphasizes the traditional Christian themes in his *Flannery O'Connor: A Critical Essay* (Grand Rapids, Mich., 1966). Ronald Berman has caught the intellectual currents of the 1960's well in his *America in the Sixties* (New York, 1968), but the book is difficult reading. William L. O'Neill's *Coming Apart* (Chicago, 1971) is lively; he disagrees with Berman and thinks the era of change is over.

The arguments of those who continued to emphasize race as a factor in achievement can be found in Audrey M. Shuey, *The Testing of*

Negro Intelligence (London, 1958) and Carleton Putnam, *Race and Reason: A Yankee View* (Washington, D.C., 1961). I. A. Newby's *Challenge to the Court: Social Scientists and the Defense of Segregation, 1954–1966* (Baton Rouge, La., 1965), is a continuation of his *Jim Crow's Defense*, although this book covers a shorter time period than the earlier one. He includes the ideas of those persons who reacted negatively to the decision on *Brown* v. *Board of Education.*

The new hereditarianism and the disenchantment with environment appear in J. S. Coleman, et al, *Equality of Educational Opportunity* (Washington, D.C., 1966); Richard Herrnstein, "I.Q.," *Atlantic* September, 1971: 43–64; and Bryan Bott, "Jensen, Race and Genes," *Times Higher Educational Supplement,* March 3, 1972. The ideas of Arthur R. Jensen can be found in his *Educability and Group Differences* (New York, 1973) and *Genetics and Education* (New York, 1973). Richard Herrnstein's hereditarian argument is most fully expressed in *I.Q. and the Meritocracy* (Boston, 1973). For a series of essays that are critical of these positions, see Alan Gartner, Colin Greer, and Frank Riessman, eds., *The New Assault on Equality: I.Q. and Social Stratification* (New York, 1974).

Any of the books of Konrad Lorenz, Desmond Morris, or Robert Ardrey will show the basic premises of the ethologists; the books of the latter two popularizers carry the new naturalism further than it can go. Peter H. Knapp has edited a scholarly collection on the natural base of emotions called *Expression of the Emotions in Man* (New York, 1963). Kenneth Mather's *Human Diversity* (London, 1964) and J. N. Spuhler's *Genetic Diversity and Human Behavior* (Chicago, 1967) both make cases for the genetic origin of much of human behavior. Carleton Coon's *The Origin of Races* (New York, 1962) contains his version of how each so-called race evolved from a different primate. Charles Keil's *Urban Blues* (Chicago, 1966) makes a case for a viable life-style of the lower-class black male; less ambitious is LeRoi Jones, *Blues People: Negro Music in White America* (New York, 1963). Roger Abrahams has investigated black folklore extensively. Some of his works are "Playing the Dozens," *Journal of American Folklore* 75 (1962): 209–20; *Deep Down in the Jungle: Negro Narrative Folklore from the Streets of Philadelphia* (Hatboro, Penn., 1964); and *Positively Black* (Englewood Cliffs, N.J., 1970).

Robert Blauner tries to answer the question of whether a separate black culture exists in his "Black Culture: Myth or Reality," in Peter I. Rose, ed., *Old Memories, New Moods* (New York, 1970). David A. Schulz describes interaction in urban black communities in *Coming Up Black: Patterns of Ghetto Socialization* (Englewood Cliffs, N.J., 1969). An opinion on what the term soul means appeared in Ulf Hannerz, "The Rhetoric of Soul: Identification in Negro Society," *Race: A Journal of Race and Group Relations* 9 (1968): 453–65.

The psychological scarring of Blacks by prejudice is a popular contemporary topic. Among the most noted efforts to describe this problem are Kenneth B. Clark, *Dark Ghetto* (New York, 1965); Joel Kovel, *White Racism: A Psychohistory* (New York, 1970); and William H. Grier and Price M. Cobb, *Black Rage* (New York, 1968).

The view that urban Blacks share older immigrant problems and experiences is the theme of Oscar Handlin's *The Newcomers: Negroes and Puerto Ricans in a Changing Metropolis* (Cambridge, Mass., 1959); Handlin is less optimistic in his *Firebell in the Night* (Boston, 1964), which more specifically centers on a number of people, including Blacks. The historical argument about the connection of slavery with prejudice, which argument began after World War II, started with Oscar and Mary F. Handlin, "Origins of the Southern Labor System," *William and Mary Quarterly*, Sec. 3, 7 (1950): 199–222. This argument was continued with Carl N. Degler's "Slavery and the Genesis of American Race Prejudice," *Comparative Studies in Society and History* 2 (1959): 49–66, and Winthrop D. Jordan, "Modern Tensions and the Origins of American Slavery," *Journal of Southern History* 28, No. 1 (1962): 18–32. Kenneth M. Stampp's *The Peculiar Institution: Slavery in the Ante-Bellum South* (New York, 1956) and Stanley Elkin's *Slavery* (Chicago, 1959) were the most significant book-length treatments of slavery in the decade of the 1950's. The Spring issue of *Daedalus* 103 (1974), entitled *Slavery, Colonialism, and Racism*, had as a lead article David Brion Davis's "Slavery and the Post-World War II Historians," which is an excellent survey of the historiography of the period.

Aristide and Vera Zobberg discuss the transfer of Frantz Fanon's ideas to the United States in their "The Americanization of Frantz Fanon," *The Public Interest* 9 (1967): 49–63. Lewis M. Killian takes a skeptical look at black power in his *The Impossible Revolution? Black Power and the American Dream* (New York, 1968). See especially his "The Revolutionary Myth." Harold Cruse looks at the same topic in *The Crisis of the Black Intellectual* (New York, 1967), and Christopher Lasch does so in "The Trouble with Black Power," *The New York Review of Books* (February 29, 1968) and in "Black Power: Cultural Nationalism as Politics" in his *The Agony of the American Left* (New York, 1969). Theodore Draper's *The Rediscovery of Black Nationalism* (New York, 1970) is a useful survey of various aspects of the topic of black goals. Floyd Barbour has edited a helpful anthology called *The Black Power Revolt* (Boston, 1968). Julius Lester's *Look Out Whitey! Black Power's Gon' Get Your Mama* (New York, 1968) goes about as far as it is possible to go in advocating racial separation. Stokely Carmichael and Charles V. Hamilton take a militant stance in *Black Power: The Politics of Liberation* (New York, 1965).

On the ideas of individual black leaders, see Martin Luther King, Jr., *Stride Toward Freedom* (New York, 1958) and his last book, *Where*

Do We Go From Here: Chaos or Community? (New York, 1967) for his version of the Negro as the leaven in American society; Malcolm Little, with Alex Haley, *The Autobiography of Malcolm X* (New York, 1969) for the development of a Black Muslim; Eldridge Cleaver, *Soul On Ice* (New York, 1968) and *Post-Prison Writings and Speeches*, edited by Robert Scheer (New York, 1968); as well as Bobby Seale, *Seize the Time* (New Yark, 1969) for insight into the Black Panthers. James Baldwin comments on the Black Muslims in his *The Fire Next Time* (New York, 1963), and Robert Brustein takes apart Baldwin's "Blues for Mister Charlie" in *Seeds of Discontent: Dramatic Opinions, 1959–65* (New York, 1965). Imamu Amiri Baraka's (LeRoi Jones) hegira can be traced from *Dutchman and the Slave: Two Plays* (New York, 1964) to *Home: Social Essays* (New York, 1966) to *Raise Race Rays Raze: Essays Since 1965* (New York, 1971). Finally, the dialogue between Margaret Mead and James Baldwin appears in *A Rap on Race* (Philadelphia, Penn., 1971).

Index